The Identity of Geneva

Recent Titles in
Contributions to the Study of World History

The Identity of Geneva

*The Christian Commonwealth,
1564–1864*

Edited by **John B. Roney** and
Martin I. Klauber

Foreword by Robert M. Kingdon

Contributions to the Study of World History, Number 59

Greenwood Press
Westport, Connecticut • London

Library of Congress Cataloging-in-Publication Data

The identity of Geneva : the Christian commonwealth, 1564–1864 /
   edited by John B. Roney and Martin I. Klauber ;   foreword by Robert M.
   Kingdon.
       p.   cm.—(Contributions to the study of world history, ISSN
   0885-9159   ;   no. 59)
   Includes bibliographical references and index.
   ISBN 0-313-29868-8 (alk. paper)
   1. Geneva (Switzerland)—Church history.   I. Roney, John B.
II. Klauber, Martin I., 1956–   .   III. Kingdon, Robert M.
IV. Series.
BR1038.G3I34   1998
274.94'51—DC21   97-37494

British Library Cataloguing in Publication Data is available.

Library of Congress Catalog Card Number: 97-37494
ISBN: 0-313-29868-8
ISSN: 0885-9159

First published in 1998

Greenwood Press, 88 Post Road West, Westport, CT 06881
An imprint of Greenwood Publishing Group, Inc.

Printed in the United States of America

The paper used in this book complies with the
Permanent Paper Standard issued by the National
Information Standards Organization (Z39.48-1984).

10 9 8 7 6 5 4 3 2 1

Contents

Foreword

Robert M. Kingdon

For hundreds of years the city of Geneva has been an international center, unusually hospitable to visitors from other countries, unusually influential on developments elsewhere. The international character of the city was first evident in the late middle ages, when it became an important regional center for fairs that attracted trading merchants from France and Germany and bankers from Italy. Geneva's importance as a trading center declined in the late fifteenth century, as nearby Lyon, under the protection of the kings of France, gained more and more of this business. But internationalism triumphed in Geneva in a radically different and even more influential form in the sixteenth century as a result of the Protestant Reformation. Thousands of religious refugees, most of them French, many of them Italian, some of them from yet other countries, moved into the city and effectively took over control of many of its institutions, most notably its church. The most prominent of these refugees was John Calvin. Under his leadership Geneva became the international headquarters of a new, unusually militant, and highly organized form of Christianity, a Protestant equivalent to Rome. It is upon the shape and influence of Geneva as a particularly important Christian commonwealth that John B. Roney and Martin I. Klauber, and the group of experts they have assembled for this volume, concentrate.

Much of Geneva's influence in this period, of course, was theological and much of the book, accordingly, examines the theological tradition emanating from Geneva. The founder of that tradition was John Calvin himself. His theology, and the biblical exegesis upon which it was based have been extensively analyzed elsewhere. They have not been ignored by the authors of this book. Indeed Richard Muller's essay, for one, offers a fresh contribution to our understanding of details of Calvin's exegesis. The primary focus of the book, however, is on Calvin's successors, the theologians who kept his ideas alive, refining and adapting them to the needs of later generations. They include Theodore Beza, the erudite nobleman Calvin selected as his immediate successor; Francis Turretin who, late in the seventeenth century, brought orthodox Calvinism to its most refined and sophisticated and rigid shape; Antoine Court and others in France who tried to develop a considerably simplified version of Calvinism that could be used by the poorly educated leaders of a surviving Protestant church in France that had been declared illegal and driven underground by the monarchy of Louis XIV and his successors; Jean-Alphonse Turretin, son of Francis, and Jacob Vernet who successively tried to redefine Christianity in ways that would make it acceptable to generations of intellectuals deeply influenced by the rise of modern sciences and tempted by versions of Deism and Atheism, and finally the leaders of the *Réveil*, a religious movement after the French Revolution that attempted to create a form of Christianity more open to an emotionalism that had growing appeal and more respect for the Calvinist tradition.

From the beginning, however, Calvinism has been more than theology, more than a body of doctrines. It has been a way of life. Calvin himself insisted on controlling human behavior by establishing and maintaining strict discipline, primarily through institutions like the Consistory, which had been established in Geneva at his insistence in 1541, and for whose powers he fought throughout his career. These institutions and others complementing them had been widely imitated in other Calvinist communities and became additional basic characteristics of the movement. It is appropriate, therefore, that this book includes chapters that are devoted to the impact of early Calvinism on behavior, specifically on suicide, social welfare, and education.

As in any collectively written book, there are inevitably variations in emphasis and focus. Francis Higman extracts significance from rare printed texts, hitherto overlooked. Richard Muller examines relatively well known texts using finely honed skills in technical analysis. Jeffrey Watt reports on his fresh research in the Geneva State Archives. Linda Kirk synthesizes recent archival research by historians of Geneva, many of them local scholars, some of whose work has never been printed. Others offer combinations of these approaches.

Some facets of Geneva's contributions to international history still need to be explored. One could imagine, for example, a fascinating study of the contributions of eighteenth-century bankers in Geneva to international finance, above all the desperate attempts to rescue the finances of the French royal government on the eve of the Revolution. Geneva's history as an international center, furthermore, continued to be of signal importance well after the date with which this volume effectively terminates. It was to become the initial home of the International Red Cross, the League of Nations, a number of international organizations now affiliated with the United Nations, and the World Council of churches. Many of these retain their headquarters in Geneva to this day.

This book makes significant contributions to our understanding of one noteworthy segment of Geneva's history as an uncommonly important center of internationalism. Let us hope that it attracts interest and stimulates further work on this important topic.

Acknowledgments

The editors of and contributors to this volume acknowledge the leadership and scholarship of Robert M. Kingdon to a generation of historians of Genevan religion and society. His encouragement, example, teaching, and writings have enabled a host of scholarly activities to come to fruition. At one time or another every contributor to this volume has spent considerable time in Geneva, and therefore we acknowledge the support of the Bibliothèque Publique et Universitaire, the Archives d'Etat, and the Institut d'Histoire de la Réformation. All these institutions have supported scholarship through their excellent facilities and through the many professional librarians, archivists, and directors who have assisted in research and design of numerous projects and have created a well-established center of national and religious scholarship. We also acknowledge the support of Olivier Fatio, *doyen* of the faculty of Protestant Theology at the University of Geneva, and Francis Higman, Director of the Institut d'Histoire de la Réformation, who have enabled international scholars to seek bursaries, locate archives and library materials, and encouraged cooperative projects. We would also like to thank Sacred Heart University for a small grant that contributed toward some translation costs and correspondance between editors and contributors.

Chronology of Events in Geneva

1526	Geneva *combourgeoisie* (alliance) with Swiss (Bern and Fribourg); Republic of Geneva created
1535	*Hôpital-Général* (General Hospital) founded
1536	Geneva accepts the Protestant Reformation (May 21); John Calvin settles in Geneva (July); the *Vénérable Compagnie des Pasteurs* (Company of Pastors) established (1530s); Publication: first Latin edition, *Institutes of the Christian Religion* by Calvin
1538	Calvin and William Farel expelled from Geneva
1541	Calvin returns; *Ecclesiastical Ordinances* and Genevan Consistory established
1540s	*Bourse française* (French fund) begins
1555	Calvin consolidates power; pastors sent to evangelize France
1559	(June) Genevan Academy, founded by Calvin with Rector Theodore Beza
1560	(May 10) Publication: *Geneva Bible*
1564	(May 27) Death of Calvin
1566	Publication: *Second Helvetic Confession* by Heinrich Bullinger
1572	(August 24) St. Bartholemew's Day Massacre, Paris
1602	(December 12) *Escalade*; Duke of Savoy's final attack fails [War 1589—1593]
1635	Centenary (*Jubilé*) of the Reformation
1648	Peace of Westphalia; end of the European Wars of Religion
1679—1685	Publication: *Institutio theologiae elencticae* by Francis Turretin
1685	Revocation of the Edict of Nantes

1725	Abrogation of the Confession of Faith by the Consistory of Geneva
1735	Bicentenary (*Jubilé*) of the Reformation
1792	*Egalisateurs*, under the Jacobin Jacques Grenus, form a new government
1794	New Constitution
1798	(April 15) Annexation by the French, Napoleonic Empire. Geneva, with expanded territory, becomes the *départment du Léman*
1801	Concordat (Napoleon-Pope) establishes freedom of worship for Catholics
1813	(December 30) Geneva freed from France
1815	New Constitution [written 1814]; Geneva joins Switzerland (Helvetic Confederation) as Canton and Republic of Geneva (May 19)
1835	Tercentenary (*Jubilé*) of the Reformation; inauguration of the *Ile Rousseau* in the mouth of the Rhone River
1842	New Constitution
1846	Radical Revolution under James Fazy
1847	New Constitution (democratic); Reformed Church loses status as the state church
1864	Birth of the *Convention de Genève*, which became (1888) the Red Cross (*Croix-Rouge*) under Jean-Henri Dunant, who helped establish the *Union chrétienne des Jeunes Gens* (YMCA).
1872	Genevan Academy reestablished as the University of Geneva

Abbreviations

AEG	Archives d'Etat de Genève
ARG	*Archiv für Reformationsgeschichte*
BPU	Bibliothèque Publique et Universitaire de Genève
BSHPF	*Bulletin de la Société de l'Histoire du Protestantisme Française*
CTJ	*Calvin Theological Journal*
IRRC	*International Review of the Red Cross*
MDG	*Mémoires et Documents publiés par la Société d'Histoire et d'Archéologie de Genève*
Ms.	Manuscript
NAK	*Nederlands Archief voor Kerkgeschiedenis*
RC	*Registres des Conseils de Genève*
RCP	*Registres de la Compagnie des Pasteurs de Genève*, ed. R. M. Kingdon, J.-L. Bergier et al. (Geneva, 1964–)
RHPR	*Revue d'Histoire et de Philosophie Religieuses*
RSH	*Revue Suisse d'Histoire*
RTP	*Revue de Théologie et de Philosophie*
RVG	*Revue de Vieux Genève*
SHAG	La Société d'Histoire et d'Archéologie de Genève
WTJ	*Westminster Theological Journal*

The Identity of Geneva

Introduction

John B. Roney

THE STUDY OF NATIONAL IDENTITY AND RELIGION

John Calvin was not alone in the sixteenth century when he insisted that religion was at the core of government and national identity: "for no man has discoursed of the duty of magistrates, the enacting of laws, and the common weal, without beginning with religion and divine worship. . . . Seeing then that among philosophers religion holds the first place, and that the same thing has always been observed with the universal consent of nations, Christian princes and magistrates may be ashamed of the heartlessness if they make it not their care."[1] The real attraction of religion for national identity was rooted not only in its other-worldly and transcendent concerns, but the church, rooted in a particular social environment, offered a means to order society. It connected the individual to the collective and the collective to other regions throughout Europe. National identity was also dependent on the establishment of an origin, and religion offered a means to ground social and political life to a legitimate beginning. Maintaining a social center and defining clear and relevant standards for national identity are always articulated within a changing cultural context. Robert Wuthnow has carefully outlined this process as a delicate balance between articulating closely enough but not too closely with the social environment: "The irony is the Reformation's success required it to articulate with its social environment and to disarticulate from this environment at the same time."[2] Religion, therefore, served as the heart of political and economic activity, and at the same time it offered a critique of the temporal realm and contemporary cultural expressions. We will examine to what extent the original articulation of a Christian commonwealth in the sixteenth century could find a new and appropriate response to the growth of Geneva in the changing context of the development of Europe until the nineteenth century.

Although there is a wealth of published material on sixteenth-century Geneva, and even more scholarship on the life and theology of John Calvin, there are few published works in English on the church and state in Geneva as it developed in the seventeenth, eighteenth, and nineteenth centuries.[3] We have chosen the dates carefully to denote significant identifying phenomena: 1564 marks the death of Calvin, and 1864, after 300 years, marks the birth of the Convention of Geneva (*la Convention de Genève pour l'amélioration du sort des militaires blessés dans les armées en compagne*), an organization that later became the Red Cross (*Croix-Rouge*, 1888) under the direction of Jean-Henri Dunant. These dates, especially if we expand them from 1535 to 1864, are also important because it is within these years alone that the clear majority of Genevans were Protestants; outside these dates there were more Catholics. After 1860, when the actual population of Catholics became the majority, a smaller group of Protestants still held more power and wealth, but the original nature and identity of the Reformation republic had clearly changed.

CHARACTERISTICS OF SIXTEENTH-CENTURY GENEVAN IDENTITY

There has been a continuing debate on the nature of identity in Geneva based on its relationship with the foundations set forth by Calvin. Some of the questions may be formulated as the following: Have Genevans remained faithful to these traditions? In what ways does one judge that faithfulness given the changing environment and relationship of religion and society in early modern Europe? To what degree was it necessary to build on what Calvin had started? Beyond the foundational theology and polity of Calvin, what other contributions has Geneva made to the universal Reformed church? Once Geneva ceased to be a Reformed republic, how did the Reformed churches fulfill their mission in a modern pluralist society? This volume will offer some identifying characteristics that take account of the dynamics of both internal developments and external developments.

Genevan political identity was strongly rooted in the city-republic, a patrician elite of original families that in time accepted new refuges into the community. Only in 1526 did Geneva gain independence from its feudal duties to the Holy Roman Empire and to its overlords, the House of Savoy and the prince-bishop of Geneva. Through a *combourgeoisie* (alliance) with Bern and Fribourg, who had begun to form a confederation of free cities after their own release from the empire in 1499, they were able to gain external protection. Although Bern and Fribourg had given their protection to the free city and republic of Geneva, William Monter reminds us that "Calvin's city was neither Swiss nor French, either politically or culturally."[4] Rather, Geneva remained in a precarious position of being a small republic that enjoyed freedom only by maintaining vigilance and international protection. The new government was composed of four syndics (elected annually), the Small Council of Twenty-Five (*Petit Conseil*), the executive branch of government, the Council of Two Hundred

(*Conseil des Deux Cents*)—an elected legislative body—and the General Council (*Conseil générale*). The idea of a republic was not entirely new, but the juxtaposition of the more direct rule of God through his Word added a distinctive element to this Protestant republic. Calvin recognized different types of government; however, for the political climate of Geneva, out of the three forms of *monarchie (roy ou duc), aristocratie (les principaux et gens d'appearance)*, and *democratie (une domination populaire)*, he preferred aristocracy as the most appropriate political system in Geneva.[5] It is important to underline the thesis of Joshua Mitchell, that for all major political thinkers the "politically authoritative history is biblical history, that is the salient events of the two Testaments: Creation, Adam's fall, Abraham's faith, Moses' covenant with God, Christ and the New Dispensation, and the final Redemption."[6] The legitimacy of the body politic in Geneva rested firmly in this biblical story, not in the recent tradition of medieval Christendom and feudal estates.[7]

In July 1536 Calvin came to Geneva upon the request of the Genevan reformer William Farel. Calvin was little known at the time, and he only slowly made an impact on the city. W. Fred Graham has found that early references to Calvin "identifies him merely as *ille Gallus*, 'that Frenchman', who had begun lecturing at St. Pierre's."[8] Within a few years, however, Calvin's strength and leadership would bring new identity to the city. Arising within Augustinianism and conciliarism, and schooled in Renaissance humanism and protest against the abuses in late medieval religious practices, Calvin stressed the absolute authority of Scriptures (*sola scriptura*) and a new method to unlock its meaning. The certainty and authority of knowledge was transformed from ecclesiastical tradition, principle, and image to the free examination of the Word of God, through an observation of the word, philologically understood. One of the fruits of Calvin's theological development was its application to Genevan society. In 1541 Geneva accepted his *Ecclesiastical Ordinances*, which established the important offices of pastors, teachers, elders, and deacons, and gave another body of pastors and elders, forming the Consistory, the charge to guard doctrinal and disciplinary matters. In this way Geneva created a unique Christian commonwealth whereby church and state cooperated in preserving religion as the key to their new identity. Geneva was not the first city to develop Reformed theology and polity, however, and much of Calvin's theological thinking was indebted to his early contact with Martin Bucer and his residence in Strasbourg. Strasbourg, already referred to as the "New Jerusalem" by the international Reformed movement, was twice the size of Geneva, and prior to Geneva's ascendancy in the 1550s, it was the internationally recognized center for Reformed thought.[9]

The Reformed community in Geneva considered itself to be a better expression of the pure church than the corrupted Catholic Church it replaced. The Genevan motto that came to dominate iconographic crests, documents, and commemorative events was *post tenebras lux* (after darkness light). Naming themselves and their enemies became an important part of developing a new identity: The Genevese called themselves "Evangelicals," a direct reference to

Scripture as the sole authority, and to the early Christians who had suffered martyrdom for their faith—paralleling their own persecution. Whereas Catholics labeled them "Lutherans," an immediate sentence of heresy and, in French lands, a statement of foreign conspiracy. The essence of an identifying name was to legitimate their claim as the uncorrupted church, indigenous to the age-old faith from whence they came. This assertion attempted to refute the consistent Catholic claim that their movement produced only "novelty," change, and rebellion.[10]

Calvinists believed that they were a people chosen by God in the tradition of both the primitive church and the original covenant given to the Israelites. Despite the French Catholic rejection of Calvin as tainted with foreign (especially Lutheran) ideas, his vision of a chosen people comes directly out of the Gallican tradition. The sixteenth-century French believed they were "the chosen people" ruled by "the most Christian King."[11] Like ancient Israel the French believed that God's covenant and protection was still applicable to them, and if they turned away from God, that his discipline and trial would follow. The theme of God's chosen people was further refined within Christian humanism—in historical and linguistic studies—and Calvin applied it to a select group of reformed Protestants. A strong emphasis on Christian Hebraicism became a dominant theme, especially in the Reformed churches throughout Europe; it can be clearly seen in Zürich, Basel, Bern, Strasbourg, France, England, and the Netherlands.[12] Not only was there a more direct appropriation of the Hebraic covenant, law, and image of God, but Genevans borrowed other cultural traditions. For example, the singing of psalms became a distinctive mark, and this was true in Calvinist worship, and French Huguenots even sang psalms during military campaigns to rally the troops. There was a strong identification with David, the author of Psalms, for it was David's courage and triumph in the face of overwhelming adversity that had been the result of divine favor. Conversion remained an essential aspect of faith. Like the ancient Hebrews, they avoided what they believed to be "idolatry" in the abusive use of image in late medieval religious practice.[13] This striving for purity created the reputation of a strict and austere religious piety. Yet this practice of strict regulation was common in many free cities before the Reformation, and Geneva was no exception. Gillian Lewis has found that in the context of the late fifteenth century, the pre-Calvinist period in Geneva, "the commune of Geneva, long before the Reformation, had regularly passed edicts against fraud in commerce, against usury, against excessive luxury in dress, against sexual offenses and prostitution, and against disorderly behaviour in the street."[14] This continuation of a disciplined communal life, understood as sobriety, a better term to express Calvin's position, did not reject an enjoyment of earthly delights; rather, it sought to transform society to conform to Scripture, while at the same time leaving the antinomy between the Testaments ultimately unresolved.[15]

Fulfilling one's religious duties was closely tied to an "earthly calling" whereby industry and hard work were rewarded as ways to serve God and the community. Mark Valeri has found in his study of the economy of Geneva that Calvin, in his commentary on Matthew 25:20, "described the purpose of one's worldly calling not as the interior sanctification of the individual but as the commonweal."[16] Geneva had never been a great manufacturing city, but it did manage to become quite a depot for commercial goods through its well-known fairs in the late Middle Ages. The refugees that poured into its walls by the 1550s, however, brought with them new crafts and skills—the majority were artisans—and gradually small manufacturing, printing, banking, trade, and eventually watchmaking became established.[17] By 1589 the population, despite the recent plague, had swelled to 13,000 inhabitants. The social ranking in Geneva followed a predicable pattern: A small patrician (*aristocratie*)—the title "noble" was only used to describe those in office, and not thereafter—controlled the economic structure and wealth. The *bourgeoisie*, second in rank, consisted of both native-born and immigrants who could become citizens (*citoyens*) by purchasing it or attained it free as an honor (like Calvin). Yet the records show that although Geneva received approximately 7,000 immigrants between 1550 and 1562, only about 650 became bourgeoisie.[18] The remainder were registered as *habitants*; they joined the ranks of the *natifs*, who acquired permanent letters of residence, together with the *étrangers* and *sujets* (peasantry). If these new refugees did not find their identity as full citizens in Geneva—which, in the context of the sixteenth century, we should not suppose they necessarily expected—they could, however, gain a sense of new identity as spiritual citizens of the New Jerusalem. Calvin's exegesis of the Old Testament applied God's covenant to the new church in Geneva.[19] The French Fund (*Bourse française*) began in the 1540s to aid the growing number of refugees, and it conformed to the strong notion of a Christian commonwealth. As an independent city, Geneva was also a city of Protestant refugees from France, Italy, Scotland, and other areas of religious intolerance. Education for all citizens became another distinctive element of Genevan social organization.[20] Boys and girls were instructed in the basics of a humanist education and Christian catechism. Geneva guarded its own patrician sovereignty, but this Reformed conference remained international in perspective and sought a pan-Protestantism that would share a common confession of faith.

THE STUDY OF GENEVAN HISTORY AND IDENTITY, 1564–1864

The strength of Geneva was contained in its tenacious resistance to outside domination and its efficient aristocratic rule. Calvin strengthened Genevan identity by uniting a distinctively Protestant religion with a strict discipline, especially after 1555, which permeated society.[21] His ascendancy came only after a bitter struggle between the rival Perrinists, who represented the traditional Genevese, and his own supporters, very often the newer refugees or the rising bourgeoisie. Calvin also encouraged an international focus, and through the Genevan printing trade in the middle of the sixteenth century—at the height some 40 printers were kept busy in the 1550s—the voice of Geneva (*voix de Genève*) could be heard throughout Europe. In addition to Calvin's published works, especially the *Institutes of the Christian Religion*, Geneva attracted attention through the Academy of Geneva founded by Calvin (1559) in order to educate a new generation of Protestant theologians and pastors who found their way to many parts of Europe, especially France.

Geneva became identified as *la Rome protestante*, and this exemplified an alternative holy city in sixteenth-century Europe.[22] The phenomenon of Geneva as *la Rome protestante* grew to mythic proportions by the late sixteenth century, and the myths were the result of positive as well as negative propaganda. The Protestant churches, especially in France, the Netherlands, and Great Britain, identified with Geneva because it became a very powerful example of the Kingdom of God on earth, or holy commonwealth. At the same time, Calvin was ambivalent about dominating other national churches. He was reluctant to meddle too much in the affairs of the new French church, yet the authors of the new Reformed confessions in France and the Low Countries were eager to secure Genevan approval.[23] For Protestants under persecution, the contrast between a powerful Reformation city and their own precarious position further enhanced the reputation of Geneva. Similarly, Catholics, as equally outraged by this tenacious heresy as the Protestants were supportive of its orthodoxy, indirectly focused attention on Geneva by their repeated references to its debauchery and concupiscence.[24] Geneva stood as a symbol of defiance, a Protestant enclave in territory predestined for Catholic rule. The most famous French Catholic preacher in sixteenth-century Paris, Simon Vigor, described the Reformed with the phrase the "wild beasts of Geneva."[25]

The myth of Geneva is perhaps best understood by the claim that Geneva developed into a theocracy ("*théocratie calvinienne*").[26] Despite the dream of Christ's disciples for an earthly kingdom, the *Deus Absconditus* of many of the Protestant Reformers could not allow its fulfillment. This is not to say that Calvin envisioned a hidden God—it is the opposite, but his emphasis is on the importance of divinely appointed earthly rule. Sixteenth-century European national identity in general, as Barbara Diefendorf has eloquently stated, was rooted in collective religious unity: "Just as one might benefit from the prayers of others, so might one be threatened by their sins, which could bring down the wrath of God upon an entire people."[27] What is special about Geneva is the assumption that both the church and the state conformed to the will of God, and each had its proper sphere in the Christian commonwealth. Calvin's addition of a universal religious discipline in Geneva, administered by the Consistory and enforced by the civil magistrates, however, has been often criticized as the primary problem of a "theocracy" of this nature. In examining the *Registres du Consistoire*, Robert Kingdon has found that although discipline was essential, in addition to acting as a court, the Consistory played a vital role in education and compulsory counseling to resolve conflicts.[28] Reconciliation was as equally important as punishment. Despite the strength of the Consistory, and its critique of all moral issues in Geneva, it never possessed the political clout to enact permanent laws.[29] Thus the notion of a true theocracy cannot be assigned to Geneva.

Francis Higman, in Chapter 1, begins with a study of the myth of Geneva by examining some important texts—previously rarely studied—circulating at the time. Higman has offered an important study of the nature of these texts as they contributed to positive a well as negative identifying characteristics. Chapter 2, by Richard Muller, tackles the foundational problem that the Christian Church has always faced: What is the balance between the two swords, the spiritual and the secular? Muller uses the debate over Romans 13:1—7—the divine establishment of earthly rulers—between John Calvin and Theodore Beza to show how Geneva established its identity as a Christian commonwealth, which became manifest in a strong republican city-state.

Geneva's independence was precarious given their small territory, which was surrounded by large Catholic lands. The ever-present fear of extermination or servitude came to a crossroad at the end of the struggle (1589—1593) with Catholic Savoy, where Genevan independence had never been accepted. During the evening of December 11, 1602, the duke of Savoy made his last great attempt to forcibly take Geneva by storming the city, but his attack was successfully repelled. This *Escalade* became a premier symbol of Geneva's great endurance as an independent city, and it was celebrated with patriotic fervor every year continuing throughout the nineteenth century. To this day the yearly celebration of the Escalade is of greater local importance than Christmas. Political weakness in the international balance of power did not necessarily mean a reduction in Geneva's theological cohesiveness.

Seventeenth-century Geneva ceased to offer other Protestant cities the attractions of education and the book trade that it once commanded in the golden years of 1559—1580.[30] The faculties of Heidelberg and Leiden surpassed its Reformed educational significance, and Geneva played only a minor role in the Synod of Dordrecht (Dort) in 1618—1619.[31] The two leaders from the Church of Geneva who were delegates to Dordrecht, Bénédict Turrentin and Jean Diodati, were in agreement with the dominant continental, orthodox Calvinist positions. Chapter 3 examines the development of theology at the Academy of Geneva after Calvin. By concentrating on the doctrine of predestination, a central identifying Calvinist doctrine, Joel Beeke shows that Geneva maintained its international focus by cooperating with Reformed theologians at the Synod. Beeke argues that Beza did not depart from the doctrine and intention of Calvin, nor was he coldly deterministic and scholastic. Rather, from Theodore Beza to Francis Turretin, theologians of the Genevan Academy attempted to be faithful to Calvin's theology and to the pastoral concerns of the Genevan congregations. Geneva's independence as a republic became increasingly precarious in the seventeenth century when the French kings Louis XIII and Louis XIV restored Catholic worship throughout France, and through a *tour de force* instituted the Mass in the French diplomatic enclave in Geneva. For this reason Geneva had to ensure that its identity as a Reformed republic remained intact. In Chapter 4 Timothy Phillips examines the role Turretin played as exponent of a theologically communal expression of identity. He has studied Turretin's notion of theology as a way to collective identity. A common theology was grounded in revelation through Scripture—the standard for truth—and through the Christian common-wealth—the "communal discernment of truth." In Turretin's opinion, all the newer expressions or "novelties" of theology ran the risk of allowing individual-ism to dictate belief, a system that could not build a community that produced works of love and charity.

Geneva continued to find its identity in a multitude of sources: The original patrician families and the particular culture that had become established before the sixteenth century combined with the various refugee cultures from many parts of the French- and Italian-speaking world. Many of the wealthy merchant families kept extensive international identity through their extended families. For example, the interrelated families Calandrini-Burlamachi-Diodati-Turrentin had family members and houses of business in Geneva, Nurenburg, Frankfurt, Stade/Hamburg, Antwerp, Amsterdam, and London. Although Geneva remained a very important center, it was the strong ties of family and Calvinist, Reformed Protestantism that linked these cities together.[32] One member of this extended family, Cesar Calandrini, became a minister and through schooling and ministry managed to live in almost every city where he had family, plus other Reformed cities, like Leiden, where close family friends resided.

Otto Selles, in Chapter 5, investigates the connection between the Reformed churches in Geneva and France as a measure of Genevan identity. Although in terms of numbers the French church was by far a much larger body, the experience of the French Wars of Religion (1562—1629) and the Revocation of the Edict of Nantes (1685) left them an outlawed and "Desert" church. Through an analysis of Bénédict Pictet (Geneva) and Antoine Court (France), the two most important theologians of the time, Selles demonstrates how Geneva maintained its ecclesiastical leadership.

Throughout the eighteenth century, religion and society in Geneva went through major changes, and a growing heterodoxy fragmented traditional identity. Already in 1725 a new trend in theological thinking had developed when the Consensus Helveticus was abolished by the established church.[33] Preachers in Geneva, and there are some parallels with Bern and Zürich, concentrated on the development of good morals; they attempted to offer Christian values that responded to the demands of Enlightenment scholarship and avoided the excesses of scholasticism. They were also quick to oppose religious fanaticism in an effort to live peacefully and in toleration. They were key supporters of cultural activities, education, and the enjoyment and study of nature. Despite their conservative political considerations, they were surprisingly progressive in their intellectual thinking. This new "Enlightened Orthodoxy,"[34] however, was not universally agreeable as a new identity, and it was often equated with Socinianism. Many foreigners praised the Genevese for their progressive thought;

for example, D'Alembert praised them in the *Encyclopedia*. Others, following the Calvinist confessional tradition, used "Socinian" as a term of derision, claiming that it manifest similar elements to English Unitarianism.[35] There were small groups of pastors and parishioners, for example, who considered themselves traditionally orthodox; however, in general religion in Geneva was quite heterodox and no longer a model of Reformed theology. Herman de Goltz, a conservative historian from the early nineteenth century, was not alone in the opinion that by the late eighteenth century the traditional designation of *la Rome protestante* had been changed to *"petit Paris."*[36]

The changing feelings toward Geneva's famous son, Jean-Jacques Rousseau, offers an example of the development of Enlightened Orthodoxy and the newer identifying elements of Geneva by the late eighteenth century. Although Rousseau's writings were rejected (1762) by the government, his development of a more modern and natural religion had a close affinity with Enlightened Orthodoxy, unrecognized at first. With revolutionary ideas permeating Europe in the 1790s, the Genevese freely partook of Rousseau's ideas, and he inspired a new generation to develop a love of nature and a sense of individual religious conscience. Fred Graham defines the movement that Rousseau began as a "second revolution" following the first revolution of Calvin.[37] Rousseau understood the social context of the Genevan tradition. For this reason Rousseau became unpopular with his Enlightenment colleagues when he disagreed with Voltaire's suggestion that Geneva allow a theater to open. According to Karl Barth, Geneva's rejection of Rousseau seems to have partially grown out of some of the "inner conflicts" inherent in the civilization of the Enlightenment that was established in Geneva.[38] Jean-Louis Leuba also points directly to a theological paradox: Rousseau's conflict with the Genevan hierarchy was due precisely to his pushing just beyond where Enlightened Orthodoxy wanted to go, and in this way he exploited the "ambiguities of the religion of the Reformed."[39]

In 1791 the General Council forgave all prior condemnations, and in 1793 it even commemorated his birthplace. The opinion of Isaac-Salomon Anspach is significant. As a pastor and counselor of state, Anspach was the moving force behind the Constitution of 1794. In a commemorative speech on June 28, 1793, he pointed to the need for a revolutionary morale that had been Rousseau's gift of "true equality, of a real liberty," and anyone who cared for Genevan patriotism, he declared, became Rousseau's "true Republicans."[40] In another sermon commemorating the *Escalade* of 1602, Anspach redefined the uniqueness of Geneva by its combination of religion, patriotism, and industry. Anspach affirmed the Reformation as the foundational event and pointed not to Calvinism or dogma but, rather, to the simplicity and reasonableness it engendered in Genevans. Certainly this understanding fit with the acceptance of Rousseau by church and government. Anspach pointed to yet another key to the original understanding of Geneva's Christian commonwealth, and this would become the foundation of a new Genevan unity in the nineteenth century: "It is your duty to have a compassionate heart, gentle manners, and charity which forms the honor of your national character."[41] Geneva exemplified the revolutionary ideas of liberty, equality, and fraternity, which had existed there for centuries. In 1835 Rousseau's renown earned him the honor of having the central island in the Rhone River renamed *Ile Rousseau*.[42] By the beginning of the nineteenth century, Geneva had to find its identity in something other than the ecclesiastical system of Calvin.[43] Henri Babel has offered a most intriguing list of the people who contributed most to Genevan identity in his book entitled *Les Quatre Hommes qui ont fait Genève: De Calvin à Beze et de Rousseau à Dunant* (The Four Men Who Have Made Geneva: From Calvin to Beza and from Rousseau to Dunant).

In Chapter 6 Jeffroy Watt has examined Genevan identity by concentrating on Reformed piety and the practice of suicide. Although the morose, strict, and austere side of Calvinism has often been connected with the development of a great anxiety among its adherents, Watt shows the increase of suicides by the end of the eighteenth century suggests the opposite. When identity as a Reformed republic was stronger at the beginning of the century, there were clearly fewer reasons for breaking with group identity through suicide. Martin Klauber continues the analysis of the changing Genevan identity through the development of theological ideas in the eighteenth century. In Chapter 7 he concentrates on two of the most important theologians, J. A. Turretin and Jacob Vernet, to record the changes. Linda Kirk, in Chapter 8, has analyzed yet another important indicator of identity in the industry and wealth that brought pride and community at the same time it helped fuel a growing perception that Geneva had, as a result, "gone soft."

By the 1770s the older ruling elite began to lose control of the Republic, and this eroded the 200-year-old reliance on patrician rule. Before to this the aristocracy controlled the city of Geneva through its sole membership in the Small Council. France, Bern, and Zürich had given legitimacy to the Act of 1738 that allowed the government to be administered by a smaller group of four syndics, the Small Council of Twenty-Five, the Council of Sixty, the Grand Council of Two Hundred, and the General Council. The *aristocratie*, automatically citizens, and the *bourgeoisie*, represented about 36 percent of the population in 1781, with a total population of only 26,140.[44] Many of the citizens of Geneva embraced the Enlightenment, perfecting its culture and taste, and enlightened ideas carried with them the seeds of political change. With traditional ties to many Swiss cantons, the Republic of Geneva began to feel the strength of the coalition of diverse cantons. The Enlightenment, Jonathan Steinberg has found, "reinforced a strong sense of 'Swissness', a common identity, which challenged the traditional patrician right to rule. . . . 'Swissness', on the other hand, glossed over the fact that the sturdy Alpine peasants and William Tell himself were inconveniently Catholic and hence not ideal representatives of progress." Long before any official membership in Switzerland, therefore, some "institutional compromises" on the part of the Genevan patricians became necessary if they were to survive.[45] Between 1770 and 1780 the majority of the Grand Council were called constitutionalists (*ultra-négatifs*), the Small Council were called *négatifs modérés*, and the General Council had strong representation by the bourgeoisie; even the *natifs* increased their political power. In December 1792 Jacques Grenus, a Jacobin, led some bourgeoisie, *natifs*, *habitants*, and *sujets* to form a new party, called the *égalisateurs*. They revolted and soon eliminated the revived patrician government. The Edict of December 1792 gave civil rights to all permanent inhabitants, yet the Constitution of 1794 allowed only full equality to members of the established Reformed Church of Geneva.

On April 15, 1798, the once-proud and independent city of Geneva was annexed by the French Empire and became the capital of the *département du Léman*.[46] The church still exercised its duties, and the Academy of Geneva, despite a limitation of the number of professors and monetary support, continued its education. In fact, education remained one of the most important distinctive elements of Genevan identity (within the extremes of Calvin and Rousseau) and Swiss renown (through Jean-Henri Pestalozzi). This was one area France did not seek to control. In 1814 George Mallet wrote, in *Genève et les genevois*, that one of the greatest establishments in Geneva was public instruction, open to even "the most poor." Although Mallet characterized Geneva's moral education, supported by the family, as possessing a "beauty and delicacy of language" developed with "memory and good taste," he was also aware of international opinion that often singled out its almost "severe examination," which produced a particular character, preparing students for the republic and nation.[47] By the beginning of the nineteenth century, Geneva had to find its identity in something other than the ecclesiastical and instructional ideal of Calvin.[48]

The Enlightenment had sufficiently dismantled the hierarchy and exclusiveness of patrician rule; what remained was a reconstruction of a commonwealth built on modern principles. The commonwealth of Rousseau encouraged the development of a community of coequal citizens whose common goal, while it embraced a diversity of economic and religious values, was political unity. The nineteenth-century became a period of compromise and of the construction of smaller interest groups that possessed greater access to political power. This great shift in orientation and the loss of political power by the church produced many fears and tensions in early-nineteenth-century Geneva. The success depended on the ability of rethinking the basis of the Christian commonwealth as a diverse community committed to the new order: equality, charity, and peace. This new community did not come easily; bitter religious rivalries, social agitation, and political wrangling became commonplace, yet this was accomplished through public opinion and discussion rather than by imposition and revolution. The original sixteenth-century community called by God and embodied in the New Jerusalem now embraced the gentiles. Although the work of God in the modern world was now seen as less direct, it included Rome and Athens; the new Genevese had a mission to bring God's light to the nations of the world.

In 1813 Geneva was freed from the Napoleonic Empire, and with their expanded territory—including a new population of Catholics—the Genevese sought an alliance with the Swiss Helvetic Confederation, which they eventually achieved in 1815. They became the Canton and Republic of Geneva. Lively debates over the reorganization and identity of Geneva and its positive and negative advantages of joining Switzerland filled the period of restoration. Ulrich Gäbler has pointed out that the great "centrifugal tendencies" of linguistic, ethnic, geographical, and religious differences that once divided the Swiss cantons before the French Revolution could be bridged only by the creation of the "myth of Switzerland."[49] Genevans came under the influence of the new diversity that was Switzerland, and they enthusiastically embraced the older myth of William Tell and other, newer movements that expanded their identity. A religious revival (Réveil) fueled by Swiss and international support quickly gained many Genevese adherents with its call for a renewal of piety, orthodoxy, and ecclesiastical reform. The Réveil had a great diversity of support from the long established, yet marginalized, Moravian brethren in Geneva and from the visits of well-known continental literary figures, such as Madame Germaine de Staël, or from other revival leaders from Great Britain, such as Robert Haldane from Scotland. By contrast, the National Protestant Church of Geneva (Église Nationale Protestante de Genève), as it became known, attempted to restore order and regain its traditionally central position. Any religious dissent and departure from their eighteenth-century standards was seen as a threat to the Republic itself. Inundated with the flood of revolutionary ideas, growing democratic practices, religious diversity, and capitalist economies, the National Church attempted, with only limited success, to steer an institutionally conservative course in the early nineteenth century. Many following the Réveil saw the opportunity for increased religious and political freedom under the restoration, and they received support from the growing international movement for an increased separation of church and state.

In 1830 the French revolutionary fury once again produced armed resistance throughout Europe and in some of the cantons of Switzerland. Geneva remained stable, but the political situation kept it in an uncertain position.[50] There was growing international interest in Geneva in the first half of the nineteenth century, and this was sparked by a revival of interest in the Reformation. The Protestant churches in France, the Netherlands, Great Britain, and North America, where Calvinist heritage was established, wanted to know more about the origins of modern institutions, and Geneva became the source. There was a wide range of opinion about whether revolutionary France had left indelible marks on the state and church of Geneva. Some conservative churches feared apostasy. For example, Rev. Edward Bickersteth, a well-known English Evangelical, warned that: "A prayer for the Emperor was introduced into the liturgy: the consistory resumed its functions, and a full and free demission was given to French intercourse and manners, so that the stern Presbyterianism of Calvin was reduced to such a state as to allow the opening of the theaters on a Sunday evening, and every other kind of Sabbath desecration, from which the once favoured city has never yet recovered."[51] Others found the new customs and cosmopolitan culture in Geneva a welcome relief to the strict and austere tradition that had dominated the city for 300 years.

Jeannine Olson, in Chapter 9, begins an analysis of identity and change in the nineteenth century by focusing on the traditional identifying theme of social welfare. Olson has surveyed the history of the *Bourse française* and showed how it was resistant to the changes in government until the nineteenth century and then eventually absorbed into the new state. John Roney, in Chapter 10, focuses on the Tercentenary of the Reformation in 1835 as yet another way to measure the traditional identifying factors in the Republic. Although Geneva was still recognized as the Reformation city of Calvin, to fulfill the requirements of a new era in European church and state relations, as well as a growing pluralist society, opinions about the relevance of sixteenth-century ideas varied greatly. Gabriel Mützenberg, in Chapter 11, has concentrated on the growing pluralism and loss of identity in his study of the reorganization of the Catholic Church in the historic city of Calvin. Finally, in Chapter 12, William Edgar concentrates on the role of education and the attempt to come to terms with modernity. Although the church lost its monopoly in education—a parallel to the Catholic Church in France—moral instruction and the virtues gained by a study of the classics went hand in hand with a new focus on practical subjects that would prepare students for citizenship and commerce.

The Revolutions of 1848, which erupted throughout Europe, came earlier to Geneva. In 1846, under the leadership of James Fazy, liberal and democratic forces were consolidated in Geneva as never before.[52] By 1847 a new constitution was written under the leadership of Fazy, and for the first time a democratic political system became established (1848). The new Constitution had revoked the status of the National Church as the dominant religion in Geneva, and by 1848 unity of Protestant belief had sufficiently splintered. As a result, some Protestants of the *Réveil* formed a free church (1849), the *Eglise évangélique libre de Genève.* By comparison, free churches had become a common phenomena in Scotland and England, the Netherlands, France, and other parts of Switzerland, as well as North America. In the years following, however, the Free Church and the National Church shared projects and ideas.[53] The revolutions and war in mid century increased the need for a new expression of the Christian commonwealth that could support plurality and respond to philanthropic needs on the international context. Already in 1828 members of the *Réveil* had set up an organization called the Public Welfare Society of Geneva (*Société genevoise d'utilité publique*).[54] Many members of the National Church also helped with these new projects, and the second half of the nineteenth century, saw far fewer religious tensions. On the Tercentenary of the founding of the Academy of Geneva by Calvin (1859), everyone was acutely aware of the vicious war being fought in Italy, and the historian Jean Henri Merle d'Aubigné proclaimed that "it is especially in the times of war, that Christians must show themselves children of peace, to demand that God conserve the peace when the war approaches, and to demand that he reestablish peace when the war rages."[55] He further demanded that as creatures in God's world, humans are to follow the example of Christ, who though a Jew demanded compassion even to the Samaritans.[56] As an immediate response to suffering, a temporary organization was set up called the Committee for the Wounded (*Comité pour les blessés*) for the purpose of collecting gifts and sending volunteers. Jean-Henri Dunant, instantly famous for his book *A Souvenir of Solferino*,[57] was one of the first members of the committee and was involved in the international Young Men's Christian Association (YMCA, and the *Union chrétienne des Jeunes Gens*), the Convention of Geneva; out of this, he became the founder of the Red Cross (*Croix-Rouge*).[58]

Geneva in the nineteenth century no longer represented *la Rome protestante* of the sixteenth century, but it fulfilled some of the older functions. Genevan identity, like those of modern North American states, did not necessarily locate its center in ethnic history, and it even began to embrace a religious pluralism. Although Geneva was no longer a center for Protestant theology, few churches of the nineteenth century wanted a complete return to the confessions and practices of the Reformation. In fact, from conservative to liberal, almost all Protestant churches saw themselves as more modern equivalents of Reformation thought.[59] Geneva never regained the status of having the first among theologians, nor could it boast of a homogeneous Protestant population with theocratic rule. Interest in theology by the second half of the nineteenth century, however, had changed from questions of dogma and uniformity as a measure of identity to questions of practical theology and social concern that had to be accomplished within a new environment of pluralism. In this regard, Geneva renewed its role as an important center for Protestant activity, despite its loss of identity as a Calvinist republic.

Throughout the nineteenth century Geneva became recognized as a model of Christian social and philanthropic activity that had continuity with the historic Reformation church of Calvin, which had formed the basis for modern political and religious institutions. The city and churches of Geneva sponsored many programs for social welfare, and because of their political neutrality and pluralistic base, Geneva was able to become the headquarters and meeting place for international religious, economic, and political organizations. Merle d'Aubigné, who helped establish the *salle de la Réformation* in 1867, liked to repeat the phrase of Jules Michelet, "*l'Europe sera sauvé par Genève*." Indeed, there was an element of truth in the prophetic voice of Michelet.

NOTES

1. John Calvin, *Institutes of the Christian Religion*, trans. Henry Beveridge, 2 vols. (Grand Rapids, MI: Eerdmans, reprinted 1983), 2: 657–658.

2. Robert Wuthnow, *Communities of Discourse: Ideology and Social Structure in the Reformation, the Enlightenment, and European Socialism* (Cambridge, MA: Harvard UP, 1989), 4.

3. See W. Fred Graham, ed., *Later Calvinism: International Perspectives, Sixteenth Century Essays and Studies*, vol. 22 (Kirksville, MS: Sixteenth Century Journal Publishers, 1994).

4. E. William Monter, *Calvin's Geneva* (New York: John Wiley and Sons, 1967), 22.

5. See Calvin, *Institutes of the Christian Religion*, 2: 656–657.

6. Joshua Mitchell, *Not By Reason Alone: Religion, History, and Identity in Early Modern Political Thought* (Chicago: U of Chicago P, 1993), 5. See also W. Fred Graham, *The Constructive Revolutionary: John Calvin and His Socio-Economic Impact* (Atlanta: John Knox Press, 1971), 24: "An underlying persuasion of this writer is that social, political, and economic change—secular change, to sum up in one catchword all that we persist in seeing as nonreligious—needs religious meaning and zeal to provide the dynamic to bring it about."

7. This needs some qualification: Calvin's primary concern was to reconstruct a holy community on the New Testament and Hebraic models, but invariably he was also rooted in the context of sixteenth-century France. Calvin took allegiance to the present political power very seriously; his first edition of the *Institutes* was dedicated to the King François I of France. The political events and persecution in France brought some changes in Calvin's theories when the *monarchomachs*—François Hotman, Theodore Beza, and Philippe Dupleiss-Mornay—more clearly relied on a link to a feudal past to support the notion of the sovereignty of the people based on communities represented by local magistrates. See Miriam Yardeni, "French Calvinist Political Thought, 1534–1715," in *International Calvinism, 1534–1715*, ed. Menna Prestwich (Oxford: Clarendon Press, 1985), 324.

8. Graham, *The Constructive Revolutionary*, 31.

9. See Mark Greengrass, *The French Reformation* (New York: Basil Blackwell, 1987), 29–32.

10. William G. Naphy, "'No History Can Satisfy Everyone': Geneva's Chroniclers and Emerging Religious Identities," in *Protestant History and Identity*, ed. Bruce Gordon (Aldershot, UK: Scolar Press, 1996), 2: 32.

11. See Joseph Strayer, "France: the Holy Land, the Chosen People, and the Most Christian King," in *Action and Conviction in Early Modern Europe: Essays in Memory of E. H. Harbison*, ed. Theodore K. Rabb and Jerold E. Siegel (Princeton, NJ: Princeton UP, 1969), 3–16.

12. See Ulrich Gäbler, "The Swiss: A Chosen People," in *Many Are Chosen: Divine Election and Western Nationalism*, ed. William R. Hutchinson and Hartmut Lehmann (Minneapolis: Fortress Press, 1994), 257–276; Paul Regan, "Calvinism and the Dutch Israel Thesis," *Protestant History and Identity*, ed. Gordon, 2: 91–106; see also 19, 27–30, 36, 38; Roelof Bisschop, *Sions Vorst en Volk: Het tweede-Israëlidee als theocratisch concept in de Gerformeerde kerk van de Republiek tussen ca. 1650 en ca. 1750* (Veenendaal: Kool Boeken Distributie, 1993); Gerrit Groenhuis, "Calvinism and National Consciousness: The Dutch Republic as the New Israel," in *Britain and the Netherlands*, vol. 7, *Church and State since the Reformation* (The Hague: Martinus Nijhoff, 1981): 118–133; C. Huisman, *Neerlands Israël. Het natiebesef der traditoneel-gereformeerdenin de achttiende eeuw* (Dordrecht: Van de Tol, 1983); and elsewhere: M. I. Lowance, *The Language of Canaan: Metaphor and Symbol in New England from the*

Puritans to the Transcendentalists (Cambridge, MA: Harvard UP, 1980). There was also a long tradition within French monarchial thinking that combined temporal power with Hebraic spiritual power given to "God's Chosen people." In this way, Calvin displayed a deeply rooted French perspective. See Dale Van Kley, *The Religious Origins of the French Revolution: From Calvin to the Civil Constitution of the Clergy, 1560–1791* (New Haven, CT: Yale UP, 1996), 16–30.

13. For the binding nature of the Old Testament covenants and for the issue of the "incommensurability of God" (the key to the idolatry of all images), see David C. Steinmetz, *Calvin in Context* (New York: Oxford UP, 1995), and David Willis-Watkins, "The Second Commandement and Church Reform: The Colloquy of St. Germain-en-Laye, 1562," *Studies in Reformed Theology and History* 2, 2 (spring 1994).

14. Gillian Lewis, "Calvinism in Geneva in the time of Calvin and of Beza (1541–1605)," in *International Calvinism, 1541–1715*, ed. Menna Prestwich (Oxford: Clarendon Press, 1985), 48.

15. See John T. McNeill, *The History and Character of Calvinism* (New York: Oxford UP, 1974 [1954]), 201–202. McNeill rightly points to the paradoxical nature (*complexio oppositorum*) of Calvin's thought, perhaps best seen in his belief in both predestination and human responsibility.

16. Mark Valeri, "Religion, Discipline, and the Economy in Calvin's Geneva," *Sixteenth Century Journal* 34, 1 (1997): 135.

17. See Monter, *Calvin's Geneva*, 2–5, 21–22.

18. Ibid., 169.

19. See Calvin, *Institutes* [Book IV, Chap. 1,4], 283–284. See also Calvin's commentaries on Deuteronomy.

20. See Karin Maag, *Seminary or University? The Genevan Academy and Reformed Higher Education, 1560–1620*, St. Andrews Studies in Reformation History (Aldershot, UK: Scolar Press, 1995).

21. See Arthur David Ainsworth, *The Relations between Church and State in the City and Canton of Geneva* (Atlanta: Stein Print Co., 1965); André Biéler, *La Pensé économique et sociale de Calvin* (Geneva: H. Georg, 1961); Hermann de Goltz, *Genève religieuse au dix-neuvième siècle*, trans. C. Millan-Sillem (Geneva: H. Georg, 1862), 1–22; René Guerdan, *Histoire de Genève* (Paris: Mazarine, 1981), 75–169; Henri Heyer, *L'Église de Genève, 1535–1909* (Geneva: A. Jullien, 1909), 7–39; Robert Kingdon, *Geneva and the Consolidation of the French Protestant Movement 1564–1572* (Madison: U of Wisconsin P, 1967); Monter, *Calvin's Geneva*, and "De L'Évêche à la Rome protestante," in *Histoire de Genève*, ed. Paul Guichonnet (Toulouse: Privat; Lausanne: Payot, 1974), 127–183.

22. Guerdan, *Histoire de Genève*, 98, claims that "if one wants to fix a date for the birth of *la Rome protestante*, one is able to say, without doubt, that it came on June 5, 1559 . . . [when Calvin] gave the word to the secretary of the council, Michel Roset." For a variety of direct references see: Jean-Claude Favez and Claude Raffestein, "De la Genève radicale à la cité internationale," in *Histoire de Genève*, ed. Guichonnet, 302–303; Goltz, *Genève religieuse*, 3; Monter, "De L'Évêche," 93–99; Robert B. Mowat, *The Romantic Age: Europe in the Early Nineteenth Century* (London: George C. Harrop, 1937), 182; Albert Py, Jean Paul Barbier, and Alain Dufour, *Ronsard et la Rome protestante* (Geneva: BPU, 1985); David Tissot, ed., introduction, *Les Conférences de Genève 1861: Rapports et discours publiés au nom du comité de l'Alliance évangélique*, 2 vols. (Geneva: H. Georg, 1861), 1: vi.

23. See Kingdon, *Geneva and the Consolidation*, 43—148.

24. See Monter, "De L'Évêche," 149, "La Puissance du contre-mythe."

25. Barbara B. Diefendorf, *Beneath the Cross: Catholics and Huguenots in Sixteenth-Century Paris* (New York: Oxford UP, 1991), 158. Diefendorf offers an enlightening history of the identity of Huguenots in Paris. See also Guido Marnef, *Antwerp in the Age of Reformation: Underground Protestantism in a Commercial Metropolis, 1550—1577*, trans. J. C. Grayson (Baltimore: Johns Hopkins UP, 1996), for a parallel study of Calvinist identity.

26. See Monter, "De L'Évêche," 152. Cf. Heyer, *l'Église de Genève*, 14—15, and Eugène Choisy, *La théocratie à Genève au temps de Calvin* (Geneva: Ch. Eggimann, 1897).

27. Diefendorf, *Beneath the Cross*, 37.

28. See Robert M. Kingdon, "The Geneva Consistory in the Time of Calvin," in *Calvinism in Europe, 1540—1620*, ed. Andrew Pettegree, Alastair Duke, and Gillian Lewis (Cambridge: Cambridge UP, 1994), 24.

29. See Lewis, "Calvinism in Geneva," 54.

30. See Nicholas Bouvier, "Geneva," in Nicholas Bouvier, Gordon A. Craig, and Lionel Gossman, *Geneva, Zürich, Basel: History, Culture, and National Identity* (Princeton, NJ: Princeton UP, 1994), 26—27. As a Genevois, Bouvier paints an unflattering picture of seventeenth-century Geneva: "No doubt the Calvinist experience, along with the *bise noir* (Geneva's icy north wind), has given a darker cast to the Genevan character and endowed it with strength and endurance. No doubt it shaped a moralistic and puritan society (fostering also hypocrisy that naturally accompanies moral rigor and puritanism), which, for a time at least, was closer to Sparta than to Athens—a city of pedagogues, scientists, and introverts."

31. See Lewis, "Calvinism in Geneva," 64—66. Even French schools, at Orléans and Nîmes, or Sedan and Saumur, as well as Cambridge, Basel, Ghent, and Herborn, offered a competition to the Academy of Geneva. See Gillian Lewis, "The Genevan Academy," 51, and Ole Peter Grell, "Merchants and Ministers: The Foundations of International Calvinism," 258, in *Calvinism in Europe*, ed. Pettegree et al., 51; and Maag, *Seminary or University?*

32. See Grell, "Merchants and Ministers," 254—273.

33. See Goltz, *Genève religieuse*, 47—52, 67—70; Émile G. Léonard, *Histoire génerale du protestantisme*, 3 vols. (Paris: Presses Universitaires de France, 1964), 3:50—53; Jean-Louis Leuba, "Rousseau et le milieu calviniste de sa jeunesse," in J.-L. Leuba et al., *Jean-Jacques Rousseau et la crise contemporaine de la conscience* (Paris: Beauchesne, 1980), 14—15, suggests that the Consensus had superseded the original intent of Calvin, demanding answers to Calvin's mysteries, and sees this as a new anthropocentric view of theology. See also Anne-Marie Puiz, "La Genève des Lumières," in *Histoire de Genève*, ed. Guichonnet, 218—219; Bernard Reymond, "Les débuts du libéralisme dans la théologie protestante d'expression française," *Sciences religieuse/Studies in Religion* 11, 2 (1982): 181—187. One cannot forget that a detailed and official confession had difficulty of enforcement even after 1564, and in 1576, only twelve years after Calvin's death, the Company of Pastors substituted Calvin's extensive confession for a summary. See Lewis, "The Geneva Academy," 53.

34. Leuba, "Rousseau," 11—46. See Maria-Cristina Pitassi, *De l'orthodoxie aux Lumières. Genève 1670—1737* (Geneva: Labor et Fides, 1992).

18		The Identity of Geneva

35. See Peter Gay, *The Enlightenment: An Introduction*, vol. 1 (New York: Alfred A. Knopf, 1976), 1:336—337, "d'Alembert's supreme compliment—'some Geneva pastors have no religion other than a perfect Socinianism.'" Heyer, *L'Église de Genève*, 112—113n. Auguste Breyton, *Le Pietisme à Genève* (Geneva: Wyss et Duchene, 1896), 44; C.-B., "Protestantism in France," *Christian Examiner* 37 (November 1844): 305, "silent and sure spread of Unitarianism." Socinianism was founded by Lelio Sozzini (1525—1562), who used the Latin name *Socinus*, and his nephew Fausto Sozzini (1539—1604), as a rationalist movement, they believed that Jesus was only human.

36. See Goltz, *Genève religieuse*, 3.

37. Graham, *Constructive Revolutionary*, 23.

38. See Karl Barth, *Protestant Theology in the Nineteenth Century: Its Background and History* (London: SCM, 1972), 218.

39. Leuba, "Rousseau," 40—41. He suggests that there is a good argument that the *Consensus* had superseded the original intent of Calvin; that is to say, it demanded answers to those areas Calvin would have wanted to remain a mystery. For Leuba this movement was based on a new anthropocentric view of theology as opposed to Calvin's theocentric one (14—15). Puiz, "La Genève des Lumières," 218—219.

40. Isaac-Salomon Anspach, "Discours du citoyen Isaac-Salomon Anspach, pro-noncé le 28 juin 1793 à la fête de l'anniversaire de la naissance de J.-J. Rousseau" (BPU, 1793), 4, 8.

41. Isaac-Salomon Anspach, "Sermon pour l'Escalade, sur Psaume XXXIII, verset 12" [Prêché à Saint Gervais, le douze décembre 1793] (BPU, 1793), 6.

42. See Henri Babel, *Les Quatre Hommes qui ont fait Genève: De Calvin à Beze et de Rousseau à Dunant* (Geneva: Tribune, 1981), 92—93. See also Pierre Burgelin, *Jean-Jacques Rousseau et la religion de Genève* (Geneva: Labor et Fides, 1962); Alexandre Jullien, *Histoire de Genève, des origines à 1798* (Geneva: SHAG, 1951), 447.

43. See Linda Kirk, "Eighteenth-Century Geneva and a Changing Calvinism," in *Religion and National Identity*, ed. Stewart Mews (Oxford: Basil Blackwell, 1982), 380.

44. See Goltz, *Genève religieuse*, 45; Robert Steimer, "L'Evolution démographique Genèvoise," in *Genève Le Pays et Les Hommes: Étude géographique* (Geneva: Société de Géographie de Genève, 1958), 191; Heyer, *L'Église de Genève*, 125; Puiz, "La Genève des Lumières," 240.

45. Jonathan Steinberg, *Why Switzerland?*, 2d ed. (Cambridge: Cambridge UP, 1996), 215.

46. See Éduard Chapusiat, *De la Terreur à l'annexion. Genève et la république française, 1793—1798* (Geneva: ATAR, 1912). With a policy of equal departmental jurisdictions, the territory of Léman grew to include the old Republic of Geneva, parts of Savoy, Piedmont-Sardinia, and other neighboring villages. The result was that the once exclusively Protestant republic was wed together with much larger Catholic regions. See also George Andrey, "La Suisse d'ancien régime face à la grande révolution," in *Les Résistances à la Révolution*, ed. François Lebrun and Roger Dupuy, Acts du Colloque de Rennes, 17—21 Septembre 1985 (Paris: Editions Imago, 1987), 255—263; Heyer, *L'Église de Genève*, 95—102; Palmer, *The Age of Democratic Revolutions*, 2: 395—421; J.-C.-L. Sismondi, *Statistique du Département du Léman*, ed. H. O. Pappe, *MD* (Geneva: Jullien, 1971); Steimer, "L'Evolution démographique Genèvoise," 191.

47. George Mallet, *Genève et les genevois* (Geneva: J. J. Paschoud, 1814), 141—142.

48. See Kirk, "Eighteenth-Century Geneva and a Changing Calvinism," 380: "1798 did not destroy the city's protestant tradition, and church and state were not formally separated until 1907, but the republics' Calvinist identity—laboriously imposed—was destroyed."

49. Gäbler, "The Swiss," 269.

50. See *Genève protestante en 1831*, ed. Olivier Fatio, Publication de la Faculté de Théologie de l'Université de Genève, no. 6 (Geneva: Labor et Fides, 1983).

51. Introduction by the Rev. E. Bickersteth, ed., in Jean Henri Merle d'Aubigné, *A Voice from the Alps: or, A Brief Account of the Evangelical Societies of Paris and Geneva* (London: R. B. Seeley and W. Burnside, 1838), 25—26.

52. See Favez and Raffestein, "De la Genève radicale," 299—314; Guerdan, *Histoire de Genève*, 283—296.

53. See also Heyer, *L'Église de Genève*, 123—124, who notes that by mid-century the doctrines the *Réveil* had "formaient la majorité du corps pastoral national."

54. See, for example, Paul Guichonnet and Paul Waeber, "Révolutions et Restauration (1782—1846)," in *Histoire de Genève*, ed. Guichonnet, 293.

55. Jean Henri Merle d'Aubigné, *La pierre sur laquelle l'académie de Genève fut posée en juin 1559* (Geneva: Émile Béroud, 1859), 3.

56. Ibid., 18.

57. See Jean-Henri Dunant, *Un Souvenir de Solférino* (Berne: Croix-Rouge suisse, 1980 [1863]).

58. The "départment d'Evangélisation à l'extérieur." See Gabriel Mützenberg, *Henry Dunant: le Predestiné* (Geneva: Robert Estienne, 1984), 100-102. The Comité was composed of Merle d'Aubigné, Jean-Henri Dunant, Adrien Naville, W. Turretin, Louis Brocher, Geymonat, Charles Barde, Dr. Louis Appia, under the presidency of Adrien Naville. In 1864 they founded the International Committee for the Amelioration of the Condition of the Wounded, which in 1880 changed its name to the *Croix-Rouge*. The first board was composed of members of the *Société évangélique de Genève*: General Guillaume-Henri Dufour, Gustave Moynier (President), Dr. Louis Appia, Dr. Théodore Maunoir, and Jean-Henri Dunant (secretary). See Pierre Boissier, "Henry Dunant," *International Review of the Red Cross* (*IRRC*) 14, 161 (August 1974): 44; Bernard Gagnebin, "Henry Dunant," *IRRC* 3, 27 (June 1963): 287; Guichonnet and Waeber, "Révolutions et Restauration," 293; Guerdan, *Histoire de Genève*, 299—300; J. H. Rombach, "Two Great Figures in Red Cross History," *IRRC* 2, 16 (July 1962): 351-361.

59. See Brian Gerrish, *The Old Protestantism and the New: Essays on the Reformation Heritage* (Chicago: U of Chicago P, 1982).

1

The Origins of the Image of Geneva

Francis Higman

In 1966 Alain Dufour published an important study entitled "The Myth of Geneva in Calvin's Lifetime."[1] In fact, he presented two aspects of the myth, the one positive or "Calvinist," the other negative, hostile to Geneva; this latter image was the work of Roman Catholic writers such as Pierre de Ronsard (in his *Discours*, 1562–1563) or Artus Désiré (in the *Grandes chroniques et annales de Passe-partout*, of 1558). Contrary to what might be expected, the negative myth of Geneva does not present the city as a center of puritan boredom and moralizing repression; the city is described primarily as a cauldron of debauchery and lust, as a refuge for all the fugitives from justice and all the hedonists of France. It is also seen, especially by Ronsard, as the center from which political and religious destabilization is spread throughout France.

Alain Dufour discusses the dating of the origins of this negative myth. "The reply is worth noting: there is no sign of it before 1555, but many examples date from that moment."[2] This is because 1555 is the year of the definitive triumph of Calvin's followers in Geneva; it is also, and for that very reason, the time when those who had been banished from Geneva, the Bolsecs, the Perrinists, are living in exile in Bernese lands around Geneva and doing their best to discredit the new government of the city. Dufour concludes: "The history of Geneva, until then simply that of a city allied to the Swiss, becomes autonomous, takes its own direction and acquires its own image in history: it is, and it will remain, the city of Calvin."[3]

Alain Dufour was "opening a file" on the subject and invited other scholars to add contributions encountered in the course of their research. This is the invitation I am here accepting by presenting—for the first time in English?—a few little-known, and sometimes amusing, texts. I hope to show that the negative myth of Geneva did not come into being at a precise moment, but it evolved slowly over a period, and that there are reasons for its development beyond those adduced by Alain Dufour.

JEAN GACY, *La Deploration de la Cité de Genesve* (1536?)

Our first text shows that the negative image of Geneva actually goes back right to the origins of the Reformation in the city, before even the arrival of Calvin. Friar Jean Gacy of Cluses, "the least of the Minims," was the confessor of the Franciscan nuns of Geneva (and consequently one of the major sources for the famous diary of Jeanne de Jussie). He had already distinguished himself by publishing one of the first anti-Lutheran compositions in French, the *Trialogue nouveau* (1524) [4] He presents a lamentation on the events in Geneva in 1535 in the *Deploration*, a poem that must have been composed in the first half of 1536 (he mentions the departure of the Franciscan nuns in December 1535, but not the arrival of John Calvin in July 1536). The text, which survives in only two copies, one in the Paris Bibliothèque nationale and the other in the Columbine Library of Seville, was reedited in the nineteenth century in an edition now difficult to find; it deserves to be made available again.

[Jean Gacy]: *The Lamentation of Geneva concerning the heretics which tyrannically oppress her*; and, *La Deploration de la Cité de Genesve sur le faict des hereticques qui l'ont Tiranniquement opprimee.*[5]

Lovely Rachel[6] shed tears and cried aloud,
Seeing the horrors which death would bring
To her children; and Naomi,[7] remembering Elimelech,
Joined to her in marriage, who died young,
And her two children for whom she wept so much,
Likewise Eli[8] questioned Hannah the mother of Samuel
Who sighed so bitterly, lamenting her fate
That she was infertile; but in misfortune
I, who am called suffering Geneva, have no rival
Among women born of Adam and Eve.

Once I was famous, rich and strong;
But at present there is no one to comfort me,
Ruined, poor, and starved, and defamed by land and by sea.[9]

[A 2r] A voix excelse plora par cris et larmes
Rachel la belle, prevoyant les alarmes
Que ses enfans par mort devoient venir,
Et Noemy, ayant le souvenir
D'Helimelech, lequel par mariage
Luy fut consors, et morut en jeune eage,
Et deux enfans pour lesqueulx tant plora,
Pareillement Hely bien explora
Anne la mere de Samuel, que tant
Amerement souspiroit, regretant
Le sien meschief, que elle estoit infecunde;
Mais en malheur je n'ay pas ma seconde,
Que suys nommee la dolente Genesve,
Trop plus que dame qu'aye produit
Adam ne Eve.

Jadis j'estoie renommee, riche et forte,
Mais present n'y a qui me conforte,
Calamiteuse, indigente, affamee,
Par mer, par terre suys par tout diffamee.

When Julius Caesar wrote his commen-
tary,[10]
He did me honour; now I must be silent.
Then I was once called Aurelia,[11]
But I am now bound by the folly of the
wicked.
I was once a delightful city;
The *anguenots*[12] have made me sedi-
tious.
These blind ones, with scales on their
eyes,
Summoned the scum of their children,
And have filled me with factions and
quarrels,
Divisions, and all sorts of bands.

I had built great halls in the
Molard;[13]
They used to hold universal fairs there.
People came from all climates to the
market;
But my inhabitants were not worthy of
that:
By their rebellion they were deprived of
them,
And the fairs were transferred to Lyons
the beautiful.[14]
I had pre-eminence among the
Allobroges,[15]
Triumphant, reigning; and because I was
great,
Very opulent and beautiful,
The wicked, cunning heretics made my
subjects rebel
Against my sovereign lord of Savoy,[16]
Who kept me in peace and in his way.

If you enquire of me
What is the cause of my destruction,
Why I weep, casting my voice into the
air,
I reply briefly:
It is the cruel, wild bear,[17]
Destroying all fruitful works,
Which has so robbed me under the pre-
tence of protecting me,
With its evil cunning,
Usurping with its hairy paw

Julles Cesar, faisant son commentaire,
M'a honnoree; maintenant me fault tayre.
Puys appellee jadiz fus Aurelie,
Mais des meschans la folie me lie.
Estre soloye cité delicieuse;
Les anguenotz m'ont fait sedicieuse.
Ces aveugles, ayant aux yeulx la maille,
Ont appellés leurs enfans la marmaille,
Puys m'ont ramplye de factions et
brigues,
Divisions, diversités de ligues.

J'avoye bastiz au Molard grandes
halles;
On l'en tenoit foyres universales.
[A 2v] De tous climatz on venoit aux
nundines;
Mes habitans de ce furent non dignes:
PrivÈ en furent par leur rebellion,
Et translatees furent au bel Lyon.
Des Allobroges j'avoye preeminence
Pour triumpher, regner; et mesmes en ce
Qu'estoye grande, tresopulente et belle,
Et2 mes incoles m'ont faict estre rebelle
A mon seignieur souverain de Savoye,
Qui me tenoit en paix et en sa voye,
Les hereticques malicieux et fins.

Si vous me faictes interrogation
Qui est la cause de ma destruction,
Pourquoy je pleure, gettant ma voix en
l'air,
Je vous respons à succincte parler:
C'est l'ours cruel et beste furieuse,
Exterminant toute oeuvre fructueuse,
Qui m'a pillee soubz umbre de tutelle,
Par façon telle, et maligne cautelle,
En usurpant à sa patte vellue
Tout mon avoir, comme faulce bellue,

All my goods, like a false monster,
Whence now, in this poor, vile age,
I am no more regarded than a poor vil-
lage;
So I am done down, full of woes,
Suffering a thousand ills day and night.

    Alas! to my dam I fed the little ass,
And received the bear, the ass and the
mule,[18]
Animals hated by everyone,
Whose detestable and vile sect
Has flourished; and under a wolf's pelt
They have planted the festering thorn
By a seditious, bizarre, fanatical
Pharel,[19]
Who pretends to be an angel;
It was already clear that he was Belial[20]
In Neuchâtel and in Montbéliard;[21]
Oecolampadius,[22] even though he was
of the same sect,
Upbraided him in word and in writing,
Saying he was born to be an obstacle:
By such works one knows the workman.

    Then the traitor called Froment[23]
Has mixed yeast into my white flour;[24]
To corrupt the whole body of the faith,
He cumulates and piles up all errors;
He is not tardy or lazy in spreading
them.
And his accomplice, the virulent
Viret,[25]
Who thought by his errors to mire down
The inhabitants and subjects of Orbe;
But at last, the heroes of the Christians
Banished him, driven out like a leper.[26]
By their great evil-doing they are cause
That most of my buildings are deserted,
And only wrongdoers remain; that is why
My songs are weeping and lamentation.

    Now, all of you, hear the great mir-
acles
Which these devils have wrought,
Deserving the fire and torments of hell,
With their false and disloyal accomplices:

Don maintenant en ce pouvre et vil eage
On ne m'estime ains que ung pouvre
village;
Pource confite suys, ramplie dennuys,
Cent mille maulx en souffrant jours et
nuytz.

    Las! à malheur j'ay nourry
l'asnichon,
Et receu l'ours, baudet et baudichon,
Les bestiaulx haiz par tout le monde,
Desquelx la secte detestable et immunde
[A 3r] A pullulé; et dessoubz peau vul-
pine
A faict planter la pungitive espine
Par ung Pharel sedicieux, estrange,
Demoniacle, en se faignant estre ange;
Bien apparut qu'il estoit Belial,
A Neufchastel et à Mont belial;
Ecolampade, quoy qu'il soit de sa secte,
En ses escrips et parolles l'insecte,
Disant qu'il est né pour faire encombrier:
A telles oeuvres on congnoit tel ouvrier.

    Puys le perfide qu'on surnomme
Froment
En ma farine blanche a mis le ferment;
Pour myeulx corrumpre de foy toute la
masse
Toutes erreurs accumule et amasse;
A les semer n'est paresseux ne lent.
Et son complice Viret le virulent
Qui a cuydé d'erreur mettre en bourbe
Les habitans et les incoles de Orbe;
Finablement, des crestiens les preux
L'en ont banny, chassé comme lepreux.
Ilz ont causé par leurs grandz malefices
Que la plus part de tous mes edificces
Plus on n'habite, et n'y a que meschans;
Parquoy de pleurs et regres sont mes
chantz.

    Or, ouyés tous que sont les beaulx
miracles
Lesquelx ont fait ces faulx demoniacles,
Dignes de feu et d'infernaulx supplices,
Avec leurs faulx et desleaulx complices:

They have committed unspeakable evils,
Gross actions, abominable to name;
They have polluted a multitude of
temples,
Cast down the sacred treasures, the chal-
ices,
Profaned the noble sanctuaries,
Pillaged the reliquaries,[27]
And without respect, fear of God or
shame,
Have melted down all the bells,
To make cannons and artillery for
Mars,[28]
While they thieved and pillaged.

What more can I say? These vile
sacrilegious men
Have sacked convents and colleges,
And attacked the virginal houses
In order to practice their vile bacchanalia,
More lubricous than mud or swamp,
More than Epicurus or Sardanapalus,
They incited the modest nuns
To apostasize and become immoral;
But God protected his virgins, burning
like candles
In his love, by his hand.[29]
They iniquitously held as prisoner
A zealous believer,[30] they cannot deny
it,
And unjustly put the good to death:[31]
Liars must surely be punished.

More hardened than marble or tor-
toiseshell,
They made every effort, going from bad
to worse,
To wipe out the holy, divine service,
Cast me into an abyss of all vice,
Suppress the holy sacraments,
Saintly doctrines and good teachings;
The loyal faithful who did not consent
Have suffered and felt infinite ills.
The good Christians, of whom I had a
multitude,
Have abandoned me, seeing the enormity
Of the heresies: for those who ally with
the bear

Il ont commis choses innominables,
Enormes cas, à dire abhominables;
[A 3v] Grand multitude de temples ont
pollu,
Tresors sacrés, calices, ont tollu,
Et prophané les dignes sainctuaires,
Emble pillé tous les reliquiayres,
Et n'ayant crainte, timeur de dieu ny
honte,
Ont mys les clouches et campanes en
fonte,
Pour faire à Mars canons, artillerie,
En perpetrant larrecins, pillerie.

Que diray plus? Ces villains
sacrileges
Ont saccagé les couvens et colleges,
Et assailly les maisons virginalles
Pour exercier villaines baccanalles,
Et plus lubriques que fange ne palludz,
Plus que Epicure ne Sardenapalus,
Ont incité les Clarines pudiques
D'apostater, devenir impudiques;
Mais de leur main Dieu a gardé ses
vierges,
En son amour ardantes comme cierges.
Iniquement ont tenu prisonnier
Ung zelateur, ne le peuvent nyer,
Et fait mourir les bons injustement:
Il est certain que à poine justement.

Plus endurcys que marbre ne testude,
De mal à pis ont tout mis leur estude
D'exterminer le sainct divin service,
Et me getter au gouffre de tout vice,
A supprimer les divins sacremens,
Sainctes doctrines et bons enseignemens;
Les bons loyaulx, que n'y ont consentu,
Infinis maulx ont souffert et sentu.
[A 4r] Les bons crestiens don j'avoye
multitude
M'ont deleissee, voyant la magnitude
Des heresies; car qui à l'ours se allye,
Il pert la foy et prend pour le vin lye.
Las! je soloye estre cité d'empire;
Mays n'est possible que soye de l'an

Lose their faith and take the dregs for   pire.
wine.
Alas! I was an imperial city;
But now it is not possible to be in worse
state.

I am a city so wrongly counselled   Je suys cité par tropt mal advisee
Not to have followed the example   De n'avoir pris exemple à la visee
Of the constant, faithful, Catholic   Des catholicques, constantes et fidelles
Christian cities and their devotion: Cités crestiennes, et devotion d'elles;
Paris, Lyon, Rohan, Tours, Orleans: Paris, Lyon, Rohan, Tours, Orleans:
The holy faith prospers well there: La saincte foy bien prospere leans,
In Troyes, Blois, Bourgogne, Grenoble,   A Troye, à Bloys, en Bourgoigne, à
In the whole of noble, very Christian   Grenoble,
France,   En toute France trescrestienne et noble,
And in my ancient capital Vienne.[32]   Et à l'antique ma metropolle Vienne.
I deserved that this evil fall upon me;   J'ay merité que ce grief mal me
For which I fear that I shall shortly sink   advienne;
Into the lake, in a deep abyss,   Parquoy je crains qu'en brief je ne
More, in the Stygian waters of the under-   parfonde
world,   Dedans le lac, en abisme profunde,
And in the flames of hell.   Et, que plus est, aux undes gehennales
                                                 Et stigiennes, ou flammes infernales.

Stay, all you who pass by in the   Arrestez vous, par le chemin passans,
road,[33]   Considerés que je ne suys pas sans
See that I am not bereft   Extreme dueil et tresgriefve souffrance;
Of deep mourning and terrible suffering;   Mieulx me seroit si je estoie soubz
It would be better it I were subject to   France,
France,   Ou obeisse à mon naturel prince;
Or obeyed my natural prince;   Je ne eusse pas forvoyé, ne prins ce
I would not have gone astray, nor taken   Chemin oblicque, devenant anguenotte,
This crooked way, becoming 'anguenot',   De deshonneur perpetuelle note.
Mark of eternal dishonour.   Las! je ne fusse par ces maulditz livree
Alas! I would not have been handed over   A heresie, ains de mal delivree.
to heresy   [A 4v] Suppliés donc Jesus à joinctes
By these accursed men, but rather   mains
delivered from evil.   Qu'il me delivre des tirans inhumains,
Pray then with joined hands to Jesus   Faulx hereticques pleins de toute fallace,
That he deliver me from these inhuman   Et de bon cueur à Dieu J'en feray grace.
tyrants,   *J'en feray grace.*
These false heretics full of all lies,
And with all my heart I shall give thanks
to God.
J'en feray grace.[34]

This is not the place to discuss the literary merits of this text. But Gacy's criteria are clear: The traditional church services have been interrupted, and therefore religion has been suppressed; Geneva should have followed the traditional path of Catholic France or of Savoyard domination (Gacy himself was from Savoy); yet, he refuses even to listen to the Reformers. The passage of Geneva to the Reformation is seen as an unqualified disaster.

ARTUS DÉSIRÉ, *Les Combatz du fidelle chrestien* (1550)

Alain Dufour quoted a text by Désiré dated 1558. But it turns out that the ideas found in Désiré's execrable verses of 1558 had already been said in part, in his prose of 1550;[35] indeed, he bases his observations on a visit he had made to Geneva in 1549. In the preface to the *Combatz du Fidelle Chrestien* he says:

[The primary source texts supplied throughout this chapter are followed by alternate, parallel paragraphs in French.]

I composed the present book, entitled *Combats of the faithful Papist against the apostate Antipapist*, the one following the path of the Roman Church, the other that of the synagogue of Geneva, otherwise called the house and refuge of the Lutherans. . . .[36] Before beginning this work I wanted to visit the place, to know better what to say about their detestable life. Having arrived there, I went straight to the church of St Peter, to see and consider the huge injuries and insults to God. When I went in, my hair stood on end at the terrible wretchedness of the place; I said to myself, thus is the prophecy of Daniel accomplished, when he says in chapter 9: "Deficiet hostia et sacrificium, et erit abominatio desolationis in templo." For I saw the greatest abomination possible: first the holy sacrifice undone, the altars shattered and broken, the images destroyed, divine service stopped, the sacred vessels polluted, the holy oil poured out, the precious relics burned.[37] In this synagogue there were only benches, and the plague-pulpit from which lies are preached, with two boards on which are written the psalms of David in French, which are sung by men and women;[38] they have no images of the saints in paradise. Alas, Christian! If you knew the great poverty and wretchedness they have there, you would be amazed. And, believe me, there are six thousand French men and women who would have given each one a pint of their blood to escape having to go there; for since their birth they have never been so stunned and lost as they are, because of the wretchednesses and sufferings which God daily sends them, so that they appear stunned, pallid, rigid, miserable, paler than Jews. And know that they have had the plague for three years, with many people dying (and God knows what happened to their souls).[39] Moreover, last year, 1548, hail destroyed all their crops. And this year, 1549, their land is so sterile that they have difficulty in surviving, and also they are always in fear of being destroyed by the Christian princes. For this reason they are fortifying their city daily, and most of the walls are built and reinforced by reliquaries from France, and by apostates who steal chalices and other sacred vessels, which they sell to the treasurer, and this provokes a thousand thefts in this country, and great harm to the very Christian king, whom I affectionately beseech, for the preservation of the Church and the kingdom, to close the borders. For from there comes the ruin and destruction of Christianity. And that he give such justice to those who are found on his lands, that a good example will be set for everyone. By so doing the fire will be gradually extinguished, and those who have been misled will come to recognize their error and ask God's pardon.

J'ay composé ce present livre intitulé les Combatz du fidelle Papiste, contre l'apostat Antipapiste, dont l'un tient le chemin de l'Eglise Rommaine, et l'autre le chemin de la synagogue de Geneve autrement nommée la maison et refuge des Lutheriens. . . . Et premier que commancer ceste oeuvre j'ay voulu aller jusques audit lieu, afin de mieux scavoir parler de leur detestable vie. Et moy estant arrivé là, pris mon chemin droict à l'Eglise de sainct Pierre, pour voir et contempler les grans opprobres et injures faictes à Dieu. Et en entrant dedens icelle tout le poil me dressa, de la grande paoureté. Et dy en moymesme, voicy la prophetie de Daniel accompli disant en son neufiesme chapitre. *Deficiet hostia et sacrificium, et erit abominatio desolationis in templo.* Car je vy la plus grande abomination qu'il est possible de voir. Premierement le sainct sacrifice deffaict, les autelz rompuz et brisez, les images cassez, le service divin cessé, les sacrez vaisseaux pollutz, la saincte unction respandue, les precieuses reliques bruslez. Et en icelle synagogue n'y a seulement que des bancs, et la chaire de pestilence où se font les predications de mensonge, avec deux tableaux où sont escrit les pseaumes de David en francoys que les hommes et femmes chantent, et n'ont aucunes images des sainctz et sainctes de paradis. Helas, chrestien! si tu sçavois la grande paovreté et misere qu'ilz ont, tu ne fus onc si esmerveillé. Et soys asseuré qu'il y a six mille françoys que hommes que femmes qui voudroyent leur avoir cousté à chascun une pinte de leur sang et n'y avoir jamais mis le pied: car depuis qu'ilz naquirent de mere ne furent si esbahyz ne esperduz qu'ilz sont: à raison des paouvretez et tribulations que Dieu leur envoye de jour en jour. Dont ilz semblent estre espouventez, blesmes, transiz, melancolieux, et plus palles que juifz. Et doys sçavoir qu'ilz ont eu trois ans la peste, dont il est mort grand peuple. (Dieu sache qu'en sont devenuz les ames.) Outre plus l'annee passée qui fut mil cinq cens quarante et huyt, tous leurs biens furent greslez. Et ceste annee cinq cens quarante et neuf, les terres ont esté si steriles qu'ilz ont beaucoup affaire à vivre, et avecques ce, sont tousjours en doubte d'estre destruictz des princes chrestiens. Et pource ilz fortifient tous les jours leur dite ville, dont la plus part des murailles sont basties, et renforcees des reliquaires de France, par les apostatz qui desrobent calices et autres sacrez vaisseaux, lesquelz ilz vendent au maistre des monnoyes, qui est cause de faire cent mille larcins au pais de pardeça. Et au prejudice du Roy treschrestien, lequel je supplie affectueusement pour la conservation de l'Eglise et de son Royaume, faire fermer les passages. Car de là vient la ruyne et perdition de la chrestienté. Et faire si bonne justice de ceux qui se trouveront en sa terre, que tout le monde y prenne exemple. Et en ce faisant petit à petit le feu s'esteindra, et les desvoyez viendront à recongnoistre leur faute et à demander pardon à Dieu. (fols. A 3v—4v)

By contrast with Gacy's view of Geneva as a "poor village," it is surprising to see, as early as 1549, that *"from there comes the ruin and destruction of Christianity"*—and that Désiré felt the need to go to Geneva before denouncing it. The place occupied by the city in Catholic demonology has evolved fast.

JOHN CALVIN, *Sermons on Isaiah* (1557)

Before tracing the further evolution of the Geneva anti-myth, one may wonder whether Calvin read Désiré. Certainly he knew the Catholic insistence, seen in both Gacy and Désiré, on the idea that the suppression of the symbols and instruments of Catholic worship indicated the suppression of religion itself. In a sermon on Isaiah 36.7, Calvin amusedly recalls the profusion of objects involved in Catholic worship:[40]

> For the Papists have their temples well stuffed with dolls, there's not a wall which hasn't got a lovely painting. Then they have their idols of wood and of stone, all grand as if they were kings or emperors. Then when you come to the high altar, there is this idol shut up in a hiding place. And there's a million more idols, to be impressive. Then when they sing mass, the altar will be well decorated, there's the lights, and the perfume, and this and that. The organ rings out, the priest is in costume as if to act in a farce. And then there's not just one altar, but thirty or so. This is the chapel of such and such a saint. That is the chapel of another one. This is the altar of such and such a patron. And there's another.

> Car les Papistes auront leurs temples bien farciz de marmousetz, il n'y aura paroyt là où il n'y ait quelque belle peincture. Aprés ilz auront leurs idoles dressees et de bois et de pierre, qui feront la morgue comme si c'estoient des rois ou des empereurs. Et puis quand on viendra sur le grand autel, on verra ceste idole qui est là enclose en une cachete. Et puis on verra ung million d'autres idoles, qui sont pour faire parade. Aprés si on chante la messe on verra l'autel bien paré, on verra le luminaire, on verra le perfum, et cecy et cela. Les orgues sonneront et puis le prestre sera là deguisé comme pour jouer une farce. Et puis il n'y aura point seullement ung autel mais une trentaine. Voilà la chappelle d'un tel saint. Voilà la chappelle d'une autre saincte. Voilà l'autel d'un tel patron. Voilà celuy d'un autre.[41]

In contrast, the papist who visits a Reformed church is disorientated—and here we find the very expressions used by Désiré:

> When you come into a church where the word of God is preached and the sacraments administered according to the Gospel, what do you find? Nothing! That's how the Papists talk today, just like Rabshakeh: "What? Do these people trust in God? For they've knocked down all the images. Will God stand for that? For they have suppressed all his worship. There are no candles, or torches, or crosses or holy water. There are no priest's vestments, no altar ornaments, there's neither mass nor worship. In short they've wiped everything out, even down to the paintings. There are no more altars for private devotions, so that you can run from one place to another, when you've said your prayers in one place you have to run to the next. They haven't even got any pilgrimages; and confession has been taken away from them. In short, there's nothing there, the whole worship of God has been abolished."

> Quand on vient icy en ung temple là où la parole de Dieu se presche et où les Sacremens sont administrez selon l'Evangile, et quoy? Il n'y a rien! Voilà donc comme les Papistes parleront aujourdhuy de nous à la façon de Rabsacés: "Comment? Ces gens là ont-ilz leur fiance en Dieu? Car ilz ont abbatu toutes les images. Et Dieu les endurera-il? Car ilz ont rejecté tout son service. Ilz n'ont ne sierges, ne torches, ny chandelles, ny croix ny eau benite. Il n'y a ne vestemens de prestre, ny ornemens d'autel, il n'y a ne messe ne devotion. Bref, ilz ont tout raclé, mesmes jusques aux peinctures. Il n'y a plus

d'autelz là où il y devoit avoir devotion particuliere, pour courir de lieu en lieu, et quand on aura fait sa devotion en ung lieu il faudroit courir à l'autre. Ilz n'ont point mesmes de pelerinages et puis la confession leur est ostÈe. Bref, il n'y a plus rien, tout le service de Dieu est aboly."[42]

In the Reformer's eyes the anti-myth has become a positive quality, a matter of pride. For Calvin, of course, the old abuses have been replaced by right worship, preaching, and the sacraments rightly administered; this concept is inconceivable in Désiré's perspective.

PIERRE DE RONSARD, *Discours des miseres de ce temps* (1562)

Although Ronsard's *Discours* were central to Alain Dufour's study, we cannot avoid looking at them again (and, to the best of my knowledge, this is the first time any part of them has been presented in English). In the *Continuation du Discours* of September 1562, Ronsard specifically attacks Geneva, in some oft-quoted lines (it is a vision of France that speaks):

There is a city in the fields of Savoy Which treacherously drove out its former lords, Wretched home of all apostasy, Stubbornness, pride and heresy, And which (while my kings increased My bounds, and fought abroad for my honour) Drawing exiles into its damned sect, Has made me poor and wretched as you see.[43]	Une ville est assise ès champs Savoisiens, Qui par fraude a chassé ses seigneurs anciens, Misérable séjour de toute apostasie, D'opiniâtreté, d'orgueil, et d'hérésie, Laquelle (en cependant que les rois augmentaient. Mes bornes, et bien loin pour l'honneur combattaient) Appelant les bannis en sa secte damnable M'a fait comme tu vois chétive et misérable.
My kings, seeing well that such a city Would one day bring them calamity, Had oft resolved to cast it down; But they never went to war against it, Either through neglect, or by fate, They left it standing; and hence my undoing.	Or mes rois, voyant bien qu'une telle cité Leur ferait quelque jour une infélicité Delibéraient assez de la ruer par terre; Mais contre elle jamais n'ont entrepris la guerre: Ou soit par négligence, ou soit par le destin, Entière ils l'ont laissée: et de là vient ma fin.
Just like a peasant whose idle hands, All winter long, leave hanging a cluster of grubs In some dry leaf atop an apple tree:	Comme ces laboureurs dont les mains inutiles Laissent pendre l'hiver un touffeau de chenilles

So soon as the sun's first rays
Warm the leaf, and the tender dew
Dampens it twice or thrice,
The venom which seemed consumed by
winter
Springs suddenly to life as caterpillars
Which fall from the leaf, and painfully
crawl,
Broken-backed, across the plain;
One climbs an oak, another a beech,
And, eating all the way, drag themselves
to the treetop,
Then return to earth, feeding so well
That no greenery survives anywhere.

Dans une feuille sèche au faîte d'un
pommier:
Sitôt que le soleil de son rayon premier
A la feuille échauffée, et qu'elle est
arrosée
Par deux ou par trois fois d'une tendre
rosée,
Le venin qui semblait par l'hiver
consumé,
En chenilles soudain apparaît animé,
Qui tombent de la feuille, et rampent à
grand peine
D'un dos entre-cassé au milieu de la
plaine,
L'une monte en un chêne et l'autre en un
ormeau,
Et toujours en mangeant se traînent au
coupeau,
Puis descendent à terre, et tellement se
paissent
Qu'une seule verdure en la terre ne
laissent.

Then the peasant, seeing his ruined
field,
Laments fruitlessly that he had not made
haste
To stifle such a brood in the nest:
He sees it is his fault, and blames himself;

Alors le laboureur, voyant son champ
gâté,
Lamente pour néant qu'il ne s'était hâté
D'étouffer de bonne heure une telle
semence:
Il voit que c'est sa faute, et s'en donne
l'offense.

So while my kings were absorbed in
wars,
These caterpillars all grew in a heap,
So that, in less than three months, this
furious mob
Has spread throughout my bounds and
consumed me.[44]

Ainsi lorsque mes rois aux guerres
s'efforçaient,
Toutes en un monceau ces chenilles
croissaient,
Si qu'en moins de trois mois, telle tourbe
enragée
Sur moi s'est épandue, et m'a toute
mangée.

The myth is developing: At first Geneva was seen as a pole to which evil-
doers were attracted; but now Geneva is exporting its evil, and—"in less than
three months"—the whole of France has been infected. It will, moreover, be
noticed that here the threat of Geneva is treated much more as a political matter
than as a religious one.

In his funeral oration for Ronsard, Jacques Davy Du Perron praised the poet for having been the first to respond in French to the writings of the Reformers. This is in fact far from the case (apart from Gacy and Désiré, one could cite Guillaume Petit, Pierre Doré, Pierre Du Val, Gentian Hervet, René Benoist, and many others). It is certainly the case, however, that Ronsard brought to his compositions a literary quality attained by none of his predecessors. The magnificent image of the caterpillars to represent the Genevan plague strikes the imagination more than chapters of prosaic argument. This can be seen, moreover, in the relative weakness of the Calvinist responses to Ronsard's *Discours*.

BERNARD DE MONTMÉJA, *Response aux calomnies* (1563)

The pastor and poet Bernard de Montméja replied to Ronsard's attacks in two poems, refuting respectively the *Discours* and the *Continuation du Discours*. In the second piece, he pours scorn on Ronsard's habit of seeing visions—the ghosts of Hugues Salel, Joachim Du Bellay, Cassandre, and now France, telling Ronsard all the ill Geneva has caused her:

It is rather the Papacy that you saw,	Plutôt la Papauté à toi s'est apparue,
Hideous, dishevelled, filled with fear,	Hideuse, échevelée et pleine de frayeur,
As if close to some profound disaster,	Comme voyant près d'elle un extrême
Saying that she felt the wounds inflicted	malheur,
By the farmers who till the shores of	Disant qu'elle a senti des laboureurs
Lake Geneva,	l'outrage
And that she can bear no more, so over-	Qui du lac genevois cultivent le rivage,
thrown	Et qu'elle n'en peut plus, tant elle est
By these Savoyards who shatter her	mise bas,
arms—the arms,	Par ces Savoisiens qui lui froissent les
one could say, of her revenues,	bras:
The domain which the Roman wolf	Ses bras, peut-on nommer, les rentes, le
Has usurped from the common people.	domaine
	Usurpé du commun par la louve
	Romaine.
For Geneva has made war on the	Car Genève a fait guerre à la
principality	principauté
Of this God on earth, head of the papacy,	De ce Dieu terrien, chef de la papauté,
And has so cast it down that it is no	Et l'a tant abattu que plus on ne le
longer called	nomme
Head of the Church, except in Spain and	De l'Église le chef, qu'en Espagne et à
in Rome.	Rome.
It is Geneva, Ronsard, of which you	C'est Genève, Ronsard, dont tu dis mille
speak so ill,	maux,
Who has made so many attacks on the	Qui à la papauté a livré maints assauts;
papacy;	Genève qui ressemble à une belle rose
Geneva which resembles a lovely rose	

Which, in the morning, was not yet open; But, the sun warming it with its clear rays, It bursts and opens in its scarlet folds, Then its scent diffused through all the garden Reveals the corner where it was hidden.	Qui n'est, sur le matin, aucunement déclose; Mais de ses clairs rayons le soleil l'échauffant, En ses replis vermeils se divise et se fend, Lors par tout le jardin son odeur Èpanchée Découvre le recoin où elle était cachée.
For at first the name of Geneva Was unknown to us, it had no fame; But for some years past we have noted it, As the rays of the sun of justice Shine in the midst, and their great splendour Spreads in many places the scent of Geneva, But especially in France, where the holy doctrine Has almost entirely extinguished idolatry; And would have done so altogether, were it not For the cruel tyrants who willy-nilly, Grasping for honours, have deprived the French people Of the privileges which they enjoyed by royal edict.[45]	Car du commencement de Genève le nom Nous était inconnu, elle était sans renom; Mais depuis certains ans nous en avons notice, D'autant que les rayons du soleil de justice Reluisent au milieu, et leur grande splendeur Épand en divers lieux de Genève l'odeur, Mais par surtout en France, où la doctrine sainte A presque entièrement l'idolâtrie éteinte, Et l'eût jà fait du tout, sans les cruels tyrans Qui à droit et à tort, aux honneurs aspirant, Otent le privilège aux habitants de France, Dont les édits du roi leur donnaient jouissance.

For the most part this is versified argument rather than poetry: It shows in the almost total absence of adjectives. The writer is determined to denounce the pope, to underline the imminent victory of Godly doctrine over idolatry, and to underline the royal edicts granted to the Reformed community: Montméja is dealing in ideas, not images. But this passage illustrates the parallel development of the myth and the anti-myth of Geneva: If Gacy sees in Geneva a "poor village" and Désiré attributes to it, only 14 years later, the "ruin and destruction of Christianity," Montméja evokes the same movement from a Geneva "without fame" to the shining of the rays of the sun of justice (compare the motto of Geneva, *Post Tenebras Lux*), and to its sweet scent diffused everywhere and "especially in France." If the Huguenot poet escapes from total banality, it is thanks to an image that he consciously borrows from the most popular of all Ronsard's poems, "Mignonne, allons voir si la rose. . . ."

J. LE FRERE DE LAVAL, *La Vraye et entiere histoire des troubles et guerres civiles* (1573)

We may add a further, later, document to the negative myth of Geneva.[46] We again find the image of a Geneva rotten with moral debauchery and resolved on the extermination of "true religion":

> Indeed, when, many years hence, men will read that, in the reign of Charles IX in France, there emerged from Lake Geneva, as from a sort of evil Lerne,[47] I know not what unknown monsters which looked on the outside like men, but inside were only huge beasts, called ministers, who imitating the gravity of Xenocrates,[48] arrogantly claimed, on no evidence, to have dropped from the clouds just in order to draw from the abyss the erstwhile hidden truth,[49] to remould the Church, like Aeson,[50] in its first youth, and restore a lost evangelical perfection. But all the while they dogmatized and perpetrated everything diametrically opposed not only to the former piety of the Christian Church, but even to the duty of the common reasonable man; they accommodated the Gospel to their desires, as if Jesus Christ had come to preach the sect of Aristippus;[51] their only activity was to muddle the world with mutinies, civil wars, factions and plots, to debauch and corrupt the former discipline, overturn the state and government, pillage the desolate provinces, profane everything that is holy, and abolish all true religion.

> Certes quand apres une longue suite d'années les hommes liront comme, regnant en France Charles 9, saillirent du lac de Genefve, non autrement que d'une Lerne de tous maux, ne sçay quels monstres incogneuz, qui par dehors avoient semblance d'hommes, et par dedans n'estoient que grosses bestes, qu'on appelloit ministres, lesquels, feignans la gravité de Xenocrate, se vantoient arrogamment sans autre preuve estre tombez expres des nuÎs pour retirer des abysmes la verité pieça cachée, refondre l'Eglise, comme Eson, en sa premiere jouvence, et remettre sus la perfection evangelique decheuë. Cependant toutefois ils dogmatisoient et perpetroient toutes choses diametralement eloignées non seulement de l'ancienne pieté de l'Eglise Chrestienne, ains aussi du devoir d'homme civil et raisonnable: accommodoient l'Evangile à leurs appetis, comme si Jesus Christ fust venu prescher la secte d'Aristippe: et ne prenoient autre deduit qu'à brouiller le monde de mutineries, guerres civiles, factions et conjures: qu'à desbaucher et corrompre la discipline ancienne, bouleverser estat et police, butiner les Provinces desolées, profaner les choses sacrées, et aneantir toute vraye religion.

The enormous influence attributed, rightly or wrongly, to Geneva in these comments is a remarkable tribute to the place occupied henceforth by the city-state in the French view of the world. That some sixteen members of the Genevan Company of Pastors, or even the few hundred missionaries sent into France, were able to "muddle the world with mutinies, civil wars, factions and plots, to debauch and corrupt the former discipline, overturn the state and government, pillage the desolate provinces, profane everything that is holy, and abolish all true religion" looks like a striking overstatement!

CONCLUSION

By choosing to provide more quotation than discussion, I have hoped to give the reader the most direct access possible (even in labored translation) to the exchanges of vituperation in which the anti-myth of Geneva in particular was forged, and to add to the corpus of material already known on the subject. Finally, some brief comments may be made.

The anti-myth began to form at the earliest possible moment, immediately after the adoption of the Reformation by the city. It was certainly given further impetus by the changes in the city government in 1555 and by the existence of a group of exiles stemming from that evolution, but it was already in place earlier, and therefore based on other factors. The most basic form of the myth, as in Gacy, is the vision of destruction the Reformed city presents. One can express the thought underlying both Gacy's and Désiré's denunciations in syllogistic form: (1) The destruction of altars means the destruction of all religion: Geneva has destroyed its altars; therefore Geneva has no religion; and (2) a place that has no religion is a center of all immorality; Geneva has no religion; therefore Geneva is a center of all immorality.

Hence the sheer horror expressed by both writers at the state of the churches in Geneva. Désiré goes further and is perhaps the first writer to perceive Geneva not only as a center of attraction for evil-doers from elsewhere but also as a source of evil going outward: The "ruin and destruction of all Christianity." This is a remarkable statement to make in 1550. It bears witness to the immense place Geneva had already established as a source of the "new" teaching; that teaching was being spread essentially by the printing press[52]—and that means essentially by the writings of Calvin, who took up residence definitively in the city in 1541. Only eight years later Désiré knows where his principal enemy lies.

For Désiré, the threat is mainly religious; it is Christianity that is menaced. But the religious and the social and political were so closely intertwined that they cannot really be distinguished: Désiré appeals to the king to take action to stop the rot. Ronsard takes this further: Throughout the *Discours* he shuns discussion of religious matters and bases his appeal to the reader on patriotic sentiment. It is the civil disorder introduced by the "innovators" that he denounces; in our extract the Geneva-based caterpillars have ravaged and laid waste the provinces of France. The implication behind his lament that France had not suppressed the menace long since is clear: It should be done now.

By the time of Le Frère (well into the civil wars and just a year after the massacre of St Bartholomew's Day), Geneva is perceived as the potential source both of the total destruction of all society and of the abolition of all true religion. The only solution must be its total suppression. Which leaves one large question: How, in a century when the trend was almost universally for the absorption of small city-states into larger entities, did Geneva ever survive and maintain its independence and identity? To this the succeeding chapters of this book will seek answers.

NOTES

1. Alain Dufour, "Le Mythe de Genève au temps de Calvin," in his *Histoire politique et psychologie historique* (Geneva: Droz, 1966), 63—95.

2. Ibid., 90.

3. Ibid., 94.

4. *Trialogue nouveau contenant l'expression des erreurs de Martin Luther. Les doleances de Ierarchie ecclesiastique Et les triumphes de verite invincible* (Geneva: Wigand Koeln, 1524).

5. Jean Gacy, *La deploration de la Cité de Genesve sur le faict des hereticques qui l'ont Tiranniquement opprimee* (Lyons: Pierre de Sainte Lucie, 1536?). In the French transcription I have modernized the punctuation, introduced the modern distinction between *j* and *i*, *u* and *v*, and added accents on accented final *é* and on the preposition *à*.

6. Rachel: see Jer. 31:15.

7. Naomi: see Ruth 1.

8. Eli: see 1 Sam. 1.

9. The destitution of Geneva, once flourishing, is an important element of this myth.

10. See Caesar, *De Bello Gallico* I, 6,7.

11. Marcus Aurelius was said to have rebuilt Geneva after it had been destroyed by fire and to have named it Aurelia. See W. Deonna, "Le nom de Genève," *Geneva* 19 (1941), 80—81.

12. *anguenots* (in the French): early form of *huguenot*, possibly attested here for the first time. The word is a deformation of the German *Eidgenossen*, "confederates": the supporters of Berne.

13. The "place du Molard," in the commercial center of Geneva, was in the sixteenth century a port giving directly onto the lake.

14. Somewhat approximate history! The competition of the Lyons fairs dates from 1470, well before any "rebellion" of the Genevans.

15. Allobroges: a Celtic tribe in the region of Geneva, Grenoble, and Vienne, conquered by the Romans in the second century B.C.

16. The rejection of the authority of the dukes of Savoy dates from the 1520s and was unconnected with the Reformation.

17. The symbol of Berne: The Bernese had come to the aid of Geneva in 1530.

18. "the ass" (French *baudet*): an allusion to Baudichon de la Maisonneuve, Genevan merchant and first protector of the Reformed preachers in 1533—1534.

19. Guillaume Farel had preached several times in Geneva in 1532—1533 and was the main Reformed participant in the Dispute of Rive (June 1535), which determined the religious fate of Geneva. Gacy himself also participated. See Théophile Dufour, "Un opuscule inédit de Farel. *Les Actes de la dispute de Rive*," in *MD* 22 (1886): 201—240.

20. "Belial": "worthless man"; see, for example, 1 Sam. 2:12.

21. Farel had preached in Montbéliard, on the advice of Oecolampadius, in 1524 and had introduced the Reformation to Neuchâtel in 1530.

22. Johann Oecolampadius, Basel Reformer and supporter of Farel. For his attempts to moderate Farel's passion in 1524, see the letters quoted in *Guillaume Farel (1489—1565): Biographie nouvelle* (Neuchâtel: Delachaux et Nieslé, 1930), 134—135. Gacy is well informed, since Oecolampadius's correspondence was not publicly known.

23. Antoine Froment (*froment* means "wheat" in French) was, with Farel, the main Reformer of Geneva.

24. See Matt. 16:6, 11–12.

25. Pierre Viret also took part in the Rive Dispute and in the evangelization of Geneva. Farel had established him as preacher in his native Orbe in 1531.

26. A.-L. Herminjard, *La Correspondance des Réformateurs de langue française*, II, 479, gives a fragment of a letter from Farel that he dates to 1532 or 1533, but referring to this accusation and seemingly to this text: "Les preux des Chrestiens [dit-il] ont banny Viret d'Orbe comme ung lepreux." The letter is probably misdated.

27. In August 1535, following some sermons by Farel, the Genevan churches were stripped of their statues, treasures, and ornaments.

28. But the bells of St Pierre continued to ring after the Reformation!

29. After implying the worst outrages against the Clarisses, Gacy recognizes that they were allowed to leave the city (December 1535) unharmed. The preachers had tried to persuade them to leave the convent and marry; but only one accepted the proposition.

30. The Dominican Guy Furbiti, invited by the Council to preach the Advent sermons in 1533, had been imprisoned by the Genevans for speaking against the Bernese government.

31. Reference to the death of Canon Werli of Fribourg, killed in a riot in 1533.

32. The Reformation had indeed made little progress in France in 1533. In the Middle Ages Geneva had been attached to the Archbishopric of Vienne.

33. Echo of Lam. 1:12, *O vos omnes qui transitis per viam, attendite et videte si est dolor sicut dolor meus*.

34. *J'en feray grace*, anagram of "Frère Jean Gacy."

35. I quote from Artus Désiré, *Les Combatz du Fidelle Chrestien, dit Papiste, contre l'Infidelle apostat antipapiste* (Lyons: Jean Pullon, 1551), sole known copy in London British Library. Another edition, by Robert and Jean Du Gort of Rouen, in 1550: copies in Paris Bibliothèque Nationale and Paris Beaux Arts.

36. There is no need to underline the reciprocal insults traded by the denominations, each calling the other "synagogue"; note that the term "Lutherans" is still used to indicate any sort of Protestants.

37. Désiré's vision is identical to that of Gacy: All that constituted "divine service" has been suppressed, therefore no religion remains.

38. Three interesting details about Reformed worship appear here: Already in 1549 there are *benches* (in the medieval church one remained standing); the *pulpit* is absolutely central: One spoke more often of "going to the sermon" than of "going to worship"; the day's psalms were written on *boards.*

39. Désiré's information on the plague, famine, external threats, and the constant work on the fortifications of Geneva are all well documented independently. That these works were financed by the theft of reliquaries and church treasures is less well documented.

40. Published in *Supplementa Calviniana*, vol. 3 (Neukirchen: Neukirchener Verlag, 1995).

41. Op. cit., 281.

42. Ibid.

43. So far Ronsard gives the same view as Gacy and Désiré: having driven out their former lords, the Genevans have attracted to them "exiles," fugitives from justice.

44. The extract is quoted in the modernized text of the Livre de Poche Classiques edition, 1993, 91–92.

45. Ibid., 217–218.

46. J. Le Frère de Laval, *La vraye et entiere histoire des troubles et guerres civiles, avenuls de nostre temps, pour le faict de la religion, tant en France, Allemaigne, que paçs bas* (Paris: Guillaume de la Noue, 1573).

47. Leerne: legendary swamp, the lair of the hydra.

48. A Greek philosopher.

49. Perhaps a reference to Conrad Badius's printer's device, with its motto: "Des creux manoirs et pleins d'obscurité, /Dieu par le temps retire verité" ("From the hollow lairs full of darkness, God, by Time, brings back the truth").

50. Aeson, father of Jason and Medea. A reference rather to Jason, who had a spell cast on the daughters of Pelias by which they killed their father and boiled his dismembered body, hoping thereby to rejuvenate him.

51. Greek philosopher who preached that pleasure is the supreme good.

52. From 1547 on, French regulations concerning the book trade make ever more specific references to Genevan books as a source of heresy.

2

Calvin, Beza, and the Exegetical History of Romans 13:1—7

Richard A. Muller

Throughout the history of the church, the text of Romans 13:1—7 has provided a foundation for the discussion of church-state relations and of Christian obedience even to non-Christian rulers, and it has placed a limit on the Christian conception of the right of resistance. The Reformation in Geneva is case in point: Divergent perceptions of the nature of church and state drew considerable attention to the apostolic mandate that "every soul be subject to the higher powers."[1] Despite the Reformers' recourse to the original Greek of the improved texts of Erasmus and Stephanus, they maintained clear continuities with traditional patterns of exegesis and the Vulgate text. Indeed, for both John Calvin and Theodore Beza, the Vulgate remained the fundamental point of reference for Latin translation.[2] Beza's reading of Romans 13:1—7 and its significant continuity with the tradition and with Calvin's exegesis are of interest both because of the enormous influence of the *Annotationes*[3] and because of the eventual divergence between Beza and Calvin, particularly in the anonymously published *De iure magistratuum*[4] and the earlier *De haereticis a civili magistratu puniendis.*[5] It can even be argued that the stability of exegesis of this particular text led theologians elsewhere for justification of various theories of resistance to authority.[6]

CALVIN AND BEZA AS TRANSLATORS OF ROMANS 13:1—7

As in virtually all Calvin's commentaries, the commentary on Romans presents an emended translation of Scripture in which some of Calvin's exegetical and interpretive decisions are evidenced prior to his discussion of the text.[7] Granting Calvin's humanistic training and his typically Protestant distaste for the Vulgate, the differences between his version and that of Jerome are surprisingly few, often drawn from Erasmus, and, in most cases nonsubstantive.

Thus, in verses 1 and 2 the Pauline phrase *exousiais hyperechousais*, "to higher powers," rendered by Jerome as *potestatibus sublimioribus*, is given by Calvin as *potestatibus supereminentibus*—a potentially substantive alteration.[8] Nonsubstantive changes are more abundant: Calvin's use of *verò* rather than *autem*, his addition of the implied *potestates* in the last clause of verse 1, and his change of the tense of the verb in the final clause of verse 2. Martin Bucer, it is worth noting, had chosen to indicate the breadth of the category "higher powers" by omitting the prefix *super* and rendering *hyperechousais* as *eminentibus*.[9] All these changes, moreover, reflect Erasmus's Latin translation. Although Calvin alters Jerome's *sibi damnationem adquirunt*, "acquire condemnation for themselves," perhaps to provide a more specifically legal connotation with *judicium sibi accersent*, "summon judgment on themselves," the theological implications of the change are minimal in the light of his commentary—and the choice of the word indicates an acceptance of Erasmus's rendition of *krima* as *judicium* over Jerome's. The choice of *accersent* rather than Jerome's *adquirunt* or Erasmus's *accipient* probably reflects Bucer's paraphrase.[10]

Beza's approach to verses 1 and 2 is hardly radical, but it does manifest a certain degree of independence from Calvin as well as from Jerome and Erasmus. The phrase "be subject to the higher powers" is given as "potestatibus supereminentibus subjecta esto"—following Erasmus and Calvin on the words "higher powers." He then offers, perhaps with a nod to Bucer, *subjecta* instead of the *subdita* of Jerome, Erasmus, and Calvin. Beza also disputes all previous renderings of verse 2: rather than the standard *resisto* (Jerome, Erasmus, Calvin) or *oppono* (Bucer), he uses *obsisto*, which connotes a more distinctly negative act—a standing in the way of something; and for "receive condemnation to themselves," Beza gives *ipsi sibi condemnationem auferent*, reflecting neither Erasmus nor Calvin—but perhaps returning to the less judicial sense of Jerome's *damnationem*, without using so theologically loaded a term.[11] Indeed, Beza comments that the *Vetus interpres* was more accurate than Erasmus in his rendition of *krima*—although he fails to note Calvin's acceptance of Erasmus's reading.[12] Beza also renders *lempsontai* as *auferent* (they shall obtain) rather than follow the Vulgate's *acquirunt* or *adquirunt* (they acquire).

In the third and fourth verses Calvin's emendations are somewhat more extensive, but again, with little effect on the theological implication of the translation. Jerome's rendition of verse 3, "For rulers are not a terror to the good work but to the evil," *Nam principes non sunt timori boni operis sed mali*, finds Calvin exchanging *terrori* for *timori* in the rendition of *phobos*, and putting good and evil "work" into the plural, *operibus* for *operis* and *malis* for *mali*. The use of *terrori* reflects Erasmus, but the other changes do not.

On the latter point Jerome was arguably correct: good and evil "work" are in the singular in the Greek and function virtually as hypostatizations that preclude legal inquiry into individual acts, detail, or motivation.[13] Calvin offers no argument here, but Beza briefly defends the plural form: "*To good works, ton hagathon ergon*. The Vulgate, *Boni operis*, is excessively obscure. Erasmus, *Bene agentibus*, correctly expresses the meaning."[14] The point remains debatable. Apart from this, Beza offers two alterations worth noting: first, he makes explicit to his readers the middle ranking of the "rulers" by rendering *archontes* as *magistratus* rather than the *principes* of Jerome, Calvin, and Erasmus. Second, for *phobos* he offers *metus*, perhaps because *metus*, like the Greek word, indicates not only fear and apprehension but also reverence and awe—from the perspective of translation, a distinct improvement. It is worth noting that although on purely lexical grounds *timor* lacks the dimension of religious awe associated with *metus*, the churchly tradition, with its distinction between *timor servilis* and *timor filialis* and its positive understanding of *timor Dei* as the first degree of wisdom—an understanding rooted in Augustine's hermeneutics—justified Jerome's use of *timor*, leaving Calvin's *terror* as the least useful option for the translator.[15]

The next phrase—"Will you, then, not be afraid of the power?"—Calvin takes from Jerome replacing Jerome's *autem* with an *ergo*: *Vis ergo non timere potestatem.* What is significant here is that Calvin follows Jerome in assuming that the phrase is a question; indeed, he accepts Jerome's *timere* despite the fact that he has broken with the parallelism in translation offered by Jerome with the *timori* of the preceding phrase. In the final phrase of the verse, "Do what is good, and you will have praise from it [i.e., from the *potestas*]," Calvin merely substitutes *bene* for Jerome's somewhat clearer *bonum*, yielding "Do well, and you will have praise," and *ab ea* for Jerome's *ex illa*. Here Erasmus is not at the basis of the changes. Beza parallels his use of *metus* in the first clause with a rendition of *phobeisthai* as *metuere* in the second clause. Beza then accepts Erasmus' *quod bonum est facito* but quite independently renders the final verb of the verse as *obtinebis*, "you shall obtain," rather than the colorless but arguably more accurate *habebis* of Jerome and Calvin or Erasmus' *feres*.

Calvin follows the Vulgate precisely in the first clause of verse 4—*Dei enim minister est tibi in bonum*—and alters the second clause only slightly without affecting the meaning, substituting *vero* for Jerome's *autem* and giving *quid mali* for Jerome's *malum*. Beza follows Erasmus rather than Calvin or Jerome in the second clause—*quod si feceris id quod malum est*—but retains his use of *metuere* for "fear" as distinct from Jerome, Erasmus, and Calvin, all of whom use *timeo*.

Calvin's alterations in the third and fourth clauses, however, are potentially substantial: *non enim frustra gladium gerit* (Calvin) for *non enim sine causa gladium portat* (Jerome); and *Dei enim minister est, vindex in iram eos qui malè agunt* (Calvin) for *Dei enim minister est, vindex in iram ei qui malum agit* (Jerome). Indeed, Jerome's rendering of the final phrase, "execute wrath on him who does evil," in the singular is correct, and his use of *porto* (as distinct from Calvin's *gero*) for the magistrate's bearing (*phoreo*) of a ceremonial sword is arguably more idiomatic and may lead to a nuancing of the text's meaning of the text in a somewhat different direction than that offered by Calvin—just as Calvin's plural (*eos*), when juxtaposed with the more war like bearing of the sword, might be taken to indicate a broader and less purely judicial exercise of power.[16] Of these changes, only Calvin's use of *frustra* reflects Erasmus. Beza here accepts Calvin's *gero* without comment on the translation.[17]

Calvin engaged in more extensive revision in his rendering of verses 5 and 6. In place of Jerome's *Ideo necessitate subditi estote*, Calvin offers *Itaque necesse est subjici*: in place of "For that reason you shall be subject of necessity," he gives "And thus it is necessary to be subject." Calvin's choice of *subicere* provides a clearer indication of the legal theme of the verse than Jerome's more general *subdere*. More interesting still, from the perspective of the Renaissance and Reformation work of text criticism, is the difference between Jerome's second-person plural future imperative, *estote*, with the perfect participle, *subditi*, coupled with the ablative of *necessitas*, and Calvin's use of *necesse* as an adjective (*necesse est*), with *subjici*, the present passive infinitive. Although there is little verbal resemblance between Calvin's reading and Erasmus's *Quapropter oportet esse subditos*, perhaps indicating a reliance in translation on Bucer's *Propterea necessarium est subijci*, Calvin clearly reflects, without noting the problems of the Greek text, the emendations made to the Greek original by Erasmus.[18]

Beza gives us a clear view of the reason for moving away from Jerome's version. In his translation, Beza follows Calvin with a nod toward Erasmus' relative adverb: *Quapropter necesse est subjici*. Jerome's translation, Beza comments, assumes the Greek to be *anagke hypotassesthe*, a second-person plural form (present middle/passive), but this reading, Beza adds, goes against all of the best codices.[19] In any case, Calvin's present passive infinitive (*subjici*) is a better rendition of the present middle/passive infinitive, *hypotassesthai*, than either Erasmus' or Bucer's alternatives—and better than Jerome's as well.

Calvin also altered the translation of the sixth verse significantly. In the first clause, Calvin offers *Propterea enim tributa quoque solvitis*, a compromise between Jerome's *Ideo enim et tributa praestatis* and Erasmus's *Propter hoc enim et vectigalia solvitis*, retaining, significantly Jerome's rendering of *phoros* as *tributum* (contribution, tax or tribute) rather than accepting Erasmus' *vectigal* (toll, tax or duty). Beza follows Calvin's rendering of *phoros* but accepts Erasmus's version of the rest of the clause (*Propter hoc enim tributa solvitis*), while nonetheless referring to the *phorous* as *vectigalia* in his comment. The second clause, *ministri enim Dei sunt* is taken over by Calvin from Jerome without change. Beza, however, follows Erasmus's *siquidem ministri Dei sunt*.

These differences would perhaps be minor from the point of view of meaning were it not for the parallelisms of verse 7: "Render to all their dues: tribute (*phoros*) to whom tribute [is due]; custom (*telos*) to whom custom; fear to whom fear; honor to whom honor." Granting that *phoros* can indicate tribute—as most probably in Luke 20:22 and 23:2—whereas *telos* has also the implication of an indirect tax or customs payment, the echo of verse 6 in verse 7 demands, at least for aesthetic reasons, that *phoros* be rendered the same way in both verses—and *vectigal* is ruled out in verse six by its better use in verse seven as the translation of *telos*.

In the final clause of verse 6, Calvin rejects Jerome's rendering of *proskarterountes* (attending constantly) as *servientes* (watching over or protecting), borrowing on Erasmus's *incumbentes* (applying or concentrating upon): Yielding, thus, *in hoc incumbentes*, rather than *in hoc ipsum servientes*. Arguably Jerome's *in hoc ipsum* (retained by Erasmus) is a better reading of *eis auto touto*: By dropping *ipsum*, Calvin loses the intensity of Paul's *auto*—yet his choice of *incumbentes* more clearly reflects the apostle's meaning. Here Beza protests quite pointedly against the Vulgate as distorting the sense of the text. His alternative, *laborantes*, simply indicates in a rather neutral fashion that taxation is the task of the magistrate. Beza does, however, restore the intensifier—*in hoc ipso laborantes*.

In the seventh verse Calvin again follows Jerome with virtually no variation. Calvin's only variation is to offer *Reddite ergo omnibus quod debetur* as a substitute for Jerome's *Reddite omnibus debita or*, as some texts have it, *Reddite ergo omnibus debita*. The difference, again, is insignificant—and Jerome, again, arguably provides the better translation. Beza following neither, offers *quod deberis* (what you owed) and then, to make the point clear, adds *debetur* in the second clause, "tribute to whom tribute *is due*."

By way of conclusion concerning Calvin's approach to the text of Romans 13:1—7, it is worth noting that his work stands in relation to the Vulgate much as modern English translations, like the Revised Standard Version, stand to the King James Version: Calvin constantly had the Vulgate in mind and used it as the primary ground of his own efforts. This in itself is a significant conclusion granting the rather different impression often gathered from Reformation era polemic aganst the Vulgate and from Calvin's own immersion in the Renaissance study of classical languages.[20] Beza exercised a bit more freedom over the previous translations, and on such points as the problem of rendering a Greek third-person singular present imperative into Latin and the translation of *phobos* as *metus*, he showed himself to be the virtuoso translator.

CALVIN AND BEZA AS COMMENTATORS

Calvin's primary purpose in his commentary on Romans was theological, and the tendency of his commentary is to set forth normative doctrine.[21] In addition, Calvin's method held him extremely close to the text of Romans, to the virtual exclusion of the considerable array of Old Testament references, classical sources of political theory, patristic references, and comments on canon law cited by many of the medieval commentators and by contemporaries of Calvin like Martin Bucer, Philip Melanchthon, Heinrich Bullinger, and Peter Martyr Vermigli.[22] The textual and linguistic concerns of the Renaissance humanist, although often evident by implication in Calvin's effort as a translator, do not occupy a prominent place in the text of his commentary. Although it is clear that Calvin was attentive to the literary style of his exposition and that he reflected the humanistic attentiveness to lucid, polished Latin prose, it is also clear that unlike his humanist contemporaries, he expressed comparatively little interest in establishing, by means of a critical argument, a definitive rendering of the text. This task he left to others, notably to his lieutenant and successor, Theodore Beza. Of the humanist scholars who contributed to the discussion of the epistle, Calvin referred only to Erasmus.

By way of contrast, when we approach Beza's exegetical labors, we find that Calvin's lieutenant set for himself a different exegetical task, evidenced immediately in the title of his work: *Annotationes Maiores.* There are explicit references to John Faber, Lorenzo Valla, and Erasmus as well as quite a few implicit references to Calvin's translation. In general, Beza is most concerned to establish his own rendering of the Greek as superior both to the Vulgate and to the work of his contemporaries. There is considerable theological comment upon the text, but the commentary is not Beza's central concern, nor is it a continuous doctrinal exposition as was Calvin's. There is a sense, therefore, in which these longer explications take the place of a continuous, balanced commentary: They are inspired by a single phrase, but they move out into the broader context of the chapter or pericope.

Calvin's exegesis of Romans 13:1—7 moves from an assessment of the historical context of Paul's remarks, to a consideration of terms, to a setting forth of principles. His exposition of verse 1 begins with a statement of the apostle's purpose that stands in positive relationship to the tradition of comment on the text. Like Nicolaus of Lyra and Melanchthon, Calvin assumes that the thirteenth chapter relates directly to the themes of Christian life stated earlier in the epistle: The thirteenth chapter offers an example of the application of previously enunciated general principles, and it moves from personal to public morality.[23] These considerations concerning the movement from general to specific also led Calvin to identify verses 1 through 7 of the thirteenth chapter as the basic unit of text to be examined. Melanchthon noted specifically that the eighth verse marked the resumption of discussion of general principles, now related specifically to the issue of civil conduct.[24]

One of the problems facing the exegete of the early sixteenth century was the identification of the boundaries of the pericope or unit of text. The chapter divisions were, of course, a product of the Middle Ages, and the exegetical efforts of the Renaissance and Reformation did little to alter these major textual divisions. The versification, however, was another matter: Identification and numbering of verses was an innovation in the sixteenth century, usually credited to Robertus Stephanus, whose 1528 edition of the Vulgate included a system of verse numbers.[25]

In the case of Romans 13, not only was there difference of opinion concerning versification; there was also difference of opinion over the unit of text—the discussion of political obedience. Calvin clearly viewed the unit of text as extending from verse 1 through verse 7, whereas many exegetes, both before and after, divided the text elsewhere. Peter Lombard, rather, understood verses 1 through 10 as a unit, but he then divided his argument after what would become the sixth verse and saw verses 7 and 8 as part of the same line of argument; Abelard, in contrast, understood the unit to be so clearly demarked by the end of verse 7, that he began the fifth book of his commentary with the eighth verse.[26] Bullinger and, significantly, Beza understood the Pauline argument as including verse 8.[27]

Despite his identification of the unit as concluding with verse 7, Calvin is sensitive to the connection between the two themes—political obedience and love. "I think," he writes, "that Paul meant to refer the precept respecting the power of magistrates to the law of love, lest it should seem to anyone too feeble."[28] The requirement to obey the magistrate is simply an example of the requirement that the faithful follow the law of love, to work for the good. "He that introduces anarchy," Calvin concludes, "violates love; for what immediately follows anarchy is the confusion of things."[29]

Calvin, moreover, like Thomas Aquinas and Martin Bucer before him, felt constrained to anchor in the historical context of the epistle the discussion of the obedience due to rulers.[30] For Calvin, however, this decision to emphasize the problem of the *sitz im leben* precluded a more generalized exposition of the theological *locus de magistratu* pointed toward his focus on the text and his methodological principle of reserving discussion of his *disputationes* and *loci communes* for the *Institutes.* Aquinas and Bucer, by contrast, had not only offered a precise definition of the *sitz im leben*, but also developed an extended meditation on Romans 13:1—7 in the light of collateral texts. In addition, both Aquinas and Bucer offered a more clearly objective and historically rooted identification of the *sitz im leben* than Calvin. Aquinas noted, with considerable accuracy, the political problems of "the primitive church" as indicated by the New Testament witness; Bucer offered an extended discussion, based on Josephus, of the political difficulties caused by Jewish sects in the first century A.D.[31] Calvin's exposition of the *sitz im leben*, however, echoing the hermeneutical interest, so evident in his Old Testament commentaries,[32] to point from past situation to present significance appears to have the sixteenth more in mind than the first century.

Calvin avers that such an explicit and carefully worded statement at this point indicated that Paul's letter was in response to "some great necessity" in the Church of Rome: "There are indeed always some tumultuous spirits who believe that the kingdom of Christ cannot be sufficiently exalted, unless all earthly powers be abolished, and that they cannot enjoy the liberty given by him, except they shake off every yoke of human subjection."[33] The rulers of the time, whether of the Jews or of the Gentiles, continues Calvin, "not only hated piety, but also persecuted religion." Christians could easily reason that it was not necessary to obey such evil men, who attempt to deprive "the only Lord of heaven and earth," Christ Jesus, of his rightful kingdom. In such a situation, Paul found it necessary to treat the authority of magistrates with great care.[34] Although unlike Melanchthon, Beza, and Vermigli he makes no direct mention of the Anabaptists in his commentary, it is certainly the case that the Anabaptist problem was on Calvin's mind when he commented on Romans 13:1 in the *Institutes*.[35]

It is significant, says Calvin, that the comparative and not the superlative form is used in the phrase "Let every soul be subject to the higher powers." The magistrate, Calvin continues, is higher than others because he has been placed in a particular civil or legal relationship with them, not because he is greater in his own right. It is sufficient in Paul's terms, notes Calvin, that they are in such a relationship; we need not ask how they came to be there. Their position is due to the Lord's will. There is no exception: All people are in subjection, as is shown by St. Paul's words "every soul." God has willed that there be magistrates and that all people accept their authority. Calvin, like the medieval commentators, immediately denies that anyone can "claim an immunity from this common subjection."[36]

Calvin moves on to a concise statement of his political theory under the clause "For there is no power but of God." It was seen that the magistrate is not intrinsically better than other men and that nevertheless, all must submit to his authority. This, says Calvin, is because all authority comes from God and the magistrate is "appointed by God's ordination." The language of "ordination" and its reflection of the providential *potentia ordinata* of God is quite typical of the tradition.[37] To resist civil government, Calvin writes, is to resist God himself, "since to despise the providence of him who is the author of political jurisdiction, is to carry on war with him."[38]

At this point Calvin clarifies his theory by making a distinction between ordinances and punishments. Government is established by an ordinance of God, but it is not any particular type of government that receives the divine sanction. God wills only that there be an order in the world "for the well-being of mankind," and therefore he ordains the "right of government." As for punishments, these too are from God, even though they are not "properly" called "ordinances" but exist for the punishment of sin and for the preservation "of legitimate order."[39] In this statement Calvin presents what may be his strongest argument against civil disobedience, for here he explicitly connects God's own providential acts, and particularly God's alien work, with the punishment of civil offenders.

Beza makes no reference to conditions at the time of Paul (as had Calvin) or to the various political models—kingship, aristocracy, democracy, and their perversions—covered by Paul's argument (as had Bullinger and as Vermigli subsequently would argue).[40] He then inquires into the use of the words "every soul." This, he says, echoing Bucer, is a "Hebrew synechdoche"—that is, a figure of speech in which a part is used with reference to the whole.[41] Beza's point of obedience is much like Calvin's, but it refers specifically to the commentator's contemporaries rather than to Paul's; and quite unlike Calvin, Beza adds an element of polemic against Rome.

Beza here reflects an exegetical debate of the age both in his choice of *magistratus* as the rendering for *archontes* and in his reference to Rome. Beza and Vermigli after him appear to reflect negatively on the medieval understanding of "two swords," the secular and the spiritual, in the context of verse 4.[42] Whereas *principes* might be extended to spiritual rulers—the "princes of the church"—*magistratus* could not. Beza specifically notes churchly power in order to exclude it from the Apostle's injunction to obedience. As David Steinmetz has pointed out, Melanchthon and Calvin had already shifted the discussion away from the problem of the "two swords" to the problem of obedience secular rulers.[43]

Church leaders, argues Beza, who "boast of special privileges" are answered by this verse. There are even certain individuals, says Beza in an oblique reference to the debate with Rome over the authority of Scripture, who cannot accept the word of the apostle alone, but who must be brought to the interpretation of the Fathers before they are convinced. He quotes Chrysostom to the effect that the Pauline principle applies to all people, be they apostles, Evangelists, or anyone who ever lived. Were Chrysostom with us today, Beza continues, in apparent anti-papal polemic, "he would have bitterly attacked anyone who would in no way be subject to kings, who would transfer kingship and rule to himself, and who nevertheless wishes to seem to be the vicar of Christ."[44] The anti-papal polemic does not reflect Calvin, but it would be a central issue addressed by Vermigli, whose commentary may here have been influenced by Beza—and certainly who, more than Calvin, was immersed in the medieval tradition.

Beza moves on to comment on his translation: he has followed Calvin by rendering the Greek *hyperechousais* as *supereminentibus* rather than follow the Vulgate's *sublimioribus*, that is, as "standing out above" rather than "lofty" or "elevated." All magistrates, he argues, even those of inferior rank, can claim authority over their subjects: Thus, *supereminens* is a better term than *sublimis.* Of course, it might well be argued on Jerome's behalf whether the comparative form *sublimioribus* actually conveys this meaning better than Calvin's and Beza's version—so that Beza qualifies the point, noting that the Vulgate is problematic not because of its mode of translation, but because of the dangerous implication it conveys.[45]

Like Martin Luther and Martin Bucer as well as John Calvin, Theodore Beza interprets the final clause of the verse as stating that those powers that exist are ordained by God, implying that no powers exist that are not ordained by God. In order to justify the objectionable reading, comments Beza, one would have to alter the Greek text in a manner not justified by any of the ancient codices.[46] One would have to convey, in short, that all power is by either the positive or permissive will of God.[47] In any case, Beza's comment is to the effect that not only the powers, but also the ordering of the powers is of divine origin. God has ordained the "right and power" of the magistrates and also their "manifold stations." Even so, the apostle's argument implies that "the distribution of the power and its right ordering (*eutaxia*) are protected by God."[48] Beza more clearly excludes tyranny from the Pauline demand for obedience than Calvin. "Two things," he argues, "must be remembered, concerning the legitimate powers" that do not apply to "those which result from Tyranny or are brought forth from impiety": namely that God is the author of order, by which the human race is governed, and that it is "not without the judgment and ordination of God" that even the evil magistrate governs.[49]

Beza refrains from any further comment on verse 2 than what was necessitated by the work of translating the passage, refraining, as Calvin also had, from following the earlier tradition and commenting at this point on the issue of resistance to the unjust magistrate.[50] This is a significant interpretive moment, inasmuch as the medieval commentators had, almost immediately, relativized the implications of the command to be subject, whereas Calvin and Beza press the point of subjection to the magistrate. William of St. Thierry is quite typical of the medieval commentators: "If, however, the power commands what God prohibits, then, Christian, spurn the power. For the former threatens punishments, the latter, hell."[51] Aquinas offered the words of the apostle Peter as a qualifier: "It is necessary to obey God rather than men."[52] Significantly, the traditional qualification of power at this point in the exegesis of the text did pass over from the medieval exegetes to the Reformation exegetes.

Calvin devotes a passage of considerable length to verses 3 and 4, but his exegesis, unlike that of many of the more extended comments offered by predecessors and contemporaries like Haymo of Halberstadt, Aquinas, Melanchthon, Bullinger, and Vermigli, draws no examples from the biblical history.[53] The first phrase, "For rulers are not a terror to good works, but to the evil," is a reference, says Calvin, to the "former proposition" and not to later, similar sentiments of the apostle—it refers to the ordinance of God that gives power to rulers. Here, however, the justification of power is made on a slightly different ground: Rulers are to be obeyed because they perform a useful, double function in providing peace for good people and restraints for the wicked. In short, rulers preserve humanity from "universal destruction." There is, therefore, no reason for fearing the magistrate unless one is engaged in evil doings. "Indeed, it is an implied proof of an evil conscience, and of one that is devising some mischief, when anyone wishes to strike off this yoke from himself."[54] In the line of the medieval commentators, Calvin declares that obedience is also due to the evil or unjust ruler, since the wicked ruler is a punishment inflicted by God. God himself turns the blessing of civil order into a curse upon wicked nations.[55] Moreover, even the wicked ruler preserves the order of the state and therefore serves a valid function: Calvin here goes somewhat beyond the cautious language of other commentators of the day, notably Pellican and Vermigli, to argue that "princes never abuse their power so far . . . that they do not retain in their tyranny some kind of just government."[56]

In verse 4, according to Calvin, the focus shifts from the citizen's duty to the magistrate's office. Not only are citizens enjoined to learn from the words of the apostle, but the magistrates also are to be instructed in task. Paul demands that they "minister . . . for good," making them responsible both to God and to their fellow human beings. This responsibility, Calvin holds, is as much an "obligation" to the people and as an answerability to God. Because of their weighty responsibility, the magistrates are armed with the sword—"that they ought forcibly to repress the waywardness of men." It may well be the case that Calvin's rendition of the Greek *phoreo*, "bear," as the more warlike *gero* rather than the somewhat ceremonial *porto* is reflected in the rather militant prose of the commentary. Magistrates are required to punish the wicked "as God's judgment requires": Paul calls the magistrate "an avenger to execute wrath" because he exercises the vengeance of God. "Those, then, who think it contrary to divine command to shed the blood of the guilty contend against God."[57] Here again, Calvin states what his contemporaries noted with some reservation: In a reading of Romans 13:4 in his *Loci communues*, Vermigli cites Acts 5:29 and notes that when the magistrate ceases to be "minister of God to the good," Christians ought to "obey God rather than men."[58] Beza's sole comment on verse 4 is that "wrath" (*ira*) echoes a Hebraic style, indicating the punishment justly effected by God in the rule of the magistrate.[59]

In verse 5, the command to obedience is repeated, but on a higher level, notes Calvin, we obey not simply out of necessity but on account of the conscience that is bound by God's word. In agreement with Bucer, Melanchthon, Bullinger, and the tradition in general, Calvin indicates that the Christian submits voluntarily, not out of fear of wrath or judgment, but for the sake of conscience.[60] This passage, Calvin maintains, is no justification of a "sacrilegious tyranny" over human souls. This surely points toward the *Institutes*, where Calvin maintains a freedom—indeed, a duty—to disobey "impious edicts" on the ground that the unrighteous ruler has "himself abrogated his power." Here Calvin finally adumbrates the qualification on obedience provided much sooner by other commentators.[61] In his comment on verse 5, Beza again follows Calvin closely in theological implication, but he bases his comments directly on textual criticism.

Beza theologizes also briefly and introduces the traditional disclaimer in virtually the same place that Calvin had done: "The exception: [only] as far the altar (*usque ad aras*)." The apostle here indicates that "it is better to obey God than men," Beza comments in an obvious reference to the Petrine dictum of Acts 5:29: "It is another thing, for a magistrate to advise impiety, or also to bring about godlessness by means of [his] subjects." Such acts of "manifest tyranny" do not carry with them the true power of a magistrate, but are a usurpation of power—and remedy is required, if only in the form of non compliance.[62] As for Calvin, so also for Beza, the requirement of obedience to the magistrate cannot justify "sacrilegious tyranny."[63] In a probable reflection of Calvin's reference to "tumultuous spirits" in his comment on verse 1 and of Melanchthon's specific identification of the Anabaptists as enemies of civil obedience addressed by the text, Beza notes that his advocacy of non compliance does not indicate—as some have inferred from a reading of Origen—that the "madness" of the Anabaptists is justified. Vermigli would make a similar point.[64]

Beza's argument thus remains generally within the scope of Calvin's

Commentary on Romans (1539/1540) and opens the question of resistance only as far as the discussion offered in the *Institutes*, where Calvin offers the traditional qualification that rulers cannot be obeyed when they enjoin disobedience to God.[65] The Beza of the *Annotationes*, writing between 1552 and 1556 on the freedom of the conscience from religious tyranny and the right "not to comply," is certainly not the Beza of the *De iure magistratuum*, the Protestant reacting to St. Bartholomew's Day, or even the Beza of the early *De haereticis a civili magistratu puniendis* (1554), where the "inferior magistrate" represents the people and where the magistrate, albeit not the body of the people, is given the limited right to revolt against unjust princely authority.[66]

In the last two verses (vv. 6–7), Calvin argues that Paul mentions the necessity of public support of the government in the form of taxes and revenues. This justifies the public use of collected funds, says Calvin, but not the private squandering of revenues. Finally, in confirmation of all that has been said, Paul may be seen to note that the fear of magistrates should be accompanied by respect for their office. Subjects should hold magistrates in honor and respect, manifested by a continued obedience to the laws, edicts, and judgments, and by a willingness in the payment of taxes.[67] Beza, like Calvin, would call the ministers *incumbentes*, "helpers," those who further a cause, rather than follow the Vulgate's *servientes*. It is only proper, therefore, that we pay taxes of all kinds, tithes, rents, duties, to the end that the community be served. "With fear" Beza explains as a Hebraism indicating the sincere respect in which magistrates ought to be held. Here, as in other places, Beza follows Calvin's interpretation, but he anchors his comment more firmly in the text—in the very connotations of Paul's words.[68]

EPILOGUE

In conclusion, there are few theological differences to be found between Calvin and Beza, although both argue the need for obedience with somewhat less qualification concerning unjust and irreligious rulers than had much of the earlier tradition and several of their contemporaries, notably Bullinger and Vermigli. Even Calvin's concern for the original historical context of the passage and for its connection with the previous issues addressed in the epistle had its clear predecessors in Aquinas, Lyra, Melanchthon, and Bucer. Concern for the *sitz im leben* places Calvin's exegesis and hermeneutics into the tradition of emphasis on the literal-historical meaning of the text that originated in Aquinas, was mediated to the later Middle Ages by Lyra, and was, to a certain extent, mediated to the Reformation by Bucer.

Many of the formal differences between Calvin and Beza—such as the application of Acts 5:29 to the problem of civil obedience in the exegesis of Romans 13:1–7—raise not so much an ultimate question of substance as a question of model: Calvin uses the text in the *Institutes*, but not in the commentary, whereas other commentators who might have provided models for Beza, such as Bucer and Bullinger, use the Petrine criterion as an immediate qualification on the Pauline text. The point is an aesthetic one: What bears on the interpretation of the text at hand? Both the citation of Acts 5:29 in the *Institutes* and Bullinger's citation in his commentary pre date Calvin's exegesis of Romans. Calvin—whether for exegetical and aesthetic or theologico-political reasons—simply chose not to cite the traditionary qualifier from Acts 5:29 in the commentary. Beza, on this point, chose to look to an alternative and more traditional model for the construction of his exegetical argument. A similar issue is raised by Beza's citation of Chrysostom.

Of course, the text is not so much about resistance to authority as it is about obedience; and the pattern of exception to the rule was already well established before the Reformation. The need to develop some clearer form of a theory of resistance, as evidenced in Beza's *De haereticis a civili magistratu puniendis* and *De iure magistratuum*, was either not directly indicated by the text—as in the case of the specific focus of the former treatise— or, as in the case of the rather pointed theorizings of the later treatise, not demanded as yet by the political context.

However, in the less stringent critique of those who would "strike off the yoke" and in the somewhat stronger statement of the exception of tyranny against true religion, we may detect the beginnings of the view that would eventually bring Beza to the teachings of *De iure magistratuum*. The differences between Calvin's and Beza's perspectives can also be explained in part by the brevity of the latter's comments and, perhaps, in part by a movement by Beza to restore some of the qualification of the argument for obedience resident in the earlier tradition of exegesis and in the work of contemporaries like Bullinger and Vermigli. Calvin would move in a similar direction in his late commentary on Daniel.[69]

These contrasts between Calvin's commentaries and, even more, between the exposition in the *Institutes* and the commentaries raise rather pointedly the question of the aesthetics of the commentary and of the impact of aesthetic concerns on theological implication. Calvin's aesthetic concern to locate his exegesis in one place (the commentary) and his *disputationes dogmaticae* or *loci communes* in another (the *Institutes*) frequently makes an assessment of his theology impossible on the basis of an examination of the *Institutes* alone. In the case of Romans 13:1—7, the opposite is the case. In a very restrictive sense, the text is concerned with obedience to the "higher powers"; thus focused, the text, allows little room for qualification of the argument. The exegetical tradition found its primary qualifier in Acts 5:29 and a series of other qualifiers, primarily examples drawn from the history of Israel, such as the story of Daniel and Nebuchadnezzar. To provide the reader of Romans 13:1—7 with the larger biblical and theological view, the tradition had expanded the discussion of obedience beyond the strict limits of the exegesis of Romans. By reserving his very traditional use of the various qualifiers for the *locus* developed in his *Institutes*, Calvin—most probably on purely aesthetic grounds—gave the readers of his commentary not only a partial view of his own doctrine of political obedience but also one of the most rigid and unyielding definitions of that obedience in the history of exegesis. Beza's slight reversal of the pattern restored the qualifier without resorting to the development of a dogmatic *locus* within the commentary. Like Calvin, Beza tended to observe the limits of the text, to offer polemic only when the text itself and its basic significance were at issue, and to avoid over-arching systematic concerns in his work of exegesis.[70]

Beza also differs from Calvin in his overriding concern for the text. Here he shows himself—more clearly than had Calvin—to be the humanist, the textual critic who is willing to bring the best opinion and the best knowledge of his day to bear on the task of exegesis. And for all his obvious relationship to Calvin's exegesis and theology, Beza also evidences, both textually and intellectually, a considerable independence from his mentor. What the *Annotationes* offers, more than anything else, is a text adequate in its critical apparatus for the work of defending Reformed Protestantism in the sixteenth century. Far more than Calvin, Beza attempts to reach a high critical level in his study of the words of the original text and their meanings. Both in his attempt to offer a definitive text and in his more nuanced and somewhat more traditional qualification of the Pauline demand for obedience, Beza can be seen as pointing consciously toward the "right teaching" of the early orthodox era, of which he was one of the notable teachers.

NOTES

1. See, for example, Henri Strohl, "Le Droit à la resistance d'après les conceptions protestantes," in *RHPR* 10 (1930): 126–144; J.-F. Collange, "Droit a la résistance et Réformation," in *RHPR* 65 (1985): 245–255; On Calvin's political theory see William A. Mueller, *Church and State in Luther and Calvin: A Comparative Study* (Garden City, NJ: Doubleday, 1965 [1954]); Wilhelm Niesel, *The Theology of Calvin*, trans. Harold Knight (Grand Rapids, MI: Baker, 1980 [1956]), 229–245. On Beza's political thought see A. A. van Schelven, "Beza's *De Iure Magistratuum in Subidos*," in *ARG* 45 (1954): 62–81; Robert M. Kingdon, "The First Expression of Theodore Beza's Political Ideas," in *ARG*, 46 (1955): 88-99; Irmgard Höss, "Zur Genesis der Widerstandslehre Bezas," in *AFR* 54 (1963): 198–214; Richard C. Gamble, "The Christian and the Tyrant: Beza and Knox on Political Resistance Theory," in *WTJ* 46 (1984): 125–139; and W. Fred Graham, "Calvin and the Political Order: An Analysis of Three Explanatory Studies," in *Calviniana: Ideas and Influence of John Calvin*, ed. Robert V. Schnucker, *Sixteenth Century Essays and Studies*, 10 (Kirksville, MO: Sixteenth Century Publishers, 1988), 51–61.

2. On Calvin's texts, Greek and Latin, see T.H.L. Parker, *Calvin's New Testament Commentaries* (London: SCM; Grand Rapids, MI: Eerdmans, 1971), 93–151.

3. The *Annotationes* first appeared in two volumes (1552–56) and were reissued with some revision in 1582; in this chapter I have followed Theodore Beza, *Jesu Christi Domini Nostri Novum Testamentum, sive Novum Foedus, cuius Graeco contextui respondent interpretationes duae: una, vetus; altera, Theodori Bezae. Eiusdem Theod. Bezae Annotationes, in quibus ratione interpretationis vocum reddita . . .* (Cambridge, 1642). On Beza's exegesis and its relation to the curriculum in Geneva, see Theodore

Beza, *Cours sur les Épitres aux Romains et aux Hébreux 1564—1566 d'après notes de Marcus Widler; Thèses disputées à l'Académie de Genève, 1564—1567,* ed. Pierre Fraenkel and Luc Perrotet (Geneva: Droz, 1988); Luc Perrotet, "Chapter 9 of the Epistle to the Hebrews as Presented in an Unpublished Course of Lectures by Theodore Beza," in *Journal of Medieval and Renaissance Studies* 14, 1 (1984): 89—96; Pierre Fraenkel, "De l'Ecriture à la dispute: le cas de l'Académie de Genève sous Théodore de Bèze," *RTP* 1 (1977); and Irena Backus, *The Reformed Roots of the English New Testament: The Influence of Theodore Beza on the English New Testament* (Pittsburgh, PA: Pickwick Press, 1980).

4. Theodor Beza, *De iure magistratuum,* ed. Klaus Sturm, *Texte zur Geschichte der evangelischen Theologie,* 1 (Neukirchen: Neukirchner Verlag, 1965), and idem, *Du droit des magistrats,* ed. Robert M. Kingdon (Geneva: Droz, 1970). Evidence suggests it was written in 1573. After the Council refused publication, it was translated into French (Lyons, 1574) and Latin (Lyons, 1576). See van Schelven, "Beza's *De iure magistratuum,*" 62—65, and in Sturm's edition, 9—13, 21—23.

5. Theodore Beza, *De haereticis a civili magistratu puniendis* (Geneva, 1554); also found in Theodore Beza, *Tractationes theologicae,* 3 vols. (Geneva, 1582), 85—169.

6. Romans 13 (v. 5) is cited only once in Beza's *De iure magistratuum* as a note. Although prescribing individual obedience or deference, the text does not rule out resistance to magistrates; rather it teaches obedience on grounds of conscience (*De iure,* ed. Sturm, 40—41); cf. *Annotationes.*

7. I have followed John Calvin, *Commentaries on the Epistle of Paul the Apostle to the Romans,* trans., ed. by John Owen (Edinburgh: Calvin Translation Society, 1849; repr. Grand Rapids, MI: Baker Books, 1979), making emendations as necessitated by Calvin's Latin text in *Ioannis Calvini opera quae supersunt omnia,* 59 vols. (vols. 29—87 of *Corpus Reformatorum*), ed. Guilielmus Baum, Eduardus Cunitz, and Eduardus Reuss (Brunswick: Schwetschke, 1863—1900), vol. 49. Subsequent references to the *Calvini opera* will be cited *CO,* followed by volume and column numbers. See also *Joannis Calvini commentarius in epistolam Pauli ad Romanos,* ed. T.H.L. Parker (Leiden: E. J. Brill, 1981).

8. See below, 17, 20.

9. Martin Bucer, *Metaphrases et enarrationes perpetuae Epistolarum D. Pauli Apostoli. . . Tomus Primus. Continens metaphrasim et enarrationeem in Epistolam ad Romanos* (Zürich: Argentorti, 1536), 479a (*interpretatio*);Cf. the analysis and collation of texts in Martin de Kroon, "Bucer und Calvin—Das Obrigkeitsverständnis beider Reformatoren nach ihrer Auslegung von Römer 13," in *Calvinus Servus Christi,* Die Referate des Internationalen Kongresses für Calvinforschung vom 25 bis 28 August 1986 in Debrecen, ed. W. H. Neuser (Budapest, 1988), 209—224.

10. Cf. Bucer, *Metaphrasis et enarratio,* 455b: "Qui vero resisterint, ii poenam ipsi sibi accersent."

11. Cf. Nicolaus of Lyra, in *Biblia sacra cum Glossa interlineari, ordinaria, et Nicolai Lyrani Postilla. . . ,* 7 vols. (Venice, 1588), VI, 28: "*Qui autem resistunt, ipsi sibi damnationem* aeternam unde dicit Salvator: Qui vos spernit me spernit & c." [herein after cited as Lyra, *Postilla*].

12. Beza, *Annotationes,* 446, col. 1.

13. See Heinrich Meyer, *Critical and Exegetical Hand-Book to the Epistle to the Romans,* 5th ed., trans. William P. Dickson (New York: Funk and Wagnalls, 1884), 490; C.E.B. Cranfield, *A Critical and Exegetical Commentary on the Epistle to the Romans,*

2 vols. (Edinburgh: T. & T. Clark, 1975—1979), II, 664, note 5.

14. Beza, *Annotationes*, 446, col. 1.

15. Cf. Augustine, *De doctrina Christiana*, II.vii.9 (PL 34, col. 39).

16. Cf. Calvin, *Commentaries on Romans*, 13:4 (CTS, 481), and below, 25.

17. Beza, *Annotationes*, 445—446, col. 1.

18. Cf. de Kroon, "Bucer und Calvin," 224.

19. Cf. Aland and Nestle—where Beza's argument is sustained at the second highest degree of certainty, but where the variant has several Greek attestations ("p[46]," "D," and "G" from the second or third, the sixth, and ninth centuries, respectively) and almost as many attestations in the Old Latin as the preferred reading.

20. Cf. Benoit Girardin, *Rhétorique et théologie. Calvin: L'Epître au Romains* (Paris: Beauchesne, 1979), 156 167, 187, with Parker, *Calvin's New Testament Commentaries*, 143, with idem, 132—139, on Erasmus: Parker modifies his view of Calvin as dependent primarily on Erasmus, offered in "The Sources of the Text of Calvin's New Testament," in *Zeitschrift für Kirchengeschichte* 73 (1962): 272—298. It is worth noting that in both places Parker examines rather select passages and that had he examined Romans 13:1—7, his conclusions would probably tilt still further toward the Vulgate.

21. On Calvin's exegetical methods see, for example, Hans Joachim Kraus, "Calvin's Exegetical Principles," in *Interpretation* 31 (1977): 329—341; Alexandre Ganoczy and Stefan Scheld, *Die Hermeneutik Calvins: Geistesgeschichtliche Voraussetzungen und Grundzüge* (Wiesbaden: F. Steiner, 1983); T.H.L. Parker, "Calvin the Exegete: Change and Development," in *Calvinus Ecclesiae Doctor*, Die Referate des Internatl. Kongresses für Calvinforschung vom 25 bis 28 September 1978 in Amsterdam, ed. W. H. Neuser (Kampen: Kok, 1978), 33—46; Richard Gamble, *"Brevitas et facilitas*: Toward an Understanding of Calvin's Hermeneutic," in *WTJ* 47 (1985): 1—17; idem, "Exposition and Method in Calvin," in *WTJ* 49 (1987): 153—165; and on Calvin's interpretation of Romans see Girardin, *Rhétorique et théologie*; for an examination of his comments on Romans 13:1—7, see David C. Steinmetz, "Calvin and Melanchthon on Romans 13:1—7," in *Ex Auditu* 2 (1986): 74—81.

22. Cf. Thomas Aquinas, *Commentaria in epistolae Pauli* (Venice, 1498), fol. 45v, col. 2; Martin Bucer, *Metaphrases et enarrationes*, 479a—b, 481b (*interpretatio*), 483—484, 486—490 (*quaestio*); Philip Melanchthon, *Commentarii in epistolam Pauli ad Romanos* and idem, *Enarratio epistolae Pauli ad Romanos*, in *Philippi Melanthonis Opera quae supersunt omnia*, ed. C. G. Bretschneider (Halle: Schwetschke, 18?), vol. 15, cols. 709—710 and 1009—1010 [here in after cited as *Opera*]; Heinrich Bullinger, *In omnes apostolicas epistolas, divi videlicet Pauli XIII. et VII. canonicas commentarii* (Zürich: C. Froschouerum, 1537), 101; Vermigli, *In epistolam s. Pauli apostoli ad Romanos commentarii*, 641.

23. Cf. Calvin, *Commentaries on Romans*, *CO* 49, col. 248, with Lyra, *Postilla*, 28, and Melanchthon, *Commentarii in epistolam Pauli ad Romanos* and idem, *Enarratio epistolae Pauli ad Romanos*, in *Opera*, vol. 15, cols. 709—710 and 1009—1010.

24. Cf. Melanchthon, *Commentarii in epistolam Pauli ad Romanos*, col. 717, with idem, *Enarratio epistolae Pauli ad Romanos*, col. 1018.

25. See the discussion in S. L. Greenslade, ed., *The Cambridge History of the Bible: The West from the Reformation to the Present Day* (Cambridge: Cambridge UP, 1963), 436—437, 442—443.

26. Cf. Lombard, *Collectanea in omnes D. Pauli apostoli epistolas*, PL 191, col. 1306—1307; with Peter Abelard, *Commentariorum super S. Pauli epistolam ad Romanos libri quinque*, PL 178, col. 947—948.

27. Cf. Calvin, *Commentaries on Romans*, 13:7—8, CO 49, col. 252 (CTS, 483—484), with Bullinger, *In omnes apostolicas epistolas*, 105, and Beza, *Annotationes*, 446, col. 2.

28. Calvin, *Commentaries on Romans*, 13:8, CO 49, col. 252 (CTS, 484).

29. Ibid., col. 253 (CTS, 484).

30. Cf. Calvin, *Commentaries on Romans*, 13:1, CO 49, col. 248—249 (CTS, 478), with Aquinas, *Commentaria in epistolas Pauli*, fol. 45v, col. 2.

31. Bucer, *Metaphrases et enarrationes*, 77a—b (*expositio*).

32. See Richard A. Muller, "The Hermeneutic of Promise and Fulfillment in Calvin's Exegesis of the Old Testament Prophecies of the Kingdom," in *The Bible in the Sixteenth Century*, ed., intro. David C. Steinmetz (Durham, NC: Duke UP, 1990), 68—82.

33. Calvin, *Commentaries on Romans*, 13:1, CO 49, col. 248 (CTS, 477).

34. Ibid., col. 248-249 (CTS, 478).

35. Calvin, *Institutes*, IV, xx, 1—2; see Girardin, *Rhétorique et théologie*, 114; and cf. Vermigli, *In epistolam ad Romanos*, 640; and note Melanchthon, *Enarratio epistolae Pauli ad Romanos*, in *Opera*, 15, col. 1010.

36. Calvin, *Commentaries on Romans*, 13:1, *CO* 49 (CTS, 477); cf. Peter Abelard, *Commentariorum super S. Pauli epistolam ad Romanos libri quinque*, PL 178, col. 946; Haymo of Halberstadt, *In divi Pauli epistolas expositio*, PL 117, col. 478; Lombard, *Collectanea in omnes D. Pauli apostoli epistolas*, PL 191, col. 1503—1504.

37. Cf. Haymo of Halberstadt, *In divi Pauli epistolas expositio*, in PL 117, col. 479—480; and Lombard, *Collectanea in omnes D. Pauli apostoli epistolas*, PL 191, col. 1504—1505 with Lyra, *Postilla*, VI, 28.

38. Calvin, *Commentaries on Romans*, 13:1, CO 49, col. 249 (CTS, 479).

39. Ibid.

40. Bullinger, *In omnes apostolicas epistolas*, 101; Vermigli, *In epistolam s. Pauli apostoli ad Romanos commentarii*, 641.

41. Beza, *Annotationes*, 445, col. 1; cf. Bucer, *Metaphrases et enarrationes*, 479a (*interpretatio*).

42. Cf. Lyra, *Postilla*, VI, 28.

43. Steinmetz, "Calvin and Melanchthon," 76. Steinmetz identifies Cardinal Cajetan and Seripando as Roman Catholic exegetes standing in agreement with Melanchthon and Calvin on this point, with Martin Luther and Jacopo Sadoleto arguing a reference to both spiritual and secular rulers.

44. Beza, *Annotationes*, 445, col. 1.

45. Ibid., col. 2.

46. Cf. Martin Luther, *Lectures on Romans: Glosses and Scholia*, ed. Hilton C. Oswald, in *Luther's Works*, vol. 25 (St. Louis: Concordia, 1972), 109—110 with Bucer, *Metaphrases et enarrationes*, 478a (*expositio*).

47. Cf. Haymo of Halberstadt, *In divi Pauli epistolas expositio*, PL 117, col. 479; with Lombard, *Collectanea in omnes D. Pauli apostoli epistolas*, PL 191, col. 1504—1505.

48. Beza, *Annotationes*, 445, col. 2.

49. Ibid., col. 1, and 446, col. 2.

50. Cf. Beza, *Annotationes*, 446, col. 1.

51. Cf. William of St. Thierry (Guillelmus S. Theodorici), *Expositio in epistolam ad Romanos*, 13:2 (PL 180, col. 675); cf. Lombard, *Collectanea in omnes D. Pauli apostoli epistolas*, PL 191, col. 1503; also note Aquinas, *Commentaria in epistolae Pauli*, fol. 46r, col. 1.

52. Aquinas, *Commentaria in epistolae Pauli*, fol. 46r, col. 2.

53. Cf. the references to incidents of political significance in the Old Testament are in Haymo of Halberstadt, *In divi Pauli epistolas expositio*, PL 117, col. 479–480; Aquinas, *Commentaria in epistolae Pauli*, fol. 45v, col. 2, and fol. 46r, col. 2; Melanchthon, *Enarratio epistolae Pauli ad Romanos*, in *Opera*, vol. 15, col. 1013–1016; Bullinger, *In omnes apostolicas epistolas*, 102–104; Vermigli, *In epistolam s. Pauli apostoli ad Romanos commentarii*, 641–642, 644-645.

54. Calvin, *Commentaries on Romans*, 13.3, CO 49, col. 250.

55. Ibid., col. 250 (CTS, 480); cf. William of St. Thierry, *Expositio in epistolam ad Romanos*, 13:1 (PL 114, col. 675).

56. Calvin, *Commentaries on Romans*, CO 49, col. 250 (CTS, 480); cf. also Vermigli, *In epistolam s. Pauli apostoli ad Romanos commentarii*, 645. Pellican, *In omnes apostolicas epistolas*, makes a distinction between the tyrant and the office of the magistrate that parallels Calvin; Bullinger, *In omnes apostolicas epistolas*, 102–103, avoids the issue.

57. Calvin, *Commentaries on Romans*, 13:4, CO 49, col. 251 (CTS, 481–482).

58. Peter Martyr Vermigli, *P. M. Vermilii loci communes* (London, 1576; editio secunda, 1583), IV.xiii.27; Peter's words are cited by Calvin as a ground for refusal to obey a magistrate in *Institutes*, IV.xx.32; cf. the discussion in Höss, "Zur Genesis der Widerstandslehre Bezas," 203.

59. Beza, *Annotationes*, 446, col. 1.

60. Calvin, *Commentaries on Romans*, CO 49, col. 251 (CTS, 482); and cf. the same point in Bucer, *Metaphrases et enarrationes*, 477b (*expositio*) and 482a (*interpretatio*); Melanchthon, *Commentarii in epistolam Pauli ad Romanos*, in *Opera*, 15, col. 714; and Bullinger, *In omnes apostolicas epistolas*, 103.

61. Calvin, *Commentaries on Romans*, 13:5, CO 49, col. 251 (CTS, 482); cf. Calvin, *Institutes*, IV.xx.32.

62. Ibid.

63. Calvin, *Commentaries on Romans* 13:5, CO 49, cols. 251–252 (CTS, 482).

64. Beza, *Annotationes*, 446, col. 1; cf. Melanchthon, *Enarratio epistolae Pauli ad Romanos*, in *Opera*, vol. 15, col. 1010, and Vermigli, *In epistolam s. Pauli apostali ad Romanos commentarii*, 640.

65. Cf. Calvin, *Institutes*, IV.xx.32.

66. Beza, *De haereticis a civili magistratu puniendis* (1554), 133 (in *Tractationes*, I, 126); cf. Kingdon, "The First Expression of Theodore Beza's Political Ideas," 90-92; and Höss, "Zur Genesis der Widerstandslehre Bezas," 203–204.

67. Calvin, *Commentaries on Romans*, 13:6–7, CO 49, col. 252 (CTS, 483).

68. Beza, *Annotationes*, 446, col. 2.

69. See Calvin, *Praelectiones in librum prophetiarum Danielis*, CO 41, col. 25.

70. Perrotet, "Chapter 9 of the Epistle to the Hebrews," 94–96.

3

The Order of the Divine Decrees at the Genevan Academy: From Bezan Supralapsarianism to Turretinian Infralapsarianism

Joel R. Beeke

"Calvin versus the Calvinists" is the battle cry in vogue with much of modern Reformation and post-Reformation scholarship. Since the 1960s many scholars have argued that the supposed Calvin-Calvinist cleavage finds its real culprit in Theodore Beza (1519–1605)—Calvin's hand-picked successor and apparent transformer of his theology. From Ernst Bizer through Johannes Dantine and Walter Kickel to Basil Hall, Brian Armstrong, Robert Kendall, and Philip Holtrop, the thesis is championed that Beza, as the father of Reformed scholasticism, spoiled Calvin's theology[1] by reading him through Aristotelian spectacles.[2] Beza's departure from Calvin has been described repeatedly as scholastic, non-Christological rigidity—not only in ecclesiastical discipline and doctrinal *loci* in general but also, more specifically, in the Bezan innovation of supralapsarian predestinarianism.[3]

In this chapter, which examines the major Genevan Academy theologians from Theodore Beza to Francis Turretin on the narrow question of the order of God's decrees in predestination, I have two goals: first, to answer the accusations of present-day academia by revealing the Christological emphases of Bezan and Turretinian predestinarianism; second, to shed some light on the movement from Beza's supralapsarianism to Turretin's infralapsarianism in terms of theology and church history. To reach these goals, I will first describe the views on the order of God's decrees in late-sixteenth- and seventeenth-century Protestantism, after which I will present the teaching of the Genevan Academy's major theologians on this doctrine, focusing primarily on Beza and secondarily on Turretin.

LAPSARIAN OPTIONS

Although the "lapsarian question" (*lapsus* = the fall) has roots predating the Reformation,[4] it first came into focus during this period. Concerned with the question of the relationship between divine predestination and the fall, first- and second-generation Reformers asked: Was the fall of man in Paradise *actively willed* or only *passively foreseen* by God in his eternal counsel and decree? Martin Luther, Huldrych Zwingli, John Calvin, and the majority of the Reformers argued for an *active* willing of God in the lapsarian question. Heinrich Bullinger and a few minor Reformers refused to go this far, teaching instead that only God's foreknowledge could be linked with the fall. Subsequent Reformers and Puritans realized that Bullinger's reasoning could not offer a solution for the relationship between the counsel of God and sin. Eventually a Reformed consensus developed that the fall must not be divorced from the divine decree.[5]

This consensus generated additional questions: Was divine reprobation ultimately based on the mere good pleasure of God, or was it an act of divine justice exclusively connected with sin? Were both election and reprobation to be considered equally ultimate as acts of pure sovereignty, or was election to be viewed as an act of divine grace and reprobation as an act of divine justice? In connection with questions such as these (i.e., questions that concerned the moral order of God's decree related to humankind's eternal state), the main difference between what came to be called *infralapsarianism* and *supralapsarianism* (often abbreviated as "*infra*" and "*supra*") came more sharply into focus.

Infralapsarians maintain that the decree of predestination must morally *follow* the decree of creation and the fall, believing it to be inconsistent with the nature of God for him to reprobate any individual being without first contemplating that being as created, fallen, and sinful. The infralapsarian proposes that God's election is in its deepest sense a loving act of grace in which God decreed to save certain individuals whom He already contemplated as created and fallen, whereas God's reprobation is a righteous passing by of others, leaving them to their eternal rejection and condemnation. Thus the decree of predestination must come after or "below" the decree of the fall (*infra* = below).

Supralapsarians believe that the decree of divine predestination must morally *precede* the decree concerning humankind's creation and fall. They teach that God's predestination is in its deepest sense a pure, sovereign act of good pleasure, in which God elected certain individuals and reprobated certain individuals, contemplating them in his decree as "creatible and fallible," but not as already created and fallen. Supralapsarians stress that everything, including all decrees, flows out of sovereign good pleasure. Thus the decree of predestination must come before or "above" the decree of the fall (*supra* = above).

The point at issue in the infra-supra debate is the *conceptual* and *moral* order of the decrees of God antecedent to creation and the fall. Neither infras nor supras find their distinctives in a *chronological* ordering of God's decrees. All God's decrees are from eternity; it is impossible to posit a chronologically first or last decree. Both infras and supras agreed that predestination was "before the foundation of the world" (Eph. 1:4), notwithstanding their different emphases.[6] Although both decretal orders stress God's sovereign grace in Christ toward His elect, supralapsarianism places its stress on the sovereignty of God and decretal theology. Infralapsarianism accents the mercy of God and soteriological theology, in conjunction with the responsibility of humankind.

With the innovations of Möise Amyraut (1596–1664) and the Academy of Saumur, a third option, dubbed "postredemptionism," entered seventeenth-century Reformed theology. By placing election after redemption in God's decree, Amyraut allowed for universal atonement. Postredemptionism never found expression in Reformed confessions nor gained respectability in circles of Reformed orthodoxy.[7] Ultimately, infralapsarianism won the day, perhaps not so much because it was the most orthodox of the Reformed lapsarian options as because it was the most effective in refuting the charges of Arminianism. Nevertheless, as we pursue the thought of the Genevese from Beza's supralapsarianism to Francis Turretin's infralapsarianism, and ultimately to the abandonment of Calvinism in Jacob Vernet (1698–1789), we must ask: Does infralapsarianism tend to weaken a thoroughgoing Reformed theology?

THEODORE BEZA

Calvin's Genevan legatee, Theodore Beza (1519–1605),[8] pursued humanism, classical studies, literature, and law before he converted to Protestantism during "a crisis of mind, heart and body" in the late-1540s.[9] He then taught Greek at Lausanne Academy for ten years; all the while he retained close ties with Calvin, seldom, if ever, publishing anything that was not first submitted to Calvin for approval.[10]

Beza accepted a call to the new Genevan Academy to serve as its first rector (1559–1563) and as professor of theology (1559–1599). He moderated Geneva's Venerable Company of Pastors *(Compagnie des Pasteurs)* from Calvin's death until 1580, served as chief counselor to the French Reformed churches, and produced a varied literary corpus. When he died at age 86, he had outlived by decades all the Reformers who had labored to establish Protestantism throughout Europe. His long life, his position in the Genevan Academy, his extensive correspondence and activity on behalf of the Reformed cause throughout Europe, and his graceful style and prolific writings assured his transitional role between the turbulent era of Calvin and the new age of Protestant orthodoxy, as well as his profound influence on many seventeenth-century theologians and pastors. In this chapter we will examine Beza's doctrinal treatises that deal most explicitly with predestination: *Tabula praedestinationis, Confessio christianae fidei,* and *De praedestinationis doctrina.*[11]

Tabula Praedestinationis (1555)

The *Tabula praedestinationis,*[12] which contains Beza's influential diagram of the order of predestination, was probably written as a polemical tract to counter the arguments of Jerome Bolsec (c. 1524–1584), a French physician and opponent of Calvin. In his diagram Beza divides humankind into elect and reprobate, and he posits God's decree as foundational for such cardinal doctrines as divine calling, conversion, grace, faith, justification, sanctification, the glorification of believers and the damnation of sinners, and eternal life and eternal death.

From this *Tabula* modern scholarship gathers most of its material against Beza, labeling him as rigidly theocentric, coldly deterministic, and overwhelmingly scholastic.[13] Beza is judged to be the transformer of Calvinian thought into a Reformed scholasticism that structured all theology under supralapsarian predestination, but most modern scholars have neglected to take into account two important considerations: First, Beza wrote the *Tabula* in response to severe attacks on Calvin's doctrine of predestination, consequently, Beza would naturally focus on predestination more in this work than if he had written a nonpolemical work of Christian theology.[14] Second, modern scholars have erred in dwelling more on the diagram than on his exposition. Without adequate support, Kickel suggests that Beza's diagram forms the base of a necessitarian system and summarizes his Christian theology.[15]

Beza's appended commentary, however, reveals that the *Tabula praedestinationis* was written with a very different emphasis. In Chapter 1, Beza explains why predestination must be preached: "in order that those who have ears may hear and be assured of God's eternal gracious purpose."[16] From the outset Beza's concern with predestination is pastoral and consolatory; it centers upon the election of the individual. His stated purpose in preaching the "double decree" is the elect's assurance.[17]

This strong soteriological note runs throughout the entire work, despite the fact that in Chapters 2 and 3 he unfolds an implicit supralapsarianism. In fairness to Beza, note that he did not intend to set forth an explicit "ordering of decrees" in these chapters or anywhere else in the *Tabula*. His focus is on salvation and damnation as present, temporal, and individual concerns.[18]

Chapters 2 and 3 anticipate the supra position by their systematic balance between election and reprobation. Beza argues that the secret "first cause of [the reprobate's] damnation is God's decree," and he affirms that from humanity's perspective the reprobate are damned for their own sins and stubborn refusal to break with the yoke of unbelief.[19] He distinguishes the public promulgation of the decree of reprobation from reprobation per se.[20] Beza reasons that the eternal decree necessitated the fall of humankind into sin and disobedience. Although the decree of reprobation always leads to *just* condemnation, and the decree of election always leads to *merciful* salvation, they both flow ultimately out of God's sovereign pleasure.[21]

In Chapter 4 and onward, Beza deals with the *execution* of the decree, and he stresses Christ as foundational in election. In Chapter 5 he states forthrightly, "Christ is the second heavenly Adam, the foundation and very substance of the elect's salvation."[22] The Christocentric character of Beza's theology is crystal clear.[23] Beza also argues for a larger Christological structure. Christ is both the efficient cause of predestination together with the Father and the Spirit and the first effect of predestination itself on account of those who are mercifully elected in Him. As Richard Muller points out, this formulation demonstrates Beza's soteriological impulse which offsets deterministic implications of some of his other formulations.[24]

Confessio Christianae Fidei (1558)

Beza wrote his *Confessio* to persuade his father of the reasonableness of his renouncing Romanism and embracing the Reformed faith, as well as to make a personal statement of faith.[25] *Confessio* represents Beza's most comprehensive and systematic theological work, arranged as (1) the unity and trinity of God, (2) the Father, (3) the Son, (4) the Holy Ghost, (5) the church, (6) the last judgment, and (7) the contrast between "the doctrine of the Papists and those of the holy Catholic Church."

In this work the only reference Beza makes to predestination deals with angels as "messengers for the preservation of the elect."[26] Providence is connected with the Trinity but separate from predestination. Creation, the fall, and the decrees of God are placed under the third head of Christology. These connections provide a foundational ground for the mediatorial ordination of Christ rather than to subsume predestination under providence.[27]

Three important observations may be made at this juncture: First, in Beza's most comprehensive doctrinal treatise, predestination serves as one basic concept, not as the overarching principle of all theology. Dantine attempts to sidestep this contradiction of his basic view of Beza by noting that Beza's lack of emphasis upon predestination in *Confessio* may have arisen out of fear of offending his Roman Catholic father.[28] But as Tadataka Maruyama argues, this theory does not explain why the entire *Confessio* is so polemically anti-Catholic or why its Latin edition, designed for the educated, retained a nonpredestinarian scheme.[29]

Second, instead of Beza parting roads with Calvin on soteriological predestination, is it possible that Beza himself influenced Calvin in the location of predestination in the last edition of the *Institutes* (1559)? Not only was *Confessio* written three years before Calvin's soteriological placement of predestination in the *Institutes*, but we also know that Beza discussed his work with Calvin prior to publication.[30] Although both sides of this question could be argued, one thing is certain: In the late 1550s Beza himself viewed predestination from a primarily Christological-soteriological context.[31]

Finally, modern scholarship's accusations against Beza as being rigid and cold in his doctrine of predestination run contrary to even a cursory reading of *Confessio*. Throughout this treatise Beza refuses to divorce predestination from the Christian's comfort, the walk of godly piety, and the work of redemption as a whole. As Beza explains: "Seeing that good works are for us the certain evidences of our faith, they also bring to us afterwards the certainty of our eternal election. For faith necessarily depends on election. . . . This is why all that we have said of faith and of its effects would be useless if we would not add this point of eternal election as the sole foundation and support of all the assurance of Christians."[32]

De Praedestinationis Doctrina (1582)

In this last treatise on the doctrine of predestination, Beza appears to have moved in a more supralapsarian direction than previously. On several occasions he asserts that the elect and reprobate are predestined from a mass "yet unshapen." In an exposition of Romans 9, he writes: "Paul . . . alludes to the creation of Adam, and rises up to the eternal purpose of God, who, before he created mankind, decreed of his own mere will and pleasure, to manifest his glory, both in saving of some whom he knew, in a way of mercy, and in destroying others, whom he also knew, inrighteous judgment."[33]

Nevertheless, even this treatise does not prove that the doctrine of predestination was the central dogma of Beza's thought or theological method.[34] Interestingly, Maruyama attributes an increasing rationalization of predestination in Beza's writings more to his "traditionalism" than to his "scholasticism."[35]

Three major conclusions about Beza's supralapsarian predestination may be drawn from his own writings: First, Beza's supralapsarianism can easily be overestimated. Carl Bangs's argument that Beza went beyond supralapsarian is incorrect; rather, Robert Kendall's observation that he showed supralapsarian tendencies that would later emerge into full-fledged supralapsarianism is more accurate.[36] These tendencies are most apparent in his polemical writings, in which he felt obliged to defend Calvinian predestination and ultimately moved increasingly into supralapsarian thought. Interestingly, supralapsarian tendencies are wholly absent in his 87 extant sermons.

Second, Beza's departure from Calvin can easily be overestimated. Neither viewed them as substantially in agreement. The sixteenth-century Reformers. In England, for example, O. T. Hargrave notes: "After those of Calvin, the works of Theodore de Beza were the most important for the Calvinist predestinarian movement in England. As with Calvin, Beza . . . was one of the ablest defenders of the Calvinist position, going even further if anything than Calvin himself."[37] Here lies the key to the Calvin-Beza debate: *going further than Calvin himself.* Beza was prone to lean toward supralapsarianism, scholasticism, and rationalism to a greater extent than Calvin; nevertheless, the times and the defense of the Reformed faith called him to take this route. Increasing pressure was placed on the second- and third-generation Reformers to expound questions relative to God's decrees and will. Beza's interest in expounding such questions does not apply to his whole thought but only to a few treatises, and even those treatises manifest no greater interest in that subject than shown by other sixteenth century Calvinist theologians, such as Wolfgang Musculus (1497–1563), Peter Martyr Vermigli (1499–1562), and Girolamo Zanchi (1516–1590).[38]

In no case does Beza's theology differ *qualitatively* from Calvin's; in fact, a quantitative distinction is the only cleavage an accurate historian could safely place between them. It is most remarkable that the work from which modern scholarship builds its case against Beza, the *Tabula*, was not published without Calvin's approval.

Finally, some of the confusion must be charged to Beza himself, for, as Muller notes, "Beza is by turns polemical and homiletical, rigid and flexible, speculative and soteriological."[39] Rather than being inconsistent in this tension, however, he walks the tightrope of Scripture. When he does begin with predestination, he is motivated by his core belief that predestination is foundational in Scripture. Beza warns against a metaphysical use of predestination. If reason contradicts Scripture, he is adamant that reason must be sacrificed. Like Calvin, he maintains that not only the will but also human reason has been seriously impaired by the fall—he calls reason "blindness." Consequently, he warns against vain speculation about predestination. "The secrets of God," he writes, "are to be highly reverenced, rather than to be searched into deeply." Following Calvin's hermeneutical principle of interpreting Scripture by Scripture, Beza spells out the limits of theology: "We may go no farther than God's Word limits us in setting forth a doctrine of Scripture in a spirit of edification."[40]

BEZA'S SUPRALAPSARIAN SUCCESSORS

Although the immediate heirs of Beza's chair of theology at the Genevan Academy were all professed supralapsarians, the theological pendulum gradually swung away from supralapsarianism for some years prior to Francis Turretin's unequivocal stand for infralapsarianism.

After Beza's death Geneva's leading theologian, Giovanni Diodati (1576–1649), was a lifelong devotee.[41] He studied avidly under Beza and received a doctorate in theology from the Genevan Academy when he was only 19 years of age. Diodati served as professor of theology from 1599 to 1645 at the Genevan Academy. Beza also delegated the teaching of Hebrew to him, a position Diodati held until 1618, when he assumed the rectorship of the Genevan Academy.

Diodati's reputation increased internationally when he served the Synod of Dort (1618–1619) as one of Geneva's two representatives.[42] At Dort he played a prominent role in defending the orthodox position. When he movingly addressed the synod on the doctrine of perseverance, Dort's supralapsarian president, Johannes Bogerman, declared that the address appeared to have been divinely inspired![43]

In addressing the issue of predestination, the statement of the Genevan delegation to the Synod of Dort, composed by Diodati and three Genevan pastors, contains no surprises. Beza's basic doctrine of predestination is presented, emphasizing the role of Christ and a trinitarian doctrine of providence. Decretal theology is not presented as the overarching structure of all theology. No mention is made of the supra-infra debate. The Genevan statement and Head I of the Canons of Dort on predestination have much in common.[44]

Doctrinally Diodati was a Bezan protegé. Doctrinal orthodoxy and biblical piety blend throughout his *Pious and Learned Annotations Upon the Holy Bible.* He took a Christological supralapsarian stand, as evidenced in his Romans 9 exposition:

[Rom. 9:11 on *according to election*] Namely, by which he had determined to chuse the one, and leave the other.

[Rom. 9:20 on *Nay but*] To answer the wicked objections of the reprobate, . . . that the work of grace is of Gods meer free will. . . .

[Rom. 9:20 on *Made me*] not that God doth indeed make a man a sinner, or that he is author of sinne; but by this word of making, is here meant the appointing of mans last end.[45]

When Diodati assumed the rectorship in 1618, *Theodore Tronchin* (1582—1657), his able Genevan associate at the Synod of Dort, took his place in teaching Hebrew. Son-in-law of Theodore Beza, Tronchin was by no means a novice at Dort or Geneva; he had been professor of Oriental languages at the Genevan Academy since 1606. Like Beza and Diodati, Tronchin maintained the high Calvinistic position of supralapsarianism as evidenced in his *De peccato originali.*[46] With the assistance of Diodati and Tronchin, supralapsarianism was the common position in the Genevan Academy throughout the first half of the seventeenth century.[47]

Although overshadowed by his son Francis and his grandson Jean-Alphonse, Benedict Turretin (1588—1631) played an important role in reaffirming the supra line of thought at Geneva. From 1612 to his premature death in 1631, Benedict Turretin carried on the Beza-Diodati tradition in his well-attended lectures. Together with the Genevan delegates, Diodati and Tronchin, the eldest Turretin held the Canons of Dort in high esteem and was influential in their adoption by the Genevan and French churches.[48]

It is difficult to determine precisely when the winds of infralapsarianism began to blow through the Genevan Academy. Muller asserts that a mild form of infralapsarianism began to filter through Geneva's students and even faculty prior to its gaining a foothold in the academy's theological chair.[49] Although supralapsarianism was formally adhered to by Genevese theological professors from Beza down to Francis Turretin, heart adherence to thorough supralapsarianism may have been waning ever since Dort's infralapsarian stand in 1619—particularly in Diodati, Theodore Tronchin, and Benedict Turretin. Frederick Spanheim (1600—1649), who assumed the chair of philosophy at Geneva in 1626 and took Benedict Turretin's place in theology in 1631, asserted that he was supra in praying and studying but infra in preaching and teaching.[50] Nor did Spanheim speak tongue-in-cheek; he was a faithful adherent of the Genevan tradition, which is amply confirmed by his major theological writings.[51]

Spanheim is credited with being the first (1635) to open the Genevan attack against Amyraut's unorthodox view on predestination, and he was subsequently joined by Diodati and Bénédict Turretin in admonishing the French Synod against "innovations."[52] Nevertheless, Spanheim's confession reveals the tension of attempting to show allegiance to both the tradition of Geneva and the position of Dort. Spanheim's transitional position helps explain the apparent suddenness of Francis Turretin's advocacy of infralapsarianism as a widely accepted alternative.

FRANCIS TURRETIN'S INFRALAPSARIANISM

When infralapsarianism prevailed at Geneva in the mid-seventeenth century, Francis Turretin (1623—1687) stood in the front ranks. All four of Beza's major supralapsarian successors—Diodati, Tronchin, Spanheim, and Francis's own father—had a strong hand in forming his background.[53] After completing the course of study at Geneva under the Academy's pillars of orthodoxy, Turretin traveled to Holland and France. In 1648 he was ordained to pastor the Italian church in Geneva, and held a professorship in theology from 1653 until his death in 1687.[54]

Turretin located the decrees and predestination in the realm of theology proper in his renowned *Institutio Theologicae Elencticae*.[55] Predestination, his "Fourth Topic," follows a discussion of the existence, attributes, and trinitarian essence of God, and precedes a consideration of creation, providence, angels, and humankind. He believed that the decrees, predestination inclusive, are properly examined immediately following the essence of God as representing his "essential internal acts." For Turretin, predestination is the major decree of God.[56] In his last question that he addresses predestination: "Question XVIII: Concerning the Order of Decrees of God in Predestination: Whether any order should be recognized in the decrees of God, and what it should be."[57] The gist of Turretin's pungent 14 pages devoted to the options of lapsarianism may be summed as follows: Supralapsarianism is too sharp and unmitigating; Arminianism is too unorthodox and unbiblical; Amyraldianism is too weak and compromising; infralapsarianism is scriptural and edifying. All outside of infralapsarianism must be, at best, respected but rejected.

Supralapsarianism is the first option Turretin rejects. He advances four objections: First, supralapsarianism is untenable in teaching that "the first act of God's will towards some of his creatures is made to be an act of hatred, . . . which does not appear to agree sufficiently with his unspeakable goodness." Second, "It is also harsh because, according to this order, God is considered to have imparted to them by far the greatest effects of love from a principle of hatred, while he is made to create them in a state of integrity for the purpose of illustrating his justice in their damnation." Third, "It is falsely supposed that God exercises an act of mercy and justice towards his creatures in the destination of salvation and destruction who are neither miserable nor guilty; yea, who are not even conceived of as yet existing." Fourth, "It is also gratuitously asserted that the creation and the fall are the means of election and reprobation, since they are antecedent to them."[58] He argues that supralapsarianism, though not heretical, is not edifying for the church. Interestingly, Dijk remarks that at this juncture Turretin has difficulty avoiding predestination as divine foreknowledge rather than as divine sovereignty.[59] For Turretin, sin in the object is the only condition worthy of the decree of rejection. Justice and mercy supersede sovereignty in divine predestination.[60]

Second, Turretin demolishes the lapsarianism of *Arminianism*. He outlines Arminian lapsarianism thus: "(1) The destination of Christ as Mediator who should acquire for sinners the right to salvation; (2) the ordination of faith and perseverance as the condition of the salvation to be communicated; (3) the ordination of the means to the end by the help of which sinners may believe and persevere; (4) the ordination of salvation itself, made for particular persons as believing and persevering."[61] Subsequently Turretin accuses Arminianism of corrupting the doctrine of gratuitous predestination, of denying God's good pleasure, of limiting God's knowledge to mere *praescientia*, of denying all election to faith, of leading back to Pelagianism and popery. In sum, Arminianism does not at any point "touch upon the true meaning of election."[62]

Third, Turretin has no more sympathy for Amyraldian *postredemptionism* than he does for Arminianism. If Arminianism is guilty of conditional election and love, Amyraldianism enters its errors at least half-way by advocating semi-Pelagianism. He argues that it is foolish to assume that (1) God can zealously love people in one decree (general), whom he equally hates in another (special); (2) God determined means before end, before he thought of the salvation of the elect; (3) "Christ has not merited faith for his own because the satisfaction for all is conceived to precede the decree to give faith to some"; (4) calling precedes election; (5) God's decrees can be based on the distinction between "God as legislator" and "Father" or "manager" and "disposer of events."[63]

Finally, Turretin proposes and defends the final and fourth lapsarian option, *infralapsarianism*, as the "mediating" view between Amyraldianism and supralapsarianism and as "the common one among the Reformed," who teach that there is a double decree.[64]

According to this order, the first decree with us concerns the creation of man. The second concerns the permission of his fall. . . . The third concerns the election to salvation of some certain ones from the fallen human race and the leaving of others in their native corruption and misery. The fourth concerns the sending of Christ into the world as the Mediator and surety of the elect. . . . The fifth concerns effectually calling them by the preaching of the gospel and the grace of the Holy Spirit.[65]

Turretin produces three sorts of evidence for infralapsarianism: (1) Scripture, which subordinates the mission of Christ and redemption to election and which attributes the saving gifts of the Spirit, faith, and repentance to the merit of Christ; (2) the nature of the case, in which the intention of accomplishing the end should come before the intention of providing the means; and (3) the mode of the work of each of the divine Persons that best fits the infra scheme.[66] Ultimately, infralapsarianism is most appropriate because "it may not afford any occasion either to the desperation of men or to their profane license—the two terrible rocks upon which the wicked (falsely abusing it) are accustomed to strike."[67]

In summary, Turretin opts for the infralapsarian perspective because he believes it best shows how predestination must be taught: "Not for the satisfaction of curiosity, but with great sobriety and prudence, remaining within the limits of Scripture, always giving consideration to the occasion, not simply repeating formulae. . . . [and] it must be taught *a posteriori*, ascending from effect to cause, not *a priori* from cause to effect. Its purpose is edification."[68]

From Benedict to Francis Turretin, the Genevan Academy made a full transition from supralapsarianism to infralapsarianism. But the pendulum did not stop here; Francis's son, Jean-Alphonse, would in turn view his father's lapsarianism as far too rigid, and the following generation of Genevan theologians would abandon orthodox Calvinism altogether.

FRANCIS TURRETIN'S SUCCESSORS

Francis Turretin's generation of Genevan theologians represented the last stand for orthodoxy in Geneva for many decades. When Francis Turretin visited Holland on Geneva's behalf, Theodore Tronchin's son, Louis Tronchin (1629—1705), was voted as Geneva's new professor of theology. The younger Tronchin studied at the Saumur Academy under Möise Amyraut, notwithstanding the opposition of his father and of Francis Turretin, his greatest opponent. As an astute Amyraldian who outlived Turretin by nearly two decades, Louis Tronchin was able to exert a long-term influence on the theological scene at the Genevan Academy through his attempt to merge Amyraldianism, Cartesianism, and orthodoxy. He was responsible for educating an entire generation of "Enlightened Orthodox" theologians, that is, men who sought to harmonize orthodoxy and enlightenment by creating a practical form of theology that maintained only the basic categories of Reformed thought that the average parishioner could understand. He eventually succeeded in breaking down Reformed scholasticism at the Genevan Academy.[69] With regard to the decrees of God, the younger Tronchin rejected the entire supra-infra debate as irrelevant to the intellectual developments of his day; moreover, he argued that "nothing should be affirmed that we do not perceive clearly either in nature itself or in that which God has taught."[70]

The most traditionally orthodox person to take a theological chair at the Genevan Academy after Francis Turretin was Bénédict Pictet (1655—1724). Pictet studied under his uncle Francis Turretin at Geneva and under Frederick Spanheim at Leiden, and he succeeded his uncle to the chair of theology. He served the Genevan Academy both as professor of theology (1687—1724) and as rector (1690—1694, 1712—1718). Although he remained orthodox in his theology,

Pictet held a mediating position between the Reformed scholasticism of his uncle and the Enlightened Orthodoxy of Louis Tronchin in defending the faith against the intellectual challenges of his era.[71] In foregoing the old scholastic methodology while retaining the old Reformed theology, "Pictet sought to construct an orthodox system of theology rigorous enough to meet the tougher standards of rational inquiry while forging a theology practical enough to stand the test of being relevant for the non-professional theologian."[72]

On the decrees of God, Pictet formally followed his uncle's infralapsarian approach. Although the translator of Pictet's *Theologia Christiana* admits he purposely omitted parts of his chapter on reprobation "as being too artificial in statement to be scriptural," sufficient material is included in his chapters on election to prove that Pictet's infralapsarianism contrasted with Louis Tronchin's "Enlightened Orthodoxy." Pictet writes: "God has decreed to save some men lying in the same abyss of misery as the rest, of his mere grace and favour, lest any one should imagine, that God hath chosen those only who he foresaw would be better and more deserving than others, and would believe, and perform good works."[73] Interestingly, he did move the placement of the doctrine to the commencement of Christological soteriology and would be followed on this score by Charles Hodge at Princeton.

Pictet's major opponent at Geneva was Jean-Alphonse Turretin (1671—1737), who gained the upper hand over Pictet and effectively stamped out any vestiges of conservative Calvinism at the Genevan Academy. Taking the theological chair of his mentor, Louis Tronchin, in 1705, Turretin has been described as "the liberator of Calvin's church from the tyranny of Calvinistic scholasticism."[74]

As an advocate of natural theology, J. A. Turretin had little sympathy for the decrees of God. He taught that the doctrine of predestination led only to "wild excess" in Protestant circles, and he condemned supralapsarianism: "When theologians appear who teach that God created the greater part of mankind for no other purpose than to show forth his glory in their eternal misery, and therefore formed them in a state of absolute necessity of sinning, these theologians, who are called supralapsarians, can be completely refuted by the natural ideas concerning the divine perfections, such as goodness, justice, and wisdom."[75] For J. A. Turretin, the notion of sin and humankind's unworthiness of salvation did not bear any implications for the divine decree. His *Fundamentals in Religion* reveals how completely he departed from his father's Reformed orthodoxy.[76] His struggle to abrogate the Helvetic Formula Consensus of 1675 *(Formula consensus eccleisarum Helveticarum)*,[77] which he accomplished by 1706, spelled the final defeat for Calvinism at the Genevan Academy. For the sake of unity and simplicity, he was quite ready to drop such "nonessential" doctrines as predestination, imputation of original sin, the presence of Christ in the Lord's Supper, and limited atonement. Philip Schaff alludes to J. A. Turretin as one who "was inclined to Arminianism, and favored toleration."[78] Alexander is more forthright: "His whole theological tendency was marked by a fascinating liberalism, verging on what was latitudinarian."[79]

Finally, in Jacob Vernet (1698–1789), professor of theology at Geneva for 40 years prior to his death, the Calvinistic theology of the Genevan Academy was replaced with the theology and spirit of the rationalism of the Enlightenment. In his *Christian Instructions,* Vernet emphasized that the church should only cling to the bare essentials, meaning the denial of the Trinity, stating that election is no more than God's foreknowledge of who would believe, and insisting the decrees of God can scarcely be profitably discussed.[80] Although J. A. Turretin had banned the signing of the Helvetic Consensus under his rectorship, he had never approved an entirely "confessionless" Geneva as it soon became in the hands of Vernet. James Good's words form an apt summary: "How great was the descent from Calvin to this. Geneva, the city that, under Calvin, had been a city set on a hill, whose light could not be hid—the model city, the wonder of its day—had fallen into an abyss. The church which so successfully had resisted all the plots of Romanism for centuries was finally captured by its opposite, rationalism. For two centuries and more, Geneva had held to its Calvinism; but half a century had undone it all.[81]

CONCLUSION

The history of the order of the divine decrees of predestination at the Genevan Academy underscores some important lessons: First, Beza and his colleagues must be acquitted of the labels of scholastic rigidity, of transforming Calvinian theology into a theology governed by supralapsarian predestination, and of promoting non-Christological predestination. Beza's sermons, which emphasize Christology and soteriology significantly more than theology proper, are further evidence that his theology was not subsumed *in toto* under the supralapsarian predestination. William Cunningham recognizes that "it has been often alleged that Beza . . . carried his views upon some points farther than Calvin. . . . We are not prepared to deny altogether the truth of this allegation; but we are persuaded that there is less ground for it than is sometimes sup-posed."[82]

Second, neither Beza nor his successors held supralapsarian views so narrowly that they could not commune with infralapsarians. The infralapsarian *Confessio Gallicana* was adopted by the Synod of La Rochelle in 1561 without objection from its chairman, Theodore Beza.[83] Geneva's supralapsarian delegates to the Synod of Dort, Giovanni Diodati and Theodore Tronchin, both signed the Canons with no conscientious objections. Turretin faced no opposition from his colleagues when he embraced infralapsarianism.

Third, the attempt within Geneva to move from a Christological to a trinitarian framework, which culminated in Francis Turretin, was not mere speculation but a serious attempt to make an improvement upon Calvinian theology *in toto*. Neither Beza nor Francis Turretin forfeited Calvinian Christology; on the contrary, they always insisted that predestination must be treated with salvation in Christ and the comfort of the believer.[84] Their theocentrism does not deny their Christocentrism. Rather, one could argue that Reformed soteriology remained Christocentric as a fruit of insisting on a theocentric causality, in contrast to Arminian soteriology, which fails to be Christocentric as a result of insisting on an anthropocentric causality.[85]

Finally, the move of Francis Turretin to infralapsarianism was significant for a historical-theological reason. The move to infralapsarianism may have been largely due to outside pressures compelling him to soften the angularity of Genevan supralapsarianism while simultaneously avoiding the pitfalls of Amyraldianism. Moreover, mainstreaming the Genevan Academy with post-Dort Reformed orthodoxy, which, with few exceptions, embraced infralapsarianism, kept the Genevan theologians from isolating themselves. Consequently, Turretin was convinced that his defense of infralapsarianism was, not a weakening of Calvinism, but a strengthening of it. Little could he realize that his own son would abandon his theology and help lead the Genevan Academy into a rationalistic spirit.

NOTES

1. Ernst Bizer, *Frühorthodoxie und Rationalismus* (Zürich: EVZ-Verlag, 1963), 6—15; Johannes Dantine, "Die Prädestinationslehre bei Calvin und Beza" (Ph.D. dissertation, Göttingen, 1965) and "Les Tabelles sur la Doctrine de la Prédestination par Théodore de Bèze," *RTP* 16 (1966): 365—77; Basil Hall, "Calvin against the Calvinists," in *John Calvin*, ed. G.E. Duffield (Grand Rapids, MI: Eerdmans, 1966), 25—28; Walter Kickel, *Vernunft und Offenbarung bei Theodor Beza: Zum Problem des Verhältnisses von Theologie, Philosophie und Staat* (Neukirchen: Neukirchener Verlag, 1967); Brian G. Armstrong, *Calvinism and the Amyraut Heresy: Protestant Scholasticism and Humanism in Seventeenth-Century France* (Madison: U of Wisconsin P, 1969), xviii, 38—42, 128—33, 158ff.; R.T. Kendall, *Calvin and English Calvinism to 1649* (Oxford: Oxford UP, 1979), 1—41 and 209ff., and "The Puritan Modification of Calvin's Theology," in *John Calvin: His Influence in the Western World*, ed. W. Stanford Reid (Grand Rapids, MI: Zondervan, 1982), 199—216; Philip Holtrop, *The Bolsec Controversy on Predestination, from 1551—1555* (Lampeter: Mellen, 1993).

For responses in defense of Beza, see Richard Muller, "Predestination and Christology in Sixteenth Century Reformed Theology" (Ph.D. dissertation, Duke University, 1976), revised as *Christ and the Decrees: Christology and Predestination in Reformed Theology from Calvin to Perkins* (Grand Rapids, MI: Baker Books, 1988); Herman Hanko, "Predestination in Calvin, Beza, and Later Reformed Theology," *Protestant Reformed Theological Journal* 10 2 (1977): 1—24; Ian McPhee, "Conserver or Transformer of Calvin's Theology? A Study of the Origins and Development of Theodore Beza's Thought, 1550-1570" (Ph.D. dissertation, University of Cambridge, 1979); Paul Helm, *Calvin and the Calvinists* (Edinburgh: Banner of Truth Trust, 1982); Dewey D. Wallace, Jr., *Puritans and Predestination: Grace in English Protestant Theology* (Chapel Hill: U of North Carolina P, 1982); Richard Gamble, "Switzerland: Triumph and Decline," in *John Calvin: His Influence in the Western World*, 55—73; Joel R. Beeke, *Assurance of Faith: Calvin, English Puritanism, and the Dutch Second Reformation* (New York: Peter Lang, 1991), 78-104. William Cunningham's study has never been answered (*The*

Reformers and the Theology of the Reformation [1862; reprint London: Banner of Truth Trust, 1967], 345—412).

For a mediating response on the Calvin vs. Beza thesis, see Jill Raitt, *The Eucharistic Theology of Theodore Beza: Development of the Reformed Doctrine* (Chambersburg, PA: American Academy of Religion, 1972); John Bray, *Theodore Beza's Doctrine of Predestination* (Nieuwkoop: B. DeGraaf, 1975); Tadataka Maruyama, *The Ecclesiology of Theodore Beza: The Reform of the True Church* (Geneva: Droz, 1978); Peter White, *Predestination, Policy and Polemic: Conflict and Consensus in the English Church from the Reformation to the Civil War* (Cambridge: Cambridge UP, 1992).

2. Kickel, *Vernunft und Offenbarung bei Theodor Beza,* 46—68. Kickel's attempt to prove that the influence of Aristotelian philosophy has problems, namely, (1) limited and prejudicial sources neglect Beza as preacher and pastor; (2) his zeal to dichotomize Calvin and Beza has neglected a gradual development; (3) theology and history are not properly integrated. Cf. Lynne Courter Boughton, "Supralapsarianism and the Role of Metaphysics in Sixteenth-Century Reformed Theology," *WTJ* 48 (1986): 63—96.

3. Gamble, "Switzerland," 66; Hanko, "Predestination," 3; Maruyama, *Ecclesiology,* 139.

4. For example, Charles Hodge speaks of Augustine's infralapsarianism. However, the terminology of supralapsarianism and infralapsarianism can be utilized only anachronistically prior to the Synod of Dordt, 1618—1619. See Carl Bangs, *Arminius* (New York: Abingdon, 1971), 67.

5. Gerrit C. Berkouwer, *Divine Election* (Grand Rapids, MI: Eerdmans, 1960), 254—77.

6. Arguments *against* supra and infra are well known. Cf. Francis Turretin, *Institutes of Elenctic Theology,* trans. George Musgrave Giver, ed. James T. Dennison, Jr. (Philipsburg, NJ: P & R, 1992), 1: 418; Charles Hodge, *Systematic Theology* (New York: Scribner, Armstrong, and Co., 1877), 2:318—19; John W. Beardslee, III, "Theological Development at Geneva under Francis and Jean-Alphonse Turretin, 1648—1737" (Ph.D. dissertation, Yale University, 1956), 400ff.; William Hastie, *The Theology of the Reformed Church in Its Fundamental Principles* (Edinburgh: T. & T. Clark), 242—52; G. H. Kersten, *Reformed Dogmatics,* vol. 1 (Grand Rapids, MI: Eerdmans, 1980), 126—30; Berkouwer, *Divine Election,* 254—77; Joel R. Beeke, *Jehovah Shepherding His Sheep* (Grand Rapids, MI: Eerdmans, 1982), 62—65.

Less known are the *positive* claims of supra and infra, which can be summarized as follows: (1) Prov. 16:4; Isa. 10:15; Eph. 3:9—11; Rom. 8:29, 9:21; (2) absolute sovereignty, omniscience, omnipotence, and glory of God promoted; (3) teleological method of God as divine architect; (4) if God dealt with the angels in a supralapsarian manner, why not also with humankind? Infras assert that their view (1) is Dt. 7:6, 8; Eph. 1:4—12; (2) demonstrates the righteousness and goodness of God; (3) protects Reformed theology from the charge of divine authorship of sin; (4) does not artificially separate the election of the elect from the election of Christ, thereby avoiding a "hypothetical Christ."

7. B. B. Warfield, *Calvin and Augustine* (Philadelphia: Presbyterian and Reformed, 1956), 298—99. Cf. Donald D. Grohman, "The Genevan Reaction to the Saumur Doctrine of Hypothetical Universalism: 1635—1685" (Ph.D. dissertation, Knox College, Toronto, 1971). I do not deny the existence of Arminian and Cocceian views of the divine decree.

8. For Bezan biography see Friedrich C. Schlosser, *Leben des Theodor de Beza* (Heidelberg: Mohr und Zimmer, 1809); Johann Wilhelm Baum, *Theodor Beza,* 2 vols. (Leipzig: Weidmann'sche Buchhandlung, 1843—1851); Heinrich Heppe, *Theodor Beza,*

Leben und ausgewahlte Schriften (Marburg: R. G. Elwet'scher Druck und Verlag, 1852—1861); Henry Martin Baird, *Theodore Beza: the Counsellor of the French Reformation, 1519—1605* (New York: G. P. Putnam's Sons, 1899); Paul F. Geisendorf, *Théodore de Bèze* (Geneva: Labor et Fides, 1949); Bray, *Predestination*, 22—44; David C. Steinmetz, *Reformers in the Wings* (reprint Grand Rapids, MI: Baker Books, 1981).

9. Raitt, *Eucharistic Theology*, 2; Baird, *Beza*, 32—33.

10. *Correspondence de Théodore de Bèze*, 1: 169—72; 2: 72—73.

11. See Maruyama, *Ecclesiology*, xvi—xix.

12. See Heinrich Heppe, *Reformed Dogmatics*, trans. G. T. Thomson (London: Allen and Unwin, 1950), 147—48; English as *A Briefe Declaration of the chiefe points of the Christian religion, Set Forth in a Table*, trans. William Whittingham (London· David Mopild and Iohn Mather, 1575); and better known, *The Treasure of Trueth, Touching the grounde works of man his salvation, and Chiefest Points of Christian Religion*, trans. John Stockwood (London: Thomas Woodcocke, 1576).

13. For example, Steinmitz writes: "Predestination becomes in the hands of this speculative theologian a form of philosophical determinism scarcely distinguishable from the Stoic doctrine of fate" (*Reformers in the Wings*, 168—69).

14. Bray, *Predestination*, 71.

15. Kickel, *Beza*, 99; cf. Bray, *Predestination*, 72.

16. *Tabula*, i, 1.

17. Ibid., i, 2. In a 1555 letter to Calvin he opts for the supra (*Correspondence*, I, 169—72).

18. Muller, "Predestination," 206.

19. *Tabula*, ii, 3, 6.

20. Ibid., ii, 2. Bray thinks that is Beza's "most significant original contribution to the question of predestination" (*Predestination*, 91). Cf. White, *Predestination, Policy and Polemic*, 17—19.

21. *Tabula*, iii, 1—3.

22. Ibid., v, i.

23. Cf. Hanko, "Predestination," 21.

24. Muller, "Predestination," 213.

25. *Confessio chistianae fidei, et eiusdem collation cum Papisticis haeresibus* (Geneva: Eustathium Vignon, 1587); *The Christian Faith*, trans. James Clark (Lewes, East Sussex: Focus, 1992).

26. *Confessio*, ii, 3.

27. Muller, "Predestination," 219—27; Bray, *Predestination*, 74—75.

28. "Les Tabelles," 374—75.

29. Maruyama, *Ecclesiology*, 140n.

30. Muller, "Predestination," 211. The *Confessio* was published 1558 but written at Lausanne in 1556.

31. *Confessio*, iii.

32. Ibid., iii, 19.

33. *Sermons and Tracts*, vol. 3, trans. John Gill (London: H. Lyon, 1815), 408—409. Cf. *De praedestinationis doctrina et vero usu tractatio absolutissima. Excerpta Th. Bezae praelectionibus in nonum epistolae ad romanos caput* (Geneva: Evstathivm Vignon, 1582).

34. Muller, "Predestination," 199—200.

35. Maruyama, *Ecclesiology*, 141.

36. Bangs, *Arminius*, 67; Kendall, *English Calvinism*, 30.

37. O.T. Hargrave, "The Doctrine of Predestination in the English Reformation" (Ph.D. dissertation, Vanderbilt University, 1966), 204.

38. Muller, "Predestination," 196.

39. Ibid., 219.

40. Quoted from Beza on Job and Song of Solomon respectively (Richard Gamble, class notes, Westminster Seminary, March 8, 1983).

41. For Diodati's biography, consult G.D.J. Schotel, *Jean Diodati* ('s-Gravenhage: Noordendoorp, 1844); Maria Betts, *Life of Giovanni Diodati: Genevese Theologian* (London: Charles J. Thynne, 1905); William A. McComish, *The Epigones: A Study of the Theology of the Genevan Academy at the Time of the Synod of Dort, with Special Reference to Giovanni Diodati* (Allison Park, PA: Pickwith, 1989).

42. DeJong, *Crisis*, 113.

43. James I. Good, *History of the Swiss Reformed Church Since the Reformation* (Philadelphia: Publication of the Sunday School Board, 1913), 34.

44. McComish, *The Epigones,* 80—85.

45. John Diodati, *Pious and Learned Annotations Upon the Holy Bible: Plainly Expounding the most difficult places thereof,* 3d ed. (London: James Flesher for Nichlas Fussell, 1651), exposition of Rom. 9:20 (no pagination).

46. Geneva, 1658.

47. Armstrong, *Amyraut Heresy*, 136.

48. Beardslee, "Turretin," 49; *New Schaff Herzog Encyclopedia*, XII, 43.

49. Muller, "Predestination," 241—42.

50. See H. Bavinck, *Gereformeerde Dogmatiek* (Kampen: Bos, 1908), 2: 346; Berkouwer, *Divine Election*, 255; W. Heyns, *Manual of Reformed Doctrine* (Grand Rapids, MI: Eerdmans, 1926), 53.

51. Particularly *Disputatio de gratia universali,* 3 vols. (Leyden: n. p., 1644—1648).

52. Beardslee, "Turretin," 50.

53. Calling his son Francis when but eight years old to his deathbed, Benedict Turretin stated with faltering lips, "This child is marked with God's seal!" (Alexander, "Turretin," 455).

54. See Beardslee, "Turretin"; and James T. Dennison, Jr., "The Life and Career of Francis Turretin," in Turretin, *Institutes,* 3: 639—58. For his theology, in addition to Beardslee, see Timothy R. Phillips, "Francis Turretin's Idea of Theology and Its Bearing upon His Doctrine of Scripture" (Ph.D. dissertation, Vanderbilt University, 1986); Paul T. Jensen, "Calvin and Turretin: A Comparison of Their Soteriologies" (Ph.D. dissertation, University of Virginia, 1988).

55. Turretin, *Institutes,* vol. 1.

56. Ibid., 329—31 (IV: 6, 1—11).

57. Ibid., 417—30 (IV: 18, 1—25).

58. Ibid., 418 (IV: 18, 5).

59. Cf. Klaas Dijk, *De Strijd over Infra- en Supralapsarianisme* (Kampen: Kok, 1912), 42.

60. Beardslee, "Turretin," 404, 412—13. Turretin mentions Beza's supralapsarianism only once, but without condemnation (IV: 9, 16), although he is harder on William Twisse, the supralapsarian chairman of the Westminster Assembly (IV: 9, 19).

61. Turretin, *Institutes,* 1: 419 (IV: 18, 6).

62. Ibid., 419—20 (IV: 18, 7—8).

63. Ibid., 423—28 (IV: 18, 14—19).

64. Ibid., 428 (IV: 18, 21).

65. Ibid., 429 (IV: 18, 22).

66. Ibid., 429—30 (IV: 18, 23).

67. Ibid., 430 (IV: 18, 25).

68. Beardslee, "Turretin," 419.

69. Ibid., 67; Michael Heyd, *Between Orthodoxy and the Enlightenment: Jean-Robert Chouet and the Introduction of Cartesian Science in the Academy of Geneva* (The Hague: Martinus Nijhoff, 1982); Martin I. Klauber, "Reason, Revelation, and Cartesianism: Louis Tronchin and Enlightened Orthodoxy in Late Seventeenth-Century Geneva," *Church History* 59, 3 (September 1990): 326—27.

70. Cited by Klauber, "Reason, revoleation, and Cartesianism," 329, from Louis Tronchin, *Notae in libros duos Theologiae sacrae Wndelini exceptae in praelectionibus Domini Tronchini theologiae in Genevensi Academia professoris celeberrimi* (Archives Tronchin, *BPU*, vol. 84, fols. 44—44v).

71. Martin I. Klauber, "Reformed Orthodoxy in Transition: Bénédict Pictet (1655—1724) and Enlightened Orthodoxy in Post-Reformation Geneva," in *Later Calvinism: International Perspectives,* ed. W. Fred Graham (Kirksville, MO: Sixteenth Century Journal Publishers, 1994), 93—113, and "Family Loyalty and Theological Transition in Post-Reformation Geneva: The Case of Bénédict Pictet (1655—1724)," *Fides et Historia* 24, 1 (1922): 54—67. See Eugène de Budé, *Vie de Bénédict Pictet, théologien genevoise (1655–1724)* (Lausanne: Georges Bridel, 1874).

72. Klauber, *Later Calvinism,* 113.

73. Bénédict Pictet, *Christian Theology*, trans. Frederick Reyroux (Philadelphia: Presbyterian Board of Publications, n.d.), 204. Chapter 6 (202—17) deals with "the right use" of election and reprobation. *Christian Theology* was originally published in Latin as *Benedicti Picteti in Ecclesia et acad. Genev. pastoris et S.S. Th. professoris Theologia Christiana.* See also *Morale chrétienne ou l'art de bien vivre,* 2 vols. (Geneva: La Compagnie des Libraires, 1710); *Les Vérités de la religion chrétienne* (Geneva: Pierre Jaquier, 1711); *Traité contre l'indifférence des religions* (Geneva: Cramer et Perrachon, 1716); *Lettre sur ceux qui se croyent inspirez* (Geneva: Fabri & Barrilot, 1721).

74. Gamble, "Switzerland," 70. For J.-A. Turretin's life, see Alexander, "Turretin," 458—61; Beardslee, "Turretin," 6—12, 414—16; Martin I. Klauber, *Between Reformed Scholasticism and Pan-Protestantism: Jean-Alphonse Turretin (1671—1737) and Enlightened Orthodoxy at the Academy of Geneva* (Selinsgrove, PA: Susquehanna UP, 1994), 36ff.

75. Beardslee,"Turretin," 404—405.

76. In Spark's *Collection of Essays and Tracts in Theology* 1 (1823): 1—91.

77. The Helvetic Consensus was drafted in opposition to the doctrines of the academy of Saumur (Klauber, *Between Reformed Scholasticism and Pan-Protestantism,* 143—65).

78. Philip Schaff, *The Creeds of Christendom* (New York: Harper, 1919), 1:478.

79. Alexander, "Turretin," 459.

80. Good, *Swiss Reformed,* 282—85.

81. Ibid., 292. Cf. Charles Borgeaud, *Histoire de l'Université de Genève: L'Academie de Calvin 1559—1798* (Geneva: H. Georg, 1900).

82. Cunningham, *Reformers,* 349. Although attempts have been made to classify Calvin as supra (Hastie, Kersten) or infra (Good, Bray), Calvin himself never addressed the lapsarian question. Cf. Fred Klooster, *Calvin's Doctrine of Predestination* (Grand

Rapids, MI: Baker Books, 1977), 55–86.

83. Dijk, *De Strijd over Infra- en Supralapsarianisme*, 284.

84. Hanko maintains that all the Reformed scholastics are free of this non-Christological charge ("Predestination," 21).

85. Muller comments on this debate: "It is no longer possible to view Arminius' doctrine as a Christological piety opposed to a rationalistic, predestinarian, metaphysic of causality. . . . Arminianism is a theological structure at least as speculative as any of the Reformed systems" ("Predestination," 438).

4

The Dissolution of Francis Turretin's Vision of *Theologia*: Geneva at the End of the Seventeenth Century

Timothy R. Phillips

Louis XIV's bold military and political moves to restore Catholic worship in his territories were just the culmination of a long line of cunning strategies against the Protestants in the seventeenth century. Some Reformed groups had recognized the shift in political power decades before and had already blazed a decidedly apologetic and liberal response. In France, for instance, Möise Amyraut and his successors at Saumur sought accommodation with the political authorities, secularized the public discourse by assuming a positive relation between nature and grace, and even reopened the debate on predestination and other cardinal Reformed distinctives.[1] Geneva, on the other hand, steadfastly sought to preserve its identity, established by John Calvin and Theodore Beza, as a "holy city," "the candlestick of truth" shining Christ's light to the nations. Maintaining close ties among its theological, social and political institutions, Geneva was a city consecrated to God's glory, with Christ as its head.[2]

By the second half of the seventeenth century, however, the rationalistic and liberalizing forces of the Saumur school invaded the citadel of Reformed orthodoxy, and even its Company of Pastors. Socially and politically Geneva was also caught between France's pinchers. Extravagant French fashions were beginning to enamor Geneva and reveal its social divisions. And Louis XIV's ominous political moves increasingly intimidated the Small Council. He succeeded in reestablishing the Mass at the residence of his diplomatic representative in 1679 and, after the Revocation of the Edict of Nantes, overran the city with Protestant refugees. These pressures strained and eventually disrupted the normally stable Genevan institutions, creating the context for great cultural change.[3]

During this tumultuous period Francis Turretin (1623—1687) emerged as the brightest and most articulate defender of the traditional Reformed vision.[4] He was a third-generation Italian refugee, whose family had sacrificially served the city in both church and state with distinction. Turretin possessed a first hand understanding of the contemporary intellectual scene; for after studying theology at Geneva, he toured the intellectual centers of Europe, including Saumur and Paris. In 1653 he returned to Geneva as a pastor in the French and Italian Churches and professor of theology in the Academy of Geneva. Chief among his achievements was the three-volume *Institutio theologiae elencticae* (1679—1685), widely renown as the classic summation of Reformed scholasticism.

Alarmed by the growing Saumur sympathies among the pastors and colleagues in the Genevan Academy, Turretin sought to retain the strict Genevan tradition by requiring new pastoral candidates to sign the anti-Saumur standards that had been formulated in 1647 and 1649. These tensions erupted into the "querelle de la grâce universelle" during the 1669 examination of Charles Maurice for ordination.[5] Louis Tronchin (1629—1705), a leader within the church and the Genevan Academy, boldly led the Salmurian adherents in repudiating these additions.[6] Tronchin charged that dictating such "formalities" and "pedantries" was more characteristic of the "papists and antichrist" than "our fathers."[7] The conflict between these two theologians electrified Geneva. Eventually Turretin joined with other Swiss theologians in formulating a common pastoral confession, the Helvetic Consensus Formula. Approval at Geneva was difficult in view of its vocal opponents in the Company of Pastors and a weary Small Council. Finally in 1679 Turretin succeeded. But that was the very year the Louis XIV's diplomat took up residence in the city. He provocatively exacerbated Geneva's precarious situation by inviting hundreds of Catholics to his home for Mass. Thereafter French repression and political threats as well as the overwhelming refugee problem consumed his energies.

On September 28, 1687, Francis Turretin died. As tributes poured in from the Reformed theological world, his opposition at Geneva celebrated. For his death decisively signaled the end of an era. As one pastor confided to Tronchin, after hearing such eulogies: "Good God, to recite such silliness . . . is to mock both God and man. If we had only heard the same news [of Turretin's death] some thirty years ago, your Church and Academy would have been so fortunate! God wished to confer his mercy on them and forgive the disorder that his [Turretin's] passion and lack of charity have caused them to commit."[8] Within a generation, the Company of Pastors led by Turretin's son disavowed the Helvetic Consensus Formula. In the succeeding generation Deists taught in the Genevan Academy. Geneva became the city of Rousseau, and the vision established by Calvin and Beza was lost.

As a leader in this concluding era, Turretin is usually dismissed as a defensive and intransigent reactionary who coercively sought to retain the theological status quo.[9] These sketches rarely transcend a stereotypical focus on a select few doctrines—such as particular election and the imputation of Adam's guilt—to reach his internal vision. As a result, many scholars have difficulty in precisely fingering a more substantial difference between Turretin and Tronchin, except that the latter foreshadowed the toleration of the future. Some even insist that they occupy the same theological horizon.[10]

This chapter, however, argues that this battle at Geneva marked a decisive yet opening skirmish in the European landmark that we now call modernity, which shattered Turretin's vision of *theologia,* one that had defined Geneva for more than a century. In its place theology was domesticated to the so-called universal truths of reason, its goal subordinated to social cohesion and its community dispersed into individual pursuits. This chapter attempts to articulate these challenges and Turretin's lost vision.

AN OVERVIEW OF TURRETIN'S CONCEPT OF THEOLOGY

Turretin's opening description of theology in his *Institutio* as a God-given *habitus*, that is, a cognizance and volition of God's wisdom, was a commonplace within Protestant scholasticism, a result of the pioneering work of Francis Junius, Johann Heinrich Alsted, and Amandus Polanus.[11] Relating theology and the term *habitus* is odd, given our association of habits with superficial unthinking behaviors. Even the scholarly secondary literature on Protestant scholasticism has failed to grasp its importance.[12] But recent work on *theologia* as a *habitus* and virtue theory permits recovery of this framework and helps elucidates Turretin's characteristic emphases and controversies.[13]

Turretin establishes the particular character and location of this *habitus* by analyzing *theologia* causally from its ontological ground in the Godhead. This analysis decisively structures his *Institutio* as well as his whole life. The archetypal theology is God's own knowledge and love of himself, and so it is identified as wisdom, denoting an integral union of knowing and willing. But God accommodates his own infinite wisdom to us through an ectypal theology, an image of his own wisdom, which he specifically shapes.[14]

Although God created humankind with a finite natural habitus of theologia, the fall blinded reason and alienated the sinner from God. As a result, sinful humanity is not only "weak, but evidently impotent and dead," and cannot apprehend "heavenly mysteries" nor love and worship God.[15] But God in his good pleasure bridges this chasm and intentionally shapes a salvific ectypal theology appropriate for the sinful creature. God communicates his wisdom through his salvific and revelatory acts, which culminate in the Incarnation. More precisely, Jesus Christ's ectypal theology of union establishes the theological realities and telos for us, namely, true knowledge, reconciliation, and conformity with God.[16]

These Christocentric realities are communicated to the believer through the supernatural theology of the Word in the Christian Church. The Word, however, is not in any way distanced or severed from Christ's own personal presence. For "Christ is our only teacher in such a way that the ministry of Scripture is . . . included of necessity, because he now only speaks to us in it and builds us up through it."[17]

The Word of God, as Turretin details, "regenerates the minds of the elect, creating it *de novo* . . . healing its depraved inclinations and prejudices."[18] More precisely the Word creates in the believer the wayfarer's infused supernatural habitus of theologia, a divine wisdom that includes a qualitatively new salvific knowledge of, loving delight in, and praxis for God. This infused habit then elicits the necessary acts, as evidenced by faith, repentance, and sanctification. In scholastic terminology, the acquired habitus of conclusions naturally arises from this infused *habitus* of theology. But this development requires a specific type of community: the Christian Church, where believers are nourished, instructed, disciplined, and further developed in the image of God by other believers and God's Word.[19] So *theologia* exists to reform the believer into the image of God, which is humanity's highest good.[20]

This brief overview of theology already reveals a richly suggestive context and belies the traditional picture of the Reformed scholastics as rationalistic, speculative, and non-Christocentic. The conflict between Turretin and the Salmurian adherents, however, centered on three distinctive features of theology: *theologia*'s uniqueness, its normativity as the highest good, and its communal context.

THE UNIQUE REALITIES OF *THEOLOGIA*

Fundamental to Turretin's understanding is *theologia* as an infused *habitus* of principles that provides a qualitatively new cognizance and volition for reality. The wayfarer's *habitus* is not simply "being disposed for" the possibility of salvation, as Richard Muller opines; rather, "the believer perceives things contrary to and remote from reason."[21] Moreover these *principia* are the cognitive and volitional structures foundational to the fiducial apprehension of Jesus Christ and his merits; indeed, Turretin identifies them as the fundamentals of the faith.[22] For the creative Word of God

lays the foundation for a full assurance of faith, . . . which suffices for expelling doubt, and tranquilizing the conscience and generating the hope of salvation . . . inasmuch as it is received as divine and true by all, either the infirm and the simple as well as the learned and the more advanced. And this sense of knowledge suffices for discerning the true from the false and for rejecting erroneous and fatal doctrines, inasmuch as they are unable to subsist with the truths, essentials and fundamentals of religion, which fills each of the faithful.[23]

Not only does this habit enable each believer personally to evaluate theological issues, but Turretin notes that without this "spiritual and internal persuasion," religion is nothing more than "tyranny" or "blind obedience."[24] Extending this basic insight, Turretin argues that this infused *habitus* of "*autopiston* first principles" is known per se, and not founded in any other epistemological ground.[25] This infused *habitus* provides its own unique light, reflecting a qualitatively new possibility of knowing. *Theologia* is a self-authenticating reality and needs no other confirmation![26]

More pointedly, theology is conceived primarily not as doctrines consisting of objective facts existing in books that must be learned and appropriated by the subject but as an attribute of the knowing consciousness.[27] Of course theology includes a system of doctrine, but the latter are the judgments and propositions arising from a determinate cognition of reality and therefore from the activity of the *habitus*. Outside this specific context—the relationship to reality constituted by this *habitus*—the understanding of these doctrines decisively shifts: There is no *divinitas* to learn.[28] Simply put, the unique realities of faith are internal to this infused *habitus*. This is fundamental to the Aristotelian conception of virtue: The exercise of a habit enables one to apprehend the unique goods internal to the practice.[29] Turretin's sermons repeatedly illustrate this unique internal relation to God available through the *habitus* of theology. He acknowledges, for example, that the major objection to the doctrine of grace and unconditional election is that it opens the door to licentiousness. At least that is the way secular people reason. But believers know "that grace . . . is the most powerful motive we have for turning to holiness, because holiness is the telos to which grace looks."[30] For in salvation, the Spirit "applies the promises of grace to us," "so that we not only possess the greatest good but even have the feeling for and knowledge of it."[31] Theology, then, is a particular even sui generis knowing with its own specific norms and structure, grounded solely in God's own wisdom as revealed in Jesus Christ.

The Saumur school, given its politically and socially besieged situation, understandably perceived reason as the way to demonstrate its theological plausibility in a religiously fragmented world.[32] But this apologetic response had momentous ramifications. Although the Salmurians readily acknowledged that special revelation was dependent upon God's revelation, they also insisted that the Spirit generates faith morally, not physically. In converting humans, God accommodates to us as rational beings; faith involves no physical change.[33] Rather, through the Spirit's illumination right reason now perceives the evidences of Scripture's authority. Turretin's argument—that Scripture's authority is known per se and this self-authenticating reality needs no other confirmation—were explicitly denied![34] By contrast, the Salmurians attempted to demonstrate the rational ineluctability of belief.[35] For "by [right] reason we know Scripture to be the Word of God, and by reason we come to their true meaning and sense of them, and by reason we know the obligation that is upon us therefrom."[36]

Relocating the place of revelation opened theology to reason's tangible impact and helps explain the rationalistic thrust of the Salmurian agenda. They offered significant modifications within the area of salvation and election, so general revelation now provided the possibility of salvation and Christ died for all.[37] Furthermore, the second generation subjected all theological claims to right reason. As Walter Rex summarizes Tronchin's criterion, "we must assert nothing concerning the Deity which our understanding does not require us to affirm."[38] Reason is the *via Examinis*. These theologians represented "Enlightened

Orthodoxy" and so Scripture as God's inspired Word always met that test. But they turned Scripture into a book of rationally comprehensible propositions, whose rational plausibility determines their meaning and coherence.

Turretin fingered the crux of the problem: Once revelation is domesticated to reason, its integrity is compromised and sinful prejudices distort God's revelation.[39] As he poignantly asks, Why does Scripture describe conversion as a "creation," a "resurrection" and a "new birth," "if God does not act otherwise than morally . . . as men are accustomed to act?"[40] Moreover, "Who can please human reason, which does not build up the conscience, but often annihilates the truths of the cross of Christ?"[41] The problem is that the revelation of Jesus Christ is grounded in a more basic truth, which imports alien ideas into Christian theology.

In place of the Salmurians' harmonization of reason and revelation, Turretin insists on the dynamics of the cross and resurrection. For sin is not merely the absence of a good but a positive corruption; it has destroyed the very faculties needed for understanding and obeying divine revelation. No matter what evidence or persuasive arguments attend, the sinful soul "cannot properly understand and will in the spiritual sphere" unless the "secret, ineffable, and hyperphysical operation of the Spirit attends, to affect the soul immediately and turn it by its omnipotent power."[42] As "hyperphysical," the Spirit creates newly infused possibilities so special revelation establishes its own self-authenticating realities.[43] Simply put, theology is sui generis.

THE NORMATIVITY OF THEOLOGY'S GOOD FOR ALL LIFE

By the "infusion of supernatural habits . . . humanity is reformed after the image of his Creator."[44] God's glory is in fact the highest goal for humanity, and God's good should order the conflicting demands of everyday life. And Turretin laced his sermons with rhetorical turns summoning the hearer to God: As God has given us all he is, has and does, may all that we are, have, and do be for him. But obedience to God intersects the everyday world; and Turretin's sermons pointedly uncovered Geneva's idolatries, its avarice, ambition, vanity, luxury, and profanities, and called the people to abandon everything rather than forsake God.[45]

But this praxis of God's glory was not an individualistic pursuit. For Geneva was structured toward becoming a "holy city," even a "city of God."[46] God's glory was the substantial good for the entire city. Nothing was outside the authority of God's Word, certainly not the individual's conscience.[47] In dedicating his *Institutio*, Turretin reminds the Small Council that since Geneva is a "theocracy, having God always for its . . . ruler," the city must defend "two impregnable ramparts—the culture of pure religion and the pious care of nurturing the church, which God has committed to the protection of your wings."[48]

But such a unified conception of society, in which every part of life is under

God's rule, was impossible for the Huguenots, who faced the constant charge of sedition and the Catholic King's increasingly determined opposition. Again the Salmurians employed the harmonization of reason and revelation to carve out and define a space for their toleration. Arguing that the conscience's judgment must never be violated, they established the "rights of conscience" and autonomy for Protestants.[49] Magistrates have no right to punish "heretics" simply for their beliefs.[50] Yet, they noted that religion, especially Protestantism, was a moral foundation for social cohesion and political order.[51]

The second-generation Salmurians at Geneva elevated these rights of conscience over religion's place in society. Tronchin, for example, derisively rejected the Morus standards with a resounding call for the freedom of conscience: How could the Reformation have occurred with such a blind reverence for tradition?[52] His more detailed *apologia* specifically targets the elevation of a creed over the political authorities: Once this occurs, "no pastor or professor is secure from being excluded from his charge," for one no longer lives "under the protection of the" city council.[53]

The public debate on the Helvetic Consensus Formula, especially the celebrated exchange of letters between Jean Claude and Turretin, undercovered major fault lines regarding theology's normativity at Geneva.[54] Claude's letter shows the hallmarks of Salmurian attempt to produce a Christianity harmonious with reason and subordinate to social cohesion. Claude opens by lamenting the conflicts at Geneva, acknowledging that the French church had to endure similar problems. Their solution was found not by creating newer and stricter articles of faith, but through toleration. Claude vigorously opposed Turretin's advocacy of the Helvetic Consensus Formula on two counts.

First, Claude argues, these new articles of faith do not reflect the fundamentals of Christian belief. Considered "impartially," apart from the "heat of debate," one can plainly see that these points are not decided by Scripture. These issues are mere trivialities and scholastic questions that have no impact on Christian piety.[55] Not only do we lack "God's authority to . . . make new articles of faith," but defining theological boundaries by nonfundamental issues produces a constantly "changing form of religion."[56] Thus the French church sticks to the "unalterable fundamentals" and practices Christian toleration.

Second, Claude insisted that confining the pastoral office solely to those who sign the Formula not only precludes Christian charity with other Reformed churches but actually declares "war" on their "rights and liberty."[57] Again Claude proffers the practice of the French churches, where the fundamentals defined the boundaries and imposed silence on controversial issues. Then all the Reformed churches can "retain their own sentiments, but without any break of peace or brotherly love."[58]

Claude had astutely focused on the fundamentals. For Turretin had a well-developed understanding of the fundamentals, grounded in the infused *habitus* of *principia*, and his own proposal parallelled the noble tradition of seventeenth-century Protestants seeking a fraternal union.[59] Turretin sought a "pious syncretism," which practices fraternal toleration among the Reformed, Lutherans, and Anglicans until God illuminates these lesser errors and brings about full doctrinal consent.[60] Acknowledging that the doctrines contested among these various ecclesial traditions do not touch the fundamentals, Turretin insists that each tradition should continue to "argue for" its respective positions while not condemning others as heretics.[61] So the desire for reconciliation never eclipses the fact that each group is making conflicting truth-claims. Precisely here Turretin differs from Claude. Whereas Claude's proposal reflects a rational reduction of theology, Turretin was not willing to subordinate truth claims regarding God's revelation to social peace, rationality, or even the fundamentals.

Turretin recognized that Claude's proposal to draw ecclesial boundaries at the fundamentals surrendered Reformed or Lutheran distinctives. These churches are shaped by a specific tradition, distilled in their doctrinal formularies, which construes these fundamentals as an integral whole, outlines their system of biblical interpretation, and fortifies their piety.[62] These formularies, such as the Helvetic Consensus Formula or the decisions of the French Reformed synods, naturally result from the interaction with new ideas and controversies that can easily subvert the confession's meaning. They preserve and strengthen the articles of faith, not extend them. How could the church conserve true doctrine, he asks, unless it precludes misinterpretation of its confession? Your charge of innovation and intolerance diverts attention from the substance of theology. You are wounding the church by prohibiting us from making truth-claims and opposing errors![63]

Second, Turretin turns the tables on Claude's charge of oppression. We have not declared you heretical, he retorts, nor are we imposing our views on anyone outside of Geneva.[64] But your insistence on toleration, even in Geneva, is oppressive. For it means that we cannot confess and preserve our traditional understanding of the Word of God, at least those distinctive theological claims that surpass the fundamentals. Because we are more fearful of God than of humankind, we are trying to maintain the purity of doctrine. Those who defend the Gospel need to be treated more charitably![65]

Subsequent events continued to reflect this fundamental breach regarding God's glory as the norm for all society. In the next decade the provocative acts of the Resident and the French king so frightened Geneva's syndics that they repeatedly cautioned the Company of Pastors to be prudent in their sermons. But it is Turretin and his confederates—and not Tronchin and the Salmurians—whose preaching on the threat of the "AntiChrist" and "tyranny" receive the syndics' ire.[66] And perhaps it is not surprising that Tronchin's famous apologetic letters to Mme de la Fredonnière finally resorts to crass economic allures in the hope that she will remain Protestant.[67] Turretin's preaching, to the contrary, consistently calls the people to abandon all than forsake God's glory.

THE COMMUNAL CONTEXT OF THE WAYFARERS' DEVELOPMENT

Teleologically defined, *theologia* exists to reform the believer into the image of God. Strengthening these saving volitions and cognizances occurs through the *habitus* of conclusions.[68] Building on Aristotle's understanding of the four major habits, Turretin explains that the sui generis and *autopiston* principles bestowed by the Word are further developed through *scientia*. Like *prudentia* or practical wisdom, theology directs the believer's actions because it infuses a knowledge of and a desire for certain ethical ends. This is not an individualistic project, however, for theology strives to build up others in the faith. It therefore includes *ars*, the edification of the body of Christ.[69]

How these practices work together to develop and advance the believer is best illustrated through the polemics of Turretin's day. One of Rome's chief weapons in its arsenal against Protestantism was the charge that Scripture was "deaf, dumb and blind" and therefore could not be viewed as the supreme norm regarding contemporary issues.[70] Rejecting the need for an infallible visible judge to decide all contemporary issues, Turretin claims that Scripture alone is the supreme judge: The Word creates the Church and bestows on all these wayfarers new possibilities for thinking and acting; it even enlists them as its secondary interpreters and judges! This communal process of the *via Examinis*—studying the Word, reflecting on the realities of faith by discerning what is true and good, seeking counsel from other believers, nurturing and disciplining others within the body of Christ—develops each believer's cognizance of and volition for God's wisdom![71] The *habitus* of theology is advanced not by blind submission but through praxis, inquiry and reflection.[72]

Turretin identifies two prerequisites for Geneva's communal project of living for God's glory: "truth joined with charity."[73] By truth he is referring to that "sacred trust" or that "deposit of purer religion" that Geneva's Reformation leaders had established.[74] This acceptance of tradition was not blind or stifling, nor did it despise those who brought "the truth to light" in the present. Modifications were always being made, not the least by Turretin himself.[75] Rather, this focus on tradition reflects his understanding of the communal context for discerning truth. The opposite, where individuals "cherish their own opinion" as if this were the standard of truth," he considers prideful arrogance.[76] How could a city that God had protected so often fail to learn from its godly leaders and their wisdom? Using tradition as a guide provides a "safer" path.

Turretin recognizes that charity or the communal process was also indispensable to promoting the common vision of God's glory. A "holy concord of souls shall flourish" only in a community centered on a common love for God and developing the reciprocal bonds of neighborly love.[77] Only if bound together in a "reciprocal intercourse" by love, justice, and purity of heart will individuals cherish their neighbor's life in every way and "commend [them]selves to every man's conscience in the sight of God."[78]

However, Turretin was apprehensive regarding the bonds of Genevan society.

He laments that many in the present esteem nothing but modern thinking and introduce novelties "as if those who preceded us lived in a fog and in shadows until now."[79] Turretin considers this strategy of spurning "the well-worn paths in order to cut new ones" as dangerous. Not only does it destroy the "good constitutions" but as "much sad experience" teaches us these novelties usually lead off into "precipices."[80] No doubt Turretin had the Salmurians in mind, for he recognized that the decisive role for the rights of conscience in their theology ruptures community into individualistic pursuits.

Much of Turretin's criticism of Tronchin targeted his individualism, which was fracturing the Genevan community. In his own history of the "querelle de la grâce universelle," Turretin recounts that Tronchin had previously rejected the Salmurian distinctives.[81] But now desiring to "establish freedom" for his conscience, he repudiated these elements in Geneva's standards, stating that "a vow which should not be made should not be held." Such an arrogant individualism ruins the trust and order necessary for the communal discernment of truth.[82] Then Tronchin took this agenda public, "flagrantly violating the most solemn promises," his pastoral vows, by catechizing the doctrine of universal grace. So much confusion and mistrust ensued that even pastors were ridiculed.[83] After the city council's order he promised to follow the former tradition and not teach differently. But this promise was "simply hypocrisy." He continued to promote Salmurian ideas in the Genevan Academy and these candidates for the pastorate, hoping that their political connections would prevail over the Company's regulations.[84]

Turretin knew well that prideful individualism and its associated political ploys shatters the fragile communal project of living under God's rule and glory. It was therefore no accident that Geneva fragmented into "cabals," or that this event hastened Geneva's secularization.[85]

Francis Turretin has usually been interpreted as a reactionary figure during the transition to the luminaries. Since modernity's grid of universal rational norms, religious toleration, and a state enforced civil peace scorns Turretin's particularistic vision of a "holy city," this assessment is not surprising. Admittedly the Academy of Geneva produced some of the great architects for a rationally free world; indeed Geneva herself is still a singular testimony to that vision. But the despair and disenchantment at the end of the twentieth century identifies that hope as illusory. Modernity's claim to provide a universal rational foundation for truth is now repudiated as pretence, a reaction that parallels Turretin's critique of the Salmurians. Nor would Turretin have been surprised that God's glory and community have vanished into individualistic pursuits, or that the cathedrals have been converted into museums and concert halls. Perhaps a return to Francis Turretin's vision of *theologia* as unique God-given *habitus*, which is pursued as a communal project by believers who live explicitly to God's glory, can provide theological direction for the way forward.

NOTES

1. On the Saumur school, see Brian Armstrong, *Calvinism and the Amyraut Heresy: Protestant Scholasticism and Humanism in Seventeenth Century France* (Madison: U of Wisconsin P, 1969); François Laplanche, *Orthodoxie et prédication; l'oeuvre d'Amyraut et la querelle de la grâce universelle* (Paris: Presses universitaires de France, 1965); *L'Évidence du Dieu Chréstien; Religion, culture et société dans l'apologétique protestante de la France classique (1576–1670)* (Strasbourg: Association des Publications de la Faculté de Théologie Protestante de Strasbourg, 1983); and, *L'Écriture, le sacré et l'histoire* (Amsterdam: Holland UP, 1986).

2. Francis Turretin, *Institutes of Elenctic Theology*, 3 vols, trans. George Musgrave Giger, ed. James Dennison (Phillipsburg, NJ: P & R Publishing, 1992–1997), 1: xxxiv. See also Roger Stauffenegger, *Église et Société Genève au XVIIe Siècle*, 2 vols. (Geneva: Librairie Droz, 1983), 1: 116–130.

3. For an examination of this period see Martin I. Klauber, *Between Reformed Scholasticism and Pan-Protestantism: Jean-Alphonse Turretin (1671–1737) and Enlightened Orthodoxy at the Academy of Geneva* (Selinsgrove, PA: Susquehanna UP, 1994); Maria-Cristina Pitassi, *De L'orthodoxie aux Lumières: Genève 1670–1737* (Geneva: Labor et Fides, 1992); Olivier Reverdin et al., *Genève au temps de la révocation de l'édit de Nantes 1680–1705, MDG*, vol. 50 (Geneva: Droz, 1985); Stauffenegger, *Église et Société*; Walter Rex, *Essays on Pierre Bayle and Religious Controversy* (The Hague: Martinus Nijhoff, 1965).

4. Francis Turretin was the son of Bénédict Turretin, a professor of theology at the Academy of Geneva, and nephew of Giovanni Diodati, another professor of theology at the Genevan Academy who represented Geneva at the Synod of Dort. He was the grandson of another Francis Turretin, who escaped from Lucca, Italy, in the late 1600s, and established the Grand Boutique, which brought wealth to community of Italian refugees in Geneva. Eugène de Budé, *Vie de François Turrettini: théologien genevois, 1623–1687* (Lausanne: Georges Bridel, 1981); Gerrit Keizer, *François Turrettini: Sa vie, ses oeuvres et le consensus* (Lausanne: Georges Bridel, 1900); John W. Beardslee III, "Theological Development at Geneva under Francis and Jean-Alphonse Turretin (1648–1737)" (Ph.D. dissertation, Yale University, 1957); Timothy R. Phillips, "Francis Turretin's Idea of Theology and Its Impact upon His Doctrine of Scripture" (Ph.D. dissertation, Vanderbilt University, 1986).

5. For a detailed history of this debate see Donald D. Grohman, "The Genevan Reactions to the Saumur Doctrine of Hypothetical Universalism: 1635–1685" (Ph.D. dissertation, Knox College, Toronto, 1971).

6. Louis Tronchin was the son of Theodore Tronchin, a professor of theology who represented Geneva at the Synod of Dort and who married the adopted granddaughter of Theodore Beza. See Martin I. Klauber, "Reason, Revelation, and Cartesianism: Louis Tronchin and Enlightened Orthodox in Late Seventeenth-Century Geneva," *Church History* 59 (September 1990): 326–39.

7. Keizer, *Turrettini*, 286; Grohman, *Geneva Reactions*, 262.

8. Quoted in Pitassi, *L'Orthodoxie*, 21, from Tronchin Archives, vol. 54, fol. 22, Daniel Chamier to Tronchin, 24 October 1687.

9. Pitassi, *L'Orthodoxie*, 6; Albert Montandon, *L'Évolution théologique a Genève au XVIIe siècle* (Le Cateau: J. Roland, 1894), 106; Emidio Campi and Carla Sodini, *Gli oriundi lucchesi di Ginevra e il cardinale Spinola: una controversia religiosa alla vigilia*

della revoca dell'Editto di Nantes (Chicago: Newberry Library, 1988), 58; Stauffenegger, *Église et Société*, 1: 392—402.

10. Campi and Sodini, *Gli oriundi*, 87; Rex, *Essays*, 139.

11. Turretin, *Institutio Theologiae Elencticae* (Edinburgh: John Lowe, 1847), 1.1.9; 1.2.1; 1.6.4-7; Johann Heinrich Alsted, *Methodus*, 18; Amandus Polanus, *Syntagma*, 13; Francis Junius, *De Theologia vera*, 17.

12. H. E. Weber, representing the scholarly consensus, contends that this term is symptomatic of scholasticism's objectifying stance, which transforms the sui generis realities of revelation into rationally comprehensible teachings. According to his analysis, since the creative and unique realities of faith are absent, the Protestant scholastics use the notion of a *habitus* to establish, in theory, that these realities must be subjectively cultivated and legalistically pursued by the believer. Hans Emil Weber, *Reformation, Orthodoxie und Rationalismus*, vol. 1, 2 pts.: *Von der Reformation zur Orthodoxie*; vol. 2: *Der Geist der Orthodoxie*; Beitrage zur Forderung christlicher Theologie, 2. Reihe, vols. 35, 45, 51 (Gutersloh: C. Bertelsmann, 1937—1951; reprint ed., Darmstadt: Wissenschaftliche Buchgesellschaft, 1966), 1.1: 214—217, 1.2: 73, 2: 106. On the other hand, Richard Muller, whose reassessment has incisively challenged many elements within the scholarly consensus, does not offers a real alternative. See Richard A. Muller, *Post-Reformation Reformed Dogmatics*, vol. 1, *Prolegomena to Theology* (Grand Rapids, MI: Baker Books, 1987), 227f.

13. This rehabilitation is to a large extent made possible by Johannes Wallmann, *Der Theologiebegriff bei Johann Gerhard und Georg Calixt*, Beitrage zur historischen Theologie no. 30 (Tubingen: J.C.B. Mohr, 1961). See Edward Farley's explication of the notion of theologia as a *habitus* in his pioneering work on theological education, *Theologia: The Fragmentation and Unity of Theological Education* (Philadelphia: Fortress Press, 1983), and also Alasdair MacIntyre, *After Virtue*, 2d ed. (Notre Dame: U of Notre Dame P, 1984).

14. Turretin, *Institutio*, 1.2.6.

15. Turretin, *Institutio*, 1.3.7; 1.4; 2.1.3; 15.4.12, 29.

16. Turretin, *Institutio*, 1.2.6, 7, 12.2.19. Note that these benefits parallel Christ's threefold office.

17. Turretin, *Institutio*, 2.2.12.

18. Turretin, *Institutio*, 2.1.2, 15.4.13.

19. Turretin, *Institutio*, 1.2.9; 1.6.5; 2.1.2, 18.1—3.

20. Turretin, *Institutio*, 1.2.8; 1.7.6; 15.4.13.

21. Turretin, *Institutio*, 1.2.8; Muller, *Post-Reformation Reformed Dogmatics*, 1:227, 229.

22. Turretin, *Institutio*, 1.2.8, 1.6.5, 1.14.

23. Francis Turretin, *Francisci Turrettini Opera*, 4 vols. (Edinburgh: John Lowe, 1847—1848), 4:267.

24. Turretin, *Institutio*, 2.20.25. Turretin, *Opera*, 4:97—122.

25. Turretin, *Institutio*, 1.8.1; 1.9.3; 2.1.3; 2.6.11, 18.

26. Turretin, *Institutio*, 2.6.11.2. In fact, Turretin explicitly argues "that the judgment of reason is not considered as necessary, as if theology could not do without it," 1.9.3.

27. Bengt Hagglund, *Die Heilige Schrift und ihre Deutung in der Theologie Johann Gerhards: Eine Untersuchung uber das altlutherische Schriftverstandnis* (Lund: C.W.K. Gleerup, 1951), 47. Otto Ritschl, *System und systematische Methode in der Geschichte des wissenschaftlichen Sprachgebrauchs und der philosophischen Methodologie* (Bonn: A.

Marcus and E. Webers Verlag, 1906), 25—54. Max Wundt, *Die deutsche Schulmetaphysik der 17. Jahrhunderts* (Tubingen: J.C.B. Mohr, 1939), 233ff.

28. *Institutio*, 2.17.12—20; 2.13.15, 17; 2.4.6, 12. For a further analysis of the Word's signum-signatum relationship in Turretin see Phillips, "Turretin's Idea of Theology," 510ff.

29. For instance, the intellectual virtue of biology provides insight to the relationships among living things. Certainly living things can be perceived outside the context of biology, but not with the biologist's insight and understanding. Similarly, theology as a "theoretical-practical" reality involves the knowledge of God's mercy and the desire for conformity to God. It is precisely this internal relationship and its dynamics that H. E. Weber ignores in his charge that "habitus" reflects a legalistic rationalism.

30. Francis Turretin, *Sermons sur divers passages de L'Ecriture sainte* (Geneva, 1676), 435—36.

31. Turretin, *Sermons*, 466.

32. Laplanche, *L'Évidence*, 201—210, 231—236.

33. Armstrong, *Calvinism*, 65ff., 244ff.; see Helvetic Consensus Formula, Art. XXI—XXII in John Leith, *Creeds of the Churches*, 3d ed. (Atlanta: John Knox Press, 1982), 308—323.

34. Laplanche, *L'Évidence*, 228—229.

35. Laplanche, *L'Évidence*, 106, 128.

36. Möises Amyraut, *A Discourse concerning Divine Dreams* (London, 1676), a3.

37. Klauber, "Louis Tronchin," 331; Helvetic Consensus Formula, Art. VI, XIII—XVI, XVII, XX.

38. Rex, *Essays*, 132, 114—120. The characterization of Tronchin as a second generation Salmurian derives from Laplanche, *L'Écriture*, 574.

39. Turretin charges that the Saumur theological strategy broadly parallels the Arminians in Francis Turretin, "Turretin to Claude, 16 February 1676," in *Lettre de Monsr. Jean Claude ecrite a Msr. Francois Turretin sur le sujet de "Fomulaire de consentement" . . . Repose de Msr. Francois Turretin . . .* (Geneva, 1676), 30, 45. Contrary to Beardslee, "Theological Development at Geneva," 200ff., 107 ff., Turretin does not ground his theology through natural theology; all that Turretin has to say about natural theology is first grounded in Scripture. He treats the sources of natural theology in humankind so tersely because the content of natural theology is more clearer repeated within Scripture.

40. Turretin, *Institutio*, 15.4.33.

41. Turretin, "Turretin to Claude," 49.

42. Turretin, *Institutio*, 15.4.13, 31—33.

43. Turretin, *Institutio*, 2.6.11.2; 1.9.3.

44. Turretin, *Institutio*, 1.2.8, 1.6.4, 5; 1.7.6; 2.1.2, 15.4.13.

45. Turretin, *Sermons*, 66—67, 138—141, 245.

46. Turretin, *Institutes*, 1: xxxvi.

47. Turretin, *Institutio*, 18.34. Referring to the "domain of conscience," Turretin in this question vigorously argues for the right to excommunicate heretics and for the Christian magistrates to punish, even with capital punishment, the apostate who damage the church by their teachings and actions.

48. Turretin, *Institutes*, 1:xxxv.

49. Laplanche, *L'Évidence*, 201—210. Rex identifies Jean Daillé's *Apologie des Eglises Réformées* (1633) as the earliest source for this theme, which was further developed in French Protestant thought. See Rex, *Essays*, 119—120, 149.

50. The Salmurians demonstrated their loyalty to the King by arguing that Jesus' love and submission to his political authorities had overturned any legitimacy to an Old Testament theocracy. Rex, *Essays*, 209—213. Turretin countered this in *Institutio*, 18.34.

51. Laplanche, *L'Évidence*, 201—210.

52. Grohman, *Genevan Reactions*, 269. Grohman narrates Tronchin's interpretations to the Company of Pastors (July 30, 1669) regarding his statements that the 1649 theses were "pedantries," "papist maxims," "an oath which should not be made should not be held," Tronchin "explained that his term 'maxims of the papists' was used only with regard to those who thought that one should never re-examine anything because the predecessors had decided it."

53. Stauffenegger, *Église et Société*, 1: 399; Grohman, *Genevan Reactions*, 408—409. This is quoted from Tronchin Archives, vol. 68, fol. 33r.

54. During this period Jean Claude (1619—1687) was the most respected Reformed pastor in France; he had been pastoring at Charenton since 1666, after teaching at the Academy of Nimes. Forbidden to take their case public, the Salmurians at Geneva finally prevailed upon Claude to plead their cause publicly. The resulting letters between Claude and Turretin were celebrated by each side and quickly published. Jean Claude *Lettre de Monsr. Jean Claude écrite à Msr. François Turretin sur le sujet de "Formulaire de consentement" . . . Repose de Msr. François Turretin . . .* (Geneva, 1676).

55. Claude, "Claude to Turretin, 20 June 1675," in *Lettre de Monsr. Jean Claude*, 2—6, 11.

56. Claude, "Claude to Turretin," 6, 14.

57. Claude, "Claude to Turretin," 13, 8, 11.

58. Claude, "Claude to Turretin," 4.

59. Among others Turretin explicitly highlights the 1631 national Synod at Charenton, the diligent labors of John Dury, and the 1661 Cassel colloquy called by Wilhelm Landgrave of Hesse. Turretin, *Opera*, 4.200ff. See also Richard Stauffer, *The Quest for Church Unity: From John Calvin to Isaac d'Huisseau* (Allison Park, PA: Pickwick Publications, 1986), 25ff.

60. Turretin, *Opera*, 4.202.

61. Turretin, *Institutio*, 18.15.11; Turretin, *Opera*, 4.200ff.

62. Turretin, "Turretin to Claude," 28—29.

63. Turretin, "Turretin to Claude," 26, 33—36, 40.

64. Turretin, "Turretin to Claude," 42—44.

65. Turretin, "Turretin to Claude," 49.

66. Fatio narrates this history. See Olivier Fatio, "L'Église de Genève et la Révocation de l'Édit de Nantes," in Olivier Reverdin et al., *Genève au temps de la révocation*, 161—168, 185—188. Fatio reports that the Syndics criticized Francis Turretin during July 1681 for exaggerating the present tribulations of the church; during this same month Benedict Calendrini, his fellow-pastor and supporter of the Helvetic Consensus Formula, was also attacked for "dangerous expressions." See also *RC*, 233 (25 July 1681); *RCP* 14, 110 (10 December 1680), 123 (27 December 1680), and 125 (31 December 1680). (Both *RC* and *RCP* are located in *AEG*.) Typically, in these events Tronchin remains in the background, a "partisan of France." However, when Michael Turretin—a pastor, Professor of Hebrew, and nephew of Francis—was severely disciplined for remarks regarding the

staging of *Cid*, Tronchin used his great diplomatic skills to mediate between the Company of Pastors and the Small Council. For this incident see Fatio, "L'Église," 191—193.

67. Tronchin suggests that she begin to send her goods outside France, to which she astutely asks why concealment is part of Protestantism! Tronchin admits that it is because abjurations are usually decided on economic grounds. See Fatio, "L'Église," 224.

68. Turretin, *Institutio*, 1.2.8, 11.12.1.

69. Since theology is a supernatural and *theosdotos* habit, it cannot properly be identified with any of the four major Aristotelian intellectual and practical habits (*intelligentia, scientia, prudentia*, and *ars*), which are "learned and cultivated by human ingenuity." Transferred to theology's unique supernatural sphere though, these habits or virtues do identify the essential dimensions that constitute the wayfarer's *habitus* of theologia. *Theologia* is not an aggregate but one integral habit. Indeed, Turretin argues that the uniqueness of theology's habit is reflected in its integral union of theory and praxis: theology "always conjoins the theory of the truth with praxis of the good." Turretin, *Institutio*, 1.6.6, 4, 5, 1.7.2, 6, 8.

70. Turretin, *Institutio*, 2.20.

71. Turretin, *Institutio*, 2.20.33—35; 17.1; Turretin, *Opera*, 4: 267.

72. Turretin, *Institutio*, 18.11.34. Yet, if God provided an oracle for every question that arises, wouldn't the development and building up of the wayfarer be thwarted and even precluded? As a result, Turretin charges Rome with advocating a *via Authoritatis*, a religion of "blind and mindless" subservience, where the wayfarer cannot be reformed in God's image. Turretin concludes that the believer is obliged to pursue the *via Examinis* and thereby "confirm saving doctrine from the principles known by the light of faith" as developed and "learned within the Church." *Institutio*, 1.2.9; 1.6.1. Turretin broadly describes his own systematic work in these terms. See Turretin, *Opera*, 1: xvff., xxiiiff.

73. Keizer, *Turrettini*, 299.

74. Turretin, *Institutes*, 1:xxxvi, xxxiv.

75. Turretin, *Institutes*, 1:xlii. Geneva had made modifications in the past, when it rejected Beza's supralapsarianism (Turretin, *Institutio*, 4.9.5, 15—16). In contrast to the traditional portrayal as rejecting any innovation, recent scholarship has begun identifying Turretin's own originality within his tradition in his doctrine of God, regeneration, and scriptural authority. See E. P. Meijering, *Reformierte Scholastik und patristische Theologie. Die Bedeutung des Väterbeweises in der Institutio Theologiae Elencticae F. Turretins unter besonderer Berücksichtigung der Gotteslehre und Christologie.* (Nieuwkoop: De Graaf Publishers, 1991); Anri Morimoto, "The Seventeenth-Century Ecumenical Interchange," in *Christian Ethics in Ecumenical Context: Theology, Culture, and Politics in Dialogue*, ed. Shin Chiba, George R. Hunsberger, Lester Edwin J. Ruiz (Grand Rapids, MI: Eerdmans, 1995), 86—102; Phillips, "Turretin's Idea of Theology," 510ff.

76. Turretin, *Institutes*, 1:xli—xlii. Turretin's own systematic reflects this communal search for truth. Virtually every *questio* displays an unusual ability to uncover false options with penetrating questions and distinctions drawn from scripture and the Christian tradition.

77. Turretin, *Institutes*, 1:xxxvi; Turretin, *Institutio*, 11.11.4; 11.12.9; 11.6.3.

78. Turretin, *Institutio*, 11.11.4, 11.12.9; Turretin, *Institutes*, 1:xxxvi.

79. Turretin, *Institutes*, 1:xli, xlii.

80. Turretin, *Institutes*, 1:xli—xlii.

81. This document, dated February 20, 1675, is found in Keizer, *Turrettini*, 281—299. Tronchin's entry into the Company of Pastors was somewhat unusual. But Turretin mentions that Tronchin rejected the Salmurian distinctives when he entered the ministry and at several synods, the Synod of Bourgongne in 1646 and the Synod of Gex in 1656. Ibid., pp. 286, 290, 296. See also Grohman, *Genevan Reactions*, 263n.

82. Keizer, *Turrettini*, 286—287.

83. Keizer, *Turrettini*, 287—288.

84. Keizer, *Turrettini*, 294—296. Campi and Sodini, in *Gli oriundi*, 82, correctly describe Tronchin as practicing an "academic nicodemism." In 1671 Tronchin sought, for the Company of Pastors, Pierre Mussard, his cousin and a pastor of considerable repute who had been expelled from France. Well aware of his Salmurian sympathies, Tronchin thought that Mussard's connections to the city council could surmount the Company's regulations. But when questioned on these articles, Mussard repudiated them with such an "odious and public invective" that even the syndics acknowledged no exception could be made. See also Stauffenegger, *Église et Société*, 1: 396. Interestingly, Mussard reappears in 1678 again as a candidate for the Company of Pastors; and even though he signs the regulations, the Company is suspicious of his real allegiances and rejects him again. See *RCP* 13, 661 (12 April 1678), 665, 667—8 (26 April 1678); *RC* (1678): 154—156, 159.

85. Pitassi, *L'Orthodoxie*, 16.

5

A Case of Hidden Identity: Antoine Court, Bénédict Pictet, and Geneva's Aid to France's Desert Churches (1715–1724)

Otto H. Selles

> On our way we met the preacher and prophetess Claire who thought it right, in what she called her revelations, to fight against the plan I had made to go to Geneva, and she did so through reasons based on the good I could subsequently do for the Churches of France. (Antoine Court, *Mémoires* for the year 1713)[1]

AN AMBIGUOUS IDENTITY?

In 1724 the French pastor Antoine Court (1695–1760) wrote to his friends in Geneva concerning a letter he was about to receive: "Although I do not know the content of this letter, I was told you speak to me of the most sad and the most overwhelming thing that could ever happen to me—of the death of the famous Pictet, of this great man, of this incomparable man, of this man so tender and good that he had for me so much kindness that he treated me as if I were one of his children. Ha, what a blow my dear friends. It is so distressing for me that I have neither the strength nor the words to speak about it."[2] Pastor and professor of theology at the Academy of Geneva, Bénédict Pictet (1655–1724), was revered among French Protestants, especially because of his many polemical publications that defended Protestantism against Catholicism.[3] After an initial correspondence Court did indeed meet Pictet and developed a close friendship with him—if not a father-son relationship—during a two-year stay in Geneva from 1720 to 1722. This contact suggests that close ties also existed between Geneva and the "Church of the Desert," the clandestine Huguenot churches led by Antoine Court in France's Languedoc region.

Recent studies on Geneva's reaction to the Revocation of the Edict of Nantes have drawn attention to the attitude of the Republic's pastors to the plight of Huguenots in France after 1685. Michel Grandjean, for example, examines the aid the Genevan pastor and professor Bénédict Calandrini organized on behalf

of Protestant galley-slaves from 1695 to 1714.[4] Focusing on the Church of
Geneva's attitude to French Protestantism from 1680 to 1705, Olivier Fatio
points to the subsequent ties between Court and Pictet, stating: "Pictet symbolizes, by his simple and effective work as author of polemical texts and by his
support—laboriously acquired—for Antoine Court, Geneva's aid to French
Protestantism."[5] According to Fatio, Pictet first hesitated to help Court before
becoming his staunch supporter, thus illustrating "the ambiguity of the position
Genevans took in their support of French Protestantism."[6]

Geneva's hesitation to help Huguenots may be linked to the nature of French
Protestantism after the Revocation. Following the destruction of Protestant
churches and the exile of Protestant clergy in 1685, Huguenot laypreachers soon
led assemblies at night in the "Desert"—in areas outside of towns and villages
and hopefully outside of the military's scrutiny. Beginning in 1688 at first
children, and later men and women, claimed to be inspired by God and soon
made prophetic visions a central aspect of Huguenot piety and worship. Reacting
to the severe persecution of the time and guided by prophetic visions, Huguenots
revolted in the Cévennes area of France during the Camisard War, which at its
height lasted from 1702 to 1704.[7] When Antoine Court and a group of itinerant
preachers tried to organize the Protestant communities in the south of France in
1715, they had to combat not only resistance within their own ranks but also the
suspicion, harbored by Protestant states such as Geneva, that the Desert
assemblies only helped the cause of fanatics and rebels. Moreover, the French
king's Resident in Geneva carefully reported to Versailles any attempt to help
French Protestants.[8] As will be seen, the Genevan magistrate's fear of offending
France made any official support of Huguenots in France impossible.

Nineteenth-century and even more recent research, however, has not
determined the exact role Genevan ecclesiastical leaders played during the period
from 1715 to 1724 in what has been called Antoine Court's "restoration of
Protestantism in France."[9] First, an analysis of the manner in which the Desert
pastors looked to Geneva for aid (1715–1720), particularly with respect to
ordination, will reveal how the Desert depended on Geneva for its own
independence whereas the latter was as quick to help Desert pastors as it was to
condemn the illegal Desert assemblies. Second, a description of Antoine Court's
two-year stay in Geneva (1720–1722) and his contacts with Bénédict Pictet will
provide the opportunity to examine the degree to which an eighteenth-century
leader in Calvin's church agreed or hesitated to help Huguenots in France.[10]
Finally, the French Resident's reprimand of Pictet's involvement in the Desert
in 1723 will indicate to what extent and manner Genevan pastors and professors
were free—politically—to help the Desert. During this period, at stake was not
only the principle of charity but also the very identity of Geneva. As French
pastors such as Court looked for aid and also a model on which to restructure the
Reformed churches in France, Geneva's pastors and professors had to determine
whether they could overcome political and theological hesitations to be as in the
past a guide to French Protestantism.

GENEVA AND THE DESERT CHURCHES (1715–1720)

It can be asked whether Geneva had any influence, directly or indirectly, on Antoine Court's decision to bring some order to a Protestant community in great disorder after the Revocation and the Camisard War. Born into a Protestant family in 1695, the young Court attended the Desert assemblies with his mother. He soon became involved in the organization of assemblies and began a career as a preacher in 1713 at the age of 18. At first Court's only teachers were *prédicantes* and *prophétesses*, women who often based their sermons on visions and prophecies that pointed to a possible liberation of Huguenots. Later he came into contact with *prophètes* and also some former Camisards who continued to soldier on as preachers. Court's own interest in the *inspirés* turned into definite disbelief when he began to question the prophets' conduct and the truth of their predictions.[11]

Not long after this change of heart, Court tried to convince his fellow preachers to unite together during what would be the first Desert "synod," held August 21, 1715, in Montèzes, near Monoblet at the edge of Languedoc's Lower Cévennes mountains. Whether a meeting of seven itinerant preachers and two laypersons should be called a synod is perhaps debatable, yet Court claimed he had been chosen as both moderator and secretary of a meeting that made various decisions to "lay the foundations of order and discipline which have been observed since that time."[12] In his *Mémoires* Court maintained that among the synod's decisions—of which the acts have been lost—"some were aimed at the extinction of fanaticism [prophecies] and others at imposing silence upon female preachers."[13]

Court gave no indication of the source for his idea to hold a "synod," but it should be noted that Pierre Corteiz, perhaps the most important preacher of the group, was in fact not at the synod but in Geneva to visit his wife.[14] In all probability he spoke with Bénédict Pictet and Jacques Vial de Beaumont (1678–1746), a Huguenot refugee from Grenoble who had become a pastor in Geneva and even the secretary of its *Compagnie des pasteurs* in 1716–1719.[15] From Vial, Corteiz received financial help for himself and religious books that he subsequently distributed in France.[16] But the help Corteiz received from Geneva was not simply material, as he noted in a letter of April 1, 1716, written in all likelihood to Vial:

Myself and my colleagues . . . considered what we must reply to those who say to us that the sacraments go with and are tied with preaching and that consequently one should not refuse them. I communicated to them [the other preachers] how Mr. P. . . . had advised me not to do so. And for that reason I would not dare to embark on anything until a *nouvel ordre*. They advised me, and with another [one of us], to come to Geneva to express it [the question] a second time, which I promised and I hope to go with the help of G[od] to your country at the end of May.[17]

Corteiz had gone to Geneva seeking theological help from "Mr. P,"—no doubt

Bénédict Pictet—to find out whether the Desert preachers, who had never been consecrated, could baptize and, especially, offer communion.

In spring 1716 Corteiz did indeed return to Geneva to see his wife and "to speak to the people sensitive to the troubles of dear Zion."[18] Although the results of these discussions are not clear, Corteiz met on his return to France with Jacques Roger, pastor in the Dauphiné region, to whom he showed the regulations the pastors of Languedoc had drawn up at the first "synod."[19] Corteiz and Roger subsequently drew up an improved list of regulations that began with this article: "In conformity with the Reformed Churches of Geneva, the commandments of God will be read before the sermon."[20] The following year, a synod in Languedoc, held March 2, 1717, added a number of articles, the first being that "Pastors will not continue to preach beyond an hour or at most five quarters [an hour and a quarter], in conformity with the Reformed Churches of Geneva, and formerly the Reformed Churches of France."[21]

To solve the question of whether unordained preachers could offer sacraments, the synod of March 1717 decided to grant to Corteiz, Court, and the preacher Jean Rouvière the right to administer communion.[22] Although Geneva had apparently approved of this measure, Court felt some French Huguenots would question the Desert synod's legitimacy.[23] If Geneva did not initiate the Desert synods, it clearly provided not only a liturgical reminder of the Reformed tradition but also theological and ecclesiastical direction through the advice of someone like Pictet.

Court was right in his fears. Both Corteiz and he met with opposition from Huguenots who requested their pastoral credentials.[24] Consequently, a synod in 1718 sent Corteiz off to Geneva again, carrying letters of recommendation for Bénédict Pictet and Antoine Léger (1652—1719), pastor and professor at the Academy of Geneva. Corteiz met secretly with Léger and other Genevan "friends" refused his request because the "magistrate did not want it."[25] They sent him to Zürich, where he received his ordination. Upon his return to France in the autumn of 1718, another synod decided to have Corteiz ordain Court immediately, much to the latter's chagrin. Court feared his ordination would be considered inferior, and perhaps he also regretted the missed opportunity to visit Geneva.[26] Both consecrations highlight the aid Geneva's pastors and professors gave to the Desert. While respecting the commands of the Republic's magistrate, they secretly guaranteed the very existence of the Desert churches.

The Desert's friends in Geneva still remained quick to suspect that Protestants in France would revolt. In the spring 1719 Vial wrote an open letter on behalf of the French court to French Protestants, calling upon them to obey the duc d'Orléans, France's regent.[27] A few months later, in August 1719, the regent still feared an uprising and sent an envoy, Génas de Beaulieu, a Protestant nobleman, to Languedoc. Court received from Beaulieu a package of letters, which included a message from Bénédict Pictet.[28] As strange as such a Huguenot-Spaniard plot may now seem, Vial made clear that he wrote on behalf of the French court.[29] The research of Gerald Cerny has shown that the abbé (and later cardinal) Guillaume Dubois, minister in charge of France's foreign affairs, had in fact contacted Jacques Basnage, the prominent Huguenot pastor living in The Hague, with regard to the rumor of a Spanish-inspired Huguenot revolt intended to destabalize the regent. Basnage cooperated by writing *Instruction pastorale*, a pamphlet calling the Huguenots to obedience.[30] Yet unclear, however, is how Vial was enlisted by the regent; but sufficient contacts existed between The Hague, Paris, and Geneva for this to occur.[31] Such contacts must have existed because Vial's letter, in an expanded form, was published in Holland with the title *Lettre pastorale aux fidelles reformez de France*, dated June 15, 1719.[32]

The Alberoni affair apparently had the positive effect of creating a link between Court and Pictet.[33] The Desert pastor began his correspondence with Pictet in autumn 1719 through the help of Pierre Rey, a Huguenot businessman living in Geneva. On August 26, 1719, Rey wrote that he had visited Pictet and that the theologian had beseeched Court to continue his ministry. Moreover, Pictet suggested that if faced by any difficult case, Court should write "preferably" to him first, that is, above any other Genevan pastor. Pictet also offered to write special texts, in the form of "exhortations" that would help Court understand better "the meaning of Holy Scripture and the ignorance of the pope."[34] Pictet would later express reservations about the assemblies, but he showed little hesitation to support the Desert pastors.[35] If Pictet symbolizes the ambiguity in Geneva's aid to France's Protestants, he seems exceptional in the extent to which he offered help.

Responding to Rey, Court thanked Pictet for the offer and praised the theologian's books: "God knows the fruits his works have produced in our parts." Court added: "if he wants to give me the liberty to write to him at your address he would give me great pleasure."[36] In a letter of May 1720, probably not his first to the theologian, Court asked Pictet for further ecclesiastical advice, particularly with regard to the preachers Jean Huc (also known as Mazel or Mazelet) and Jean Vesson. Both had taken part in the synod of August 1715, but both would rebel against the *nouvel ordre*. In fact, Huc had been deposed in September 1719, charged with "loose morals" notably with regard to what was seen as lenient teachings concerning the Catholic Church.[37] Court indicated to Pictet that a letter from Vial "dated April 1 and signed for all" had been read at the recent synod yet its advice was not being followed, as Huc had misinformed Geneva. It appears the rebel preacher had written to Pictet giving a favorable impression of himself.[38] Court informed Pictet that Geneva would receive a letter from the elders at the synod describing Huc's true character.[39] As would be the case in subsequent years, Geneva's involvement in the Desert created some confusion.

As to Jean Vesson, Court described him as "a man full of fanaticism," that is, a prophet known for his *extases*.[40] Like Huc, Vesson had also been deposed. In February 1718 he was accused of having falsely claimed that the "*Messieurs de Genève*"—the pastors and professors of Geneva—had sent him to preach in

France, a claim that reveals the weight Geneva still carried in the minds of Huguenots.[41] After promising to censure any signs of prophecy in his assemblies, Vesson was reintegrated into the church.[42] At the synod of May 1720 however, he refused to compose his own sermons or memorize printed sermons.[43] To avoid a schism, the synod allowed Vesson to have his way on the condition that another preacher would monitor his extemporaneous preaching.[44]

Court commented to Pictet that both Vesson and Huc caused the Desert leaders "to endure what happened to many, and especially to the famous Calvin, when he established in Geneva a *corps de discipline.*"[45] Aware that he himself was no Calvin, Court called on Pictet, the Reformer's eighteenth-century successor, to provide advice and concrete help.[46] As in the case of ordinations, Court's plan to organize the Desert required an outside—Genevan—authority. The aid Court could or could not obtain from the Republic became clear when he traveled to Geneva.

ANTOINE COURT'S STAY IN GENEVA (1720–1722)

In his *Mémoires* Antoine Court provided a short description of his trip to Geneva: "In 1720 I resolved to make a trip to Geneva to rid the people there of their prejudice against our assemblies because the letters we had just received from this city, and which blamed things unknown to them, were damaging our plans and slowing the progress of the Gospel."[47] The letters Court referred to were of course those written by Bénédict Pictet and Jacques Vial in 1719 during the Alberoni affair. Court then explained how a simple public relations journey turned into a lengthy stay: "I left without requesting leave from the Churches, for fear that they would not grant it to me. I only thought of being a month in Geneva or five weeks at most. But the plague that appeared at that time in Marseille and caused painful losses kept me locked up there for two consecutive years."[48] In admitting he skirted the synodical authority he had helped establish, Court revealed his own independent nature and also that the trip was not just for the churches but to satisfy a long-standing desire, already expressed in 1713, to go to Geneva.[49] Court probably left in the middle of July 1720, as the outbreak of the plague became common knowledge by the end of that month.[50] Because the French military soon established extensive quarantine lines, it was impossible for Court to return to France.[51]

According to his *Mémoires* Court took advantage of his Genevan prison. He had such success with his public opinion campaign that "the people the most biased against us," that is, Genevan pastors such as Vial, became the Desert's devoted supporters. After this success, he claimed to have moved on to develop a European-wide correspondence in favor of the Desert churches. Court was particularly proud of a letter he had written to the archbishop of Canterbury, a letter that was apparently presented to the British king.[52] Although Court did in fact write such letters, the bragging tone of his *Mémoires* hides the extent to which his correspondence was devoted to solving divisions in the Desert churches and to what degree Geneva did and did not support him.[53]

Stranded in Geneva, Court could count on the aid of the Republic's Huguenot community.[54] However, Pictet also helped Court survive in Geneva. The professor spoke up on Court's behalf in a meeting of the *Compagnie des pasteurs*, which decided to give to the Desert pastor 10 *écus* and a recommendation for the *Bourse française*.[55] Court seems to have had an open access to Pictet and his home, enjoying meals at the theologian's table.[56] Pictet's concern and esteem for the young pastor went to the point of suggesting that Court could probably find a charge in a French church in Germany.[57] No proof exists that Court, who had received only a very basic education in France, studied at the Genevan Academy.[58] Pictet did advise Court to study Latin, which he tried abortively.[59] In that light it is not impossible that Pictet, if not another professor, guided Court in his studies and provided some form of private lessons.[60]

Court did not exaggerate when he said Pictet had treated him as one of his own children. And at the risk of sounding sentimental, one may wonder whether Court, who had lost his own father a very young age and was raised in his faith by his mother and the *prophétesses*, had found in Pictet the spiritual and even natural father he had never known.[61]

From the beginning of Court's stay, Pictet also supported the Desert cause. It was chiefly Pictet, for example, who encouraged Court to write to the archbishop of Canterbury about the Desert churches.[62] Pictet contributed to a collection Court organized in favor of a group of Protestant prisoners in La Rochelle.[63] Via Court, the professor also provided advice to other Desert pastors on various theological questions.[64] How much Pictet was willing to help the Desert is very much evident in the case of his writings against Jean Vesson and the other *inspirés*, as well as his advice given with regard to Jean Huc.

The question of the *inspirés* was far from having been resolved when the Desert pastor left for Geneva. In December 1720, for example, a synod deposed the prophet Jean Vesson, using a letter by Pictet on the necessity of discipline—a letter perhaps written upon Court's arrival in the Republic.[65] Pictet also took the time to write personal letters to Huguenots who had questions about the prophets.[66] Even more significantly, Pictet wrote for the Desert his *Lettre contre ceux qui se croient inspirés*, a short pamphlet against the Huguenots prophets.[67] Court obviously inspired much of the text's content as passages of the *Lettre* describing various *inspirés* correspond to the Desert pastor's own experiences.[68] Pictet even gave Court the chance to proof the text and propose corrections; the Desert pastor also took care of the printing arrangements before the *Lettre* was sent out to France in the spring of 1721.[69] As dry as the text may now seem, it had the effect of drawing the lines between *prophètes* and *pasteurs*.[70] Up to that time, and contrary to Court's *Mémoires*, the Desert synods were fairly conciliatory toward the prophets.[71] In fact, one of Court's close colleagues, Benjamin Du Plan, wrote directly to the *Compagnie* in May 1721 to assert that true *inspirés* existed. The *Compagnie* in turn charged Pictet to pen a reply to Du

Plan.[72]

In December 1721, repeating a tactic he had used a few years before, the prophet Jean Vesson claimed to have a letter from Pictet saying that a church could consecrate its own pastors. Vesson's followers consequently ordained him.[73] In light of the plague, Pictet, Vial, and Jean-Alphonse Turrettin had agreed that Du Plan's church in Arlès could ordain its own pastor without the participation of a previously ordained pastor.[74] It is possible that Vesson heard about this decision or even had a copy of it. To clarify the matter, Pictet was asked to write more letters to those living in Vesson's stronghold, a request the professor dutifully honored.[75]

The preacher Jean Huc also had to bear the brunt of Pictet and Court's letter-writing campaigns.[76] In summer 1721, Huc and his followers wrote to Pictet letters attacking the Desert synods, putting into question Corteiz's ordination and his contacts with Geneva. In penning his replies, Pictet again relied on Court, who provided a longish report on the errors of Huc's pro-Catholic ways. Court even summoned into Pictet's office three Huguenot refugees living in Geneva who supported Huc.[77] The professor gave them a severe tongue lashing, following Court's prompts. Subsequently, Court wrote a letter against Huc's followers on their behalf, a letter that confirmed, for example, that Pictet had written against "mixed" Protestant-Catholic marriages.[78] Huc, however, again claimed the letters from Geneva were false and refused to show them to anyone.[79]

Vesson and Huc seem to have lost their supporters by the beginning of 1722.[80] In December 1722 Vesson became part of a sect in Montpellier known as the Multipliants.[81] He was arrested in March 1723 with other members of the sect.[82] In no way attached to the Multipliants, Huc was also arrested in spring 1723 through the treachery of an informer.[83] When the two Desert preachers were forced to meet each other in a judicial confrontation in April 1723, Huc claimed he did not know Vesson despite the latter's assurances to the contrary.[84] Vesson was executed April 22, 1723, and although Huc converted to Catholicism, the intendant Bernage still carried out his execution May 5, 1723.

At the deaths of Vesson and Huc, one could hail the vindication of Geneva's triumphant rescue of the French Reformed from the twin foes of fanaticism and diluted Protestantism. But the situation was more complex than that. Both Huc and Vesson, for all their sectarian faults, represented currents in French Protestantism, namely accommodation with Catholicism and the prophet's subsequent call to repentance—currents without which French Protestantism would not have survived the Revocation. The new current proposed by Du Plan, namely, blending the positive aspects of an increasingly marginalized prophetic movement with the new Desert order, became impossible when the Protestant nobleman was himself implicated in the Multipliant affair and forced to flee France.[85] If Court and Corteiz seem to come out as the winners, there would be supporters, for years to come, of both the prophets and, more significantly, of a Protestantism that made do in some form or other with the Catholic rites of baptism and marriage.[86]

Even Pictet and Court were not completely of one mind. If the numerous letters Pictet sent to the Desert and the various anecdotes Court provided in his own correspondence show the theologian's committment to the Desert churches, there were limits to what Pictet could and wanted to do and what Court would ask of him.[87] To accompany a letter by Pictet on the question of whether Huguenots should participate in the illegal Desert assemblies, Court attached an apology declaring that: "The ties and care that this republic [of Geneva must] keep with France do not allow *Mr. le professeur* to say all he thinks with regard to the assemblies: that is why he must very often speak in veiled terms, as it is easy to understand."[88] By trying to clarify the matter, Court in fact covered up the ambiguity in Pictet's position; that is, his strong support for Huguenots in France combined with his hesitation to condone the assemblies.[89]

On a related topic, Court wrote in 1721 a polemical letter, with "rather embarrassing questions" for Geneva's *Compagnie des pasteurs*, arguing that if Geneva accepted the Huguenots' right to hold assemblies, it would have to follow through by sending pastors to France.[90] Examined by Pictet, Vial and the professor Antoine Maurice,[91] Court's letter seems to have received little support.[92] In December 1721, Court wrote to Corteiz: "I admit that this small republic has to deal very carefully with France but also perhaps this policy is pushed too far. Whatever that may be, I do not see the day that we will be able to have pastors from foreign countries. They don't have enough courage or enough zeal to preach *sous la croix* [under persecution]."[93] Although Court readily passed on "embarrassing questions" to Pictet, nothing indicates that he would have questioned the theologian's own zeal. Yet Court severely criticized the pastor Pierre Durand for asking Pictet how to decide when a preacher should be consecrated. Court wrote to Corteiz: "Haven't you dealt with that, do you have to have recourse to Geneva to learn how?"[94] If Court tried to obtain from Pictet whatever support he could get, this comment reveals that he did not want Geneva's charity to take away the Desert's hope for independence.

THE RESIDENT'S INTERVENTION (1723)

As Court admitted, Geneva did need to be wary of France. He even stated in his *Mémoires* and his correspondence to have been "well known" by La Closure, France's Resident in Geneva, whose tasks included the monitoring of Geneva's relationships with French Protestants.[95] In 1722 one of Court's letter's was intercepted and the Resident apparently made the Desert pastor's planned departure impossible.[96] Court claimed to have finally tricked the Resident's vigilance to make his way out of Geneva on August 9, 1722.[97]

Although no reference to Court exists in La Closure's correspondence with Cardinal Dubois, Pictet's contacts with Protestants in France are prominent. In a letter dated June 21, 1723, Dubois wrote that Bernage, intendant of Languedoc, had discovered proof that Pictet had written letters providing support for the

Desert pastors and their assemblies. Dubois instructed the Resident to threaten the Syndics, Geneva's chief magistrates, with the loss of the "king's protection"—in other words, an invasion—if the Genevan pastors continued to correspond with French Protestants.[98]

La Closure proceeded by having a private conversation with the first *syndic* Antoine Tronchin who in turn spoke to Pictet. Upon hearing the accusation, Pictet was reportedly very surprised saying, "he had always disapproved of the assemblies, but that he could never refuse letters of consolation to those who requested them." And if he had written to France on how a pastor should be selected, he had done so "according to the opinions of Calvin and our [Geneva's] other doctors." Pictet told of the letter he had written a few years before urging French Protestants to be loyal, a letter which the then abbé Dubois had apparently seen. The theologian added that perhaps the letters found by Bernage where, as had happened in the past, counterfeits. Pictet even proposed to speak directly to the Resident to justify himself.[99] In short, if he had written letters to France, it was only in response to those he had received.[100]

In Pictet's arguments one finds the various strands of his involvement in the Desert, from his letters on the assemblies and the Alberoni affair to Vesson's counterfeit letter and the advice on ordination given to Du Plan. Judging from the number and content of Pictet's letters in Court's correspondence and especially the close collaboration between the theologian and the Desert pastor, it would be easy to accuse the honorable professor of no small amount of voluntary ambiguity in his reply to the syndic. But Pictet could not be charged with hypocrisy as he clearly felt he was only doing what charity and his role because a Genevan pastor and theologian required. Such an open participation in France's religious affairs, however, was at odds with the post-Revocation politics of the time.

According to La Closure's correspondence and the minutes of Geneva's *Conseil*, First Syndic Tronchin obsequiously obliged the Resident by reprimanding a deputation of the *Compagnie des pasteurs*. Tronchin also ordered the deputies that Geneva's pastors must never engage again in any correspondence with Protestants in France.[101] The minutes of the *Compagnie* itself tell a slightly different story. In fact, Tronchin had exhorted the deputies that the *Compagnie* would have to: "Conduct itself towards Reformed Protestants in France with all the moderation and prudence possible and in a manner that would give no rise to any complaint on the part of the French court against this state."[102] The advice was clear: Follow Pictet's example by continuing to help the Desert churches, but this time as secretly as possible.

A HIDDEN IDENTITY: THE *COMITÉ GENEVOIS POUR LE PROTESTANTISME FRANÇAIS*

Back in France, Court wrote to Geneva during winter 1723 asking Pictet for new books in favor of the Desert.[103] The theologian responded, saying he was more than willing but no printer supported him and his health was waning.[104] After Pictet was reprimanded in summer 1723, Court's attitude to Genevan politics became even more critical than before. Writing from the Desert in October 1723 to Corteiz, who was then in Geneva, Court mentioned the Desert's recent decision to write to the intendant of Languedoc: Geneva—"our most honored fathers and brothers the pastors and professors of the learned academy of the Church of the Holy City"—would have been consulted, were the Republic not so afraid of being invaded by the French. After his ironic statement Court lamented that Geneva, home of the sixteenth-century reformers, had become more concerned with "temporal interests" and "worldly politics" than the church's interests: "Ha, cowardly children of so generous fathers, why do you not imitate the zeal of these glorious ancestors and why do you not have for the posterity [of the Reformation] the same love these great men had for us."[105] In Court's eyes the Genevan pastors had lost their identity; France was forgotten in the name of politics alone. For the Desert pastor, who risked his life everyday, Calvin's descendants had hidden themselves in a cloak of prudence, a costume worn by cowards.

Yet Court did not see the whole picture; even La Closure was not fooled by the reprimands given to Pictet and the *Compagnie*. La Closure wrote to Dubois in July 1723 after his meeting with the *premier syndic*:

The magistrate couldn't really do much more substantial than what it did. Such a step of disapproval may well honor it in the eyes of *V[otre] É[minence]*, but it didn't remedy anything, and any man, be he a minister or another given to an indiscreet zeal, as it happens far too often, will soon have forgotten the magistrate's remonstrances, and it will be easy for him to continue secretly the same intrigues, without it coming to his [the magistrate's] knowledge: moreover, *Monseigneur*, the canton of Bern, which is not lacking in ministers, or others of the same temper as Pictet, will provide enough people fit to second him in the same practices.[106]

In view of a permanent solution, La Closure called for an extremely tight surveillance of border crossings by Huguenots living both in France and in Geneva, a measure that was probably easier to request than to implement.[107] After Pictet's death in 1724, Court prayed someone would be found to continue to the theologian's aid to the Desert.[108] He had little reason to worry, for even after the regent's death in 1723 and the proclamation of the Edict of 1724, which confirmed existing anti-Protestant legislation, Pictet's successors managed to circumvent France's surveillance—as the Resident himself had predicted.

In fact, from the time of Calindrini before 1714 to that of Léger, Vial, Maurice, and Jean-Alphonse Turretin in 1715—1724, not just Pictet but a distinct group of Genevan pastors and professors were involved in the affairs of the Desert. As in Vial's act of signing "for all" in 1719 and the group of pastors consulted on Court's and Du Plan's questions, it is easy to see the beginnings of what would be known as the *Comité genevois pour le protestantisme français*.[109] In the past this "Genevan Committee for French Protestantism," formed by the likes of Vial, Maurice, and J.-A. Turrettin, provided advice on ecclesiastical problems. And added to its ecclesiastical wisdom and Genevan prestige, the *Comité* controlled the financial aid given by various Protestant countries to help French Protestants. Raised by the exiled Benjamin Du Plan, the majority of these funds were used to allow Desert preachers to study in Lausanne, at what would be called the "Seminary of Lausanne."[110] Like Bénédict Pictet, *Messieurs les pasteurs et professeurs de Genève* would manage to obey officially the principles of international politics while secretly honoring, throughout the eighteenth century, the Desert's request for charity. In that context, Antoine Court's stay in the Republic was essential in helping to establish the personal contacts and confidence necessary to overcome any Genevan hesitation.

In 1729 Antoine Court fled France and made once again for Geneva to settle finally in Lausanne. Antoine Court continued in his exile to play a significant role as a member of Lausanne's own *Comité* until his death in 1760. And so both Court and the pastors and professors of Geneva would benefit from the weight given to hidden but not forgotten identities.

NOTES

1. Antoine Court, *Mémoires pour servir à l'histoire et à la vie d'Antoine Court (de 1695 à 1729)*, intro. Patrick Cabanel, ed. Pauline Duley-Haour (Paris: Les Éditions de Paris, 1995), 40—41.

2. *BPU*, Collection Court, ser. 7, vol. II, 65 (7/II, 65), [Court] to his "friends," [July] 1724. See 8, f.202 for Court's résumé of this letter, dated July 1724. As to the letter he mentions, see 1/III, 209—212, f.105—106v (verso), [Gaillard] to Mlle de Gibolinoire [Court], June 10, 1724. It should be noted that unless otherwise mentioned (1) manuscripts cited in this paper are located in the Collection Court; (2) Court's own letters are copies or drafts; (3) all translations are my own; and (4) original spelling is retained in French quotations. Research for this study was made possible through a Redeemer College Internal Research Grant and a bursary of the *Comité genevois pour le protestantisme français* (June-July 1996).

3. See Olivier Fatio with Louise Martin-van Berchem, "L'Église de Genève et la Révocation de l'Édit de Nantes," in *Genève au temps de la Révocation de l'Édit de Nantes 1680-1705, MD*, vol. 50 (Geneva and Paris: Droz and Champion, 1985), 294—297, especially, 296, note 47. See also 17/H, 279, f.140, Campagne to Pictet, November 25, 1717: This correspondent of Pictet claimed in 1717 that his family had managed to remain Protestant in France chiefly because of the professor's published sermons.

4. Michel Grandjean, "Genève au secours des galériens pour la Foi (1685—1718)," in *Genève au temps de la Révocation de l'Édit de Nantes 1680—1715*, 400—438.

5. Fatio and Martin-van Berchem, "L'Église de Genève et la Révocation de l'Édit de Nantes," 162.

6. Ibid., 297.

7. For sources on the prophets and the Camisard War, see Maximilien Misson, *Le Théâtre sacré des Cévennes*, ed. Jean-Pierre Richardot (Paris: Les Éditions de Paris, 1996), and the various studies by Philippe Joutard, such as *Les Camisards* (Paris:

Gallimard, 1976, 1994), and *La Légende des Camisards. Une sensibilité au passé* (Paris: Gallimard, 1977), as well as Henri Bosc's mammoth *La Guerre des Cévennes 1702-1710*, 6 vols. (Montpellier: Les Presses du Languedoc, 1985—1993). For a sociological study of prophetism, see Daniel Vidal, *Le Malheur et son prophète: Inspirés et sectaires en Languedoc calviniste (1685—1725)* (Paris: Payot, 1983). See as well Hillel Schwartz, *The French Prophets. The History of a Millenarian Group in Eighteenth-Century England* (Berkeley: U of California P, 1980), Chapter 1, "The Desert," 11—36.

8. For Residents, see Georges Livet, *Recueil des instructions données aux ambassadeurs et ministres de France des Traités de Westphalie jusqu'à la Révolution française. Suisse . . .* , vol. 2 (Paris: Éditions du Centre national de la Recherche scientifique, 1983) and Jacques Flournoy, *Journal 1675—1692*, ed. Olivier Fatio with Michel Grandjean and Louise Martin van Berchem, *Publications de l'Association suisse pour l'histoire du Refuge huguenot*, vol. 3 (Geneva: Droz, 1994), 30, n.21. Fatio suggests that Louis XIV's decision in 1679 to have a permanent diplomatic representative in Geneva coincided with the king's plans to rid Protestantism from France. At the same time, Fatio indicates that the Resident played a purely political role, indicating to Savoy and Bern that Geneva was under French protection.

9. Edmond Hugues, *Antoine Court, Histoire de la restauration du protestantisme en France au XVIIIe siècle*, 2 vols. (Paris: Michel Lévy, 1872).

10. For studies of Court and Pictet, see Edmond Hugues, *Antoine Court*, vol. 1, 213—233; Eugène de Budé, *Vie de Bénédict Pictet, théologien genevois, 1655—1724* (Lausanne: Georges Bridel, 1874), 214—243 and, more recently, Jean-Daniel Candaux, *Histoire de la famille Pictet* (Geneva: Etienne Braillard, 1974), vol. 1, 114. On Pictet, see Martin I. Klauber, "Reformed Orthodoxy in Transition: Bénédict Pictet (1655-1724) and Enlightened Orthodoxy in Post-Reformation Geneva," in *Later Calvinism: International Perspectives*, ed. W. Fred Graham (Kirksville, MS: Sixteenth Century Studies, 1994); "Family Loyalty and Theological Transition in Post-Reformation Geneva: The Case of Benedict Pictet (1655—1724)," *Fides et historia* 24 (1992): 54—67.

11. See Court, *Mémoires*, 31—67.

12. Ibid., 68. See also Collection Court, 37, "*Mémoire aux arbitres*," f.125—[126], 5—6. See also Charles Bost, "Les deux premiers synodes du Désert, 21 août 1715—13 janvier 1716," *BSHPF* 65 (1916): 10—54, especially, 30ff.

13. Court, *Mémoires*, 68.

14. Corteiz (1683—1767) played an essential role in the early years of the Desert churches. A former Camisard, he lived in Geneva from 1706—1709. For Corteiz and the period 1699—1715, see Bost's pertinent comment, "Les premiers synodes," 24: Pierre Corteiz, *Mémoires et lettres inédites*, ed. Paul Dombre et al. (Mende: Société des Lettres, Sciences et Arts de la Lozère, 1983), 23—33; Charles Bost, "La Première Vie de Pierre Corteiz, pasteur du Désert," *RTP* 23 (1935): 5—31, 89—121.

15. See Sven and Suzanne Stelling-Michaud, *Le Livre du Recteur de l'Académie de Genève (1559—1878)* (Geneva: Droz, 1958—1980), vol. 6, 151.

16. 17/G, 1, f.1, Corteiz to [Vial], "du deser [from the Desert]," April 1, 1716.

17. Ibid.

18. Corteiz, *Mémoires*, 33.

19. On Jacques Roger (c. 1675—1745), see Eugène Arnaud, *Histoire des protestants du Dauphiné aux XVIe, XVIIe et XVIIIe siècles* (Geneva: Slatkine Reprints, 1970, [1875—1876]), vol. 3, 96ff.

20. Edmond Hugues, *Les Synodes du Désert. Actes et règlements des synodes nationaux et provinciaux tenus au Désert de France de l'an 1715 à l'an 1793* (Paris: Fischbacher, 1885), vol. 1, 2.

21. Ibid., vol. 1, 6.

22. Ibid.

23. Court, *Mémoires*, 88.

24. Ibid., 91.

25. 1/II, 25, f.13, Corteiz to [Court], August 27, 1718.

26. Court, *Mémoires*, 93.

27. 1/II, 69-72, f.35—36v, 73—[76], f.37—38v and especially 71, f.36. For the printed version, dated June 15, 1719, see [Jacques Vial de Beaumont], *Lettre pastorale aux fidelles reformez de France* (Rotterdam: Abraham Acher, 1719), 12. The letter is signed "J.V.D.B." Compare Gerald Cerny, *Theology, Politics and Letters at the Crossroads of European Civilization: Jacques Basnage and the Baylean Huguenot Refugees in the Dutch Republic* (Dordrecht: Martinus Nijhoff, 1987), 154—163. Although Cerny speaks of Basnage, he does not mention Vial. The correspondence between La Closure, France's Resident, and Dubois makes no mention of this affair. See Archives du Ministères des Affaires étrangères (Paris), Correspondence politique, Geneva (A.E., C.P., Geneva), 34, 1719 January—1720 December.

28. See Court, *Mémoires*, 105—106, and 1/II, 109—[120], f.55—60, [Court and Duplan] to Pictet and Duquesne, August 14, 1719.

29. 1/II, 71, f.36.

30. Cerny, *Theology, Politics and Letters*, 154—163. See Jacques Basnage, *Instruction pastorale aux reformez de France, sur la perseverance dans la foi, et la fidelité pour le souverain* (Rotterdam: Araham Acher, 1719).

31. Cerny does not speak of the Genevan side of this episode nor of Vial's *Lettre* mentioned below. Court's correspondence provides no clear explanation either. A probable link would be Henri Duquesne or Henri de Mirmand. See Marie Alexandre de Chambrier, *Henri de Mirmand et les réfugiés de la Révocation de l'Édit de Nantes. 1650—1721* (Neuchâtel: Attinger-Frères, 1910), Appendix, 105—107.

32. Cf. 1/II, 69—72, f. 35—36v and [Jacques Vial de Beaumont], *Lettre pastorale aux fidelles reformez de France* (Rotterdam: Abraham Acher, 1719), 12. The letter is signed "J. V. D. B."

33. In his *Mémoires* Court claimed to have written to Calandrini in 1715 to counter the professor's condemnation of the Desert assemblies. See Court, *Mémoires*, 69, and Grandjean, "Genève au secours des galériens pour la Foi (1685—1718)," 437.

34. 1/II, 135—136, f.68—68v, Rey to Court, August 26, [1719].

35. 17/G, 189—192, f.99—100v, [Pictet] to [Corteiz], received January 12 [1720]. See Hugues, *Antoine Court*, vol. 1, 375—378 for a transcription.

36. 7/I, 1—2, f.2—2v, [Court] to [Pictet], [May 1720].

37. 7/I, 1—2, f.2—2v, [Court] to [Pictet], "August 1719" [May 1720].

38. 7/1, 1, f.2. It is possible that Pictet even responded to Huc. A general letter by Pictet on the prophets was discovered among Huc papers upon his arrest in 1723. See Archives départementales de l'Hérault, Montpellier (A.D.H.), C.197, n.136, document 115. Apparently Huc also had at the time of his arrest a copy of a letter from Vial (C.197, n.136, f.35, interrogation of Huc, March 23, 1723). See Charles Bost's excellent use of these documents in his "Les deux premiers synodes du Désert," 29ff.

39. 7/I, 1, f.2. Cf., *Synodes*, vol. 1, 18, article II.

40. 7/I, 1-2, f.2—2v.

41. *Synodes*, vol. 1, 10 (original manuscript, 1/II, [20], f.10v).

42. *Synodes*, vol. 1, 11—15 (original manuscript, 1/II, 23—24, f.12—12v) and *Synodes*, vol. 1, 17.

43. 7/I, 2, f.2v.

44. Ibid. also cf. *Synodes*, vol. 1, 18—19, article IV.

45. 7/I, 2, f.2v.

46. Ibid.

47. Court, *Mémoires*, 112—113.

48. Ibid., 113.

49. See above and ibid., 40—41.

50. For the 1720—1722 plague see Monique Lucenet, *Les grandes pestes en France* (Paris: Aubier, 1985), 213—274.

51. Cf. Lucenet, *Les grandes pestes en France*, 257—265; Court, *Mémoires*, 113—114.

52. Court, *Mémoires*, 113. For a description of this letter's content, see 7/I, 273—[276], f.137—138v, Court to Roger, February 15, 1722. I have as yet not found a copy of the actual letter in the Collection Court.

53. From his time in Geneva, almost 300 letters of Court's active and passive correspondence have been saved (Collection Court, ser. 1/II, 1/III, 7/I, and 17/G). Pictet stands out as being Court's most important contact with Geneva. See Klauber, *Between Reformed Scholasticism*; Maria-Cristina Pitassi, *De l'orthodoxie aux Lumières. Genève 1670-1737* (Geneva: Labor et Fides, 1992), 51—66, and on a similar although later topic, Olivier Fatio, "Le Christ des Liturgies," in *Le Christ entre orthodoxie et Lumières. Actes du colloque tenu à Genève en août 1993*, ed. Maria-Cristina Pitassi (Geneva: Droz, 1994), 11—30.

54. See Court's mother's letters in Antoine Court, *L'Assemblée de la Baume des Fées, près Nîmes. Relation d'Antoine Court, avec lettres et pièces justificatives*, ed. C. Saignier, intro. J. Bonnet (Paris et Nîmes: Grassart et Lavagne-Peyrot, 1891), 231—233.

55. *AEG*, Archives de l'Église nationale protestante de Genève, Registres de la Compagnie des pasteurs, 21, 50 (*AEG*, R 21, 50), December 20, 1720.

56. See, for example, 7/I, 217, f.108, Court to Pierredon, December 15, 1721 and 7/I, 219, f.109, [Court] to Corteiz, December 21, 1721.

57. 7/I, 22, f.12v, Court to Corteiz, March 1, 1721.

58. Compare Stelling-Michaud, *Le Livre du recteur*, vol. 2, 1191.

59. 7/I, [182], f.90v, Court to Durand, October 23, 1721.

60. Since Court did not know Latin, he could not have followed the courses given at the Genevan Academy (see 1/III, 77—[80], f.39—40v, Raoulx to Court, June 1722: This correspondent, from Vevay, addressed his letter to Court, "theological student at the Academy of Geneva"; cf. Hugues, *Antoine Court*, vol. 1, 226—227).

61. Court, *Mémoires*, 32.

62. See 7/I, 11—12, f.7v, [Court] to [the Desert churches], December 25, 1720 (see 8, f.191); and 1/II, [416], f.209v, Secretan to Court, April 27, 1721.

63. 1/II, 351, f.177, transcribed in Antoine Court, *L'assemblée de la Baume des Fées, près Nîmes*, 232.

64. See, for example, 1/II, 553—554, f.278—278v, Delors and Bétrine to [Court], September 1721; 1/II, [562], f.282, Durand to Court, September 25, 1721 and 1/II, 599, f.301, Pictet to Court, [November 4, 1721].

65. 17/G, 205—208, f.107—108v, "Copy of a letter by Mr. Pictet on order, 1720," and 17/G, 211—214, f.110—111v, "Resignation of Jean Vesson, sent to me [Court] by Corteiz, December 13, 1720."

66. Note especially 17/G, 257—259, f.133—134, Pictet to [Simard], March [28], 1721, a letter to a woman whose servant was an *inspirée* (transcribed in Hugues, *Antoine Court*, vol. 1, 385—387).

67. Bénédict Pictet, *Lettre sur ceux qui se croyent inspirez par Bénédict Pictet, pasteur et professeur en theologie* (Geneva: Fabri et Barrillot, 1721).

68. Cf. Pictet, *Lettre*, 48, and Court, *Mémoires*, 48—49, regarding the prediction made by the *prophétesse* Claire that the English would arrive in France's Vivarais region on Christmas Day, 1713.

69. 7/I, 23, f.13, Court to Corteiz, March 1, 1721; *AEG*, R 21, 56, January 17, 1721. See Pictet, *Lettre*, 94, for the text of the *approbation*, signed by P. Gallatin, A. Maurice, and A. de la Rive, January 24, 1721. See Pitassi, *De l'orthodoxie aux Lumières*, 67—76, and 72—74 on Pictet's *Lettre*. Samuel Turrettin, *Preservatif contre le fanatisme ou refutation des pretendus inspirez des derniers siécles*, trans. [Jacques-Théodore Le Clerc] (Geneva: Du Villard et Jacquier, 1723), and Pitassi, *De l'orthodoxie aux Lumières*, 74—75.

70. 1/II/631, f. 317, Corteiz, Rouvière, and Pierredon [written by Corteiz] to Court, December 5, 1721, and 1/11/[602], f. 302v, Valadière to Court, November 10, 1721.

71. *Synodes*, 1, 4, article 4; and 1, 26, article XII.

72. *AEG*, R 21, 73.

73. 1/II, 641, f.322, Bétrine to Court, December 12, 1721; and 1/II, 651—653, f. 327—328, Roux to Court, January 2, 1722.

74. 17/G, 215—218, f.112—113v, "Opinion of Mrs. Alphonse Turretin, Pictet, Vial consulted by the church of Alais [Alès], 1721 [dated by Court]."

75. 7/I, 269—[270], f. 135—135v, Pictet to Fourmeaux [copy], "concerning Master Vesson fanatic," February 14, 1722.

76. See 17/G, 197—198, f.103—103v, Pierredon to Court, September 24, 1720.

77. On this matter, see 7/I, 63—[66], f.33—34v, 67—[70], f.35—36v, documents by Court [August 29, 1721] advising how to respond to Huc's letter of July 20, 1721; Pictet's letters to Mazel's [Huc's] partisans (7/I, 71—74, f.37—38v) and to Mazel [Huc] (7/I, 75—[78], f.39—40v [c. August 29, 1721]).

78. 7/I, 105—107, f.54—55, [Court] to Corteiz, September 15, 1721 and see 7/I, 93—[96], f.48—49v, Boury, Hours and Rouveyran to Mazel's [Huc's] partisans, September 6, 1721.

79. 1/II, 662, f.332v, Corteiz to Court, January 24, 1722; and 1/II, 685, f.344, Combe to [Court], February 12, 1722.

80. With regard to Huc, see 1/II, 662, f.332v, and 1/II, [684], f.353v; as for Vesson see, 1/111, [58], f.29v, Roux to Court, May 17, 1722.

81. André Vigne, *Jean Vesson et les Multipliants* (Montpellier: Thèse présentée à la Faculté Libre de Théologie Protestante de Montpellier et publiquement soutenue le 6 juillet 1934), Chapter 3, and A. Germain, "Nouvelles recherches sur la secte des Multipliants," *Mémoires de la section des Lettres de l'Académie des Sciences et Lettres de Montpellier* 2 (1855—1857), 413—416; reeditions (Nîmes: Lacour) with Hubert Bost, postface, "Les Multipliants de Montpellier. Parcours historiographique." See also Schwartz, *The French Prophets*, 118—119.

82. See Vigne, *Jean Vesson*, Chapter 9.

83. A.D.H., C.197, n.136, f.31—32v, "Diverny" to [Bernage], March 23, 1723.

84. A.D.H., C.197, n.136, f.70, April 21, 1723.

85. Daniel Bonnefon, *Benjamin du Plan, gentilhomme d'Alais, député général des synodes des Églises réformées de France, 1688—1763* (Paris: Sandoz et Fischbacher, Grassart, [1876]), 55ff.

86. Cf. Daniel Vidal, "Antoine Court à Contretemps. Champ calviniste et horizon prophétique," *Entre Désert et Europe, le pasteur Antoine Court (1695—1760)* (forthcoming). See also Émile G. Léonard, "Le problème du mariage civil et les protestants français au XVIIIe siècle," *Études de théologie et d'action évangélique* 2 (1942): 241—299.

87. See 7/I, 219—220, December 21, 1721.

88. 7/I, 354, f.177v, Court to [Pagès], May 15, 1721.

89. 7/I, 355, f.178, Pictet to [Pagès], May 15, 1721.

90. 7/I, 133—[144], f.63—73v, Court to the Pastors of Geneva, October 6, 1721 and for another version, 7/I, 145—[160], f.74—79, and 7/I, 193, f.96, [Court] to Corteiz, November 8, 1721).

91. 7/I, [144], f.73v.

92. 1/II, 611, f.307, Pictet to Court, November 20, 1721.

93. 7/I, 227, f.113, [Court] to Corteiz, December 21, 1721.

94. 7/I, 193, f.96, [Court] to Corteiz, November 8, 1721.

95. Court, *Mémoires*, 114; and 7/I, 23, f.13, Court to Corteiz, March 1, 1721.

96. 7/I, 371, f.186, Court to the Elders of Nîmes, June 20, 1722; and cf. 8, f.198.

97. Court, *Mémoires*, 113—114.

98. A. E., C. P., Geneva, 36, f.102, [Dubois] to La Closure, June 21, 1723.

99. *AEG*, Registres des Conseils (RC), RC 222, 1723, 356—357, July 2, 1723. Cf. La Closure's account, AE, C. P., Geneva, 36, f. 118—124v, La Closure to [Dubois], July 2, 1723.

100. *AEG*, R 21, July 8. 1723, 303.

101. AE, C. P., Geneva, 36, f.120, La Closure to [Dubois], July 2, 1723 and *AEG*, RC 222, 357, July 2, 1723.

102. *AEG*, R 21, 303, July 9, 1723.

103. 7/I, 427—[430], 214—215v, [Court] to Pictet, [February?] 1723.

104. 17/G, 319, f.165, Pictet to A. C. Gebelin [Court], March 1, 1723.

105. 7/I, [426], f.213v, Court to [Corteiz], October 1723.

106. AE, C. P., Geneva, 36, f.122, La Closure to [Dubois], July 2, 1723.

107. Ibid.

108. 7/II, 66, [Court] to his "friends."

109. Philippe Monnier, "Les archives du Comité genevois pour le protestantisme français," *BSHPF* 119 (1973): 575—596; as well *BPU*, Archives du Comité genevois pour le protestantisme français, C. F. 1, "Notice sur la fondation du Comité, son office, et l'étendue de ses droits, rédigée par Mr. [Louis Manoël] de Végobre en septembre 1809, revue et augmentée par le même en janvier 1811," 15—21.

110. See Bonnefon, *Benjamin du Plan*, 127ff.; and Claude Lasserre, "Antoine Court et le séminaire de Lausanne," *Entre Désert et Europe, le pasteur Antoine Court (1695—1760)* (forthcoming).

6

Reformed Piety and Suicide in Geneva, 1550—1800

Jeffrey R. Watt

Studies have tended to show that Protestants, especially Calvinists, commit suicide more often than Catholics. In his pioneering work the sociologist Emile Durkheim found that in the nineteenth century in which he lived, suicide was invariably more common in Protestant than in Catholic areas. Asserting that suicide is the result of social forces that produced anomie, Durkheim suggested that Protestant societies were more individualistic and less strongly integrated than Catholic societies. Accordingly, Protestants were more likely to commit "egoistic" suicides, occurring when an individual is not adequately integrated into society.[1] Maurice Halbwachs argued that this was more an urban-rural than a Protestant-Catholic distinction, but even he found higher suicide rates among rural Protestants than among urban Catholics.[2] Markus Schär went so far as to blame Reformed religiosity itself for the increasing numbers of suicides in the Zürich countryside in the late seventeenth century. He maintained that people felt an emotional and spiritual void as a result of Protestants' elimination of many rituals, such as fasts and prayers to saints. Those most likely to take their lives, he argued, were those who had most internalized Reformed morality; after hearing so many Reformed sermons, they became obsessed with their own sinfulness and convinced that they were predestined to eternal damnation.[3] For similar reasons, Calvinism, with its predestinarian theology, has been blamed for an epidemic of suicides in seventeenth-century Puritan England.[4]

The Republic of Geneva, obviously the most Calvinistic state ever, is ideal for studying whether the Reformed faith nurtured suicidal tendencies.[5] The Geneva state archives have a series of source collections that are exceptionally well preserved and precisely catalogued. They provide a unique opportunity to study early modern suicide, even allowing one to determine suicide rates, so important to the work of Durkheim. With Calvinistic precision, authorities in Geneva consistently investigated and recorded unnatural deaths. Among the most valuable sources are inquests following unnatural deaths, which are contained in the criminal proceedings. These sources provide valuable detailed information about events surrounding the untimely deaths. Upon learning of an unnatural death, an *auditeur*, a type of police officer, went to the scene of the death to investigate. A physician examined the body, giving a detailed account of the state of the corpse and probable cause of demise, and witnesses described the circumstances leading up to the death. This very rich testimony sheds much light on popular piety in the daily lives of Genevans and on the attitudes of both the authorities and the rank and file toward suicide. Although fully extant from the late 1600s, some criminal proceedings have been lost for the sixteenth and seventeenth centuries

Other sources, however, fill these gaps and effectively complement the criminal proceedings. Most important are death records. For every death in Geneva, a surgeon examined the body and recorded the name, age, profession, and political status of the deceased; the date, hour, and place of death; and, most important for this study, a brief description of the cause of death. Extending as far back as 1549, these death records have few lacunae—none after 1616—and provide most reliable evidence on the total number of unnatural deaths. Also important are the registers of the Small Council, which, serving as the chief tribunal, heard the *auditeurs'* reports and often passed sentences against the bodies and estates of suicides.

These various records show that whereas suicide was quite rare in Reformation Geneva, *la Rome protestante* experienced a veritable explosion in self-inflicted deaths in the late eighteenth century. From 1542, the date of the first Geneva suicide, through the end of the Republic in April 1798, 405 deaths were beyond a reasonable doubt self-inflicted. Of these, 288, almost three-fourths the total, occurred after 1750.[6] The suicide rate reached a crescendo toward the end of the century: from 1781 on, 160 Genevans took their lives, and the year 1793 witnessed more suicides than any other year (17). Surprisingly, for the period 1751–1798 suicides far outnumbered homicides: 288 to 108, including 42 cases of infanticide. The ratio of suicides to murders was even greater in the 1780s and 1790s: 160 to 46, 18 of which were infanticides. Contemporaries were aware that suicide was becoming more common. Members of the Small Council expressed alarm already in 1758, as did the Consistory in 1774.[7] Voltaire wrote in a letter in 1767 that Genevans were more melancholic than the English and, he believed, that there were proportionally more suicides in Geneva than in London.[8] This dramatic increase in suicides far outpaced population growth and cannot be dismissed as simply the result of better records or more aggressive investigations in the late eighteenth century than before. Investigative procedures were established in the Reformation period, and there are no lacunae from the late seventeenth century.

Why were the contemporaries of Rousseau and Voltaire so much more likely to kill themselves than the residents of Calvin's Geneva? This chapter will look at the role of increased secularization and changing attitudes toward suicide.

Simply put, during the course of the early modern period, Geneva experienced a secularization of suicide.[9] A more secular mentality removed key religious deterrents to "self-murder" and ultimately represented one of the most important reasons that Geneva experienced an explosion in suicides after 1750.

From the Reformation through 1650, magistrates and common folk alike viewed suicide as resulting from demon possession. Thus, in 1561 Bonaventure Gronbon, a native of Burgundy employed as a soldier in Geneva, jumped to his death from a bridge to avoid being arrested for the capital crime of counterfeiting. Declaring that Satan had incited Gronbon to kill himself, magistrates ordered his body to be dragged through the streets, then stuffed in a barrel and thrown into the Rhone River.[10] Since in Reformation Geneva demon possession was considered the root cause of suicide, contemporaries surely were not surprised that during this period of intense witch-hunting, four people accused of witchcraft killed themselves while in custody in Geneva. In 1547, for example, Perrod Bouloz a farmer in nearby Avussy, was detained and interrogated because he was suspected of being responsible, through witchcraft, for the sudden deaths over several years of at least two people and a number of heads of livestock. Bouloz refused to confess to sorcery even under torture. Held prisoner in a private home, Bouloz managed to get hold of a knife and stabbed himself five times, dying four hours later. Before expiring, Bouloz begged God for mercy and on one occasion screamed, "Devil, get away from me."[11] Although he had emphatically denied under torture that the devil was his master, Bouloz nonetheless associated self-murder with diabolical possession.

Demon possession was also alleged in the suicide of Jean Jourdain, 26, who took his life in 1555 because he was upset on three counts: He was distraught that he had contracted venereal disease, for which he could not afford medical treatment; he felt guilty for having passed this illness to his sister (though no evidence suggests that he was guilty of incest); and he was especially worried about having to appear before the Consistory of the village of Thonon because of his fornication. On a Sunday morning, rather than going to church, Jourdain went into the woods to kill himself. Immediately after stabbing himself, Jourdain heard the ringing of the church bell. Feeling remorse, he asked forgiveness from God and walked to a nearby village, where he survived another eight days. The most important question asked of the dying Jourdain was whether he had given himself to the devil or heard a voice in the woods. Jourdain replied that he had indeed asked the devil to come kill him. He heard no voice, however, and the devil did not put Jourdain out of his misery.[12] This testimony suggests that even suicides themselves assumed that "self-murder" was under the purview of the devil.

Even when witnesses mentioned mental illness as the possible cause of suicide, it was not as yet dissociated from demon possession. This should come as no surprise, as a host of theologians from the Reformation era, both Protestant and Catholic, saw "melancholy" and other mental infirmities as resulting directly from diabolical possession. Moreover, various historians see a dramatic increase in the incidence of melancholy during the Reformation, which they attribute to Protestant and Catholic preachers' obsessive warnings against sin, damnation, and Satanic possession.[13] In Geneva the rather wealthy Elisabeth Paschal had been mentally deranged for several weeks before committing suicide in November 1625. Often incoherent, Paschal repeatedly said she felt possessed by demons and was frequently so violent, swearing and occasionally even biting those around her, that she dared not be left alone. A witness reported that several days before her death Paschal declared that "the evil spirit wanted to make her kill herself and she prayed to God to protect her from it." One evening, after reading from the Bible, Paschal managed to jump out a window to her death, despite the efforts of her niece and chambermaid to restrain her. A fascinating document in this criminal proceeding is a report made by Dr. Dauphin, a physician who made numerous house calls over a period of months. In treating her "melancholy," Dauphin resembled more a pastor than a physician, praying with her and asking her to think of God. On one occasion Dauphin was leading her in reciting the Lord's Prayer, and Paschal had trouble getting past the words "lead us not into temptation." When asked why, she replied that the devil was trying to prevent her from praying. In concluding, Dauphin reported he had seen other tragic cases involving people whom God allowed to behave in such a bizarre way that one could not cure the ills of their souls. These cases might be initiated by avarice or some other sin, which produced a corporal illness as "the melancholy humor took root and through its vapor . . . took over the brain."[14] Paschal herself was convinced that the devil possessed her; Dauphin at least agreed that sin was the root cause of her mental illness and seemed to imply that it was divinely rather than diabolically inspired. Although the devil is not mentioned in every investigation of suicides in Reformation Geneva, evidence nonetheless shows that authorities and common folk shared the conviction that suicide was of diabolical origin; prayer was therefore the best medicine.[15]

Throughout the seventeenth century, suicides usually involved people who had been suffering from mental or physical illness for weeks or months before their untimely deaths. Many of these individuals, like Paschal, desperately sought refuge in religion during the difficult weeks prior to their suicides. Religious devotions both at church and in the home were an important part of the daily life of Jean Mermillod, a pastrycook who took his life in February 1644. Mermillod, 35 and evidently a widower, had suffered from melancholy and a feeble spirit for about a year. Witnesses reported that Mermillod was at times furious, having more than once drawn his sword and threatened to kill people. Physicians and surgeons had been treating him during the previous months for "an extraordinary malady." The day before his death, a Tuesday, however, Mermillod appeared most joyous after attending the morning church service. He awoke about five the next morning, sleeping in the same bed with his eldest son, whom he awoke and asked to say the morning prayer. A few minutes later, however, Mermillod shot himself in the chest in his room.[16]

The suicide of a merchant in the late 1670s shows that religion still permeated the daily life of many Genevans at that time. Jacques Rigoumier, 45, was a wealthy jewelry merchant who took his life in March 1679 after suffering periodically from an unspecified physical illness. On March 14, a Friday, Rigoumier went to the morning church service and later asked his servant-girl to let him know when it was time to go to church for afternoon prayers. Testifying to the *auditeur*, the servant expressed no surprise at her master's request, thus indicating that it was not unusual for Rigoumier to attend church twice on a weekday. Early that afternoon he went into a room in his apartment where he read aloud from the Bible for a half hour, a habit that he performed every day. When the servant notified him at 3:30 that it was time for the afternoon prayer service, however, Rigoumier went into his room and fatally shot himself in the head.[17]

Do these cases suggest, as has been argued for Puritan England, that Reformed Protestantism helped stimulate melancholy and that "grief was exacerbated to terror by Calvinist theology"?[18] The suicide of Madeleine Sirau sheds light on this issue. Sirau, 35, the wife of the citizen goldsmith Pierre Sautier, jumped to her death in December 1636 from her upper-storey window after having suffered from alienation of spirit for five months. According to her husband and servant-girl, Sirau actively participated in the daily devotions that her husband led. The night before her death, with their young son present, Sirau's husband read from the Bible and sang Psalms, and she herself said the evening prayer. After the prayer her husband went to bed, leaving Sirau with the servant-girl and their child. Ignoring the servant's entreaties to go to bed, Sirau complained that she had offended God and asked him for forgiveness.[19]

At first glance this testimony concerning Sirau seems to lend credence to the contention that the Reformed faith nurtured guilt feelings in devout believers, ultimately pushing them to despair and suicide. Throughout the sixteenth and seventeenth centuries Sirau came closest to resembling a desperate believer who, aware of her sin, suffered from anxiety and feared that her destiny was reprobation.[20] What is most striking, however, is the fact that so few people reacted in the manner of Sirau, Paschal, and Mermillod. Simply put, suicide was rare in sixteenth- and seventeenth-century Geneva. True, diligent private devotions, church attendance, and Scripture readings ultimately did not prevent this handful of people from taking their lives. If commonly followed by the population at large, however, such practices would have, one would think, a strong deterring effect on suicide. More important, although the widespread belief in diabolical power led to a witchcraft craze in Reformation Europe, the contemporary view that the devil was responsible for suicide—a view expressed, as we have seen, by judicial authorities, witnesses, and even some of the suicides themselves—put a brake on carrying out suicidal impulses. By the time of Rigoumier's death, the devil, although much less visible than in the Reformation era, was still a palpable part of popular religious culture. Geneva's last execution for witchcraft, the diabolical work par excellence, occurred in 1652; its last witchcraft trial occurred in 1681, two years after Rigoumier's death; and we still find references to suicide as diabolical after 1650.[21] In short, even as the widespread belief in diabolical power led to a witchcraft craze in Reformation Europe, the contemporary view that the devil was responsible for suicide served as one of the most important deterrents to taking one's life.

The belief that the devil caused suicide, however, disappeared along with the fear of witchcraft. In 1686 two men believed that God, not the devil, had afflicted them with maladies that eventually pushed them to kill themselves. François Cartier, 48 and a gardener, took his life in January of that year after suffering from hemorrhoids and, for the past two months, from a fever that left him frequently deranged and paranoid. Pastor Dupan, who served as Cartier's minister, reported having consoled Cartier many times during his illness. He declared that Cartier had "a genuine piety and fear of God, with a constant faith and utter confidence in divine mercy, always . . . resigning himself to his will."[22] Because of his illness, Dupan argued, the incoherent Cartier no longer had control of his actions. During lucid moments Cartier even thanked God for the affliction, always assured of his eternal salvation. Dupan described Cartier as a good, hard-working man who attended church on Sundays and was dedicated to his family. The pastor argued that Cartier had not been abandoned by God but had simply succumbed to his illness. He pleaded that Cartier should receive a good Christian burial, claiming that his physical ills and alienation of spirit were of this world—he did not suffer "the rage or despair of the soul."[23] Pastor Dupan was in effect medicalizing this suicide. Not for a moment did he suggest that this suicide could have been diabolical in origin. Similarly, François Dunand of the rural village of Avully drowned himself in September 1686 after suffering from a serious fever. According to his wife, Dunand had stoically said that he had to accept his illness, as it was God's will.[24]

Although quite distinct from the view that suicide was diabolical, this belief that suffering is divinely inflicted also served as an effective deterrent to suicide. From Augustine to Calvin and beyond, theologians warned Christians that they must, like Job, bear hardships patiently and never hasten their own end. Calvin saw no justification for a terminally ill person to end his or her life, even if caused simply by abstaining from eating. The key reason against self-inflicted deaths was, according to Calvin, that since it was God who gave life, only he can take it away. Moreover, Calvin held that one gives better evidence of obedience to God through long suffering than through dying a dozen deaths.[25] Although it did not prevent either Cartier and Dunand from ending their lives, this Calvinist emphasis on the judgmental nature of God effectively deterred self-inflicted deaths in Geneva's population at large; the fear of God's judgment was enough to discourage most Genevans from voluntarily ending their lives.

In any event, the fact remains that suicide was quite rare through the end of the seventeenth century. Certainly there is no evidence to suggest that Calvinistic piety itself contributed to suicidal behavior. On the contrary, evidence indicates that throughout the seventeenth century the religious convictions of Geneva's

Reformed Christians served as one of the most important restraints on suicidal proclivities. Regular church attendance, family devotions, and above all fear of both God and the devil fostered an abhorrence for suicide.

A decidedly more secular atmosphere prevailed, however, after 1750, when Genevans killed themselves in unprecedented numbers. To be sure, eighteenth-century Geneva was still a Reformed republic, and most of its residents were still self-avowed Protestants. Be that as it may, Reformed Christianity did not pervade the everyday lives of Genevans anywhere near the extent that it had during the Reformation. By the late eighteenth century, the Consistory had long lost its ability to require all residents of Geneva to attend church and take communion regularly. More important, although Genevans generally still embraced Protestantism, it played a much less dominant role in shaping mentality than it had in the sixteenth and seventeenth centuries. Like contemporary England, early modern Geneva witnessed the transformation from a religious culture to a religious faith. By the eighteenth century, religion had become one aspect of Genevan culture rather than the very basis of its culture, as had been the case in Calvin's time.[26]

During this "Age of Reason," Genevan intellectuals were more influenced by Enlightened than Calvinist thought. In the first half of the 1700s the jurist and law professor Jean-Jaques Burlamaqui (1694–1748) introduced the discipline of Natural Law at the Genevan Academy. Like earlier jurists, such as Hugo Grotius of Holland (1582–1645) and Samuel Pufendorf (1632–1694) of Germany, Burlamaqui insisted that reason was the ultimate ground on which laws were to be based. In his *Principes du droit naturel* (1747), Burlamaqui described Natural Law as "the rules that reason prescribes for men in order to lead them . . . to true and secure happiness."[27]

The Reformed faith itself assumed a much more "liberal" character, as Geneva's most prominent pastors and theologians appeared influenced more by the *jusnaturalistes* and philosophes than by the thought of Calvin. Jean-Alphonse Turretin (1637–1737) and Jacob Vernet (1698–1789), professors of theology at the Genevan Academy, both gave great importance to reason in defining their religious views. Though rejecting the atheism and deism of various Enlightenment thinkers, Turrettin and Vernet embraced a form of "Enlightened Orthodoxy" or natural theology, accepting only those aspects of the Christian faith that were in accord with reason. Vernet's interest in Natural Law can be seen in his editing Burlamaqui's *Principes du droit politique*, which was published in 1751, three years after Burlamaqui's death. Having spent time in Paris, the pastor Vernet was on familiar, if not always friendly, terms with Voltaire, Rousseau, and Montesquieu. Although he complained about the unbelief of his contemporaries (for which he held the philosophes partly responsible), Vernet was rather evasive on the divinity of Jesus and thus ultimately contributed to the unintentional movement toward Deism that had begun in Geneva with Turretin. Another pastor, Jacob Vernes (1728–1791), who has often been confused with the theologian Vernet, also had close contacts with several philosophes and edited the journal *Choix Littéraire*, which catered to those with Enlightened, though Christian, tastes.[28] By the late eighteenth century, theologians at the Genevan Academy went so far as to deny the Trinity and Incarnation.[29]

Most important with regard to suicide, whereas Calvin had viewed the devil as responsible for self-murder, eighteenth-century educated people in effect killed Satan. Among the various tenets of Christianity, the belief in the devil, whose existence could not be verified through sense experience, was surely among the most difficult to reconcile with the new scientific mentality that came to predominate among eighteenth-century intellectuals.[30] Turretin and Vernet tacitly rejected the very existence of Satan, and Vernet suggested that an eternal hell was irreconcilable with the benevolence of God.[31] Also absent in their theology is the fear of God, so prevalent in Calvinist thought, as Vernet and other pastors stressed the benevolent as opposed to the judgmental side of God. As he and others questioned the traditional belief in an eternal hell, the fear of damnation obviously declined. Significantly, the most fundamental of these new religious trends clearly filtered down. In the second half of the eighteenth century, Reformed authors published works for the religious education of children that made no mention of the devil and emphasized God's love over his wrath.[32] In short, the religious ambience of Geneva of the 1700s reflected "Enlightened" mores as church leaders promoted religious values that seemed better suited than Calvin's for the more secular world in which they lived. Geneva was experiencing in the eighteenth century an important "desacralization" of society, whereby people began downplaying the importance of the supernatural in worldly affairs, seeking rational or scientific explanations in human affairs and natural phenomena.[33]

In passing sentences Genevan authorities reflected the more lenient attitudes towards suicide espoused by eighteenth-century intellectuals. In 1764 Beccaria called for the decriminalization of suicide, and philosophes such as Voltaire and Montesquieu defended the right of individuals to choose death, so long as they acted rationally.[34] Even before the publication of Beccaria's *Crimes and Punishments*, Genevan magistrates in effect decriminalized suicide, even though they still viewed it with abhorrence. Many magistrates no doubt shared Pufendorf's view that suicide was wrong because it violated Natural Law.[35] But eighteenth-century authorities understandably did not punish violators of Natural Law with the same rigor that their sixteenth-century counterparts had shown towards the diabolically possessed. Judicial authorities no longer confiscated the property of suicides, thus removing an incentive for survivors to try to conceal suicides. They also had long ceased desecrating corpses by having them dragged through the streets on a hurdle or impaled and left exposed.[36] By 1792—when a new regime was established, providing citizenship to those who before had simply been residents—the de facto decriminalization became de jure, and magistrates even stopped denying funerary rites to suicides.

By the late eighteenth century, suicide was thoroughly secularized and medicalized. Physicians, *auditeurs*, and witnesses all offered medical explanations as to why people took their lives. This medical concern was not altogether new. Throughout the early modern period we can find cases of physicians trying to treat the "melancholy" of people who eventually took their lives. By the late 1700s, however, Genevans, including the suicides themselves, no longer attributed mental or physical woes to sin, diabolical possession, or divine judgment. This is not to say, however, that eighteenth-century Genevans were entirely secular. But the faith of common folk, like that of Turrettin, Vernet, and Vernes, was less closely tied to the traditions of Calvin. Their testimony no longer reveals much "fear of God," so typical of traditional Calvinism; and many, including people of rather humble backgrounds, were clearly imbued with the spirit of the Enlightenment.

A case in point is the suicide of Jaques Aimé Mellaret, a 22-year-old employed in the watchmaking industry, who shot himself in the head in his room in July 1769. Although he apparently felt quite alone following the deaths of both parents, Mellaret seems to have suffered from a general unhappiness that did not stem from any one cause. At any rate, Mellaret was a very religious young man and an avid reader, as evidenced by the number of printed works which the *auditeur* found on his desk. These included a number of books of devotion but also works that showed a keen interest in the Enlightenment. Included in his reading material was a French translation of poetry by Albrecht von Haller (1708–1777), a physician and native of Bern. Well known among Swiss Enlightenment thinkers, Haller wrote, among other creative works, an epic poem in which he celebrated the natural beauty of Switzerland, which he described as the home of liberty.[37] Also present was an issue of Vernes's journal, *Choix Littéraire*. In that particular issue was an article by Voltaire ("Sur l'Esprit," taken from the *Encyclopédie*) and, appropriately, the "Philosophical Reflections on the Moment of Death" by the French naturalist Buffon.[38]

Of greatest interest, however, is a 15-page manuscript that Mellaret himself wrote just before killing himself. More a treatise than a suicide note, his "Reflections on Suicide" is fascinating and, though a bit rambling, even eloquent. A strong religious theme runs throughout this treatise, in which Mellaret defended the taking of one's life, which, he admitted, at first glance seems revolting and contrary to nature and reason. Mellaret avowed that the desire to live is divinely inspired, stemming from the incertitude the individual faces with regard to his or her destiny:

The Creator acted very wisely by imprinting in our hearts the love of life, hiding from us the Book of Destinies. As a result, we cling to life and, ignoring what will be our destiny when we leave this world, we prefer to put up with pains and chagrins. . . . We have countless examples before us. Regardless of how bitter life can be, humans are so attached to it that even when in the middle of suffering, an old man in the face of death still desires to prolong his life at any price. Where does this come from? It is a result

... of the incertitude of our fate, which always causes people to tremble when faced with the prospect of leaving this world.[39]

Although acknowledging the natural instinct of survival, Mellaret asked why suicide is considered a crime. He concluded that the criminal nature of suicide stems from the fact that we do not give ourselves life. Many argue, therefore that we are no more masters of our lives than of those of our neighbors; killing oneself is therefore just as bad as killing another person. But where does this logic come from? Mellaret rightly insisted that one cannot find this antagonism to suicide in either the Old Testament or the New Testament. Life, he argued, is simply one of the many favors that God has bestowed upon us. As God created us free and made us the masters of nature, life is one of the myriad things over which God has given us dominion.[40]

Mellaret asked rhetorically whether God would punish someone for being too sensitive to "life's calamities." If experiencing excruciating pain from a certain part of the body, would not a sensible person amputate that limb in order to be rid of the pain? According to Mellaret, the same applies to the body and the soul if one becomes unbearable to the other. The forced separation of the soul from the body must not obliterate the former, for the body is simply the recipient in which the soul is placed. The soul will survive the death of the body if its sentiments are pure and its inclination noble and kind, and if "one of the causes of its anxiety was not being able to use its noble faculties for itself or for others."[41] Surely God would not condemn that soul to more punishment than it deserves; he would not place such a soul in the same class as the degraded soul of a totally wicked person.

Needless to say, Mellaret did not believe that God always approved of self-inflicted deaths. He wrote that humans, though sublime as far as the soul is concerned, are base from the point of view of carnal desires. Accordingly, he spoke very disparagingly of the "sensual man" who is totally dominated by base desires. Such a man pursues only frivolous things, which, once attained, leaves his heart no more fulfilled than before, ultimately ruining his health and his character. Having enjoyed hedonistic pleasures, he will experience great pain once his senses are exhausted. In such a state, he cannot even delude himself into thinking that he can find peace and deliver himself from his evils by taking his life. Repose after death can come only to those who have a clear conscience. Mellaret thus clearly believed that God still had a judgmental side.[42]

Yet, Mellaret revealed an affinity for Enlightened thought in his celebration of nature. With religious passion, he sang the praises of nature and, like the philosophes, of God as creator of an ordered, beautiful universe. According to Mellaret, a person who is dominated by the intellect, rather than by animal-like passions, has a real appreciation of nature:

He is enraptured in considering the magnificent spectacle of nature. . . . In getting closer and closer to nature, he feels rejuvenated; his soul acquires a more noble taste than when he pursues vain objects which are the perpetual occupation of the sensual man. He begins to broaden his view. He discovers the beautiful things which until now he had been unaware of. He delves deeper into the secrets of nature. He discovers everywhere the power and infinite goodness of the Creator who displays before his eyes the harmonious vastness of the world; the laughing greenness of meadows, flecked with flowers; the healthy and abundant food that is everywhere available. . . . Transported with admiration and full of love for his Creator, he cries out [with joy].[43]

The sensitive person "lifts up his eyes to the immense azure sky." There he sees the sun, "the most beautiful ornament, whose warmth gives life to plants and revives all of nature and whose splendid light cheers up and revitalizes all beings."[44]

Appropriately, this young watchmaker praised God as the author of order in the universe much as Enlightened thinkers likened God to a clockmaker. For Mellaret, the sensitive person admires the "regular, constant and unvarying" movements of the planets, stars, heavens, and the earth. These planets and stars, which "faithfully following their orbits, without ever straying from them, continually announce to the intelligent man, the boundless power, the admirable wisdom and the immense goodness of a God Creator." Reflective people will be "overjoyed to the point of ecstasy by seeing this beautiful order of creation," their hearts flooded with an inexpressible joy, their souls ennobled. Constantly meditating on the wonders of creation, such people endeavor to perfect their "noble faculties" by imitating the "perfect Being."[45]

All told, Mellaret was inspired by Enlightenment thought strongly tempered by Christianity. The young artisan ended his "Reflections on Suicide" with a lengthy prayer. Invoking the name of Jesus Christ, Mellaret asked for God's compassion, acknowledging his faults and also his fears concerning the life to come. Begging for mercy, Mellaret besought God "to efface my transgressions and my hidden faults with the blood that cries for grace for us." In begging for mercy, however, Mellaret also reminded God of his good side: "Lord, if the extent of my loathing of life pushes me to this point, you know, Lord, . . . the integrity of my heart. . . . Oh, Lord, will your goodness be offended by the great desire that I have to leave this world? I do this not out of scorn for life. On the contrary, I thank you for giving me a soul that was capable of knowing you and of lifting itself up to you." Mellaret celebrated above all God as creator of nature and the universe, emphasizing his goodness over his power: "It is your goodness that has guided your power. It is you who keeps the sun, that blazing star, to stay at the center and orders it not to stray from it. You determine the limits of the waves of the sea, preventing them from passing beyond. From the shores of the Tagus to the banks of the Ganges, from one end of the universe to the other, is manifest the greatness of your marvelous deeds which shine everywhere to the eyes of the attentive man."[46] Begging God, his "tender Father" not to be angry, Mellaret wrote his last words: "My Lord, I submit to your judgment. . . . Lord, forgive me; Lord, have mercy. Let yourself be swayed by my prayer that the blood of your Son cleanse me of all sins, that he be my intercessor—hear my prayer!—and servant of almighty God! It is in throwing myself in the arms of Jesus, my Savior, that I implore your mercy."[47]

Simply put, the religious convictions expressed in this treatise are quite different from those of John Calvin. Although there is an element of the fear of God in these words, Mellaret concentrated much more on the benevolent than the judgmental side of God. Not depicted as the remote clockmaker described by some philosophes, God appears as the compassionate creator of a beautiful world and the author of natural order. With some misgivings about the afterlife, Mellaret convinced himself that God's love was greater than his wrath. In short, although Mellaret's values can hardly be described as entirely secular, his religious convictions were quite different from those of earlier generations. His religion—and that of other contemporaries—did not offer much of a deterrent to suicide.

Another watchmaker with strong literary interests was Pierre Dombre, 47, who committed suicide in June 1787. Dombre was a very cultivated man and an amateur poet who left behind many writings that revealed the causes of his despair. He complained of being a victim of technological change: The component he had manufactured had become obsolete, subjecting him to a life of poverty. He also bitterly criticized his estranged wife, whom he accused of adultery, and bemoaned the fact that he was now hopelessly in love with an unidentified married woman who had rejected his overtures. Although Dombre, unlike Mellaret, was more absorbed with mundane concerns than religion, he nonetheless composed a prayer shortly before pulling the trigger. In words that resonated with Enlightened themes, Dombre wrote:

God or Heavenly Being, Creator and Preserver of all things, have mercy on this soul that is burdened with worries and stifled by the miseries of this life. I have broken the tower in which it has been held captive. In doing this, have I offended you, as people of little faith allege? As you know, how many times have my eyes, filled with tears, eager to see your glory, asked you for death as an act of grace? Today it will all come to an end. And may I be assured that my arm is merely the instrument that carries out your will? The power that animates my soul and moves it is a spirit that emanates from you. If I have not dishonored [this spirit], it will recover its rights.[48]

There is nothing decidedly Christian about this prayer, and the fear of God is all but absent. His generic reference to "God or Heavenly Being" sounds vaguely similar to the Cult of the Supreme Being, celebrated a few years later during the French Revolution. At any rate, the religious sentiments expressed in this last appeal offered little restraint to suicidal tendencies.

To be sure, most Genevans were not as well read and, most likely, not as imbued with Enlightened mentality as Dombre and Mellaret. Still, the claim that traditional Reformed morality nurtured suicidal proclivities could not be farther from the truth. The fear of God, the devil, and damnation served as most effective deterrents to "self-murder." As the experiences of these two watchmakers reveal, "Enlightened" religious convictions and a more secular mentality was not limited to an educated elite. When intellectuals, judicial authorities, and common folk alike dissociated killing oneself from both demon possession and divine judgment, suicide seemed less terrible. Surely the belief that voluntary death simply transgressed Natural Law was much less a deterrent to suicide than the conviction that it was diabolical. When suicide became secularized, medicalized, and decriminalized, exhortations alone proved inadequate in trying to dissuade people from taking their lives.

True, a more secular mentality was not exclusively responsible for the explosion in suicides in the late eighteenth century. The peak in suicides overlapped with a period of economic and political crisis (1785–1798). This crisis hit watchmaking, the largest sector in Geneva's economy, very hard. Suffering from frustrated expectations, watchmakers such as Dombre, heretofore the most affluent artisans, were clearly overrepresented among suicides in the late eighteenth century. Such economic reversals clearly contributed to the explosion in suicide. But the dramatic increase in suicides had begun during the previous three decades, an era of unprecedented economic growth. Moreover, the more severe economic crisis of the 1690s had not resulted in any suicides at all.[49] The *auditeurs*' reports and postmortem inventories of suicides' estates suggest further that only one-fifth of post-1750 suicides were financially distressed. And although the poor were overrepresented among suicides throughout the early modern period, the percentage of suicides who were poor actually declined in the late eighteenth century.

In addition to financial reversals, frequently cited motives for suicide were the loss of loved ones and, most commonly, mental and physical illnesses. But Genevans of earlier generations had endured similar travails without taking their lives. Why were people of the late 1700s so much more willing to commit suicide for these and other reasons? Surely the decline in influence of traditional Calvinist piety and the rise of an increasingly secular atmosphere in Geneva were among the most fundamental factors. In killing the devil, early modern Genevans unwittingly gave life to suicidal tendencies.

NOTES

1. *Suicide: A Case Study in Sociology*, trans. John A. Spaulding and George Simpson, ed. George Simpson (New York: Free Press, 1951), 152–164.

2. Maurice Halbwachs, *Les causes du suicide* (Paris: Félix Alcan, 1930), 261–283.

3. Markus Schär, *Seelennöte der Untertanen: Selbstmord, Melancholie und Religion im Alten Zürich, 1500–1800* (Zürich: Chronos, 1985).

4. S. E. Sprott, *The English Debate on Suicide from Donne to Hume* (La Salle, IL: Open Court, 1961), 29–54. Jean Delumeau, *Sin and Fear: The Emergence of a Western Guilt Culture, 13th–18th Centuries*, trans. Eric Nicholson (New York: St. Martin's Press, 1990), 554, also contends that the Puritan doctrine of predestination was largely responsible for the high incidence of "religious melancholy" in seventeenth-century England.

5. Two authors have already published some very interesting work on suicide in early modern Geneva. Employing Durkheimian methodology is Laurent Haeberli, author of "Le suicide à Genève au XVIIIe siècle," in *Pour une histoire qualitative* (Geneva: Presses Universitaires Romandes, 1975), 115–129. More recently, in several articles, Michel Porret has examined suicide from a juridic-medical point of view: "'Je ne suis déjà plus de ce monde': Le Suicide des vieillards à Genève au XVIIe et XVIIIe siècles," in *Le poids des ans. Une histoire de la vieillesse en Suisse Romande*, ed. Geneviève Heller (Lausanne: Editions d'en Bas et Société d'Histoire de la Suisse Romande, 1994), 67–94; "'Je suis bien criminel de vous quitter ainsi,' ou l'adieu des suicidés. L'exemple de Genève au XVIIIe siècle," in *Savoir mourir*, ed. Christiane Montandon-Binet and Alain Montandon (Paris: L'Harmattan, 1993), 38–63; "La 'mort de la belle jeunesse' ou le suicide juvénile a Geneve au XVIIIe siècle," *Gesnerus. Revue suisse d'histoire de la médecine et des sciences naturelles* 49 (1992): 351–369; "Solitude, mélancolie, souffrance: Le Suicide à Genève durant l'Ancien Régime (XVIIe–XVIIIe siècles)," *Cahiers Psychiatriques Genevois* 16 (1994): 9–21.

6. These numbers are noticeably higher than those found by Haeberli, "Suicide à Genève au XVIIIe siècle," 117–118, whose figures are also cited by Porret, "'Mort de la belle jeunesse'," 358; and "Solitude, mélancolie, souffrance," 14. Haeberli discovered 10 suicides for 1650–1700, 42 for 1701–1750, and 248 for 1751–1798. My figures by contrast are 41 for 1542–1650, 22 for 1651–1700, 54 for 1701–1751, and, as noted, 288 for 1751–1798. I was able to uncover more suicides by not relying exclusively on the *Procès Criminels*. It was primarily through reading all the early modern *Livres des Morts* that I was able to identify 3,764 unnatural deaths from 1542 to 1798. For each such death, I investigated to determine whether a *Procès Criminel* was extant and whether mention was made of it in the registers of the Small Council. I was therefore able to identify several suicides for which no criminal proceeding is extant, all but two of which occurred before 1700. Moreover, I avoided relying too heavily on the archives' handwritten *inventaires*, prepared several decades ago by a team of scholars, for the *Procès Criminels*. Some self-inflicted deaths were specifically categorized as suicides, others were listed under generic terms such as "*noyade*" or "*levée de corps*." Putting too much faith in the inventories would thus mean missing a considerable number of suicides.

7. *AEG, RC* 259: 57; Registres du Consistoire 89: 452.

8. Haeberli, "Suicide à Genève au XVIIIe siècle," 116, n. 6; Voltaire, *Correspondence*, ed. Theodore Besterman (Geneva: Institut et Musée Voltaire, 1961), 61: 257.

9. See Michael MacDonald, "The Secularization of Suicide in England 1660–1800," *Past and Present* 111 (1986): 50–100; and Michael MacDonald and Terence R. Murphy, *Sleepless Souls: Suicide in Early Modern England* (Oxford: Clarendon Press, 1990).

10. *AEG*, Procès Criminel (hereafter PC) 983. The desecration of a suicide's corpse by placing it in a barrel which was then dumped in a river had precedents in medieval Europe. J.-C. Schmitt, "Le suicide au Moyen Age," *Annales: E.S.C.* 31 (1976): 12, finds that according to medieval popular religious culture, the barrel was "un moyen de transport des corps et des âmes maudits vers le pays des morts."

11. AEG, PC 2e série 745; *RC* 42: 149, 155. The others who took their lives while imprisoned on suspicion for witchcraft were Genon Chambet (13 November 1567, PC 1441), Jeanne Guarin (6 October 1609, PC 2002, *RC* 106: 185), and Ayma Pelloux (7 October 1615, PC 2292, *RC* 114: 259); E. William Monter, *Witchcraft in France and Switzerland: The Borderlands during the Reformation* (Ithaca, NY: Cornell UP, 1976), 207–215.

12. *AEG*, PC 552; *RC* 50: 23v, 25v, 27-28.

13. Delumeau, *Sin and Fear*; H. C. Erik Midelfort, "Sin, Melancholy, Obsession: Insanity and Culture in 16th Century Germany," in *Understanding Popular Culture: Europe from the Middle Ages to the Nineteenth Century*, ed. Steven L. Kaplan (Berlin: Mouton, 1984), 141.

14. *AEG*, PC 2681bis. By placing the origins of her illness in her sin, Dauphin differs somewhat from German physicians. According to Eric Midelfort, from the mid-sixteenth century the germans increasingly asserted that all diseases were physical in origin and accordingly prescribed humoral treatments, such as bleedings, for patients suffering from melancholy; "Sin, Melancholy, Obsession," 115—125.

15. The fear of diabolism can be seen in the suicide of Marie Chioccio. After being told that her daughter was bewitched, she jumped to her death from a garret in the building in which she lived. Chioccio almost certainly would have been able to tolerate the girl's death more easily than the possibility that the devil possessed her daughter's soul; PC 2e série 2509; Etat Civil (hereafter EC), Livres des Morts (hereafter LM) 34: 137, 20 August 1647; *RC* 146: 119v—120, 140v.

16. *AEG*, PC 2e série 2476; EC, LM 34: 39v, 14 February 1644; *RC* 143: 23v—24, 28.

17. *AEG*, PC 4451; EC, LM 43: 98, 14 March 1679; *RC* 179: 82—83, 91, 95—96.

18. Sprott, *English Debate on Suicide*, 48. Sprott goes on, "A depressive predestinarian who could not feel in his spirit the movement of grace that signified that he was called to salvation might conclude that he was elected to damnation. Why delay death? If grace were wanting, he could not repent. Further sin, in disobedience to God, heaped up future torments"; ibid., 48—49.

19. *AEG*, PC 2e série 2425; *RC* 135: 338.

20. Through the end of the seventeenth century, only one other suicide appeared to be obsessed with his own sinfulness: Abraham Dufour dit Poignant, who jumped off the roof of his home in the nearby village of Cartigny in May 1688. This obsession was tied to the alienation and paranoia that he suffered during the last two weeks of his life; *AEG*, PC 4764. In no case—including those of Dufour dit Poignant, Sirau, and Paschal—is there any mention made of predestination, a tenet that some historians claim contributed strongly to melancholy. No evidence from these suicides suggests that Genevans were bothered by or even thought about the doctrine of predestination. Studying the registers of the Consistory, Robert Kingdon has aptly shown that religion for common folk was more a matter of rituals than theology; "The Geneva Consistory as Established by John Calvin," *On the Way: Occasional Papers of the Wisconsin Conference of the United Church of Christ* 7 (1990): 41. The dispute in 1551 between Calvin and Jerome Bolsec, who attacked the doctrine of predestination, did generate considerable interest among common folk. Although they did not follow the nuances of this theological debate, a few artisans clearly had some idea of the possible implications of the doctrine of predestination, repeating Bolsec's claim that it made God the author of evil. Many of those who sided with Bolsec, however, defended not his theological convictions but his character, insisting that he was an "homme de bien" and the victim of a personal vendetta with Calvin; Kingdon, "Popular Reactions to the Debate between Bolsec and Calvin," in *Calvin: Erbe und Auftrag*, ed. Willem van't Spijker (Kampen: Kok, 1991), 138—145.

21. Michel Porret, *Le crime et ses circonstances. De l'esprit de l'arbitraire au siècle des Lumières selon les réquisitoires des procureurs généraux de Genève* (Geneva: Droz, 1995), 43. In February 1651 Jacques Sollicoffe, 19, the son of an affluent merchant,

stabbed himself after suffering from an illness. He survived for several hours, during which time he told the surgeon who treated his wounds that the devil had pushed him to commit this act; PC 2e série 2534, *RC* 149: 35. Similarly, in August 1669 Claude François Montral, 30, an agricultural laborer, hanged himself in his home in Geneva. Devastated by his death, his wife told the *auditeur* that Montral was not alienated but did occasionally get angry and at times made "winds from his mouth as do possessed people" and acknowledged that he had a brother and sister who had been possessed by demons. Taking these words quite seriously, the Small Council ordered that his assets be confiscated and that his body be dragged on a hurdle through the streets from his home to Champel where it was to be buried; *AEG*, PC 4053; *RC* 169: 311–312.

22. *AEG*, PC 4679.

23. Ibid.; the Small Council allowed Cartier to be buried in the regular cemetery, but without honors; *RC* 186: 23–24.

24. His body was never found, so burial was a moot point; *AEG*, PC 4712; Juridiction Civile F 212.

25. Jeffrey R. Watt, "Calvin on Suicide" (paper delivered at the Sixteenth Century Studies Conference, San Francisco, 27 October 1995).

26. C. John Sommerville, *The Secularization of Early Modern England: From Religious Culture to Religious Faith* (New York: Oxford UP, 1992), 9, 16–17.

27. Jean de Senarclens, "Les Écrivains politiques," in *Encyclopédie de Genève*, vol. 4, *Les Institutions politiques, judiciaires et militaires*, ed. Bernard Lescaze and Françoise Hirsch (Geneva: Association de l'Encyclopédie de Genève, 1985), 190.

28. Published in Geneva during the years 1755–1760, *Choix Littéraire* published the works of Protestant and Catholic authors, rejecting the atheism associated with some philosophes; Michel Porret, "Mourir l'âme angoissée: Les 'Reflexions sur le suicide' de l'horloger genevois J.-J. Mellaret (1769)," *Revue d'histoire moderne et contemporaine* 42 (1995): 81, n. 46.

29. Graham Gargett, *Jacob Vernet, Geneva and the Philosophes* (Oxford: Voltaire Foundation, 1994); Martin I. Klauber, *Between Reformed Scholasticism and Pan-Protestantism: Jean-Alphonse Turretin (1671–1737) and Enlightened Orthodoxy at the Academy of Geneva* (Selinsgrove, PA: Susquehanna UP, 1994). See also Martin I. Klauber, "The Eclipse of Reformed Scholasticism in Eighteenth-Century Geneva: Natural Theology from Jean-Alphonse Turretin to Jacob Vernet," Chapter 7 in this volume.

30. Jeffrey Burton Russell, *Mephistopheles: The Devil in the Modern World* (Ithaca, NY: Cornell UP, 1986), 128–131, 149.

31. Gargett, *Jacob Vernet*, 144–151.

32. In the 1770s the Zuricher Johann Rudolf Schellenberg published two volumes of illustrated Bible stories, which were immediately translated into French. Intended for young children, these stories too show a change in focus from earlier pedagogical religious works. There is still an element of the fear of God—most notable are examples from the Old Testament of the punishing of those who abandoned God, but quite evident is God's love, aptly portrayed in a picture of Jesus blessing children. Significantly, no image of or reference to the devil is found in either volume. Satan's absence, even in the depiction of the self-inflicted death of Saul, reflected the influence of rationalism; Max Engammare, "De la peur à la crainte. Un jeu subtil dans le premier recueil d'images bibliques composé à l'usage de jeunes enfants (1774–1779)," in *La peur au XVIIIe siècle. Discours, représentations, pratiques*, ed. Jacques Berchtold and Michel Porret (Geneva: Droz, 1994), 19–43.

33. See Michael Heyd, *Between Orthodoxy and the Enlightenment: Jean-Robert Chouet and the Introduction of Cartesian Science in the Academy of Geneva* (The Hague: Martinus Nijhoff, 1982), 9—10; Michel Vovelle, *Piété baroque et déchristianisation en Provence au XVIIIe siècle. Les attitudes devant la mort d'après les clauses de testaments* (Paris: Plon, 1973).

34. Cesare Beccaria, *Dei delitti e delle pene*, ed. Franco Venturi (Milan: Arnoldo Mondadori, 1991), 85—88; John McManners, *Death and the Enlightenment: Changing Attitudes to Death in Eighteenth-Century France* (Oxford: Oxford UP, 1981), 409—437.

35. Citing a wide variety of authors, primarily from ancient Rome and Greece, Pufendorf condemned those who took their lives "from mere weariness of the troubles common to life, or from disgust at the evils which would have made them objects of the scorn of society, or from fear of trials which they might have borne with fortitude . . . ." Pufendorf, however, did not issue a blanket condemnation of suicide. He condoned the self-inflicted deaths of Cato, Saul, and Samson and insisted that people who were ill and had lost the use of their reason were not guilty of suicide; *De Jure Naturae et Gentium Libri Octo*, trans. C. H. Oldfather and W. A. Oldfather, The Classics of International Law, No. 17 (Oxford: Clarendon Press, 1934), vol. 2: Book 2, Chapter 4, "The Duties of Man towards Himself," 262.

36. Only once in the entire century (in 1732) did the Small Council order the desecration of the corpse of a suicide that of a woman who hanged herself in prison after confessing to theft. She was also the last suicide whose assets were confiscated; *AEG*, PC 7890. Only three other times after 1650 did Genevan authorities order the bodies of suicides dragged through the streets, and only six other times after 1650 did the Small Council confiscate or impose fines on the estates of suicides. The last argument in favor of confiscating the property of a suicide was made by the *Procureur général* Martine in 1738 in response to the suicide of the wealthy publisher Jean-Alphonse Pelissari. In making his case, Martine referred to many ancient and modern authors, including Pufendorf. In the end, the Small Council accepted Pelissari's heirs' proposal to donate to the hospital 10,000 florins from his estate in lieu of total confiscation. This donation—tantamount to a fine for the suicide—was the last time any money was transferred from the estate of a suicide to the Republic. In effect, this marked the last punishment, apart from the denial of funerary honors, imposed on a suicide; AEG, PC 8581; RC 238: 437—438. Pelissari was also the best example of a suicide that may have been religiously inspired. Pelissari suffered intense feelings of guilt for sins that he believed could not be forgiven. This, however, was one of a very few suicides for the entire early modern period, and the only one for the eighteenth century, that appear to support Schär's analysis. In this case, witnesses make no mention either of the devil or of the doctrine of predestination.

37. *AEG*, PC 11902; Porret, "Mourir l'âme angoissée," 81, n.45.

38. In Buffon's article, Mellaret could have read that death "n'est pas une chose aussi terrible que nous l'imaginons, nous la jugeons male de loin, c'est un spectre qui nous épouvante à une certaine distance, et qui disparaît lorsqu'on vient en approcher de près"; *Choix Littéraire* 4 (1755): 200; cited in Porret, "Mourir l'âme angoissée," 81, n.46—47.

39. *AEG*, PC 11902.

40. Ibid.

41. Ibid.

42. Ibid.

43. Ibid.

44. Ibid.

45. Ibid.

46. Ibid.

47. Ibid.

48. *AEG*, PC 15188.

49. Anne-Marie Piuz, "Chertés et disettes," in *L'Économie genevoise, de la Réforme à la fin de l'Ancien Régime, XVIe—XVIIIe siècles*, ed. Anne-Marie Piuz and Liliane Mottu-Weber (Geneva: *SHAG*, 1990), 372—378; Liliane Mottu-Weber, "Les activités manufacturières," in ibid., 423—499; Mottu-Weber, "La Conjoncture de l'économie genevoise, XVIe—XVIIIe siècles," in ibid., 615—648; cf. Haeberli, "Suicide à Genève au XVIIIe siècle," 122.

7

The Eclipse of Reformed Scholasticism in Eighteenth-Century Geneva: Natural Theology from Jean-Alphonse Turretin to Jacob Vernet

Martin I. Klauber

The scholastic method in theological discourse developed out of the adaptation of Aristotelian terminology and philosophy in Western Christian thought. Scholasticism became the dominant method for theological instruction until the seventeenth century. In spite of the Reformation reaction against many aspects of scholastic thought, by the end of the sixteenth century, Protestant theologians faced many of the same conflicts between philosophy and theology as had their medieval predecessors. According to Richard A. Muller, Protestant scholasticism became the dominant organizational approach to teaching theology in the academies. Muller uses "scholasticism" to refer to the locus method of teaching theology and "Reformed orthodoxy" to refer to the specific teachings of the Reformed movement.[1]

By the mid-eighteenth century the triumph of reason over revelation succeeded in dismantling the scholastic method. In Geneva the eclipse of the scholastic method was achieved through the work of key members of the theology department at the Academy of Geneva. One of the most important aspects of the use of reason in theological discourse was an expanded use of natural theology. Natural theology was important because it provided common ground for discussion with the unbeliever or the deist. It was the least objectionable form of revelation and helped to make Christianity a reasonable faith. The most important members of the department who led the movement against Reformed scholasticism and toward an expanded use of general revelation were Jean-Alphonse Turretin (1671—1737)[2] and his successor to the theology chair, Jacob Vernet (1698—1789).[3]

Jean-Alphonse Turretin was the third in a line of theology professors at the Genevan Academy, following his grandfather, Bénédict (1588—1631) and his father, Francis (1623—1687), the famed Reformed scholastic theologian. Jean-Alphonse was educated at the Genevan Academy and became the pastor of the Italian congregation in Geneva in 1693. He joined the theological faculty in 1697 as professor of church history and later, in 1701, was named rector. He assumed the post of professor of theology in 1705. His father was the leader in attempting to protect Reformed scholasticism through the Helvetic Formula Consensus (1675).[4] Jean-Alphonse, however, undermined his father's ministry through the abrogation of the Formula in 1706.[5] Jean-Alphonse championed an approach to theology known as Enlightened Orthodoxy. This was an approach that emphasized the practical nature of the faith devoid of the speculative aspects of scholasticism. The Enlightened Orthodox theologians attempted to maintain only those aspects of the faith that squared with reason.[6]

Jacob Vernet was one of the last theologians at the Genevan Academy to defend the vestiges of Reformed orthodoxy. Vernet's family came from the Provence region of France and his father was a second-generation member of the Genevan bourgeoisie. Vernet was professor of belles lettres from 1739 to 1755 and then professor of theology from 1756 until his death. As Turretin's protégé, he attempted to carry on the tradition of Enlightened Orthodoxy.[7]

Jean-Alphonse Turretin built an apologetic system designed to convince the unbeliever of the reasonableness of the Christian faith. Turretin was critical of Reformed scholasticism because of its divisiveness and its emphasis on the fine points of theology over personal piety. He ignored many of the traditional points of Reformed theology, including predestination, reprobation, the specific nature of divine decrees, and the use of detailed theological creeds to which ordinands were required to subscribe. He preferred a practical system, reminiscent of Erasmus, and highlighted the clear, ethical teachings of Christ.[8]

Turretin's theology focused primarily on the practical advantages of the Christian faith and had much more affinity with the Socinian-Remonstrant tradition than the tradition of Calvin.[9] Reason was the primary judge of religious truth and the distinctive mysteries of the faith such as the Trinity and the Incarnation of Christ were maintained but not explained in any detail. Turretin's successors among the theological faculty at Geneva, led by Vernet, refused to speculate at all concerning biblical mysteries and, in their discussions of the nature of Christ, would not even use the language of the early ecumenical councils. It is not surprising, therefore, that many of the *philosophes* accused them of Socinianism.[10]

Turretin was a founder of this new Enlightened Orthodoxy, which relied heavily upon rational investigation. He used natural theology to a much greater extent than did his scholastic predecessors, as he tried to establish a rational basis for the Christian faith. Concerning special revelation, he employed external arguments based upon rational proofs to establish the divine origin of Scripture. He thereby provided a more rational footing for the doctrine of salvation and virtually made saving faith the equivalent of intellectual assent to the fundamental doctrines. He wrote: "The Holy Spirit does not work in us blindly, but through reasons presented in the mind. . . . Without this our faith would be mere enthusiasm."[11]

As a result of this enlarged role of natural theology, special revelation was less important for Turretin than for any of his scholastic predecessors in Geneva. Although he viewed the Bible as coming from God, Turretin limited the extent to which it could regulate Christian doctrine. One should not insist upon explicit definitions of predestination, for example, because the Bible does not clearly teach its technical aspects. One should maintain only those doctrines that are clear and necessary for salvation. As a result Turretin failed to insist upon most of the doctrines that made Reformed theology distinct from other forms of Protestant thought. This did not alarm Turretin, however, because he believed that the scholastic insistence upon minute definitions of dogma served only to cause schism and discord between the various Protestant sects.

The main source for Turretin's views on the subject of natural theology is his treatise *Theses de theologia naturali*, which makes up the first volume of his *Opera omnia*.[12] This work is divided into several sections: the existence of God, the attributes of God, the providence of God, human freedom, natural law, and the immortality of the soul.

One of the most significant aspects of Turretin's work on special revelation is his extensive use of classical, rather than Christian, authorities. His favorite sources were the great rhetoricians of Rome, Cicero (36 citations) and Seneca (26 citations). Turretin's repeated use of such authors shows his disdain for the scholastics and his humanistic shaping of the Christian faith. It is important to note that he cited Aristotle only once in this treatise and referred to the Church Fathers sparingly. In fact, the only Fathers that he cited were Ambrose (2 citations) and Tertullian (1 citation). He was thereby able to establish a common starting point with the Deist or atheist who preferred classical over Christian authorities.

Turretin's evidence for the existence of God centered on the traditional cosmological and teleological arguments. He did not assume any innate knowledge of God; instead he maintained that such knowledge must be demonstrated so that different rational inquirers would independently come to the same conclusion. As long as one reasonably examines the evidence, one will come to the conclusion that God does, indeed, exist. The first proof was the cosmological argument that posits an "uncaused cause" or a "necessary being" as the creator. Since an infinite regress of contingent beings cannot exist in reality, an original, noncontingent being must have made the world.[13] A second proof for God's existence was the teleological argument. Turretin assumed that the first premise of true religion is the existence of a perfect, infinite being. Arguing that God clearly reveals himself through creation, Turretin countered the claims of the skeptics and atheists against the self-evidence of God's existence. All one has to do, he argued, is to observe the world around us in order to recognize the handiwork as that of a wise master artisan.[14]

That the libertines questioned the existence of God led Turretin to ask how it was possible for one not to recognize the creation as the work of God. He began his argument by comparing the created order to an intricate clock. As one observes the clock, one immediately notices the movement of its hands and the ringing of the bell at regular intervals. Inspecting the inner workings, the observer has to ask himself how the machine got there. Turretin asserted that the possibility of such a complicated machine arising accidentally without any wise creator would be remote. Therefore, a rational being must have created it. Interestingly enough, Turretin employed this argument of the clock in proving the nature of God as well as his existence.[15]

Turretin asserted that the arguments of the atheists and libertines would lead one to the ridiculous conclusion that works of art do not exist. If all the great creations of the world were the work of chance, one could never recognize beauty. In fact, there would be no such concept as beauty. Turretin was mocking the skeptics here because the concept of beauty is universally accepted.[16]

Closely related to the argument from design is the proof for the existence of God based on causality. Turretin posited that it is clear that an intelligent being created the world because the face of the universe is filled with a series of essential causes that seemingly bear no relationship to one another. However, the result of such causes is a system that reflects the necessity of design. He concluded that it is therefore certain that the universe is the work of an intelligent master artisan. He condemned the arguments of the libertines and atheists as pure folly when they pointed to imperfections within the universe as proof that there could not have been an intelligent creator.[17]

The subject of divine creation of the world in time is an essential topic for establishing the existence of the Christian God. Aristotle's emphasis upon the eternity of the world posed serious problems for medieval scholastic theologians in their attempts to harmonize Aristotelian categories with orthodox theology. Turretin, not being tied to Aristotelianism, argued forcefully for the non-eternity of the world.[18] He used the teleological argument to prove the non-eternity of the cosmos as well. The evidence of design in the world, its order and regularity, points to a creation in time. Turretin wrote: "When we see a beautiful building, who believes that building to have been made by chance motion? When we see a watch, who imagines all those wheels and parts, by which the hours are measured and indicated to have come together by chance motion? When we see a magnificent poem, for example the *Aenead* of Virgil, who dreams that the drops of ink, or the printed characters, have by chance motion so impressed themselves on the paper, as to make that poem?"[19]

Although Cartesianism is evident in these arguments, Turretin's proofs for the existence of God are generally traditional, scholastic arguments. He employed, for example, the Cartesian argument of the power of God to explain the design of the world. Nevertheless, Turretin's use of the cosmological and teleological arguments are scholastic rather than Cartesian. Yet Turretin was neither a Cartesian nor a scholastic; he used whatever arguments suited his purpose, regardless of their philosophical origin.

The next important argument in favor of the existence of God comes from universal consent. The growing awareness of travel literature, which revealed significant differences in religious assumptions among pagan cultures, posed theological problems for seventeenth-century theologians. Turretin, however, merely admitted that, when first discovered by the West, not all the world's cultures advocated the existence of a divine being. He observed that most pagan cultures did believe in God. Turretin explained: "We will pass by the fact, proved by the famous theologian John Ludwig Fabricus, that the atheism of these people has not been completely demonstrated, and here we argue, not the consent of all without exception, but of nearly all. No great exception can be made of a very few, and these very savage."[20]

An important component of Turretin's arguments against atheists, who object to proofs for God's existence, lay in a comparison of systems. Turretin asserted that the beliefs of atheists fail to answer the most basic questions of life and thus serve as an inadequate explanation for the nature of creation and the maintenance of the world order.

The last section of Turretin's treatise on natural theology is devoted to the subject of the immortality of the soul. His arguments on the topic are not original: The difference between the nature of the mind and the nature of the body is evidence that when the body dies, the soul does not necessarily die with it.[21]

Turretin claimed that the nature and perfections of God point to an afterlife. Since God is the all-just, wise and benevolent being and is also all-powerful, naturally he would provide an ultimate judgment upon each individual according to his works.[22] Since God is absolutely perfect, he must contemplate himself with great pleasure and He must love those who attempt to follow after his attributes and detest those who oppose him. It follows that he must render a final judgment because, in this life, many of the wicked prosper while many of the righteous suffer.[23]

The argument in favor of human immortality stems from human conscience. Humankind universally receives a favorable inner feeling from performing good deeds, and self-condemnation from evil ones. Furthermore, since many pious individuals live miserable lives here on earth, the promise of a future reward serves as a great consolation.[24] The promise of eternal rewards for the godly and condemnation for the wicked characterized Turretin's practical and simple approach to theology. He attempted to construct a theological system that was both applicable to Christian living and defensible for the rational inquirer. His treatise on the subject of natural theology was not a mere series of theoretical statements but, a response to specific challenges to Reformed orthodoxy, a response intended to diffuse the atheism of Spinoza and the Deism of Hobbes. In addition, it laid the foundation for an acceptance of special revelation that could counteract the Socinian position on the Trinity.

In his treatise Turretin attempted to establish a non-fideistic apologetic based on reason. His was a theological system intended to support scriptural revelation but prove as much about God as possible without the necessity of resorting to the Bible. In his defense of the divine origin of Scripture, Turretin relied upon non-fideistic proofs. Such an argument difffered greatly from Calvin's approach of assuming the divine origin of the Bible based upon the interior witness of the Spirit of God.

The next generation of Genevan theologians, led by Jacob Vernet, continued Turretin's methodology of advocating a reasonable faith. Vernet was also careful to ensure that no aspect of theology would be objectionable for the Deist or unbeliever. Theological mysteries such as predestination, reprobation, or the relationship between the persons of the Trinity were difficult doctrines to defend because they went beyond the scope of reason. Vernet showed his disdain for scholastic theology by refusing to speculate at all in these areas.

Vernet has gained his reputation among historians for his series of conflicts with the French *philosophes*. He first became acquainted in 1722 with them in his capacity as tutor for the children of a wealthy Parisian family. During his nine years in Paris he took advantage of the rich, intellectual environment and initially had friendly relations with the *philosophes*. Conflicts with them came later in his career after he returned to Geneva. In *Jacob Vernet, Geneva, and the philosophes* (1995) Graham Gargett provides the details of these skirmishes.[25] Gargett argues that Vernet wanted to impress the *philosophes* with his open-mindedness and his use of reason. At the same time Vernet carefully tried to preserve his reputation within Reformed circles in his use of Enlightened orthodoxy. Vernet desired to rid traditional Calvinism of its dogmatic trappings and return to a purer form of biblical theology. Voltaire saw this methodology as leading straight to Deism.[26]

Vernet's major academic accomplishment was his French edition of Turretin's Latin theses on the truth of the Christian religion.[27] From 1730 to 1788 Vernet reedited the *Traité de la vérité de la religion chrétienne* several times and showed his affinity for his mentor's approach to defending the faith. The book is basically an apologetic piece designed to show the reasonableness of the Christian faith. Vernet argued that revelation does not contradict reason but is in accord with it. In his section on biblical revelation, Vernet changed Turretin's title from "The Necessity of Revelation" to "The Usefulness of Revelation" in the second edition of the *Traité*. This change was intended to indicate the importance of natural theology. The "heathen in Africa" who had never heard the gospel could potentially be saved without a specific knowledge of Christ by responding favorably to the revelation that God had given in nature and in conscience.[28]

In this work Vernet asserted that revelation must always be in accord with reason and can never be self-contradictory. Furthermore, special revelation complements natural theology by providing a specific knowledge of the plan of salvation culminating in the work of Christ. One can recognize scriptural revelation as divine by the presence of biblical miracles and fulfilled prophecy.[29] Vernet explained that faith and reason a important aspects of the faith: "These are two torches that God has given to us, and it is necessary to carry one in one hand and the other in the other hand."[30]

An important aspects of the external proofs for the veracity of the Christian faith is the testimony of the Apostles themselves. Vernet argued that Christianity "is not a sort of natural science, that carries its own evidence in itself. . . . It is therefore very important to see, whether in the character and life of those who announce this doctrine [the Apostles], and who attest these facts, that there exists such a thing which belies the sanctity of such a communion, and weakens the force of such a testimony; or whether on the contrary we do not find in both, materials to justify and prove the authority they assume."[31]

Another of Vernet's important works that reflects his reliance upon reason and his expanded use of natural theology was his *Instruction chrétienne*.[32] This particular treatise was designed as a theological primer and therefore provides important insights into Vernet's theological system. At the outset, Vernet argued that the goal of his theological method was to simplify the faith and to reduce divisions among Christians. He believed that the precision of Reformed scholasticism led to theological divisions. The major goal of the truly religious person is to honor God and his commandments because God is the sovereign master of the universe and is infinitely wise. In addition, religion has the utilitarian purpose of leading to personal happiness. Religion also turns us away from the transitory and carefree cares of the world and toward more noble aspirations; it provides strength in times of trouble.[33]

The enemies of true religion are impiety and superstition, which are founded on fables and provide false ideas on the nature of God. Impiety and superstition do not lead to wisdom and do not help promote the good of society. True religion, by contrast, is founded on truth and renders us righteous and happy. Furthermore, the proper fear of God helps us to live virtuously; impiety leads to corruption and the destruction of the family and civil government. Impiety leads to too much emphasis on procuring wealth and earthly gratifications. Note that Vernet focused primarily upon the practical benefits of the Christian faith for the social good, thereby condemning the growing secularization and emphasis upon worldly wealth.[34] In fact, Vernet devoted an entire treatise to his fears of the growth of materialism among Genevans.[35]

Vernet also noted that it does indeed matter which religion one chooses, and that Christianity is based upon reasonable standards. The key question for Vernet was how one can truly know God and follow his will. The first means is by following right reason: Reason is helpful in discovering truth in science and can also help us to discover truth in religion. God can also manifest himself by means of special revelation which is a more certain method of ascertaining divine truth; but Vernet clearly emphasizes that natural theology must be pursued first.[36] Vernet wrote: "Reason is the first torch that God has given man to lead him. It seems to me that one must first consult reason to see what one can discover concerning God and his will. After we have exhausted this means we will see if there is also some other divine revelation which can perfect our natural knowledge."[37] Vernet argued that there are several characteristics determine whether a doctrine or teaching truly comes from God: The doctrine must be reasonable, useful, and one that advances the glory of God and the good of humanity.

Vernet went on to list several traditional proofs for God's existence starting with the argument of first causes. Since there are animate beings in the world that are not eternal, he wrote, there must logically have been an eternal and intelligent being as the first, uncaused cause. Further, the order of the world indicates an intelligent creator. Here, like Turretin, he used the traditional illustration of the relationship between the clock and the clockmaker: It is difficult to imagine a clock being made by chance; a wise clockmaker must have put it together. Creation could not have come by chance or through some cataclysmic event. Thinking beings must have derived their existence from a being of the same nature. And it is impossible to have an infinite regress of causes, God must have been the creator. Vernet called this first cause the efficient cause, using the language of the scholastics.[38]

The next major proof for the existence of God comes from conscience. Vernet asserted that reason and justice regulate our judgments and actions. Conscience is defined as reason applied to morality to help us discern the good from the bad, the just from the unjust. It provides us with the basic notion of honoring our creator and respecting divine truth. Reason and conscience, furthermore, are natural to humanity and are not acquired though education. All peoples have the same basic notions of right and wrong. These principles are engraved upon the human spirit. Truth and justice are supported by such strong universal evidence that they cannot be contradicted. An intelligent author must have provided us with this inherent knowledge. At the same time, conscience is necessary to lead us through life and to prevent chaos from reigning in society.[39]

In his discussion on natural law, Vernet wrote that reason is given to us by God and leads us to right conduct. Morality, being common to all peoples, provides the basis for civil government. Indeed, human society is most tranquil and agreeable when its citizens are just, religious, and faithful to their promises. Proper respect for God is an important foundation for a good society.[40] In addition, since human beings are reasoning creatures, reason must show what is just and good. And because God is the ultimate author both of reason and of conscience, we are obligated to obey natural law. Vernet defined law as the imposition of the will of a superior being upon an inferior being. Since God is the supreme being, his will is infinitely respectable.

In his *Instruction chrétienne* Vernet argued that natural theology can tell us much about life after death. We can recognize the incorruptible nature of the soul, which cannot be just material because of such qualities as intelligence, sensibility, and freedom. Vernet concluded that when a person dies, the material body changes its form. Since the soul has no form, it changes in its qualities but does not perish in its substance.[41] Furthermore, the moral law provides the assurance of eternal rewards and punishments. All peoples agree that the soul survives the body and that there are eternal punishments and rewards. This universal consent shows that immortality is a reasonable idea.[42]

Vernet emphasized the supreme fairness of God in the final judgment. Without providing details on the nature of hell, Vernet argued that any ultimate punishment is in direct proportion to the deeds of the individual. To describe what form this punishment may take is useless; we should simply trust that God will be fair. Vernet denied the existence of a literal hell, arguing that it might simply be separation from God, with no literal flames of torture. Nowhere did Vernet elaborate on election or reprobation in his discussion of the final judgment.[43] At the same time he argued that God's final judgment is beneficial to society: It serves as a motivation for good citizens to behave properly and is a deterrent to crime. Also, the poor and suffering people may look forward to better times in eternity. Any reasonable person would agree with these benefits.[44]

Vernet concluded that general revelation was sufficient for humankind in a state of innocence. After the Fall, special revelation was necessary to provide the specific details of the plan of salvation. Special revelation also helps to prevent humanity from falling into idolatry, barbarous ceremonies and superstitions.[45] Special revelation, teaches us divine truth in more specific terms. It is useful to help the common people understand what God wants us to know about him. Natural revelation does not teach us everything about God. For example, natural theology tells us that God is the creator, but it does not teach the manner in which God created. Another example is prayer: Natural theology teaches us to honor God, but not the way we should pray or worship. Special revelation prevents us from worshipping in bizarre and idolatrous ways.[46]

Like Turretin, Vernet expanded his system of natural theology to include as much as possible about God without resorting to special revelation. Vernet's rationalism dominated his entire theological system. Both Turretin and Vernet claimed that natural theology is the necessary prerequisite for special revelation. Natural theology became the common ground with the deist or rational observer who would note that the Christian faith is indeed reasonable.

Desiring a return to the purity of the pre-Nicean era, Vernet argued that "true Christianity had become overlaid with additions and accretions and that it must be restored to its original simplicity."[47] He went on to demean the importance of the ecumenical councils that had given the specific theological language defining the Trinity. Further, he denied the validity of post biblical miracles, thereby providing even more rational footing for Christianity. In doing so he followed the example of Turretin, who argued that God performs miracles in only rare instances.[48] The rejection of the decisions of the ecumenical councils clarifies Vernet's weak position on the Trinity. In the *Instruction chrétienne*, he asserted that the councils represented merely the opinions of the principal bishops rather than the views of individual churches or the church at large.[49] Any talk of Christ's being consubstantial with the Father, therefore, merely represented the opinions of certain fourth-century bishops.

Vernet's theological system was freed from the rigors of scholastic methodology and lacked the precision that the scholastic framework provided.

Consequently, his statements on the Trinity were unclear and left open the possibility of charges of Socinianism. Vernet followed Turretin's system of subjecting the Christian faith to the demands of reason and thereby accepted the same presupposition as the *philosophes*. As a result, Vernet emphasized the ethical and social benefits of the Christian faith and virtually ignored the potentially objectionable aspects of the faith such as predestination and even the doctrine of the Trinity.

It is not surprising that Vernet's successors moved even further away from Trinitarian theology. By 1814 the revised Genevan catechism neglected to proclaim the traditional doctrines of redemption and the divinity of Christ, preferring to envision Jesus as the first born of all creation who should be honored, but certainly not worshipped. Through Turretin's and Vernet's monumental theological development Genevan identity had quietly and consistently dissolved its reliance on Reformation confessions and polity. In an effort to be relevant, practical, and in their own way speak of the beauty of the Christian faith, they discovered a moral high ground that would provide space for even the greatest Deist thinkers. The theological tenets Turretin and Vernet designed offered a means for a stable and just society that kept the pitfalls of unbridled reason and materialistic enterprise in check. Yet in the very year of Vernet's death (1789), much larger forces would soon engulf all Europe in a final test of the ideas developed in eighteenth-century Europe.

NOTES

1. One of Muller's major contributions is his definition of scholasticism which stresses the organization of theology rather than its specific content. Muller defines Reformed scholasticism as

a highly technical and logical approach to theological system, according to which each theological topic or *locus* was divided into its component parts, the parts analyzed and then defined in careful propositional form. In addition, this highly technical approach sought to achieve precise definition by debate with adversaries and by use of the Christian tradition as a whole in arguing its doctrines. The form of theological system was adopted to a didactical and polemical model that could move from biblical definition to traditional development of doctrine, to debate with doctrinal adversaries past and present, to theological resolution of the problem. This method is rightly called scholastic both in view of its roots in medieval scholasticism and in view of its intention to provide an adequate technical theology for schools, seminaries and universities. The goal of this method, the dogmatic or doctrinal intention of this theology was to provide the church with "right teaching," literally, "orthodoxy."

He later expands this definition by referring to scholasticism as a whole as "a discipline characteristic of theological systems from the late twelfth through the seventeenth century. Since scholasticism is primarily a method or approach to academic disciplines it is not necessarily allied to any particular philosophical perspective nor does it represent a systematic attachment to or concentration upon any particular doctrine or concept as a key to theological system. Richard A. Muller, *Dictionary of Latin and Greek Theological*

Terms (Grand Rapids, MI: Baker Books, 1985), 8, 18.

It should be noted that Muller's definition of Reformed scholasticism is by no means an innovation. The debate over the term goes all the way back to Maurice DeWulf's attempt to define medieval scholasticism as an adherence to a specific set of doctrines. Muller prefers to use "orthodoxy" to refer to "right teaching" whereas "scholasticism" refers to "the formal theology of the systems and doctrinal compendia developed out of the classroom experience of the academies and universities." Muller, *Christ and the Decree: Christology and Predestination in Reformed Theology from Calvin to Perkins* (Grand Rapids, MI: Baker Books, 1988), 11–12. See also Maurice DeWulf, *L'Introduction à la philosophie néo-scholastique* (Louvain: Institut supérieur de philosophie, 1904).

A host of scholars preceded Muller in arguing for some measure of continuity between Calvin and his followers. A sampling of some of these scholars' works includes: Jill Raitt, *The Eucharistic Theology of Theodore Beza: The Development of Reformed Doctrine* (Chambersburg, PA: American Academy of Religion, 1972); John S. Bray, *Theodore Beza's Doctrine of Predestination* (Nieuwkoop: B. de Graaf, 1975); Olivier Fatio, *Méthode et théologie: Lambert Daneau et les débuts de la scholastique réformée* (Geneva: Droz, 1976); Robert W. Godfrey, "Biblical Authority in the Sixteenth and Seventeenth Centuries: A Question of Transition," in *Scripture and Truth*, ed. Donald A. Carson and John D. Woodbridge (Grand Rapids, MI: Zondervan, 1983), 225–243; and Godfrey, "Tensions Within International Calvinism: The Debate over the Atonement at the Synod of Dort, 1618–1619" (Ph.D. dissertation, Stanford University, 1974). Several other scholars have clearly followed Muller's line of argumentation, including Stephen R. Spencer, "Reformed Scholasticism in Medieval Perspective: Thomas Aquinas and Francis Turrettini on the Incarnation" (Ph.D. dissertation, Michigan State University, 1988); Joel R. Beeke, *Assurance of Faith: Calvin, English Puritanism, and the Dutch Second Reformation* (New York: Peter Lang, 1991). For a fuller analysis of Muller's approach see Martin I. Klauber, "Continuity and Discontinuity in Post-Reformation Reformed Theology: An Evaluation of the Muller Thesis," *Journal of the Evangelical Theological Society* 33–34 (December, 1990): 467–475. See also Carl R. Trueman and Robert S. Clark, *Protestant Scholasticism: Essays in Reassessment* (Carlisle, UK: Paternoster Press, 1997).

2. The only complete biography on Jean-Alphonse Turretin is Eugène de Budé, *Vie de J. A. Turrettini, théologien genevois (1671-1737)* (Lausanne: Georges Bridel, 1880). Budé also edited three volumes of Turretin's correspondence, *Lettres inédites addressés de 1686–1737 J. A. Turretin, théologien genevois*, 3 vols. (Geneva: Jules Carey, 1887). Budé wrote several other biographies that touch on Jean-Alphonse Turretin; among them is his treatment of Bénédict Pictet, Turretin's cousin and colleague on the theological faculty, *Vie de Bénédict Pictet, théologien genevois, 1655–1724* (Lausanne: Georges Bridel, 1874). For a discussion of Turretin's position on natural theology see Michael Heyd, "Un role nouveau pour la science: Jean-Alphonse Turrettini et les débuts de la théologie naturelle Genève," *RTP* 112 (1982): 25–42. Theological analyses include John W. Beardslee III, "Theological Developments at Geneva under Francis and Jean-Alphonse Turretin, 1648–1737" (Ph.D. dissertation, Yale University, 1956); Martin I. Klauber, *Between Reformed Scholasticism and Pan-Protestantism: Jean-Alphonse Turretin (1671-1737) and Enlightened Orthodoxy at the Academy of Geneva* (Selinsgrove, PA: Susquehanna UP, 1994). See Martin I. Klauber and Glenn S. Sunshine, "Jean-Alphonse Turrettini in Biblical Accommodation: Calvinist or Socinian?" *CTJ* (April 1990): 7–27;

Maria-Cristina Pitassi "L'Apologétique Raisonnable de Jean-Alphonse Turrettini," in *Apologétique 1680-1740: Sauvetage or naufrage de la théologie*, ed. Olivier Fatio and Maria Cristina Pitassi (Geneva: Publications de la Faculté de Théologie de l'Université de Genève, 1990): 180—212; Maria-Cristina Pitassi, "Un manuscrit genevois du XVIIIe Siècle: La Refutation du Systeme de Spinosa par Mr. Turrettini," *NAKG* 68 (1988): 180—212.

3. On Vernet see: Eugène de Budé, *Vie de Jacob Vernet, théologien genevois (1698—1789)* (Lausanne: Georges Bridel, 1893); and Graham Gargett, *Jacob Vernet, Geneva and the Philosophes* (Oxford: Voltaire Foundation, 1995).

4. The Helvetic Formula Consensus was initiated in 1675 primarily by three Swiss Reformed theologians, Lucas Gernler, Johann Heinrich Heidegger and Francis Turretin in response to the modified position of the Academy of Saumur to the canons of the Synod of Dort. The most notable of the Saumur theologians was Moïse Amyraut (1596—1664), who proposed "hypothetical universalism," a concept that moderated, in theory, the Reformed doctrine of limited atonement as defined at the Synod of Dort. He maintained that God's redemptive plan includes all humanity, but it cannot be fulfilled unless men and women believe. Since they cannot believe without the power of the Holy Spirit, a second, limited election is necessary for the elect. The basis for such an election is hidden in the counsel of God. Since his concept of hypothetical universalism provided for the salvation of the elect alone, Amyraut believed that his theory would bridge the gap between Reformed and Remonstrant positions on the atonement. Most Reformed theologians, however, rejected his system as the first step toward Arminianism. See Donald D. Grohman, "The Genevan Reaction to the Saumur Doctrine of Hypothetical Universalism: 1635—1685" (Ph.D. dissertation, Knox College, Toronto, 1971); Martin I. Klauber, "The Helvetic Formula Consensus: An Introduction and Translation," *Trinity Journal* (spring 1990): 103—23.

5. See Martin I. Klauber, "Jean-Alphonse Turrettini and the Abrogation of the Formula Consensus in Geneva," *WTJ* 53 (1991): 325—338.

6. See François LaPlanche, "La Bible chez les Réformés," in *Le Siècle des Lumières et la Bible*, ed. Yvon Belval and Dominique Bourel (Paris: Editions Beauchesne, 1986), 459.

7. Charles Borgeaud, *Histoire de l'université de Genève: L'Académie de Calvin, 1559-1798* (Geneva: George & Co., 1900), 550.

8. The primary sources for Turretin's theological system are found in the *Opera omnia theologica, philosophica et philologica*, 3 vols. (Franeker: H. A. de Chalmot et D. Romar, 1774—1776), and in the *Dilucidationes philosophico-theologico-morales, quibus praecipua capita tam theologiae naturalis, quam revelatae demonstrantur ad praxin christianam commendantur accedunt*, 3 vols. (Basel: J. R. Imhoff, 1748). Both works contain Turretin's *Theses de theologia naturali*, the primary source for his views on natural theology, and his *De Veritate religionis Judaicae et Christianae*, in which he discusses his beliefs about special revelation. Both editions also include a series of Turretin's academic orations, his treatise on the essence of Christian belief, *De Articulis fondamentalibus*, and his *De Pyrrhonismo pontifico*, which is a critique of the French Bishop Jacques Bénigne Bossuet's polemics against Protestant theology. The Franeker edition contains Turretin's commentaries on Romans and Thessalonians. In addition, the *BPU* houses several unpublished treatises of Turretin, including his commentary on the Sermon on the Mount, various collections of his sermon notes, and part of his personal correspondence.

9. For more on Turretin's affinity with the Remonstrants, see Martin I. Klauber, "Between Protestant Orthodoxy and Rationalism: Fundamental Articles in the Early Career of Jean LeClerc," *Journal of the History of Ideas* (1993): 611—636.

10. James I. Good, *History of the Swiss Reformed Church since the Reformation* (Philadelphia: Publication and Sunday School Board, 1913), 282—301. One should employ the term *Socinian* with extreme caution. It was often used as a mere epithet to mean heretic, it could also be used to refer to the theological system of Socinus, namely, the excessive use of reason in scriptural interpretation to the point of denying theological mystery such as the Trinity and the Incarnation of Christ. The latter is the meaning here.

11. Turretin, *Dulucidationes*, 2.3.13.

12. I have used the Basel edition of 1748, which is divided into three volumes, the first being Turretin's theses on natural theology. The treatise on natural theology was translated into English by William Crawford in 1778 under the title *Dissertations on Natural Theology* (Belfast: James Magee, 1778). All English quotations follow these translations, with the original Latin footnoted only when deemed essential to the argument.

13. Ibid., 1.2.27.

14. Ibid., 1.2.35—1.3—37; J.-A. Turretin, *L'Existence de Dieu démontrée par la structure de l'univers*, Manuscrits de la Compagnie des Pasteurs, vol. 36, fol. 3, *BPU.*

15. Ibid., fol. 4.

16. Ibid., fols. 6—7.

17. Ibid., fols. 12—14.

18. Turretin, *Dilucidationes*, 1.2.22.

19. Ibid., 1.2.28.

20. Ibid., 1.2.59.

21. Ibid., 1.12.2.

22. Ibid., 1.12.4.

23. Ibid., 1.12.6—17.

24. Ibid., 1.12.8.

25. Secondary works on Vernet assume different perspectives on the Genevan theologian's conflicts with the *philosophes*. Early works assume a positive evaluation of Vernet; the biography written by his grandson, Michel-Jean-Louis Saladin, *Memoire historique sur la vie les ouvrages de Jacob Vernet, ministre de l'Eglise, accompagné de l'Invocation aux Muses, de Montisquieu, et de plusieurs lettres J.-J. Rousseau et Voltaire, qui n'ont pas encore été publiées* (Paris, 1790). This was followed by Jean Gaberel's work *Voltaire et les Genevois* (1857) and his article "Jacob Vernet et ses relations contemporaines," *Etrennes religieuses* 34 (1883): 120—41 and finally by Eugène de Budé's biography of Vernet. The most recent work is Gargett's *Jacob Vernet, Geneva and the Philosophes*, an exhaustive and definitive work that makes excellent use of both printed sources and archival materials to uncover significant holes in previous research. Gargett is highly critical of Vernet for his alleged hypocrisy on a number of issues.

26. Gargett, *Vernet*, 40.

27. Jacob Vernet, *Traité de la verité de la religion chrétienne. Tiré du latin de Mr. J. Alphonse Turretin* (Geneva: M. M. Bousquet, 1730—47).

28. Gargett, *Vernet*, 350.

29. Budé, *Vernet*, 74.

30. Vernet, *Traité de la vérité*, xvi. See also Gargett, *Vernet*, 56.

31. Vernet, *An Argument Concerning the Christian Religion Drawn for the Character of the Founders* (London: Hull, 1800), 2.

32. Jacob Vernet, *Instruction chrétienne*, 5 vols. (Geneva: Henri-Albert Gosse, 1756).

33. Ibid., i, 8—10.

34. Ibid., 12—14.

35. Jacob Vernet, *Réflexions sur les moeurs, sur la religion et sur le culte* (Geneva: Claude Philibert, 1769).

36. Vernet, *Instruction chrétienne*, i, 16.

37. Ibid., 18.

38. Ibid., 20—32.

39. Ibid., 32—39.

40. Ibid., 44—45.

41. Ibid., 50—52.

42. Ibid., 52—54.

43. Ibid., ii, 135—139.

44. Ibid., 140—141.

45. Ibid., i, 61—64.

46. Ibid., 58—62.

47. Gargett, *Vernet*, 55.

48. Turretin, *Dilucidationes*, 1.5.19.

49. Gargett, *Vernet*, 288; cf. Vernet, *Instruction chrétienne*, ii, 371.

8

"Going Soft": Genevan Decadence in the Eighteenth Century

Linda Kirk

Some facts are clear: Geneva prospered for much of the eighteenth century, and material prosperity is a necessary, if not sufficient, condition for the changes in eating, dressing, building, and spending leisure time that we associate with a shift from Spartan values toward the frivolous, the self-indulgent and the idle. We also know that Geneva surrendered to the French and their allies in 1782 without even attempting to fight, and that military defeat is a routine indicator of a state's lapsing into decay. No sooner are these points made, however, than qualifications have to be attached to them: Geneva may have prospered, but this did not prevent some of those who lived there from being miserably poor,[1] nor is it obvious that by the standards of contemporaries, even those furthest advanced in wealth and worldliness had gone far in the direction of decadence. We find an interesting contrast between the comments of visitors, who mostly continued to perceive Geneva as more ordered than wherever they came from,[2] and the lamentations of insiders, for whom the loss of old ways and old standards represented the tarnishing of an ideal. Likewise, Geneva had never expressed nationhood through successful wars of conquest, although the mythic importance of the *Escalade* of 1602 could be read as guaranteeing survival against military odds. We may think Genevans were mistaken in believing that their forebears used to be Godly, sober, hard-working, and successful in war, but their scandalized sorrow at the humiliations of the 1780s is real.

Given these factors, the task of this chapter is two-fold: to explore and itemize some of those changes in Genevans' behavior that can be measured; and also to address the less clear-cut evidence of values and perception, accepting that most cultures lament that things are in decay.[3] This distinction between the measurable and the impressionistic is not, of course, the same as a difference between the material and the cultural: Even indisputably "material" develop-ments, such as changes in diet or building materials, are read by observers and

actors alike as signifiers of status or virtue. The chapter will conclude by
sketching, for eighteenth-century observers, the political implications of a
conviction that Geneva was drifting toward decadence.

Montesquieu's examination of Rome's greatness and decline offers a model
that would have been recognized by many Genevans.[4] His critique was aimed
chiefly at corruption in France; nonetheless, if we check through Montesquieu's
dozen symptoms of terminal decadence, once we have discarded those of which
Geneva was plainly innocent (like depopulation, pauperization, wars of conquest,
excessive size, imperial ambitions, and cruelty), we are left with several whose
barbs catch in the fabric of Genevan life. These are luxury, avarice, hedonism,
the waning of public-spiritedness, faction, and the falling away from the simple
and austere religious practices of earlier days. It immediately becomes clear that
by Montesquieu's rules, most of what had gone wrong in Geneva had to do with
its "spirit." This was no trivial charge: Republics, he taught, were powered by
virtue and without it could not sustain themselves.[5] Through evidence of changes
in material culture, then, we gain a purchase on Montesquieu's categories while
initially, at least, addressing plain data.

How did Genevans earn their living in the eighteenth century? Consuming
while not obviously producing lays people open to the charge of decadence. We
know what a sample of male heads of household did for a living at four separate
periods of the eighteenth century, thanks to the records used for family
reconstitution.[6] Fewer of them, as the century advanced, were engaged in
agriculture and other forms of primary production. We also have a census of
1788 which notes the occupations, broadly categorized, of the 7,500 men it
recorded. By this late date there were scarcely any citizens or bourgeois were
working in the trades "considered base"; the greater number of workers and
servants came almost entirely from outside the city. The near invisibility of
agricultural workers in these figures is no surprise: Only a tiny proportion of
Geneva's surrounding countryside formed part of the city's sovereign territory.
It is striking, however, that few Genevans worked as laborers on the many
building projects of the eighteenth century. The settled population had chosen to
specialize chiefly into the skilled area of watchmaking; contemporaries used the
umbrella-term *Fabrique* to designate the many different workers and workshops,
who together produced the finished watch or clock. *Fabrique* artisans worked
with their hands, certainly, and did not enjoy continuous and unbroken
improvement in their standard of living, but their sector of the economy was
concerned with luxury rather than necessities. Higher up the social scale we find
rentiers, bankers, and financiers who did no visible work at all. By 1780, it has
been estimated, the richest 500 households enjoyed an income of 1,000 florins
a day,[7] a figure that should be contrasted with the workman's daily wage of
often less than 2 florins.

Access to necessities like bread, rent, and clothing represents an irreducible
minimum for the survival of the poorest.[8] Many Genevans lived far more
grandly than this, and surviving household account books reveal that members

of the patriciate enjoyed luxuries like game, exotic fruit, coffee, and chocolate.[9] The taste for ice and chilled foods increased; ice wells were dug to meet the demand.[10] The city's annual consumption of meat per head during the eighteenth century rose to 70 kg, and although most of this found its way to the plates of the rich, some was bought by the less well off; indeed, some went to feed the inmates of the hospital.[11] Annual bread consumption, by contrast, dropped. Not only had Genevans become less dependent upon bread, they had grown accustomed to white wheaten loaf. Dark bread, using a high proportion of rye or bran, was considered an insult to civilized consumers.[12] Another example of refined expectations can be found in the register of the committee of the city's library: In 1726 they were looking for space to expand into, and they argued that a neighboring set of rooms would be ideal. Since no one was living there, the rooms were unheated and therefore free from the risk of fire. Some 50 years later, in April 1773, successor members of the same committee noted that it was impossible to work in the library in winter because it was far too cold. They recommended an inner porch door, a glazed door on the landing, and carpets. Thanks to a sequence of generous legacies, the ammenities were added. Geneva's winters had grown no colder, but Genevans had gone soft.[13]

Magnificent town houses were being built by members of the patriciate like Marc Lullin, Gédéon Mallet, Léonard Buisson, Jean-Robert Tronchin and Pierre and Gaspard Boissier.[14] In 1765 the author of *Princes Manqués* (an anonymous pamphlet) accused J.-R. Tronchin of building himself a palace.[15] The only way of clearing ground for such buildings, in a long-settled urban area, was to buy up and sweep away older, smaller dwellings. Geneva had last demolished houses on this scale in the sixteenth century, when it had razed the suburbs and blocked up the sewers to make taking the city by siege more difficult. This time the object was comfort and display, and the outcome was further to separate the rich from the poor.[16]

Other changes in behavior are recorded at the point where sexual propriety intersects with public life: During the eighteenth century prenuptial conceptions rose. According to one study the proportion of brides who went to their weddings already pregnant rose from 11 to 25 percent.[17] Illegitimate births also increased, admittedly from virtually nil. More couples sought divorce, although the Consistory set its face against divorce by consent.[18] Since the regulations governing divorce remained unchanged, the figures showing a steep increase in the cases per year must give some real indication of marriage breakdown: Something between 1 and 7 applications were made annually from the beginning of the century until 1766, whereas the next three years saw a sudden surge to 12, 13, and 15. In the 1770s figures dropped again to a level like that of the first half of the century, but new peaks were reached in 1779 with 17 (of whom only 7 were allowed to proceed to divorce), 20 in 1781, and 26 in 1791. These raw figures are less startling when set against a population rise over the eighteenth century from under 20,000 in 1700 to some 29,000 in 1790.[19] Magistrates before the eighteenth century would probably not have encountered a couple like the Custozes, who in 1780 were almost 60 years old and married for 32 years: They had nonetheless parted on bad terms and were refusing to be reunited.[20] Known suicide rates also rose: The most recent study agrees with one of some 20 years ago in seeing a startling rise after 1750, peaking in the period 1781—1798 with a figure that resembles those of today.[21]

The long-running contention about the theater had complex resonances. The meanings of plays and players, and Geneva's identification of theatricals with decadence are twined among the bare facts of story. D'Alembert in his *Encyclopédie* article "Genève" had urged the city to allow the establishment of a theater; this would, he argued, encourage citizens to develop subtlety and discrimination and improve their taste. Many of Geneva's lower-class citizens seem, so far as we can judge, to have shared the view Jean-Jacques Rousseau advanced in his reply, the *Lettre à d'Alembert* of 1758: The values of their community would be undermined by permitting such a focus for falsehood, display and pleasure-seeking. In 1711 a troop of actors had been banned from entering the city,[22] but in the 1750s and 1760s many members of the ruling elite succumbed to the attraction of Voltaire's theatricals despite official policy; they then yielded to French pressure for a theater to be built in 1766. In January 1768 this burned down in circumstances the authorities suspected were not accidental. Genevan fire drill brought out citizens to fight the fire, but once they became aware what was burning they decided to go home. Geneva could not prevent a theater from being built on foreign territory just outside the walls so the project continued. In 1722 Samuel Mestrezat begged the Council of Two Hundred to choke the project at birth: Every member of all the councils, indeed every parent in the city, should undertake to stay away and to forbid his family to attend. People, he lamented, were willing to spend on pleasure but not on the poor, nor on the clergy's salaries. He failed: by the 1780s the state of Geneva had lent 9,000 livres to the Theater Company.[23] In 1784 a stone theater was built outside the walls, and the city gates had to be reopened to let late-night revelers back to their beds. Clergy who preached against theatricals in April and September 1784 found themselves examined and reprimanded for political unsoundness.[24] In 1785 William Beckford saw "Genevans' of the old stamp, chewing the cud of sober sermons" seated on a bench at Plainpalais (just outside the city walls), "waiting for their young ones, who had been seduced to the theatre."[25] In April 1787 the Consistory recorded its outrage that theatrical performances were still being given until the Tuesday of Holy Week, presenting a rival attraction to the confirmations taking place just before the Easter Communion, when in 1784 the Council had given its word that the performances would not continue after the Monday.[26] Popular opposition to the theater must have crumbled if these performances were drawing in audiences large enough to make the venture commercially worthwhile.

There are cultures in which a shift like this, taking most of the eighteenth century to complete, would mean little—just one more symptom of modernization or secularization—but Genevans had attached a totemic significance to their refusal to house a theater, and their flocking to see plays in the late 1780s demonstrates the distance not only their laws but their *moeurs* had moved. This was what they themselves had previously categorized as decadence. Similar changes can be charted through successive edicts governing other amusements: In 1749, for instance, the ban on balls and dancing was sustained; in 1772 dancing had to stop at 10 o'clock in the evening; in 1785 it was positively forbidden after midnight; in 1786 dancing masters had to be licensed by the city authorities. Likewise at the beginning of the century playing with cards was forbidden; by the end it was obligatory for playing cards to bear a stamp showing that tax had been paid. On his visit in 1764 James Boswell, a man who understood what Calvinist decency required, "was amused to see card-playing on a Sunday at Geneva, and a minister rampaging amongst them," asking rhetorically of his Journal "O John Calvin, where art thou now?"[27]

Not surprisingly, by the 1760s letters to and from Rousseau yield evidence that many, visitors and local people alike, shared Boswell's view.[28] As late as 1758 Rousseau had been able to gloss his city's prosperity as the deserved product of hard work, explicitly denying that there were vast gaps between the rich and the poor.[29] Once he had fallen foul of the magistracy, his disenchantment was swift.[30] Rousseau then attracted and approved a certain style of gloomy pronouncement against Genevan luxury. His friend, Paul-Claude Moultou, had already declared in a sermon on the theme "we are rich enough and need no more" that corruption was well on the way.[31] Jean Romilly, writing from Paris in May 1763, deplored Geneva's corrupt business practices, including the falsifying of places of production; he blamed Voltaire's having settled nearby for the new laxness in religion and the increased appetite for luxuries. In February 1764 Charles Pictet declared that both the republic's laws and its spirit favored commerce and so led to a torrent of dissipation.[32] Geneva was no longer a fit place to bring up children. Antoine-Jacques Roustan, a pastor, longed to leave in March 1764: The frenzy of getting and spending increased every day, and the city had become a Christian republic where you could not preach virtue.[33] In 1769 Jacob Vernet, no friend of Rousseau's by then, agreed with him that the previous 30 years' luxury, born out of commerce, banking, and annuities, had sapped Geneva's earlier piety, good discipline, hard work, charity, modesty, and steadiness. If people fell sick, their fear was now focused solely on physical recovery and their secular concerns. They were reluctant to go to church and had lost sight of the connection between decency at home and public order. It was, Vernet lamented, the *mollesse,* the softness of the times, that had caused all this. He linked these changes explicitly to the loss of theological rigor; many who liked to be called theists were, he thought, no better than atheists.[34]

It is useful to consider separately the practice and the theology of the church in Geneva. Although the magistracy economized on services and sermons later in the century, Geneva's style of worship remained close to its traditions, stark and casual to the eyes of outside observers. Admittedly, long sermons grew shorter—"not above three quarters of an hour," according to one observer.[35] The rebuilding of St. Pierre did allow the great church to present a classical west front to the world; the excess money raised for this was used to buy an organ, a more formal written liturgy was imposed, and Christmas was still celebrated. Nonetheless, unison singing remained the norm, and the clergy's idea of honorific display mostly limited itself to keeping their hats on when the lay authorities did likewise.[36] Here, at least, Montesquieu's categories did not fit: Little of the city's public religion had abandoned the simplicity and austerity of the past. How far had Geneva's religious teaching itself gone soft? And where it had, what were the effects? New looseness in understanding the Trinity or predestination need not have had a direct effect on people's behavior.

Other doctrines shaped Genevans' conduct more obviously: Was Hell a reality? Were children born tainted by original sin? Could a good pagan be saved? How these issues were understood and expounded in eighteenth-century Geneva continues to be explored.[37] Without doubt the clergy were less and less likely to press the full ferocity of Calvin's teaching upon their congregations. In any event, natural theology and natural morality flowed easily into the thinking of individuals who prided themselves not only on the victory of Scripture over corrupt tradition but also on that of reason over superstition. The pursuit of scientific knowledge appeared to threaten little that was fundamental in a culture that had already learned to laugh at transubstantiation and dismissed as nonsense tales of bowing, speaking or bleeding statues. According to J.-A. Turretin, one of the most deplorable aspects of Roman Catholicism was that it required its adherents to reject the clear light of common sense.[38] Jacob Vernes's short-lived periodical *Choix Littéraire* wooed its readers in the opening volume: Exposing one's mind to contemporary literature not only would make one thoughtful but would demonstrate to the Christian "the accord there is between his reason and his religion."[39] Gabriel Cramer offered a scientific explanation of the fate of Sodom: Perhaps that site had been perched over a sulfurous pit since the beginning of time, and God foresaw that at just the right moment a pebble would strike a spark to detonate the catastrophe.[40] Scientists also questioned traditional orthodoxies about, for instance, predestination and hell. Charles Bonnet, the naturalist, recalled discussions in a literary group about free will, determinism, and a version of hell that sounds uncommonly like purgatory: The pains, thought Gabriel Cramer, might well fit one for heaven, and how could the good Father shut the gates of heaven to someone once healed and worthy of admission?[41]

The 1543 *Liturgy* made much of the risk of the devil's seizing his chance in a sick person's last hours; eighteenth-century official prayers ask God to heal and spare if it is his will to do so, but if not, to receive the invalid's spirit into his hands or to welcome the poor soul into paradise. The devil seems to have disappeared. In his *Dissertation on Natural Theology* Turrettin ridiculed the notion that "God hath formed the greatest part of mankind in order to consign them to eternal misery."[42] Jean-Louis du Pan noted in 1762 that "when we were young they taught us that Jesus Christ came to save us from the punishment for original sin, that the water at baptism washed us free from it," but that these doctrines were no longer taught.[43] Moultou assured Rousseau in 1761 that so long as the dogmas essential to the moral order were respected, he for one would not make difficulties about the rest of the church's teaching.[44] A recent study of sermons preached to and about children has found a distinct shift in attitudes around 1750: Earlier preachers saw children's natures as actually or potentially wicked; those of the second half of the century supposed that they were naturally good.[45] Less fear, less discipline, and less expectation that God's justice will seek out the hidden faults that escape the eyes of one's neighbors,[46] all these changes need not undermine morality, but they make it increasingly likely that hard choices will be considered and resolved before the sympathetic court of the individual conscience. Conscience, in turn, had by the middle of the century, begun to be formed in a culture where happiness had been legitimized as "the chief end" of life.[47]

So far the story is straightforward. Geneva enjoyed more wealth and a less strenuous morality than before. Few would have disputed that the city had "gone soft"; many would have agreed that these changes amounted to decadence. Their political significance, though, was disputed passionately. The two different readings are easily summarized: The popular understanding, promoted by those who became known as the *représentants*, was that Geneva's political health and capacity to defend itself depended upon broadly equal rights and wealth among the citizen body. The drift toward oligarchy; the aping of French manners by those who felt themselves to be aristocrats; an increased reluctance to work for a living; a skeptical, amused, tolerant attitude to the claims of Christianity—all these developments endangered the city.[48] Most members of the ruling elite, by contrast, took the view that their fellow citizens' attempts to participate in government and to check the powers of the executive were themselves further symptoms of dangerous innovation. Faction, after all, was a traditional indicator of decadence, and in withholding obedience and organizing themselves for opposition, what were the radical groups doing if not endangering their city by splintering its unity?

In August 1764, for instance, Voltaire thought that the appetite for democracy drew individuals away from work to political activity, and that politics that included the poor could not escape corruption, since each individual would necessarily have his price. In January 1767, in contrast, Rousseau wrote to François-Henri d'Ivernois that the staunchness of the threatened *représentants* resembled the courage of Roman senators about to be cut down by Gauls.[49] Such rival accounts of the same conflict reach their peaks with the events of 1781 and 1782. There is no space to recount the story here, but as popular forces seized power and the established magistracy sought French help to put down what they perceived as revolution, so irreligion, materialism, decadence, faction, and contempt for tradition were charges hurled from each side at the other. It was possible to agree that Geneva had "gone soft"; it was impossible to agree whose fault it was and what it meant.

NOTES

1. The author thanks the British Academy and the University of Sheffield for assistance with research on and in Geneva over a number of years. See the classic study of one unskilled workman by Anne-Marie Piuz: "Jean Vian (vers 1690–1772), ouvrier italien réfugié à Genève. Contribution à la typologie de la pauvreté ancienne," *Studi in memoria di Federigo Melis* (Naples: Giannini, 1978), 4: 395–407.

2. Indeed, in 1761 George Keate noted that Geneva's young people might find the city's culture rather confining for it "frequently produce[d] a contracted Way of Thinking." Mme d'Epinay, in contrast, said that the city's *moeurs* were simple, and that even though some citizens lamented their corruption, she marveled at their purity and innocence. See George Keate, *A Short Account of the Ancient History, Present Government and Laws of the Republic of Geneva* (London, 1761), 119; and the memoirs of Mme "de Montbrillant," *Texte intégral publié pour la première fois . . . par Georges Roth* (Paris: Gallimard, 1951) excerpted in Jean-Daniel Candaux, ed., *Voyageurs européens à la découvert de Genève 1685–1792* (Geneva: Populaire, 1966), 63.

3. See Peter Burke, "Tradition and Experience: The Idea of Decline from Bruni to Gibbon," *Daedalus* 105, 3 (1976): 140; and H. G. Koenigsberger, "The Idea of Decadence in Early Modern History, or the Apples of Freia," *European History Quarterly* 22 (1992): 164.

4. Montesquieu (Secondat, Charles Louis de, Baron de), *Considérations sur les causes de la grandeur des Romains et de leur décadence* (Amsterdam, n. p., 1734); the most accessible modern translation is Montesquieu, *Considerations on the causes of the Greatness of the Romans and their Decline*, trans. David Lowenthal (New York and London: Free Press and Collier-Macmillan, 1965). For evidence that he was read and understood, see for instance, *Représentations des Citoyens et Bourgeois de Genève au Premier Syndic de cette République, 8 August 1763*, para 54 ("l'illustre Montesquieu dont nous empruntons Si Souvent le language").

5. Montesquieu, *The Spirit of the Laws*, ed., trans. Anne M. Cohler, Basia Carolyn Miller, and Harold Samuel Stone (Cambridge: Cambridge UP, 1989), 22–24; for an exploration of the term *republic* especially on the pens of eighteenth-century English speakers, see David Wootton, "Introduction: The Republican Tradition: From Commonwealth to Common Sense," in *Republicanism, Liberty and Commercial Society, 1649-1776*, ed. David Wootton (Stanford, CA: Stanford UP, 1994).

6. Alfred Perrenoud, *La population de Genève du seizième au début du dix-neuvième siècle: étude démographique. MDG* (Geneva: A. Jullien, 1979), 145–228. Whenever a man appears in the death register, his profession is given. Since a man in the prime of life can appear as the father of a dead child or the husband of a dead wife, we are not confining our attention to the job or career recorded for those (sometimes too old to work) who had already died. Alfred Perrenoud's study sought, however, to establish the demographic outcomes of a set group of marriages, so no single men were included.

7. David Hiler, "Recherches sur les finances publiques d'une cité état au XVIIIe siècle. Les Comptes de la Seigneurie de Genève (1714–1781)" (mémoire de licence, Faculté SES, Geneva, 1983), 88–90; Patrick O'Mara, "Geneva in the Eighteenth Century. A Socio-economic Study of the Bourgeois City-state during Its Golden Age" (Ph.D. dissertation, University of California, 1954), 123–24. This thesis, never published, and now superseded in part, remains the starting point for much modern work on eighteenth-century Geneva.

8. How these sums were found, and the extent to which public poor relief helped the destitute, is explored in Lawrence Wiedmer, "Pauvreté et assistance," in *L'Economie genevoise, de la réforme à la fin de l'ancien régime XVIe–XVIIIe siècles*, ed. Anne-Marie Piuz and Liliane Mottu-Weber (Geneva: H. Georg & *SHAG*, 1990), 149.

9. David Hiler, "Les sept jours gras du patriciat genevois. Le livre de ménage de Marie Gallatin," *RVG* 16 (1986): 32; and Barbara Roth-Lochner, "Les repas du graveur Fournier à l'Auberge de Grange-Canal," *RVG* 21 (1991): 42–51. Marie Gallatin spent some 12,000 florins a year on her household.

10. Lawrence Wiedmer, "Les Glacières de l'Hôpital au XVIIIe siècle," in *Sauver l'âme, nourrir le corps: de l'Hôpital général à l'Hospice général de Genève*, ed. Bernard Lescaze (Geneva: Atar, 1985), 261–266.

11. Anne-Marie Piuz, "L'Alimentation hospitalière à Genève au XVIIIe siècle," in *A Genève et autour de Genève au XVIIe et XVIIIe siècles* (Lausanne: Payot, 1985): 124–138, and "Le Marché du bétail et la consommation de la viande à Genève au XVIIIe siècle," *RSH* 25 (1975): 52, 65, 66. By the 1770s a lottery was introduced to help fund the hospital, a measure that itself points to a cultural shift.

12. Lawrence Wiedmer, *Pain quotidien et pain de disette, meuniers, boulangers et état nourricier à Genève (XVIIe et XVIIIe siècles)* (Geneva: Editions Passé Présent, 1993), 17–19; 32–39: in *coupes* of grain, consumption fell from 3.8 to 3.0 per head per year. (A *coupe* was almost 80 liters.)

13. *BPU*, Registre des Assemblées des Messrs. les Directeurs de la Bibiothèque, vol. 1, 132; vol. 2 (red pagination), 84. On December 17, 1741, the same register had recorded (71) disquiet at the possibility of books being borrowed merely for amusement.

14. Eugène-Louis Dumont, *Genève d'autrefois: Cours et escaliers des XVIIe et XVIIIe siècles* (Geneva: Le Pavé, 1969).

15. *Princes Manqués* (Geneva: n. p., 1765), 12.

16. Sumptuary laws continued to distinguish between Regarding entitlement to magnificence in clothes and furniture, sumptuary laws continued to distinguish between different "conditions" of Genevans; they did not, as Rousseau supposed, impose the same modest standards on everyone. It may well be that by the eighteenth century money-raising was the chief object of fining for breaches of these rules.

17. Yves Brütsch, "Population Genevoise du XVIIIe siècle" (*AEG*, mémoire de licence, 1973), 91. Brütsch's first sample of 319 brides was taken from records of the mid-1720s; the higher percentage was found in a similar sample for 1772.

18. Perrenoud, *La population de Genève*, 395, gives a figure of 1.1 percent for illegitimate births as a proportion of all the city's births for the period 1730–1739; Geneviève Perret, 'La Paillardise à Genève, 1760–1764' (*AEG*, mémoire de licence, 1982), 350, found 5 percent for the early 1760s. Daniel Aquillon in "Hélène Chambras, Marie Passant, Georges Parvis . . . ou le don et l'abandon d'enfants à l'Hôpital au XVIIIe siècle," in *Sauver l'âme* (see n. 10), found 2 percent for 1745–1785. Not all these babies were strictly Genevan, though.

19. See Bernard Sonaillon, "Etude des divorces à Genève dans la seconde moitié du XVIIIe" (*AEG*, mémoire de licence, 1975), 9, 11, 31, 60–64.

20. *AEG*, Registre Consistoire, Aug 1780.

21. Jeffrey Watt, in "The Family, Love and Suicide in Early Modern Geneva," *Journal of Family History* 21, 1 (1996): 63–86, records higher figures than those analysed by Laurent Haeberli in "Le Suicide à Genève au 18e siècle," *Pour une histoire qualititative: études offertes à Sven Stelling-Michaud* (Geneva: Presses Universitaires

Romandes, 1975), 115—129. According to Haeberli, expressed as a number per hundred thousand per year, the rate for the first half of the century was 3.8; for the second half, 18.5—concealing 26.4 for the period 1781—1798. Perhaps because he trawled more kinds of record than Haeberli, or perhaps because he included cases which Haeberli had excluded as doubtful, Watt gives a rate of 34.38 for this final phase of the Republic's life. Changes can also be discerned in motives for suicide and the reactions of neighbors to people who killed themselves, but these are not straightforwardly quantifiable. See also the exploration of dying messages in Michel Porret, "'Mon Père c'est le dernier chagrin que je vous donne': Jeunes suicides à Genève au 18e siècle," *Ethnologie française* 22 (1992): 61—69.

22. Only since 1617 had actors been banned; Calvin had used theater as one of many modes of propaganda.

23. This made it the largest single source of credit to the undertaking; other shareholders mostly put in just over 363 livres each. *Reconnoissance d'Action sur La Salle des Spectacles établie à Genève* (a copy of share certificate no. 98, recording Isaac-Robert Rilliet's investment in the theater: he was a member of the Two Hundred).

24. *AEG*, Registre Vénérable Compagnie, 9 April, 1 October 1784.

25. William Beckford, *The Travel Diaries of William Beckford of Fonthill*, ed. G. Chapman, 2 vols. (London: Constable and Co., 1928), 1, 320.

26. There had also been a clash of views over *Samson* in March 1784: Both the Company and the Consistory thought the performance mocked Scripture and wanted it banned; the city council refused. Reg. Ven. Co. 19, 26 March 1784. It was thus infuriating that *Samson*, probably the opera with a libretto by Voltaire, was offered again in 1787.

27. James Boswell, December 23, 1764, in Frederick A Pottle, ed., *Boswell on the Grand Tour: Germany and Switzerland 1764* (London: William Heinemann, 1953), 271. He also thought Genevan manners "monstrously familiar"; one minister "slabbered the greasy, unwashen hands of a married woman" (298). This he wrote off as "a nauseous example of the manners of republicans": not so much decadence as primitivism.

28. Rousseau's *Correspondance Complète*, ed. R. A. Leigh, 1965—1995, had different publishers and places of publication before settling at Oxford with the Voltaire foundation. References will be given as volume number, letter number.

29. Jean-Jacques Rousseau, *Lettre à M. D'Alembert sur son article Genève*, ed. Michel Launay (Paris: Garnier-Flammarion, 1967), 183—4.

30. *Du Contrat Social* and *L'Emile* were banned and burned on June 19, 1762, and it was decreed that Rousseau would be arrested if he returned to the city.

31. Paul-Claude Moultou, "Extrait d'un sermon de M. Moultou, ministre de Genève, sur le luxe," *Annales de la Société Jean-Jacques Rousseau*, 17 (1926): 171—8. The sermon was preached at Pentecost 1759; extracts were sent to Rousseau, who approved of the argument but wanted to take it further.

32. In *Lettres populaires où l'on examine la réponse aux lettres écrites de la campagne* (Geneva, 1765), the *négatif* author or authors explicitly link to the portable, valuable stock held by jewelers, the authorities' right for the arrest on suspicion.

33. *Correspondance*, 16: 2720; 19: 3133, 3164.

34. *Réflexions sur les moeurs, la religion, et le culte: Par J. Vernet, pasteur & professeur en théologie* (Geneva: n. p., 1769), esp. 95—114. For a detailed examination of this work, see Graham Gargett, *Jacob Vernet, Geneva and the Philosophes: Studies on Voltaire and the Eighteenth Century* (Oxford: Voltaire Foundation, 1995), 416—436. Graham Gargett's study explores the touchy relationships between this particular member

of Geneva's clerical elite and an important subgroup of his contemporaries. It also offers an exhaustive analysis of the shadings and reworkings of Vernet's theology prompted by respect for evidence and reason, but checked by his fear of the charge of religious laxity.

35. Andrew Le Mercier, *The Church in Geneva in Five Books . . . .* (Boston: n. p., 1732), 210.

36. They were denounced in 1707 for their powdered wigs, but they would have looked unconventional without them. See Linda Kirk, "Eighteenth-century Geneva and a Changing Calvinism," in *Religion and National Identity*, Studies in Church History, 18, ed. Stuart Mews (Oxford: Basil Blackwell, 1982), 367—380.

37. See John Stephenson Spink, *Rousseau et Genève* (Paris: Boivin, 1934); Maria-Cristina Pitassi, *De l'orthodoxie aux Lumières, Genève 1670—1737* (Geneva: Labor et Fides, 1992); Kirk, "A changing Calvinism," cited in n. 35 and work by Graham Gargett, including that cited in n. 33.

38. J.-A. Turretin, *Sermon sur le Jubilé de la Réformation* (Geneva: n. p., 1735), 5.

39. Jacob Vernes, ed., *Choix Littéraire* 1 (1755), ix—x.

40. Charles Bonnet, *Mémoires autobiographiques de Charles Bonnet de Genève*, ed. Raymond Savioz (Paris: J. Vrin, 1948), 137.

41. Ibid., 135.

42. Turretine [*sic*], *Dissertations on Natural Theology* (Belfast: n. p., 1777), 14.

43. *BPU*, Mss. Suppl., 1540, f.59; Du Pan had previously, when reacting to d'Alembert's letter, pinned the responsibility for the drift to Socianism on one man: "c'est le Vernet." *Correspondance*, 5: Appendix 193.

44. *Correspondance*, 9: 1431.

45. Philip Rieder, "Les Enfants de la Chaire . . . ou ces chers Enfants. Être Enfant à Genève au XVIIIe siècle," *RVG* (1994): 23—24.

46. This was no light matter. The records of the Consistory show the importance of neighborly surveillance throughout the century. Jean-Robert Tronchin was clear that everything done was known in the city within the hour; citizens were in instant contact with one another. See *Lettres écrites de la campagne* (Geneva: n. p., 1763): 100, 166. See also the heartening evidence summarized in "Entre tolérance tacite et intolérance collective: enfants violentés et parents dénaturés, Genève 1700—1765," *RVG* 19 (1989): 27—43. Michel Porret demonstrates that "excessive" violence against wives and children attracted disapproval and intervention from those nearby.

47. Vernet's *Instruction Chrétienne* was a five-volume work, first published in 1751, meant to fit a marketing gap somewhere between a common catechism and a full-blown work of technical theology. It opens with the question: "What is the natural end of all men or the chief end they propose in all their enterprises?" The answer he offers, "To be happy," is startling in its presumption of a hedonist, utilitarian basis for ethics, but as the argument of the book develops it quickly seeks to establish that long-term happiness is better than short-term gratification, and that since it is likely there is a life after this one, pursuing happiness in a way inconsistent with eternal felicity is ill-advised.

48. Jacques-François De Luc, *Observations sur les savans incrédules* (Geneva: n. p., 1762); Moultou's sermon of 1759, see n. 30, made explicit the link between inequality and decadence and their combined threat to the safety of the Republic. Rival understandings of the role of *cercles* illuminate this conflict. Decent working men saw them as clubs where harmless sociability maintained a civic consciousness; the authorities perceived noise, drunkenness and sedition. The military exercises of 1761, likewise, to Rousseau's supporters represented disciplined carnival, consciously following the pattern

laid out in the *Lettre à d'Alembert*. Men exercised and women watched on; they danced together in the evening. But Jean-Louis Mollet's breathless account (*Correspondance*, 9: 1429) dwelt on "de l'égalité, de la liberté, de la fraternité," Jean-Louis Du Pan had already taken fright in 1758 at the implications of the sociability Rousseau claimed to remember in Geneva (*Correspondance*, 5: 735).

    49. *Correspondance*, 21: 3458; 32: 5697.

9

Social Welfare and the Transformation of Polity in Geneva

Jeannine E. Olson

Social welfare has been a key element in the development of identity in Geneva. Through welfare Protestant immigrants and refugees were welcomed within the city walls, and in turn they contributed to the ongoing concern for the social needs of the community. This chapter will examine the place of social welfare from the *ancien régime* through the mid-nineteenth century, concentrating on the institutional adjustments to Geneva's changing political and religious context.[1] Since the sixteenth century, social welfare was strongly tied to their Protestant identity and affected practically every aspect of life, but by 1860 Geneva had evolved into a predominantly Catholic canton of Switzerland. These changes in political and religious affiliation caused difficult adjustments in the traditions and institutions of Geneva that are not fully resolved today.

In the 1530s Geneva's bid for independence from Savoy had coincided with a religious reformation and a break with the ecclesiastical hierarchy of Rome. Geneva sent packing its prince-bishop, of the Savoyard ducal family, which had ruled over it in the medieval period. After that, the newly independent city ruled itself through a council headed by four syndics, who rotated in office called the *Petit Conseil*. This oligarchy of leading burghers gave an occasional nod to the adult male citizens, assembled to confirm slates of office that the *Petit Conseil* controlled. As for the church in this newly independent state, the city took over the Genevan land that belonged to the Roman Catholic Church and Geneva's pastors become city employees, in the pay of the *Petit Conseil*. Soon leading this Company of Pastors was John Calvin, one of many French refugees, in a sense.

Independence and religious Reformation brought not only glory and status to Geneva but also problems, some of which the city created on its own. Soon after independence from Savoy, this reformed city, so close to Catholic neighbors, became a city of refuge for Protestants persecuted for their religious beliefs. They flocked to its gates and worshiped there according to their convictions.

They published Bibles and Psalters and sent them illegally back home, spearheading a movement to obtain the right to worship that led to the Wars of Religion that dominated France during the latter half of the sixteenth century. Geneva became the capitol of Protestants in France and benefited from the financial and political support of Protestants and Protestant states throughout Europe. This support helped it to survive as an autonomous political unit throughout the *ancien régime*.

Many of these refugees were poor and needed to be cared for, and the city was hard pressed to care for them. The arrangements for the poor that the city had made at the time of the Reformation were not adequate to subsidize a flood of foreign refugees. With its Reformation, Geneva had set up a new welfare system in 1535, a multipurpose city welfare institution, the General Hospital. The city council (*Petit Conseil*) had needed a building for this hospital and had taken over the convent of the Sisters of St. Clare in Geneva. The Poor Clares had moved to the neighboring town of Annecy in order to continue to live together as Catholic sisters in Savoy after the Reformation in Geneva. The city council turned their vacant convent into a hospital, consolidating into one a number of smaller Genevan hospitals that predated the Reformation. To run the new Genevan hospital, the city council set up a board of trustees and employed a hospital administrator, or hospitaller, as he was called.

This new hospital was truly an all-purpose welfare institution. The Genevan hospital cared for the sick, the elderly, the disabled, the orphaned, and the poor either in its own building or on an outpatient basis. The Genevan city hospital also placed young children with wet nurses, many of whom lived in the country.

Geneva's new hospital and social welfare arrangement might have sufficed had it not been for the foreign poor who began to overload the system in the 1540s, fleeing from areas of Catholic repression. The problem their presence caused became so great that in 1545 Geneva was about to evict them. Just then a wealthy refugee, David Busanton, was dying, with John Calvin at his side. Busanton willed a significant sum of money to the poor of Geneva and Strasbourg, solving the problem of the foreign poor in Geneva just in the nick of time.[2]

Busanton's gift apparently became the basis, in Geneva, of a pastors' discretionary fund that could be used to help the poor who came to their door. The need soon became too large for the pastors to handle alone, and lay administrators of refugee relief were appointed from among the wealthier refugees in the late 1540s, probably in 1549.[3] Within a few years these administrators came to be called deacons after the deacons in the early centuries of the Christian Church who had helped the poor. These sixteenth-century deacon-administrators of poor relief were volunteers and often men of means who donated to the poor themselves. They helped poor refugees who sought a haven in Geneva. The deacons and the funds they administered came to be called the *Bourse française* or French Fund.

The French Fund gave regular handouts to poor and disabled refugees, found jobs for the unemployed, provided training and tools, apprenticeships, midwives, medicine, doctors' visits, barber surgeons, foster homes, clothing, bedding, shoe repair, Bibles, schoolbooks, and loans to start up businesses. In general, the French Fund provided for refugees the services that the city hospital did for the poor of Genevan origin. The deacons did so not with local resources but with money from the wealthier refugees and from sympathizers for their cause in France and elsewhere who sent donations to the French Fund in Geneva. Thus their budget was not under the direct control of the city council of Geneva, but rather, was under the deacons and pastors of the city, who were French rather than native Genevan. This enabled the French Fund to diversify its activities beyond social welfare and to subsidize the copying down of John Calvin's sermons and the dispatch of Bibles, Psalters, catechisms, and pastors back into France to further the Evangelical cause there.[4]

Despite all its activities the French Fund appeared to have had no building out of which to operate at first. It seems to have functioned out of the deacons' homes, and the deacons housed the homeless in private homes and in the city's inns, even refugees who were ill.[5] The deacons employed guardians to take care of the sick.[6] They used the city hospital, too.[7] On December 30, 1583, the deacons bought a house from the widow of Thomas Courteau, a refugee printer. Here they could hold meetings and distribute alms.[8] In time the deacons gained control of buildings in exchange for care or as bequests from the deceased.[9]

Other groups of refugees followed the model of the French and organized funds for poor relief within their respective ethnic communities. Thus the Italians had their Italian Fund with deacons to administer it. Italian deacons appear to have been in place even before the Italian church had a pastor, and the Italian Fund would continue to exist after that church disappeared in the late eighteenth century (c. 1780).[10] The English came to Geneva in the mid-1550s, escaping the persecution of Mary Tudor, and stayed until after she died in 1558. Their English church in Geneva had deacons. The *Livre des Anglois* lists two in 1555, the year in which John Calvin requested the city council, on June 10, to allow the English to set up a congregation.[11] There were three English deacons in 1556, and four in 1557–1558.[12] German-speaking refugees organized a German Reformed Church in Geneva in 1580. It had deacons and eventually subdeacons and began to organize a German Fund.[13]

These deacons' funds were fundamental to the dispensing of poor relief to refugees to *ancien régime* Geneva. Organized by the refugee communities along ethnic lines, each fund took responsibility for refugees of the same ethnic origin and some others as well. Originally the French Fund appeared to have been flexible in dispensing aid, helping a native Genevan at one point and also a Jew passing through on his way to England, but by the seventeenth century the lines between welfare institutions were finely drawn.[14] A Genevan law of 1682 provided that the city hospital assist the poor of the city and the territory under its jurisdiction (those poor whom the city considered "Genevan" rather than foreign); that the French Fund assist the French; the Italian Fund assist the

Italians, Spaniards, and refugees from Burgundy; and the German Fund assist Germans, the German-speaking Swiss, and all those who were from within the Holy Roman Empire including Alsace, Lorraine, Holland and the Flemish countries, plus England, Sweden, Poland, Denmark, Norway, Hungary, and Transylvania.[15]

This division of the welfare load by nationalities led to conflicts of interest. A shifting regional boundary in Europe could realign each institution's responsibility and lead to bickering over which of the poor belonged to which fund. Welfare recipients were occasionally shuttled from one institution to another. Drawing strict nationality lines among the welfare funds, however, might have prevented abuse of the system. The diversity of sources of aid in Geneva could have allowed some people to have used first one institution and then another and perhaps even to have received aid from more than one welfare institution at once.[16] These deacons' funds, French, Italian, German, and English, were significant not only for their role in maintaining the minority ethnic groups in Geneva but also for the model they provided for an organization of aid to the poor wherever Reformed churches spread, in France, the Low Countries, and the British Isles.

Thus, self-help within ethnic communities solved the problem of the flood of refugees who came to Geneva in the early modern era. The "first refuge," as it was called, that of the sixteenth century, was followed in the seventeenth century by the second, associated with the revocation of the Edict of Nantes in France. Refugees began to arrive in Geneva from France prior to 1685 already as the gradual imposition of religious prohibitions under Louis XIV took its toll on Huguenot sensibilities. With the actual revocation the tide continued, flooding Geneva with a new population of foreign poor. Fortunately, the refugee welfare funds were already in existence although the French Fund was hard pressed to meet the need and the city encouraged refugees to move elsewhere. The deacons' minutes of September 26, 1687, discuss the boats that took refugees across Lake Geneva to other destinations.[17]

By the eighteenth century the city hospital no longer had room for the poor of the French Fund and offered the Fund a building, rent-free, on February 12, 1703. It became the hospital of the French Fund. The deacons furnished it and installed help, including a pastor. In 1707 the fund transferred its hospital to the house next door, and in 1742 the fund enlarged it with the purchase of another building. This hospital lasted less than a century. Because of financial hardship, the French Fund closed the hospital in 1798 and placed its sick people in the country or at the city hospital.[18]

Over the years the French Fund weathered periodic attempts of the city council to exercise control. On February 9, 1676, the council ordered, without success, that one of its members should preside over the French Fund to better administer it. Forty-five years later, on April 28, 1721, a member of the city council and a member of the Council of Two Hundred were to preside over the deliberative assemblies of the French Fund. The same order was made on

December 24, 1721. The Company of Pastors of Geneva resisted, and in an order of January 26, 1722, the pastors were allowed to continue to preside, but the city council took stricter control of the auditing of the accounts.[19]

At the same time, the city council gave the French Fund privileges and helped in times of need. The city council authorized collections for the fund and, in 1568 at each door in the churches put alms boxes for the fund and for the city hospital. In 1569 the council gave money, wheat, and rye to the deacons. After the Massacre of St. Bartholemew's Day on August 24, 1572, the city council lodged refugees from France in the city hospital and authorized the hospital to provide them with furniture and clothing. Members of the council gave money and instructed the preachers to prepare the people, who were convoked in one of the churches where the ministers and members of the city council led in a collection.[20] The French Fund was exempted from certain legal fees (December 3, 1573, and January 3, 1599) and from dues to master artisans when placing apprentices (April 11, 1683; May 21, 1701; and May 25, 1729). On March 17, 1671, the council ordered that French people who wanted to become inhabitants of Geneva pay a surety to the French Fund. When they married, they were to pay the Fund again. After the revocation of the Edict of Nantes, in August 1687, the city council gave the French Fund the Thursday proceeds from the alms boxes in the city's churches to the dissatisfaction of the city hospital. In 1689 the city council issued grain from the city's reserve in the *Chambre des blés*; this grain the hospital baked into bread for the poor.[21]

After the outbreak of the French Revolution the situation of Geneva and of the French Fund became difficult. France occupied Savoy in 1792 and came close to taking Geneva, sparking a revolutionary movement within the city that overthrew the government in December 1792 and provoked a new constitution in 1794. The new constitution was democratic but limited citizenship to Protestants.

During this era the financial situation of the French Fund deteriorated, and the fund was threatened with the possibility of union with the city hospital. On April 15, 1798, Geneva was occupied by French troops and joined to France. The French allowed Geneva considerable autonomy in domestic affairs, but Genevans could not prevent the reestablishment of the Roman Catholic Mass, celebrated in the old church of St. Germain.[22] The city's welfare institutions continued to function, though. The administration of the hospital came under a Welfare society, the *Société de bienfaisance*.[23] The French Fund was supposed to turn over its assets but resisted, and, in order to assure the desired allocation of its funds, it inscribed them in the name of the "poor Genevan foreigners of French origin."[24] The Italian and German Funds continued to function into the nineteenth century as well.

At the end of the Napoleonic wars, in 1814 and 1815, Geneva joined the Swiss Confederation, but at the price of a new constitution and of having to absorb Catholic territory along Lake Geneva. A treaty was negotiated protecting the Catholics in these new Genevan lands. With that, Geneva evolved from a

Protestant to a multireligious state. The transition was not easy. Many Genevans were unhappy with the religious affiliation of their new compatriots. Genevan Protestants would be uncomfortable also with an ensuing rise in the number of Catholics through immigration and the proselytizing endeavors of Jean-François Vuarin, a priest assigned to Geneva in 1806.[25] By 1860, in the canton of Geneva, would live an estimated 43,000 Catholics and 41,000 Protestants.[26]

For almost 300 years, Genevan institutions had been organized to protect and serve Genevan Protestants and those foreign Protestants who sought refuge there. Catholics were considered outsiders. At the time of the Reformation in the 1530s, Catholics had been forced to convert or leave Geneva, even Catholic nuns and priests, who in many newly Protestant cities had been allowed to live out their lives in city cloisters. Tolerance of Catholics had come only gradually and in a limited sense to Geneva. Catholicism was practiced in Geneva during the period of the French occupation, of course, but that was hardly a Genevan initiative. After the Napoleonic Wars many Genevans wanted to return to the city as it had been before the French Revolution and period of occupation. They wanted to return to the Protestant establishment.

In this desire to return to the past, Geneva was in step with the rest of Europe. Immediately after the Napoleonic Wars Geneva went through a period of reaction and conservatism that successfully held many changes at bay. Trade unions were forbidden, for instance. There had to be some changes, of course. With the addition of new territory, there was a new population for Geneva to care for.

Geneva's social welfare institutions had been set up in the sixteenth century to serve Protestants. The adjustment was an uneasy one. The old families made distinctions between inhabitants of the old and the new territories.[27] Even after Catholics in the newly attached territory were accepted as members of the canton of Geneva, there were members of Genevan institutional boards who wanted to retain religious distinctions, understandably, since the private ethnic welfare funds had emerged from the Italian, French, and German communities when these communities were Protestant. In a plea of 1819 to bring the Catholic Sisters of Charity to Geneva, Father Jean-François Vuarin accused the government of the canton of reserving for the Protestant population all the resources that the public establishments offered. He published this statement anonymously in a treatise. In reality, Catholics were admitted to the hospital but not to its external services for the poor. A separate foundation aided the new Catholic compatriots, the Tronchin Foundation (1818), reserved for indigent Catholics of the new territory. Father Vuarin was suspected of being the author of the derogatory treatise, and the government of Geneva attempted, unsuccessfully, to get him removed.[28]

Liberalism and multiculturalism eventually prevailed. The nineteenth century saw adjustments to this new state of affairs, adjustments that were painful to Genevans and to their institutions. In Switzerland as in other parts of Europe, the decade of the 1830s was decisive. Most Swiss cantons liberalized their constitutions and widened suffrage. Geneva followed suit in 1842 with a new constitution that accepted universal manhood suffrage. This gave the working classes a larger role in government and opened the way to a new genre of political leaders and to new political parties, including, in Geneva, the Radical Party, a party that was to initiate decisive changes in Genevan institutions in the decades that followed.

The best-known early leader and founder of the Radical Party was a Genevan by the name of James Fazy, a politician about whom Genevans are still impassioned today. Champion of the common man, Fazy would change the very face of Geneva. He was to govern the city from 1847 to 1861, with an interruption in 1853–1855, and to him goes credit or blame for many of the changes in Genevan institutions that the city weathered during the mid-nineteenth century.[29]

Born May 12, 1794, James Fazy (d. 1878), actually Jean-Jacob Fazy, was a descendant of French Protestants who came to Geneva in the second refuge and successfully prospered in the cotton print textile business. His father hoped he would work in the family business and sent him as a child to Germany and then France for his education, but James was more interested in arts, letters, and social sciences than in textiles. He studied law and became a journalist and newspaper editor and owner, of the genre of newspaperman who used the press to enhance his own political career.[30]

As a young man of high ideals in restoration France, Fazy developed an enthusiasm for liberal ideas, for the revolution of 1830, and for Louis Napoleon Bonaparte.[31] Jailed in Paris, Fazy eventually settled in Geneva, where he had already helped found the *Journal de Genève*, January 5, 1826.[32] This was one of a series of newspapers he helped found.[33] Launching himself in the world of politics and hoping to maintain himself there, he also had helped found the Radical Party to represent the working people of Geneva, who would vote Radical until the end of the century.[34] Genevan Catholics would also support the party for a time.

A Genevan uprising in 1846 overturned the government and gave the Radicals an opportunity to lead the government and to rewrite the Genevan constitution. Guided by his populist ideas, Fazy reshaped the institutional structure of Geneva. He opposed the power of the old families of Geneva held and the Church of Geneva as it was then constituted.

Fazy had been baptized as a child in the Reformed Church of Geneva, but as an adult he was of indifferent religious convictions. Moreover, he felt that the Church of Geneva was an undemocratic structure, that it, like the city, was dominated by the old families, whose conservative ideas and privileged position held back change and excluded the working classes from their proper role in city life. Fazy's rhetoric was highly idealistic and popular in tone although he was personally authoritarian.[35]

Once the Radicals were in power, Fazy began to put his agenda into action. Central to this agenda was his conviction that some of the old city institutions and the very city walls themselves stood in the way of progress. According to Fazy, the city walls, initiated when they made some military sense to surround a smaller city, now served as an economic barrier. The rich lived within the walls. The working classes and the poor lived outside the walls. Among the city institutions with which Fazy felt uncomfortable were the so-called Foundations. These included the privately endowed French Fund. The Italian and German funds he could do less about. Fazy wanted to bring the private foundations under Genevan control and to consolidate Geneva's medical and social welfare services into centralized institutions. He had the dream of a cantonal hospital serving all Genevans regardless of ethnic identity or religious convictions.

Fazy lost little time. By 1847 there was a new Genevan constitution that removed from the Reformed Church of Geneva its status as the dominant religion.[36] Next came legislation to put into effect his program, much of which met with active resistance, but by 1849 Geneva had voted to tear down the city walls. The demolition work began the same year.

That same year, on June 23, 1849, a law was in place establishing a cantonal hospital "to receive and care for the sick and injured," including those citizens of the canton of Geneva who could not afford to pay. No one with a grave illness or injury was to be refused entrance, even indigent foreigners. The law provided for an administrative commission for the new hospital.[37] The commission met for the first time on October 6, 1849, and had built a new hospital by July 1, 1856, when patients were transferred from the old General Hospital to the present cantonal hospital of Geneva.[38]

This new cantonal hospital was responsible for medical care. There was a separate home for the elderly, and, in 1869, the social welfare and charitable activities of the old General Hospital on behalf of the poor and needy were placed under the *Hospice général*, a continuation and augmentation of the old General Hospital of Geneva.[39] Today the *Hospice général* of Geneva continues to work with the elderly, children, and adolescents. It has become an institution of social action, aiding refugees, helping the marginal, the unemployed, the aged, and drug addicts, even delivering meals to homes.[40]

What, then, of the private foundations in all this mid-nineteenth-century reorganization? What of the French, Italian, and German funds? The fate of the French Fund was the saddest, although initially its prospects under the Radical regime were optimistic. A June 1849 project for a general law covering the foundations provided for the continued existence of the French Fund under the condition that it continue to assist French Protestant families in Geneva in need of help, that it provide a list of the families in Geneva that it assisted, and that it pay an annual sum to the cantonal hospital and the old folks home to cover people under the fund's charge. The administration of the French Fund was to submit to an election every five years under the Consistory of the Church of Geneva and the Council of State.[41] Another optimistic note for the French Fund was that the law for the establishment of a cantonal hospital of June 23, 1849, acknowledged the French Fund's continued existence by noting that it would pay an annual sum to the hospital for patients under its charge.[42]

James Fazy's intentions towards the private foundations, however, appear not to have been so benign. In a report of June 13, 1849, he read: "It is impossible to deny that in a democratic republic there is danger in allowing certain foundations to continue that, established at first with the most sincere intentions of public usefulness and welfare, finish by degenerating from their noble end and take on, often unknown even to those who administer them, a hostile character toward the democratic principle. . . . Charity is badly administered by a spirit of coterie."[43]

The upshot was that the proposed definitive law covering the foundations united the French Fund with the hospital. The deacons of the French Fund objected and offered to open their books for inspection, but it was too late. The government did not respond. Henri Grandjean recorded that on August 18, 1849, the *Grand Conseil* passed, 27 to 12, a law concerning "the Foundations" that united the French Fund to the Hospital of Geneva.[44]

Title III, Article 15, paragraph 6: The establishment of charity destined for the relief of Genevans of French origin, known under the name of the French Fund, is reunited with the Hospital of Geneva, in order to be administered according to its ends.[45] The same law allowed the German Fund to continue.

Title III, Article 15, paragraph seven: Without entering into an examination of the interior organization of the German church, and taking into consideration only the existence of a foundation in this church, the German Fund is maintained, on the condition that it submit the election of its financial administration to all the active members of the German Church to which it is attached, housed in the Canton, and of whom it will draw up a list 15 days before the elections; this list will be rectified upon appeal to the Council of State. This administration will be submitted to a new election every five years.[46]

Why were the German and Italian funds allowed to continue and not the French Fund? Was James Fazy launching an attack particularly on the established Church of Geneva and agencies affiliated with it? Did he consider these funds less important to his designs than the French Fund? Were he and his colleagues not politically powerful enough to dissolve the Italian and German funds? Did they fear antagonizing the Italians and the Germans and Swiss Germans who supported the German church? Or were the deacons of the French Fund somehow partially at fault. Were they less cooperative than they could have been in producing information when the fate of the French Fund was under consideration?

There are different opinions whether the French Fund shared in the responsibility for its own dissolution. Henri Grandjean implied in his 1927 article, *La Bourse française de Genève*, that the deacons were recalcitrant in providing information to the *Grand Conseil* when the matter was under study in summer 1849 and, in particular, that the deacons should have sent forward a treatise to plead, their cause as did most of the foundations under examination. Several deputies and councilors of state reproached the French Fund for not having furnished the requested explanations.[47]

In contrast, in his analysis of the 1849 debates over the foundations, the historian of Geneva, François Ruchon, presented a situation beyond the control of the French Fund. Those deputies who wished to preserve the fund were in the minority and could not protect it against the Radicals. The debates were long and impassioned, lasting from June 13 to August 22, 1849.[48] The reporter for the minority, Monsieur Binet-Hentsch, argued in support of the private foundations: Why "unite their funds to other establishments, conserving, it is true, their purposes on paper, without a serious examination of the facts having established that the ends would be better fulfilled by the new body to which one confides them than by the old and special body that one suppresses?"[49]

Meanwhile the minutes of the deacons of the French Fund themselves reveal that business was being conducted as usual during the summer of 1849 with gifts to the fund coming in and money dispensed as if nothing unusual was about to happen. There appears to have been no sense of foreboding that the end was in sight, but once the *Grand Conseil* took action to join the French Fund with the Hospital of Geneva, the deacons of the French Fund objected. On September 8 they wrote to the Council of State stating that, without a judicial decision, they could not give up the funds for which they were responsible.[50] The French Fund was not alone; the Committee of the Society for the religious instruction of the youth, called the Society of Catechumens, refused to hand over its funds to a *Caisse Hypothécaire* created by the Constitution.[51]

On September 11 the Council of State declared that the possessions of the Society of Catechumens were to be turned over to the *Caisse Hypothécaire* and the possessions of the French Fund were to be turned over to the General Hospital (an action that was probably illegal, in the view of François Ruchon).[52] To whom could the Society of Catechumens and the deacons of the French Fund appeal this action?

The deacons of the French Fund refused to turn anything over to the hospital. Records and valuables were removed from their office and deposited for safekeeping with one of those responsible for the French Fund, an attorney, Des Gouttes. The possessions of the fund were, after all, gifts from private individuals intended for the use of the French Fund and not for social welfare in general.[53] The deacon-administrators of the French Fund met for the last time on September 14, 1849.[54] On September 18 several members of the hospital commission, a commissary of police, and two locksmiths entered the office of the French Fund and seized what they could find. On September 20 a judge, a clerk of the court, and a police officer seized the books and valuables of the French Fund from Des Gouttes. After 300 years of useful labor, the French Fund came to an end.[55] The Italian Fund and the German Fund, meanwhile, tied respectively to the Italian community and to the German-speaking Reformed congregation in Geneva, continued. The Italian Fund voluntarily gave over its capital in 1869 to the *Hospice général*, the renamed General Hospital.[56]

Fazy had worked his wonders. On the plus side, by the latter part of the nineteenth century Geneva had a modern cantonal hospital and a centralized and rationalized social welfare system. On the minus side, private foundations and private property had been suppressed without adequately taking into consideration the wishes of the donors and whether the foundations could have been as effectively left intact.

But the spirit behind private philanthropy could not be repressed. Undaunted by the setback, the Reformed Church of Geneva instituted a new diaconate within a year of the dissolution of the French Fund. These deacons, assigned to various sections of the city, were closely tied to the pastors, helping with charity, the care of the poor, religious education, and the surveillance of the youth. In reinstating deacons the Reformed Church of Geneva attempted to avoid appearing to reinstate a Protestant welfare fund to avoid trouble with the state. In this it was successful. The endowment of the French Fund had been lost to the General Hospital, but Protestant deacons in Geneva lived on.[57]

NOTES

1. Research for this paper in the Genevan archives and university library was funded by the American Philosophical Society, the American Academy of Religion, and the *Bourse française* of Geneva through Professor Olivier Fatio of the University of Geneva.

2. *AEG, RC*, vol. 40 (February 8, 1545–February 7, 1546), fol. 161.

3. Jeannine Olson, *Calvin and Social Welfare: Deacons and the Bourse Française* (Selinsgrove, PA: Susquehanna UP; London: Associated UP, 1989), 169.

4. For details on these activities see Chapters 3 and 4, "Welfare, Refugees, Publishing," and "International Activities," in Olson, *Calvin and Social Welfare*, 37–69.

5. "Au filz du bon homme de Paris pour deux garçons qu'il a mallades chez luy, 15 sols" (To the son of the good man of Paris for two boys whom he has sick at his house, 15 sous), *AEG*, Archives hospitalières, Hj 2, [5] of October 1560 (hereafter known as Arch. hosp). "À Jehan de Sainct Denys mallade chez Henry Gon [host of the Inn of the Crescent], 12 sols (To Jean de Saint Denis, sick, at Henry Gon's place, 12 sous), ibid., [2] of January 1561.

6. "A une Provençale pour avoir gardé une pauvre fille qui est morte chez elle, 2 florins, 6 sols" (To a Provencal for having cared for a poor girl who died at her house, 2 florins, 6 sous), *AEG*, Arch. hosp., Hj 2, [2] of May 1561.

7. "A Jehan Personne pour une fille qui est à l'Hôpital, 4 florins" (To Jehan Personne for a girl who is at the hospital, 4 florins), *AEG*, Arch. hosp., Hj 2, [2] of February 1560.

8. Hélène Mayor, "La Bourse française de Genève au moment de la révocation de l'Édit de Nantes" (Mémoire de licence, University of Geneva, May 1983), 47.

9. For instance, on March 1, 1613, the deacons awarded assistance of two florins per week to the widow of Nicolas Saget on the condition that she transfer a large boutique over to the profit of the poor. "Livre Memorial des Diacres," *AEG*, Arch. hosp., Ka 1, 31.

10. Henry Heyer, *L'Église de Genève 1535–1909, esquisse historique de son organisation suivie de ses diverses constitutions, de la liste de ses pasteurs et professeurs et d'une table biographique* (Geneva: A. Jullien, 1909; reprint, Nieuwkoop: B. De Graaf, 1974), 74.

11. Dan G. Danner, "The Marian Exiles and the English Protestant Tradition," in *Social Groups and Religious Ideas in the Sixteenth Century*, ed. Miriam Chrisman and Otto Gründler (Kalamazoo: Medieval Institute, Eastern Michigan UP, 1978), 96—97; John Burn, *Livre des anglois à Genève* (London: n. p., 1831), 12—13.

12. Burn, *Livre des anglois à Genève*, 12—13.

13. "Extrait de l'Adresse présentée au Grand Conseil Constituant par la Direction et Diaconie de l'Église allemande réformée de Genève et de la Bourse allemande. (Lue au Grand Conseil dans sa séance du 15 février 1847)" in *La Communauté réformée allemande de Genève et la Paroisse protestante de langue allemande de l'Eglise Nationale: Documents divers et notices historiques*, ed. H. Fehr (Geneva: Gutenberg, 1917), 25—26.

14. "A ung pauvre Genevoys mallade par les main de . . . Bastie par ordonnance, 12 sols" (To a poor sick Genevan by the hands of . . . Bastie by ordinance, 12 sous). *AEG*, Archives hospitalières, Hj 2, [2] of September 1560; "A ung pauvre Hebreu qui s'en alloit en angleterre, 4 florins, 9 sols, 6 deniers" (To a poor Hebrew who was going to England, 4 florins, 9 sous, 6 deniers). *AEG*, Arch. hosp., Kg 14, August 18, 1553.

15. Emile Rivoire and Victor van Berchem, eds., *Les Sources du droit du Canton de Genève*, vol. 4, *1621—1700* (Arau: H. R. Sauerländer, 1935), 477.

16. Jérôme Sautier, "Politique et refuge: Genève face à la Révocation de l'Edit de Nantes," in *Genève au temps de la Révocation de l'Edit de Nantes, 1680—1705*, 1—158, MD, 50: 439—91 (Geneva: Droz, 1985), 47.

17. Cécile Holtz, "La Bourse française de Genève et le Refuge de 1684 à 1686," in *Genève au temps de la Révocation de l'Edit de Nantes, 1680—1705*, 487—89.

18. Henri Grandjean, "La Bourse Française de Genève (1550—1849)," in *Etrennes Genevoises* (Geneva: Atar, 1927), 54—57.

19. Ibid., 49.

20. Eugène Choisy, *L'état chrétien calviniste à Genève au temps de Théodore de Bèze* (Geneva: Ch. Eggimann, 1902), 69—70, 84—85, 88.

21. Grandjean, "La Bourse française de Genève," 51—52.

22. Ibid., 48.

23. *Notice publiée à l'occasion du cinquantième anniversaire de la fondation de l'Hôpital cantonal de Genève, 1856—1906*, ed. Commission administrative de l'Hôpital cantonal de Genève (Geneva: Atar, 1906), 17, 57.

24. Grandjean, "La Bourse française de Genève," 57.

25. Louis Binz, *Brève histoire de Genève*, 2d ed. (Geneva: Chancellerie d'État, 1985), 55; David Hiler and Bernard Lescaze, *Révolution inachevée révolution oubliée, 1842: Les Promesses de la Genève moderne* (Geneva: Suzanne Hurter, 1992), 139.

26. Binz, *Brève histoire de Genève*, 60—61.

27. Hiler and Lescaze, *Révolution inachevée révolution oubliée, 1842*, 141.

28. "Le gouvernement de ce canton a réservé pour les anciens genevois, c'est-à-dire pour la population protestante, toutes les ressources qu'offrent les établissements publics." Jean-François Vuarin, quoted in François Ruchon, *Histoire politique de la République de Genève de la restauration à la suppression du budget des cultes (31 décembre 1813- 30 juin 1907)*, vol. 1 (Geneva: A. Jullien, 1953), 151—53.

29. Jean-Claude Frachebourg, "James Fazy (1794—1878): L'homme, le démocrate, le magistrat," *Actes de l'Institut National Genevois*, new series of the Bulletin of the Institute National Genevois, no. 23 (Geneva: Institut National Genevois, 1979), 16.

30. Ibid., 9—12.

31. See, for instance, the 11-page pamphlet by James Fazy: *De la tentative de Napoléon Louis* (Geneva: P.-V. Oursel, 1836).

32. See also the biography of James Fazy: Henri Fazy, *James Fazy, Sa Vie et Son Oeuvre* (Geneva: H. Georg, 1887), 1–85.

33. Frachebourg, "James Fazy," 14–15.

34. Binz, *Brève histoire de Genève*, 58.

35. Frachebourg, "James Fazy," 20.

36. Binz, *Brève histoire de Genève*, 58; James Fazy, *Rapport de la Commission sur le Projet de Constitution du Canton de Genève* (Geneva: P.-A. Bonnant, 1847), 68.

37. "Loi sur l'établissement d'un Hôpital cantonal du 23 juin 1849," in *Notice publiée à l'occasion du cinquantième anniversaire de la fondation de l'Hôpital cantonal de Genève, 1856–1906*, 81–84.

38. Ibid., 21, 27.

39. Frachebourg, "James Fazy," 17.

40. Bernard Lescaze, ed., *Sauver l'âme, nourrir le corps, de l'Hôpital général à l'Hospice général de Genève, 1535–1985*, pref. Jean Imbert (Geneva: Hospice général, Atar, 1985), x–xi.

41. Grandjean, "La Bourse française de Genève," 59.

42. "Loi sur l'établissement d'un Hôpital cantonal du 23 juin 1849," in *Recueil authentique des lois et actes du gouvernement de la République et Canton de Genève*, vol. 30: *1849* (Geneva: Vaney, 1850), 286.

43. "Il est impossible de nier que, dans une république démocratique, il se rencontre quelque danger à laisser se perpétuer de certaines fondations, qui, établies d'abord avec les intentions les plus sincères d'utilité publique et de bienfaisance, finissent par dégénérer de leur noble but, et prennent, souvent à l'insu même de ceux qui les administrent, un caractère d'hostilité envers le principe démocratique . . . . La charité s'administre mal par l'esprit de coterie." Report of the *Conseil d'Etat* to the *Grand Conseil*, read by James Fazy on June 13, 1849, in Grandjean, "La Bourse française de Genève," 59.

44. Grandjean, "La Bourse française de Genève," 59–60.

45. "L'Établissement de Charité destiné au soulagement des Genevois d'origine française, connu sous le nom de Bourse Française, est réunie à l'Hôpital de Genève, pour être administré suivant sa destination." "Loi Générale sur les Fondations du 22 Août 1849," 397–408, in *Recueil authentique des lois et actes*, 30: 402.

46. "Sans entrer dans l'examen de l'organisation intérieure de l'Église allemande, et ne prenant en considération que l'existence d'une foundation dans cette Église, La [*sic*] Bourse allemande est maintenue, à la condition qu'elle soumettra l'élection de son administration financière à tous les membres actifs de l'Église allemande à laquelle elle est affectée, domiciliés dans le Canton, et dont il sera dressé un tableau quinze jours avant les élections; ce tableau pourra être rectifié sur appel au Conseil d'État. Cette administration sera soumise tous les cinq ans à une nouvelle élection." "Loi Générale sur les Fondations du 22 Août 1849," 397–408, in *Recueil authentique des lois et actes*, 30: 403.

47. Grandjean, "La Bourse française de Genève," 59–60.

48. Ruchon, *Histoire politique*, 2: 70–74.

49. "[Pourquoi] réunir leurs fonds à d'autres établissements, en conservant, il est vrai, la destination sur le papier, sans qu'un examen sérieux et des faits justifiés aient établi que la destination serait mieux remplie par le corps nouveau auquel on la confie que par le corps ancien et spécial que l'on supprime." In ibid., 73.

50. Ruchon, *Histoire politique*, 2: 74.

51. "Arrêté du Conseil d'État du 11 Septembre 1849," 421–23, in *"Recueil authentique des lois et actes*, 30: 422.

52. Ibid., 421–424; Ruchon, *Histoire politique*, 2: 74.

53. "Arrêté du Conseil d'État du 11 Septembre 1849," 421–424.

54. Grandjean, "La Bourse française de Genève," 60.

55. Ruchon, *Histoire politique*, 2: 74.

56. Heyer, *L'Èglise de Genève*, 74–75.

57. "Règlement sur l'institution de Diaconies dans la ville de Genève du 4 avril 1850," in Église Nationale Protestante de Genève, *Les Diaconies de la ville de Genève: Leur origine et leur activité de 1850 à 1900 avec le tableau des membres; Rapports présentés à la séance annuelle du Consistoire et des Diaconie, le 27 novembre 1900, par MM. Henri Heyer, ancien pasteur, et Louis Johannot, Diacres de la Fusterie* (Geneva: Henry Kündig, 1901), 27.

10

Notre Bienheureuse Réformation: The Meaning of the Reformation in Nineteenth-Century Geneva

John B. Roney

In comparison to twentieth-century scholarship, knowledge of the sixteenth-century Reformation in Geneva, and the meaning of the events for contemporary times, was not so clearly established in the early nineteenth century. It was not until the mid-nineteenth century that historians such as Jules Michelet and Jakob Burckhardt imbued the Renaissance and Reformation periods with enhanced meaning for the birth of the *modern* world. Since the sixteenth century, however, Geneva had been identified as the Reformation city, and this became, once again, a key ingredient for a new identity forged in the early nineteenth century. As a result the great changes wrought by the French Revolutionary wars, individuals and nations searched for a new understanding of the origins of this new era. With far less certainty about knowledge, and a growing recognition of the uniqueness of different historical periods, historians struggled to find continuity with the past.

Interest in the sixteenth-century Reformation in the French-speaking world increased and was influenced through the rise of French Revolution historiography.[1] Explanations, condemnations, or support very often placed the origin of modern ideas in the sixteenth century. Historians looked for a number of key concepts in the Reformation that had gained importance as a result of the French Revolution, such as liberty, freedom, conscience, popular sovereignty, the nation, and the people. Martin Luther and John Calvin either became known as heroes, for their individual and courageous proclamation of liberty and religious conscience, or were blamed for unleashing the forces of evil culminating in the breakdown of society, order, and decency. Neither those who supported the Revolution nor those who condemned it really believed that it could have happened so suddenly. Romantic thought offered a structure to early-nineteenth-century historical explanation.[2] A romantic view of history searched for long-range development and located any legitimacy in the discovery of the people or nation as it had been constituted over time. The study of the Reformation followed this same pattern: Did the sixteenth-century reform come as a result of internal forces and the will of the people, an original genius, or as an external imposition through foreign ideas and individual wills? Although the traditional appeal to the will of God was still offered as an explanation, the authoritative standards had clearly shifted to temporal and national legitimacy.

The Reformation in Genevan thought attempted to reestablish the significance of the sixteenth-century reform as a means to understand the place of religion and national identity after four decades of rapid change.[3] When the 300th anniversary (tercentenary) of the Reformation in Geneva came in 1835, a great *Jubilé* celebration was planned. This event demanded a more concrete statement about the meaning of the Reformation. National identity (referring to the Republic of Geneva) was still intricately related to religious identity, yet both had changed substantially in the last decades. By the early 1830s three distinctive groups or parties (*parti*) emerged, two Protestant and one Catholic, that had a vested interest in redefining the meaning of the Reformation. The larger and established Protestant group was represented by the National Protestant Church of Geneva (*L'Église nationale protestante*). Although they were heirs of the Reformed Church established by Calvin, after the restoration of the Republic from the French Empire and membership in the Swiss Confederation in 1815 as a Canton, they had more clearly distinguished themselves as the "National" and "Protestant" church, and only occasionally as the Reformed church (*L'Église Reformée de Genève*). This was primarily a result of the great increase of Catholics into the enlarged territory of the Canton and Republic of Geneva, and they saw their own development toward a more unified and broadly based Protestant church—they may be called "neo-Protestants"—and less an identity with Calvin or a narrowly defined Reformed church.[4] They had an interest in defending their legitimacy as the state church while recognizing a more plural society. A strong and unified state church, they believed, would be the only way to bring order and stability—the *juste milieu*—to the new Canton.

The second Protestant party were newly established as a result of the religious *Réveil* (revival) that occurred in 1817.[5] With roots in Pietism and Moravian spirituality, this group sought to reform individual religious belief and practice. Although there were degrees of variation, ranging from a very individual Pietism to doctrinal orthodoxy (Reformed), there was common agreement on the necessity of reforming the church as an institution and on an individual conversion experience. Among visiting British Protestants, who saw an opportunity for renewed Protestant activity on the continent after the defeat of Napoleon, Robert Haldane was the most successful in leading a Bible study that was attended by many students of theology.[6] Through their conflict with the National Church, in the 1820s, followers of the *Réveil* either voluntarily left the Church or were forced to leave. The conflicts were primarily with the Vénérable Compagnie des Pastuers (Company of Pastors), the regulating ecclesiastical body, and the main defenders of the National Church within the Compagnie were the pastors and professors Jean-Jacques Caton Chenevière (Hebrew) and Jacob-Elisée Cellérier (theology). The *Réveil* formed a number of separate churches, chapels, and dissenting congregations.[7] By the 1830s the most influential *Réveil* group was a congregation meeting in the Chapelle de l'Oratoire under the leadership of Louis Gaussen, Jean Henri Merle d'Aubigné, and Antoine Galland—all dismissed of their pastoral ministries in the National Church in 1831. They founded the *Société évangélique de Genève* as an organization to promote traditional orthodoxy, Bible study, and evangelization, and an École de théologie to train ministers. They represented an influential group in their size, social status, and education. In contrast to many of the other *Réveil* groups who came from the lower classes, this group claimed many aristocrats, governmental leaders, and rising (haute) bourgeoisie. The Oratoire offered a real threat to the National Church's Protestant identity because it promoted a return to the teachings of the reformers. The group claimed not to have left the Church but to have simply become a distinct party within it, much like the Puritans or Methodists had done in the Church of England. "We belong to the Reformed church," claimed the pastors of the Oratoire, "as it was founded three hundred years ago in Switzerland, Germany, Holland, Great Britain, and in Geneva."[8]

The third group represented the growing numbers of Roman Catholics who received freedom to worship under French occupation, and again under the newly established Canton and Republic of Geneva. Although they possessed little political power in the early nineteenth century, by the mid-century they began to command much more political clout. Catholic political power lagged far behind its rising population, and by 1860 they actually outnumbered Protestants in Geneva.[9] With the celebration of the *Jubilé* in 1835, the Catholic Church, and especially its outspoken priest Jean-François Vuarin, saw the necessity of setting the record straight by calling on the historically legitimate Catholic Church that had existed before the sixteenth-century religious revolution. All three groups realized that Genevan identity in general had to be extended to a diverse and religiously plural population of citizens, but each struggled to define its own set of characteristics, largely religious in nature, that expressed the core of the real historically accurate identity.

Under the direction of the National Church, a committee (*Comité du Jubilé*) planned the celebration of the Reformation in the *Jubilé* of 1835 and designed it to be a national Genevan festival and an internationally recognized Protestant festival. In this way they hoped to include all citizens, even Catholics, in some aspect of the religious and political celebration.[10] No doubt few Catholics took this invitation seriously, but approximately 160 foreign Protestant pastors did attend. It was helpful to claim some advantages to the Reformation, whether religious or political, because all knew that the Reformation had brought international renown to this small city and republic. Through a number of important histories, the official commemorative sermons delivered August 23, 1835, announcements, and brochures, agreements and disagreements about the meaning of the Reformation for nineteenth-century Genevan identity are represented.[11]

All Protestants looked to the Reformation with pride, and the consistent phrase to describe it was "our blessed Reformation" (*notre bienheureuse Réformation*). There is much agreement among Protestants that God had finally decided to bring a change to the corrupt state of Geneva in the sixteenth century. The motto of the Genevan Reformation, *post tenebras lux*, still meant "after the [Medieval] darkness came the light" of the Reformation.[12] By largely secondary means, God prepared the soil for reform, then raised up certain individuals and groups to promote political and religious changes.[13] With characteristically nineteenth-century concerns in mind, the Reformation had brought "liberty" and "freedom" to the "people" of Geneva. It once and for all eliminated an abuse of privilege and power that had been limited to the Catholic bishop-lords (*L'Évêque seigneurs*) with their medieval feudal rights. The Reformation ensured Geneva of political independence from the neighboring French or Savoyard powers that would have liked to dominate this wealthy and strategic city. Geneva's new religious adherence further cemented their relationship of political alliances, which in turn brought them protection with the help of the Protestant cities of Bern and Neuchâtel and support from many other cities throughout Europe. Political and religious liberty were thus inseparable.

A second fundamental change in the Reformation was the establishment of freedom of conscience. Within a Christian humanist tradition, all believers became free to know God through a reading of Scripture, prayer, and study, without any mediatorial assistance. The reformers had established a new tradition of knowledge and responsibility for the development of their own faith. The tradition of education remained one of Geneva's greatest achievements. All Protestants could agree that the authority of the Bible became the key accomplishment of the Reformation. In fact, the Bible was raised to the first rank. Cellérier echoed the Protestants of Geneva when he said, "Our *Jubilé*, festival of the Reformation, is also a festival of the Bible; for you have seen it: the Bible is the flag of the Protestants. As good soldiers, defend it!"[14]

The great debate over the Reformation in Geneva hinged on two central questions: Did a substantial number of the original Genevese people support the change to Protestantism in general and Calvin's interpretation in particular, and how normative were the confessions and rules of Calvin for the contemporary church in Geneva? Paralleling a French Revolution historiographical question, did the people, the true nation without any foreign meddling, choose a new social organization that would lead toward self-determination? In this light, was the Reformation a better expression of the people of Geneva? Unlike many other cities, sixteenth-century Geneva experienced a great influx of refugees who resettled there after religious persecution—Geneva, in short, became a city of refuge—could they become the people of Geneva? Throughout nineteenth-century France the indigenous nature of the Reformation was also a question.[15]

The unique contribution of Reformed theological thinking was to develop a new religious identity based, not so much on geographical or ethnic common history, but on a religious identity based on God's chosen and gathered people who possessed no land of their own. Geneva became known as the New Jerusalem, a promised land for God's people who had wandered in the desert of persecution. As a chosen people, Cellérier affirmed, they "quit their family and *patrie* in order to go as Abraham, where God led them, thinking: go to Geneva; the conscience of Protestants is free there."[16] Throughout Europe the Reformed churches often referred to themselves as a new Israel, and they accepted the original covenant of God and the normative laws given to Israel as a new support for legitimacy, rather than having to argue along Catholic apostolic, early church, or medieval authoritative lines. Whether part of the established church or the parties of the *Réveil*, reference to the Reformed Church of Geneva as the chosen people and Israel was clearly still part of their identity. They represented a new combination of Hellenic thought and Hebraic tradition that were the roots of Western culture.[17] Had God not taken back his covenant, as revealed in Scripture, and had the Catholic Church ignored the covenant, then the Reformed church, and Geneva in particular, had received the blessing! "It is the people of Geneva assembled," Chenevière underlined, "like ancient Israel at another time, before the Word of God."[18] Unlike Israel, however, the people of God in Geneva were not a blood tribe; they represented a collection of the elect from Italian-, French-, Spanish-, and English-speaking countries: "These refugees are our fathers. We carry in our veins the blood of all countries; but whether it is from the Orient or from the Occident, from the North or Middle, it matters little; it was always the blood of pious men, laborious and conscientious, completely devoted in their hearts to the *patrie* which they took as their own."[19] Rather than being a weakness, ethnic diversity further increased Geneva's international reputation and created a stronger nation.

Educated in the school of the Enlightenment, and paralleling early evolutionary views, professor David François Munier advanced his own view of development in Western civilization: "I consider therefore the apparition of Protestantism as a natural phase of progress of Christian society to the defects without number that the barbarism of the Middle Ages, and the false light of pagan philosophy, brought to this development. Since then, Protestantism and Catholicism do not offer, in my view because of their origins, two irreconcilable enemies."[20] In this viewpoint, Munier attempted to avoid a polemical history; he envisioned a natural development whereby Protestantism would eventually benefit all of society, including new light for Catholicism. Development meant progress. Like Munier, Étienne Chastel underlined that "the essence of Protestantism, . . . is progress."[21]

Many other Protestants proclaimed that the bishop-seigneurs of the sixteenth century were, in fact, foreign to Geneva. By imposing their foreign feudal rights on the independent Genevese, and by obeying the popes in Rome, they deviated from the natural sovereignty of the people. Bedot claimed that the Reformation had detached "the citizens from all foreign influence in order to connect them forever more to their magistrates and to their natural princes."[22] Cellérier claimed that the true people of Geneva wanted liberty: "This day [May 1536] truly Geneva was reformed, for the nation as a body had spoken, and no one had contradicted, saying: I don't want it, and I protest."[23] And, regarding its own legitimacy, "the Reformation was thus sovereignly decided."[24] This claim for the sovereignty of the people was justification enough for the natural development and legitimacy of the sixteenth-century Reformation.

Despite this designation, neither the National Church nor the *Réveil* wanted to exclude Catholics from Geneva, and they therefore called for a new tolerance, within the understanding that Protestantism still held the upper hand. The Reformation had brought political liberty, and this independence had allowed Geneva to develop to its potential in education, commerce, morals, and customs. If Catholics could not accept the religious arguments, certainly they should be able to recognize the political and material progress since the sixteenth century. Munier summarized these practical effects of the Reformation: "Independence, public spirit, love of liberty and order, living and true patriotism, simple and austere customs, external considerations, honorable and guardianship alliances, protection from the great states of Europe, sympathetic bonds with generous nations, Geneva has possessed all goodness, and it has only obtained it by following the Reformation."[25]

Until very recently Genevan Protestant historiography of the Reformation has avoided a focus on the degree to which a revolution occurred in the early sixteenth century. William Monter has pointed out that "the earliest such admission dates from 1926, but the official history of 1951 still refers to the decade after 1526 under the euphemism of 'political emancipation'."[26] Certainly the early nineteenth century was no exception. Protestant tradition clearly envisioned that the counselors of 1536 had acted with full legality based on ancient liberties that had been subsequently overtaken by the usurping bishops and princes. Monter, however, claims that in "this revolution, Geneva's citizens had usurped one by one the various prerogatives of their Bishop." Although at the same time he confirms that the revolution was justified because "their Bishop had in fact deserted them."[27]

Catholics did not find it advantageous to accept this New Jerusalem and argued for the legitimacy of an original population loyal to the medieval Catholic tradition. Reformation ideas were foreign to the people of Geneva. In his book entitled *Calvin à Genève*, Abbot Fleury underlined this theme of the foreign character of the Reformation. According to Fleury's reading of the sixteenth-century decision, some malcontent Catholics, who sought only political freedom, turned to foreign cities for alliance. Bern, which had become Reformed, became a good ally. When the lone Genevan reformer Guillaume Farel needed help, "a stranger came to his aid. It was Calvin."[28] At first Calvin was known only as the "Frenchman" ("*ce Français*"), and for Fleury this only proved his foreign takeover. Reminiscent of the evil in the French Revolution, Calvin was a Maximilien Robespierre: Calvin wanted an "inquisitorial chair" and a "code of terror."[29] In addition, "Calvin favored the recruitment of anti-nationals with all his force, and gave the titles of bourgeois, under the pretext of religion, to all those who came to seek asylum in Geneva."[30] To counter the wonderful Protestant image of a chosen people coming to Geneva through God's guidance, Fleury claimed that "Calvin had his plan; he wanted to infuse in the veins of the recalcitrant republic a new blood."[31] There was, therefore, no legitimate claim to the notion that the people of Geneva chose the Reformation; they were clearly coerced. In fact, it was probably the very tolerance of the Catholic bishops that allowed the Protestant powers to grow, and "if the vicar-general of the bishop would have acted the same way [intolerant] against the first religious trouble-makers in Geneva, they would have assuredly saved the ancient faith."[32] When a small group of reformers convinced the Council to accept its heresy and condemn and exile all dissenters, it became much easier to claim universal acceptance. Once Calvin became the "absolute master" the "national party only existed in the memories."[33] Catholics wanted to remain loyal to Genevan independence. Catholics preserved the idea that the original inhabitants of Geneva gained their liberty without the help of foreign powers. The one glory of the persecuted Catholic Church in Geneva was their attention to the care and needs of the people: "One had restricted the priests of their functions, but they continued to fulfill them in the shadows, visiting the sick, baptizing the local children, and encouraging the faithful to rest firm in the tempest."[34]

By mid-sixteenth century Geneva came to represent a real rival to Rome; indeed, many Protestants in the early nineteenth century still referred to the city as *la Rome protestante*.[35] Since that time, however, Geneva gradually ceased to be recognized as a leader in the Protestant world. By the early nineteenth century few Genevans believed that they should still follow all the confessions and practices of Calvin. Times had changed! Nonetheless, the degree to which Calvin had represented any normative expressions of true Christianity remained a lively issue.

The National Church universally believed that Calvin was lacking in key areas, and therefore no confessions of the sixteenth century, nor in fact, any human doctrinal statements, could be binding on any Christian. First, the sixteenth century was a time of extreme violence and intolerance. If the reformers fought fire with fire, their tactic may have been excusable given the temper of the time, but it had no place in the nineteenth century. Edouard Diodati underlined the point that "they addressed themselves exclusively to the needs of the times, and the movement produced was only an expression of those needs."[36] Second, Calvin had established a new work that highlighted the Gospel, obscured for centuries, but he never achieved a fully balanced Christian life. After all, Étienne Chastel claimed, "one would not have supposed that the reformers, despite their science and genius, would have embraced the entire truth at first."[37] Cellérier saw that "the genius of Calvin, good, certain, and admirable, was completely in his head; he did not know enough, perhaps he misunderstood, he did not search to develop the religion of the heart."[38] Although Calvin established the Bible as the new authoritative source, he could not progress beyond human formulations. The immediate successors of Calvin carried on this legacy of the Middle Ages: They relied on human authority to regulate matters of the heart.[39] It was not until the eighteenth century that the Church of Geneva abolished human confessions (1725), a practice strongly reconfirmed by the strict adherence to individual conscience in the nineteenth century.[40] Whereas Calvin had taken the important first step, but the Church of Geneva had developed his original intent to its fullest expressions. In this way, Chenevière claimed, the Genevan church had returned to the faith of the early church and found a better expression for the times.[41] Calvin's real contribution was his organizational strength in the church and in education. Accordingly, Calvin's great example of love of country, church, and Bible should be followed, not his confessions and catechisms.

This is exactly where the *Réveil* Protestants found their greatest disagreement with the National Church. In their minds, the National Church still followed Enlightenment principles of free inquiry based on the Baconian inductive method. This method started from observation; it found knowledge built on principle or inner sensibility superfluous. The *Réveil*, in contrast, embraced more fully the romantic tendency to use the deductive method. A priori assumptions became the starting point for any investigation, and only then to evidence. The inductive method used by the National church and the deductive method favored by *Réveil* Protestants were bound to create very different pathways. The two groups agreed that the times had changed, but the *Réveil* believed that the general doctrinal faith established by Calvin remained a normative standard for the nineteenth century. Calvin had reaped the full fruits of the Reformation. Without denying the needs for the times, the *Réveil* claimed that Calvin's confessions were really commentaries on the Bible, and still represented the best interpretations for the Christian life. But the real point was that the church had to promote a vibrant faith. The National Church accused the *Réveil* of uncritically promoting the ancient human confessions of Calvin. This rhetoric came from a conflict that had developed between the *Vénérable Compagnie* and a very small group of orthodox pastors who wanted to republish key Reformation confessions to discuss their relevance to the times.[42] The original intent of honoring the confessions, however, was never that they act as a fixed standard but as a resevoir from which modern statements of belief might flow—the *Réveil* downplayed the scholastic confessions of Dort, for example. Merle d'Aubigné contrasted the time-bound nature of confessions with their application. Christianity consisted of unchanging principles, an "eternal theology," that needed to find an appropriate form in every new age.[43] Moreover, the National Church not only had rejected Calvin's confessions, denying his very desires, but had ignored Scripture for the church's own humanly devised moral teachings. This accusation is highly charged given the atmosphere of polemics in the 1820s and 1830s, and is therefore difficult to judge. Evidence suggests that late eighteenth-century educators did not study the Bible with any regularity and found many passages irrelevant to contemporary issues. While a theological student, and a committed member of the National Church at the time, Merle d'Aubigné claimed that the Bible was never read at school, but that in its place the classical authors were vigorously studied.[44] To the *Réveil* leaders, it was not a matter of strict adherence to every confession of Calvin but a question of orthodoxy, centered on the divinity of Christ and his atonement for sins, that they found to be unmistakably the central teaching of the Bible and the Christian Church in every century.[45]

The Oratoire and the *Société évangélique* were not alone in their return to orthodoxy; they had widespread international support, as did the National Church.[46] In fact, the *Réveil* accused the National Church of foreign and Enlightenment influences by designating them as "latitudinarian," "socinian," or "rationalist," and "pelagian."[47] These accusations had already been used by many foreign churches where Calvinism had become an idealized form of Christianity; the churches were appalled at the stories of apostasy they had heard about Geneva.[48] During the *Jubilé* conference meetings in August 1835, a lively discussion ensued about the controversy between the National Church and the *Réveil*. Given the numerous foreign delegates who spoke—and the selection of delegates had excluded all international *Réveil* leaders—there was still equal support for both sides. Those who appealed for a reconciliation claimed that the two positions differed only on a few points and that toleration demanded a new peaceful solution. The National Church claimed that the *Réveil* came from foreign influences and was responsible for the struggles in the church and state. Although the *Réveil* did have foreign support from Britain, France, other Swiss cantons, the German lands, and the Netherlands, which would legitimately increase the National Church fears, there is no real evidence that they had any institutional or political interests outside their appeal to the central teachings of Scripture. In the end, both sides were responsible for the conflict in church and state, and during these early years of the new canton of Geneva increased tensions often came from unfounded fears rather than real intentions. In the opinion of Chenevière, the *Réveil*'s "narrow principles . . . are not those of the Reformation."[49] Professor Chastel echoed the fear of many in the National Church that the *Réveil* was perhaps a British plot: "Implanting under the religious flag, none other than the British one, they wanted to stifle as much as possible all the bad germs that had been allowed by the [French] revolution."[50] Within this framework, the *Vénérable Compagnie* constantly referred to the *Réveil* as Methodists. The real problem with the *Réveil*, they felt, was a return to human authority. They attract "simple souls, pressed to renounce their connection with heaven, who accept without enough examination the ancient doctrines."[51] For the National Church, any use of confessions of faith denied the free examination of the Bible and faith; such use denied, in short, the right of every individual conscience. Yet the *Réveil* also claimed to protect individual conscience. Merle d'Aubigné constantly returned to the principle that "conscience, which is the voice of God, is higher than all the voices of men," and it was Calvin himself who recognized that "it was God's will that he should be there, and this conviction was constantly presenting itself to his conscience."[52] In the end the National Church found that the "confessions of faith were one of the great obstacles to the diffusion of tolerance."[53]

Catholics used the Protestant controversy to undermine the integrity of the National Church and the Reformation. On the one hand, the Abbots Martin and Fleury quoted from Henri Empaytaz, an early *Réveil* leader, who had castigated the National Church for its denial of the divinity of Christ. "It was an indictment in form, calm, but irrefutable, against the Socinianism of the degenerate inheritors of Calvin."[54] Coinciding with the *Jubilé* in 1835 was an unveiling of a commemorative monument to Jean-Jacques Rousseau, and this further confirmed Catholic opinion of the apostasy of the National Church.[55] Vuarin published a scathing brochure entitled *L'ombre de Rousseau*, in which he exposed the theology of the National Church as identical to Rousseau's.[56] In this way, argued Vuarin, the National Church does not have the right to call itself heirs of the Church of Calvin; by doing so it misleads all other Protestant churches. "Truly this dear and venerable Compagnie has committed a contempt which will cause many regrets; . . . it is that they reject all the confessions of faith, all the symbols consecrated in the 16th and 17th centuries."[57] The *Réveil* was also scandalized at the homage paid to Rousseau and supported Geneva's earlier condemnation.[58] On the other hand, the Catholic authors used the opinions of the National Church to fault Calvin as well: "'Under the severe forms to which Calvin prepared himself', M. Chenevière, professor at the Academy of Geneva, has said, 'the Gospel has an iron arm; humans are determined by fatality, and Christianity, so beautiful in the mouth of its chief, becomes a cruel law.'"[59] The Catholic argument for confessions was based on a wholly different set of principles, however: Unaltered was their support for the traditions of the Catholic Church, the ecumenical creeds—with the *Réveil*—and the teachings of the pope.

Debate over the meaning of the Reformation continued throughout the nineteenth century, but the framework of the argument had changed. Opinions about the meaning of the Reformation were conceived from within their contemporary experience, hope for unity, and the desire to construct a new identity. William Bouwsma has made a convincing argument for the existence of "two Calvins": one a philosopher and rationalist, who produced a "static orthodoxy"; the other a rhetorician and humanist, who "celebrated paradoxes and mystery at the heart of existence . . . the primacy of experience and . . . tolerance for individual freedom."[60] If Bouwsma is right, the National Church and the Oratoire may have been responding to different aspects of Calvin.[61] Looking ahead to the late eighteenth century, Bouwsma claims that "the polar extremes of evangelical pietism and deistic rationalism . . . can also plausibly claim Calvin as spiritual father."[62] Despite this, both sides may well have also missed the complexity that was Calvin; at the same time, they knew they had to re-create him for the new times. There were no juridical and governmental powers behind religious beliefs and practices, and less and less pressure to conform to one religious standard as a mark of national identity. The debate became a *guerre de plume* and it appealed to a very tangible public opinion, which was based on a growing freedom of speech and belief. Accompanying the many polemical words, as well, was an increasing toleration and recognition of the necessity of works of charity and philanthropy. Chenevière proclaimed that "a new crusade is proposed; a crusade entirely inoffensive, entirely based on benevolence and charity."[63] The National Church had to set an example of social care if it wanted to promote order and unity. Even the *Réveil*, linked closely to the international Evangelical anti-papal campaign—a direct inheritance from the sixteenth-century reformers—could hold works of charity for all as a necessary aspect of their faith. It was within the *Réveil*'s youth organizations that Jean-Henri Dunant, founder of the Red Cross (*Croix-Rouge*), received his inspiration.[64] No matter the interpretation, a common call for Christian works of charity unified Genevans and helped to create a new national identity as a city that supported those in need. In addition, all Protestants recognized that the true principles of the Reformation were the free examination of the Bible, individual conscience, and the necessity of articulating the Gospel in forms appropriate for the needs of the times, enabling greater numbers to live in peace and harmony. In the end, although the debate over the interpretation of the Reformation never ceased, the controversy stimulated deeper thinking about how to interpret history and still practice tolerance and charity. It made them think further about liberty and conscience, and how to live in a more plural and democratic society. Merle d'Aubigné addressed the apparent problem of divisions as a result of a concentration on the Reformation by pointing to the free examination of history.

But is there not reason to fear that the history of the Church, and of the Reformation in particular, may revive polemics, above all against the Roman Catholics, and may re-open the wounds of the Western church, as yet but imperfectly healed? I believe the reverse. History will doubtless show us, in a general way, truth on one side, and error on the other. But she will show us good and evil mixed here and there; she will show us, on the side of Catholics, many a true Christian, although in some respects certainly but little enlightened, and on the side of the Protestants, many a man unworthy of the name. She will show us Catholicism adding, without doubt, many things to the Word of God, but preserving, nevertheless, most of the fundamental doctrines of Christianity, the depravity of man, salvation through the atonement, the essential divinity of the Redeemer, the indispensable work of the Holy Spirit in the heart.[65]

A new examination of the Reformation was a necessary aspect of developing a new Genevan identity that recognized the continuing place of the Christian commonwealth, however broadly defined, in the nineteenth century. The Reformation was "blessed" because it was the origin of the modern concerns for freedom, liberty, conscience, and progress.

NOTES

1. See Linda Orr, *Headless History: Nineteenth-Century French Historiography of the Reformation* (Ithaca, NY: Cornell UP, 1990).

2. See Stephen Bann, *Romanticism and the Rise of History* (New York: Twayne, 1995).

3. See John B. Roney, *The Inside of History: Jean Henri Merle d'Aubigné and Romantic Historiography* (Westport, CT: Greenwood Press, 1996), for a longer analysis of the Reformation and a religious history of Geneva in the early nineteenth century.

4. Bernard Reymond, "Les Premières livraisons du *Protestant de Genève* et le contexte théologique et religieux de 1831," in *Genève protestante en 1831*, ed. Olivier Fatio (Geneva: Labor et Fides, 1983), 52, has described the National Church as "neo-Protestants." This designation sets them apart from nineteenth-century liberalism and is perhaps a better term than "pre-liberal," used by Daniel Robert, *Les Églises reformées en France 1800-1830* (Paris: Presses Universitaire de France, 1961).

5. In 1810 Ami Bost and some students (Henri-Louis Empaytaz, Émile Guers, Henry Pyt, and Jean Gonthier) formed the *Société des amis* with the purpose of theological discussion and the practice of piety. See Henri Dubief, "Réflexions sur quelques aspects du premier Réveil et sur le milieu où se forma," *BSHPF* 114 (1968): 392; Ulrich Gäbler, "Der Weg zum Réveil in Genf," *Zwingliana* 16, no. 2 (1983): 142–167; Gabriel Mützenberg, *A l'Écoute du Réveil* (St-Légier: Éditions Emmaüs, 1989); Ernest Rochat, *Le mouvement théologique dans l'Église de Genève au cours du XIXe siècle* (Geneva: H. Georg, 1933).

6. Robert Haldane, a Congregational Calvinistic-Revivalist from Scotland, visited Geneva from 1816 to 1817. See Alexander Haldane, *Memoirs of the Lives of Robert Haldane of Airthrey, and of His Brother, James Alexander Haldane* (New York: Robert Carter and Brothers, 1858). Richard Wilcox, a Calvinist-Methodist, like George Whitefield, visited in 1816. Henry Drummond, London banker, former British MP, and later Irvingite, came in 1817.

7. The L'Église du Bourg-de-Four began in 1818 and soon had 300 members, including Henri-Louis Empaytaz, Henry Pyt, Jean Gonthier, Émile Guers, and Felix Neff; it was pietistic and attracted people from the lower classes. A second group, under Ami Bost, opened a congregation in Carouge, a working-class suburb of Geneva. A third group of strict Calvinists under César Malan opened the Chapelle du Témoignage in 1820. See Ami Bost, *Mémoirs peuvent servir l'histoire du réveil religieux*, 2 vols. (Paris: Meyreuis et C., 1854); Emile Guers, *Le Premier Réveil et la Première Église Indépendante à Genève* (Geneva: Béroud et Kaufmann, 1871); Henri Heyer, *L'Église de Genève, 1535–1909* (Geneva: A. Jullien, 1909), 124–133; Léon Maury, *Le Réveil religieux dans l'Église Reformée à Genève et en France (1810–1850): Étude historique et dogmatique*, 2 vols. (Paris: Fischbacher, 1892).

8. Louis Gaussen, Jean Henri Merle d'Aubigné, et al., *La Direction de l'École de Théologie établie dans L'Église Reformée de Genève* (Geneva: Susanne Guers, 1833), 22.

9. See Jean-Claude Favez and Claude Raffestin, "De la Genève radicale à la cité internationale," in *Histoire de Genève*, ed. Paul Guichonnet (Toulouse: Privat, 1974), 302–303. In 1860 there were 40,069 Protestants and 42,099 Catholics.

10. See the committee report, *Récit des principale circonstances qui ont signalé du célébration du 3e Jubilé de la Réformation de Genève en l'an 1835* (Geneva: Abraham Cherbuliez, 1835), 14.

11. The official commemorate sermons of the *Jubilé* by pastors in the National Church are published in *Jubilé de la Réformation de Genève. Août 1835*, 3 vols., vol. 1, *Liturgies et Sermons* (Geneva: Charles Gruaz, 1835), containng: Charles Bourrit, "Sermon sur psaume 121: 12, 13, prononcé le dimanche 23 août 1835, dans le temple de Saint-Gervais, a neuf heures"; Jean Jacques Chenevière, "Sermon sur psaume 126: 3, prononcé le dimanche 23 août 1835, dans la cathédrale de Saint-Pierre, à midi"; Edouard Diodati, "Sermon sur I Cor. 2: 2, prononcé le dimanche 23 août 1835, dans la cathédrale de Saint-Pierre, à neuf heures"; David François Munier, "Sermon sur I Tim. 6: 20, prononcé le dimanche 23 août 1835, dans le temple Saint-Gervais, à midi"; le pasteur Bedot, "Sermon sur Éphes. 5: 8, prononcé le dimanche 23 août 1835, dans le temple de la madelaine, à neuf heures." [vol. 1 hereafter cited as *Sermons*.] See also vol. 2: *Correspondance, historiques et conférences*, and vol. 3: *Mélanges*; and the official history: Jacob-Elisée Cellérier, *Le Jubilé de la Réformation; Histoire d'autrefois* (Geneva: Abraham Cherbuliez, 1835).

12. See Chenevière, in *Sermons*, 61, "darkness of superstition . . . the sun of the Reformation"; Bedot, in *Sermons*, 189.

13. This has universal agreement. See Cellérier, *Histoire d'autrefois*, 11, 54, 55, 58, 67, 93, 120, 122; Bouritt, in *Sermons*, 31; Chenevière, in *Sermons*, 71, 72; Diodati, in *Sermons*, 92, 93, 97; Munier, in *Sermons*, 138, 141; Jean Henri Merle d'Aubigné, *History of the Reformation of the Sixteenth Century*, 5 vols. (Grand Rapids, MI: Baker Books, 1976 [1853]), 4: ix. The romantic historical method allowed Christian historians to discuss divine activity in the world through God's immanence, without denying transcendence, and this opened up the possibility of appealing to the scientific and epistemological orientation of the age.

14. Cellérier, *Histoire d'autrefois*, 101.

15. See André Encreve, "Image de la Réforme chez les protestants français de 1830 à 1870,"in *Historiographie de la Réforme*, ed. Philippe Joutard (Paris: Delachaux et Niestle, 1977), 182–199.

16. Cellérier, *Histoire d'autrefois*, 165. See Bourrit, in *Sermons*, 24; Diodati, in *Sermons*, 89, 116; Bedot, in *Sermons*, 190, 193; Munier, in *Sermons*, 123–124.

17. William Bouwsma, in *John Calvin: A Sixteenth-Century Portrait* (New York: Oxford UP, 1988), claims Calvin initiated this new combination. Calvin did not reject the early church or Greek civilization. He respected the early Fathers and believed they would have sided with the reform (see 83, 103).

18. Chenevière, in *Sermons*, 90.

19. Cellérier, *Histoires d'autrefois*, 168. See also Bedot, in *Sermons*, 206; Bourrit, in *Sermons*, 41.

20. Munier, in *Sermons*, 128.

21. Étienne Chastel, *Conférences sur l'histoire du christianisme prêchées à Genève*, 2 vols. (Valence: Marc Aurel frères, 1839–1847), 1:241. Chastel was professor of ecclesiastical history and a pastor in the National Church. See also Jean Henri Merle d'Aubigné, *Discours sur l'étude du christianisme, et son utilité pour l'époque actuelle* (Paris: J. J. Risler, 1832), 35.

22. Bedot, in *Sermons*, 209.

23. Cellérier, *Histoire d'autrefois*, 141.

24. Ibid., 142.

25. Munier, in *Sermons*, 139.

26. E. William Monter, *Calvin's Geneva* (New York: John Wiley and Sons, 1967), 58.

27. Ibid., 57.

28. L'Abbé Fleury, *Calvin à Genève: Quelques pages de sa vie à l'occasion du 300me anniversaire de sa mort par un Genevois* (Geneva: Pfeffer et Puky, 1864), 14.

29. Ibid., 17.

30. Ibid., 89.

31. Ibid., 90.

32. Ibid., 18.

33. Ibid., 118.

34. Ibid., 11.

35. See Bourrit, in *Sermons*, 29; Munier, in *Sermons*, 141. See also André Biéler, *La Pensée économique et sociale de Calvin* (Geneva: Georg, 1961); Charles Borgeaud, *Monument international de la Réformation à Genève: Le groupe centrale* (Geneva: Albert Kündig, 1911), 5; Favez and Raffestin, "De la Genève radicale," 302–303; W. Fred Graham, *The Constructive Revolutionary: John Calvin and His Socio-Economic Impact* (Atlanta, GA: John Knox Press, 1971); René Guerdan, *Histoire de Genève* (Geneva: Éditions du Mont-Blanc, 1977), 75–169; Heyer, *L'Église de Genève, 1535–1909*, 7–39; Robert Kingdon, *Geneva and the Consolidation of the French Protestant Movement 1564–1572* (Madison: U of Wisconsin P, 1967); Émile G. Léonard, *Histoire Générale du Protestantisme*, 3 vols. (Paris: Les Burges et Les Mages, 1977), 1: 268–312; Monter, *Calvin's Geneva*, and "De l'Évêché à la Rome protestante," in *Histoire de Genève*, ed. Guichonnet, 127–183; Albert Py, Jean Paul Barbier, and Alain Dufour, *Ronsard et la Rome protestante* (Geneva: BPU, 1985).

36. Diodati, in *Sermons*, 100. See also Cellérier, *Histoire d'autrefois*, 64: "the men of old times were more rude, and the Genevans of the other times were often quarrelsome." Munier, in *Sermons*, 143, "the rudeness of the century," "the rigidity of the founders."

37. Chastel, *Conférences sur l'histoire*, 205.

38. Cellérier, *Histoire d'autrefois*, 212.

39. Munier, in *Sermons*, 145, called this human authority in confessions a "principle of the papists."

40. In 1813 the National Church forbade any preaching about original sin, the divinity of Christ, the sacrificial death and atonement of Christ, or predestination for fear that they would incite division within the church.

41. See J.J.C. Chenevière, *Principaux faits de l'Histoire Sainte et de l'Histoire de L'Église chrétienne* (Geneva: J. J. Paschoud, 1819), 196.

42. See Jean-Isaac-Samuel Cellérier and Louis Gaussen, eds., *Confession helvétique postérieure. Confession de foi de l'Églises de la Suisse: precédée de quelques réflexions des éditeurs sur la nature, le légitime usage et la necessité des confessions de foi*, trans. from Latin (Geneva: Luc Sestie, 1819; 1st ed.: Heinrich Bullinger, 1566).

43. Jean Henri Merle D'Aubigné, *Quelle et la théologie propre à guérir les maux du temps actuel?* (Geneva: Émile Guers, 1852), 13.

44. See Jean Henri Merle d'Aubigné, "Souvenir de sa vie," *BPU*, MS 560, 72.

45. In fact, Louis Gaussen claimed that since 1819 he preached only from the Bible and could freely apply it to the needs of the times. See Mützenberg, *A l'Écoute du Réveil*, 111.

46. See the record of contributions (in francs) by country to the *Société évangélique* in Merle d'Aubigné, *Vie et Doctrine, ou 325 et 1857* (Geneva: Jules G. Fick, 1858), 5: Genève, 48,424,60; Écosse, 30,101,80; Angleterre, 18,344,75; Amérique, 16,622,70; Irlande, 8,318,85; Hollande, 5,677,20; Vaud, 4,621,70; Bâle, 2,957,00; Stations en France, 2,723,45; Thurgovie-St.Gall, 1,839,00; France, 1,595,10; Savoie-Piémont, 941,60; Allemagne, 622,35; Berne, 501,00; Zürich, 60,00; Belgique, 6,00. See also Mützenberg, *A l'Écoute de Réveil*, 128, claims that when the theological school opened, 453 pastors of the Church of England and 100 pastors from the Canton of Vaud, in addition to many French pastors, sent letters of support.

47. These polemical designations were not just *Réveil* terms, but had international reputation, beginning already in the eighteenth century with d'Alembert's article in the famous *Encyclopédie* and continuing in the nineteenth century in the opinion of many ministers in the Church of England, including John Henry Newman.

48. See David Bebbington, *Evangelicalism in Modern Britain: A History from the 1730s to the 1980s* (Grand Rapids, MI: Baker Books, 1989), 77.

49. Chenevière, in *Sermons*, 85.

50. Chastel, *Conférences sur l'histoire*, 53. Chastel also believed that the *Réveil* was merely a sectarian movement: "One saw the Pietist, Moravian, Quaker, Baptist, Methodist, and even Swedenborgian agents pursue with a new ardor the work of the *Réveil*, not only in their countries of origin, but again in all the Protestant communions." (52)

51. Ibid., 63.

52. Jean Henri Merle D'Aubigné, *History of the Reformation in Europe in the Time of Calvin*, 8 vols. (London: Longman, Green, Roberts, 1863—1878), 8: 190 (see also 7: 12), and *Histoire de la Réformation en Europe au temps de Calvin*, 8 vols. (Paris: Michel Lévy frères, 1863—1878), 8: 200 (see also 7: 13).

53. Munier, in *Sermons*, 144.

54. L'Abbé François Martin and l'Abbé Fleury, *Histoire de M. Vuarin et du rétablissement du Catholicisme à Genève*, 2 vols. (Geneva: A. Jaquemont, 1861), 439.

55. In 1791 the General Council of Geneva annulled all judgments against Rousseau, in 1793 they commemorated his birthplace, and in 1835 the central island of the Rhone River was named *Ile Rousseau*. See Henri Babel, *Les Quatre Hommes qui ont fait Genève: De Calvin à Beze et de Rousseau à Dunant* (Geneva: Tribune, 1981), 92–93. See also Pierre Burgelin, *Jean-Jacques Rousseau et la religion de Genève* (Geneva: Labor et Fides, 1962).

56. Jean François Vuarin, *L'Ombre de Rousseau en réponse à l'ombre de Calvin* (Geneva: A. L. Vignier, 1835). See also César Malan, *La statue de Rousseau. Réponse d'un citoyen du Genève chrétien, à la demande qui lui est faite de contribuer à l'érection de ce monument* (Geneva: P. A. Bonnant, 1828).

57. Vuarin, *L'Ombre de Rousseau*, 77.

58. See Karl Barth, *Protestant Theology in the Nineteenth Century: Its Background and History* (London: SCM, 1972), 218, Barth claimed that Rousseau exploited the "inner conflicts" of Genevan theology. See also Jean-Louis Leuba, "Rousseau et le milieu calviniste de sa jeunesse," in J.-L. Leuba et al., *Jean-Jacques Rousseau et la crise contemporaine de la conscience* (Paris: Beauchesne, 1980), 40, confirms the same "ambiguities" that led to Rousseau's parallel thoughts.

59. Fleury, *Calvin à Genève*, 6.

60. Bouwsma, *John Calvin*, 230—231.

61. Yet it is difficult to deny that despite the tensions within Calvin, he was emphatic about the unchanging nature of the essential doctrines: "God is one; Christ is God and the Son of God; our salvation rests in God's mercy." John Calvin, *Institutes*, IV, i, 12, cited in Bouwsma, *John Calvin*, 222.

62. Bouwsma, *John Calvin*, 234.

63. Chenevière, in *Sermons*, 106.

64. See Gabriel Mützenberg, *Henry Dunant le prédestiné* (Geneva: Robert Éstienne, 1984).

65. Jean Henri Merle d'Aubigné, *Discourses and Essays*, ed. Robert Baird (Glasgow and London: William Collins, 1846), 162. Chastel, *Conférences sur l'histoire*, 1:241, recognized that Catholic orthodoxy was essentially the same as *Réveil* orthodoxy on these points. See also Munier, in *Sermons*, 130, in a statement similar to Merle d'Aubigné's: "each Christian walking freely, and under his own proper responsibility, to the light of the divine oracles . . . which has not only been won over to the profit of my *patrie* and to all Protestant states, but to the Catholic Church itself."

11

Loss of Genevan Identity and Counter-Reformation in the Nineteenth Century

Gabriel Mützenberg

COUNTER-REFORMATION AND DEMOGRAPHY

For Geneva, the nineteenth century represents a particularly difficult period of transition. Born out of Reformation, Protestant by origin, Protestant by spirit—from the mid-sixteenth century to the mid-nineteenth century a Genevan citizen had to be Protestant—the Republic underwent a profound traumatism right from the time of the *Annexion* to France in 1798. In the midst of the department of Léman, where six-sevenths of the population was Catholic, not only did the Republic lose its political independence, and consequently its liberty, but Geneva also witnessed the slow invasion of a population, both foreign in its mentality and foreign in its faith. The newcomers were French civil servants, soldiers, and little by little, poor Savoyards in need of aid and attracted by Geneva's well-earned reputation for charity. Almost all belonged to the Roman Catholic faith, and because the law of April 8, 1802, guaranteed them freedom of worship, they formed a parish, obtaining the use of the Protestant church of Saint-Germain. Their second parish priest, in office until 1843, was Jean-François Vuarin.[1] A royalist and an enemy of any republic, as well as a skillful diplomat with no mind for concessions, Vuarin wanted to dominate the city's religious scene. The Catholic community soon compromised 3,000 members, many of whom were indigent in need of help. Vuarin was able to obtain aid for them by unabashedly requesting funds from the highest-placed authorities in Europe whether French under Napoleon or Russian after 1815. The peace treaties go so far to indicate Vuarin's salary—at £5,000 almost twice that of the most well-paid pastors. Bargained at the cost of a minimum increase in territory, Switzerland's independence also made Vuarin, as owner of property ceded by Sardinia, a Genevan citizen.[2]

During the first half of the nineteenth century, the Catholic population of

Calvin's city grew steadily. Between 1822 and 1860 the annual growth rate among Catholics reached 4.12 percent in the city and 2.02 percent in the canton; that of the Protestants reached only 0.3 percent in the city and 0.65 percent in the canton. Consequently, by 1860 the population's majority had shifted: 40,069 Protestants to 42,099 Catholics. The influx of foreigners—34.7 percent of the total population in 1860—provides sufficient explanation for this change. A failure in 1602, the *Escalade* seemed a success when the pastor Jean-Jacques Chenevière appeared before the *Conseil d'État* in January 1838. Although peaceful, many viewed this change in demography as dangerous.

Toward the end of the 1830s, two city notables echoed these fears before the *Conseil représentatif et souverain*. During the *Conseil's* session of May 8, 1837, Marc-Antoine Fazy-Pasteur, a representative of the upper-class industrialists, bemoaned the current situation. While the protectionism exercised by neighboring countries hurt Geneva, the Republic allowed both foreigners and their goods to enter freely, which in turn hurt the local economy. Above all, the proportion of non-Swiss immigrants worried Fazy-Pasteur: Because of its rapid growth, spirit, and poor financial situation, as well as its lack of intellectual and political experience, the unstable Catholic population jeopardized Genevan nationality. "Genevans," he commented, "mixed among the world of foreigners, are no longer able to recognize themselves."[3]

The second notable, Alphonse de Candolle, a renowned botanist like his father, commented vigorously on this point. "We are killing ourselves," he exclaimed.[4] In his opinion, numerous immigrants, chiefly the Sardinians, brought only poverty and crime to the city. Although they represented 10.5 percent of the canton's total population in 1837, immigrants committed 29 percent of the misdemeanors and 23 percent of the felonies. Consequently, Candolle, as well as Fazy-Pasteur, saw the need to monitor the quality of the immigrants—a view shared by several deputies. But a commission that examined the question during winter 1837—1838 proposed an indefinite adjournment of a bill entertained by the *Conseil représentatif*. Deemed too difficult to enforce, none of the measures were adopted. The shift in population continued as before. In 1860 Sardinians constituted half the number of foreigners, and any attempt to check this expansion during the nineteenth century consistently met with failure.[5]

COUNTER-REFORMATION AND GENEVAN IDENTITY

The bookseller and publisher David Dunant, uncle of Jean-Henri Dunant, the founder of the Red Cross (*Croix-Rouge*), in his writings examined and reexamined the loss of Genevan identity. For the most part his works remain unpublished. Their titles alone bear witness to his preoccupation: "Grandeur, Decadence and Fall of the Old Genevan Nationality," "Old Geneva at Its Final Day," "The Heavenly Punishment," and "Geneva at its First, at Its Glorious and its Final Days." These manuscripts provide examples of bombastic, often repetitive prose or samplings of a few lines of bad poetry: "O old Geneva, dying nation!" Although a fervent admirer of Count Jean-Jacques de Sellon, founder of the *Société de la paix*, Dunant to his credit, in a beautiful edition, published François Bonivard's *Chroniques de Genève*. Dunant bogged down the sixteenth-century text with often unnecessary footnotes, though he preceded with an appeal *Aux Genevois*. Paying tribute to the Republic's ancestors, Dunant is forced to exclaim, "Where are its successors?"

David Dunant, like Alphonse de Candolle and also Fazy-Pasteur—Dunant found in the latter a model of moral simplicity, patriotism, selflessness, and an unchangeable attachment to Protestantism—could not resign himself to the influx of royalist and Catholic Savoyards. "How can an old citizen still consider himself to be Genevan" he wondered, "among these German sauerkraut eaters and beer imbibers, these frivolous French and these Savoyards, more Catholic than the pope, to whom one must never mention neither the name of Calvin nor the *Escalade*?" When he published his *Essai statistique sur le canton de Genève*, Jean Picot received a severe reprimand from the *premier syndic* for having reproduced a portrait of the Reformer and the *Ce l'ai no* in dialect. With some indignation, the curate Vuarin and two archpriests denounced the reckless professor, who was guilty of having gravely offended his fellow Catholics through his publication.

Although he felt he had a few ties with immigrants, the patriotic Dunant did not think they were the source of the city's decadence. In fact, that decadence arose from among the Genevans themselves, through their abandonment of the dynamic and vigorous Christianity that had characterized the early Christian Church and the Reformation. Therefore, the proper action to follow was to return to the Republic's roots, to Calvin, and to forego what he considered to be mind-deadening rationalism, which had held sway long enough. Too often denigrated, was it not Calvin who brought, and better than anyone else, "the admirable union of religion and liberty"?

Not a member of the *Réveil*, David Dunant, nevertheless saw in the National Church's doctrinal statement, and in the waning of piety among Genevans, one cause for the loss of identity some fellow citizens deplored. *La Rome protestante* was fading away. It had lost its center. And Catholics, the majority in the canton, but not in the city—16,000 to 24,000 in round figures—were growing in number.

David Dunant tirelessly preached a turnaround. Since the sumptuous covered market at Bel-Air was far from successful (the market, built in a style marked by Roman architecture, is the present site of the *Crédit lyonnais*), he proposed to transform it into the *Temple de la Restoration* by adding a bell-tower and inviting worshippers to services held twice daily, at 8 o'clock and noon. The market's cellars, transformed into catacombs, would be dedicated to the memory of famous Genevans. As the center of patriotic and Christian devotion, this new church, set in the midst of the city's commercial district, would be used for national celebrations. This well-meaning utopia did not come about, however. Dunant's humanitarianism and peaceful Calvinism did not fare much better. Struck by the common contempt for human life, he advocated its inviolability.

Likewise, he demanded for animals a less barbarous fate, for violence is never praiseworthy. In 1864, at the time the Genevan Convention took hold of his illustrious nephew, he proposed twelve articles to guarantee world peace. The articles made provisions for a new church based on in the early Christian model, the implementation of Christian principles by governments, the foundation of a *Société universelle de la paix* and a *Tribunal arbitral permanent*, the creation of a common market, the replacement of professional armies by well-organized militia, and the elimination of all works of art depicting violence. Admittedly, it would have not been wrong to have given, even guardedly, a little benevolent attention to this somewhat naive prophet.[6]

COUNTER-REFORMATION AND POLEMICS

In my study *L'Obsession calviniste*, published in 1979, a chapter bears the title "La Contre-Réforme continue."[7] Numerous examples show how the Roman Catholic Church's attempt to stifle the Reformation—the powerful movement advocating a return to the Bible as the sole source of spiritual authority—did not stop in the sixteenth century. In fact, the nineteenth century saw an effort, especially in the Ultramontane movement, to renew the battle between opposing sources of authority and institution. Demography, as noted above, was important. Catholic policy supported a rising birth rate, and its imperious power required troops. Catholics as a result, had to have many children, no matter what the consequences. What was important, was their presence. The state—which in this case could, and to their benefit should, be secular—would take care of them. And why should Protestants not do the same? Protestants had always respected the opinions of others. Were not these opinions to be respected—and followed? Such would be the case of Geneva.

This Catholicism, bitter and sweet for the needs of the cause, had something of the irenic spirit. It was deft and diplomatic, as had already been seen during the Reformation. The differences between Calvinism and Catholicism, according to many contemporary theologians, were not so great. There was no need, therefore, to fight about them from the barrel of an *arquebus*! But this was pretended toleration, a masquerade, unmasked only by the name with which the Edict of Nantes labeled the Protestants: *Religion Prétendue Réformée* (the so-called Reformed Religion). The charade did not stop the most bitter, indeed the most contemptuous, polemic. In nineteenth-century Geneva militant priests, such as Jean-François Vuarin, Étienne Marilley, and Gaspard Mermillod, were key players in this debate.

The first debate has been mentioned. A noted historian of the Restoration, Paul Waeber, comments about Vuarin: "[He] campaigned ardently with [Félicité Robert de] Lamennais for the advent of a modern Counter-Reformation." Waeber adds, "Even if we were to appear excessive, we would say often that he often confused his parish's interest, linked to his own, with Christianity's. A man of faith, and naturally ambitious, a lover of struggles as much as of his household's comfort, and hardworking, such are some of the character traits he never abandoned."[8]

Otto Karmin, also knowledgeable about Vuarin, completes this portrait: "The struggle against heresy was his goal, his tactic was to always present Catholicism wherever he could as a victim of Protestant intolerance."[9] Charles Pictet de Rochemont, the Genevan members of the *Conseil d'État* and diplomat, stated in a confidential letter sent to the Czar's envoy, Baron de Krüdener:

The abbé Vuarin is a man of uncommon ability, tireless activity and an ardent character, but he is a priest whose zeal is darkened by fanaticism, who has made an art of insubordination and, judging by the conduct he leads, seems to believe himself destined to overthrow the work of Calvin in *La Rome protestante*. While he may still hide his direct participation in this project, he feels free to indicate in his speeches the hopes he fosters.

All the ways, all the means of gentleness and persuasion used by our magistrates have been useless. The considerable increase in his salary that I requested personally for him at the Treaty of Turin, and obtained from our government; the efforts I made to attract his favorable consideration towards the schools of our new territory . . . nothing has had the slightest influence on him. We had the disappointment of seeing him . . . misrepresent the conduct of the government, which in its relations with the Catholic citizens, only merits thanks and praise.

To the degree that religious interests have become more and more linked to European politics, the activity and hopes of Ms. Vuarin have increased. His vast correspondence, his contacts in every court, his frequent trips, his conduct and discourse, could rightfully cause one to suspect him to be part of some vast Counter-Reformation project.[10]

Clearly this man thought he was powerful. He showed an "arrogant confidence." He subscribed, no doubt, to the ironic response given to him by Charles Maurice de Talleyrand-Périgord to Étienne Dumont, who had said in reference to the districts ceded to Geneva by France: "*Eh bien!* You gave us Catholics! Say rather that we have given to you the Catholics."[11]

Vuarin did all he could to make this comment come true. He accused the Genevans of having offended continuously, over the last three centuries, "Our Lord Jesus Christ." During the *Jubilé* of the Reformation in 1835, in which the government did not officially participate, he published a manifesto entitled *Mémoire présenté à Mgr l'évêque de Lausanne et de Genève par le clergé catholique de Genève sur les pièges tendus par l'hérésie à la foi de la population catholique*. Although the Tercentenary of the Reformation of Calvin was not officially celebrated by the government, the feast of Saint Francis de Sales was.[12]

This virulent text, published anonymously—but it was not difficult to recognize its origin—approved the ransacking of a Protestant house of worship. Roused to fanaticism by the clergy, the populace destroyed a private building in which the Protestants of Anières met, because they neither had the right to build a chapel nor the possibility, given the distance, of attending one of the nearest

Protestant churches. The pamphlet also denounced coeducation and mutual, or Lancasterian, instruction. Although used successfully in Fribourg by the great pedagogue, the cordelier father Gregoire Girard, the method was condemned as Protestant, on account of the British origins of two of its promoters, Bell and Lancaster. Clearly Vuarin felt that anything that was not fundamentally and totally Catholic had to be rejected.[13]

Vuarin always took advantage of any opportunity to speak his mind on what he would still readily call the *Religion Prétendue Reformée*. During a marriage ceremony, for example, he took advantage "of the fact that many Protestant relatives of the two spouses could hear him, and he spewed out terrible insults against Protestantism and Geneva, to the point that some of the Protestant relatives left the church, and the Catholics became furious with the care he took to cast gall upon a ceremony that should have been but sweetness."[14]

The reign of this most fanatical defender of Catholicism ended in an illegal apotheosis. After his death on September 6, 1843, he was embalmed. The funeral was delayed until September 13 so that a large number of clergy could be assembled. The procession took on an uncommon solemnity, usually not permitted in the city: There were two bishops, 157 priests, 30 Sisters of Charity, and 816 women in white and black veils—a total of 1,800 people. The *premier syndic* Jean-Jacques Rigaud lamented: "It was a painful sight to see the streets of Calvinist Geneva invaded by the mass of foreign priests who seemed to witness to the fact that the Savoyard clergy had taken hold of *la Rome protestante*."[15]

This moderate magistrate's account is striking for its incisive sobriety. He knew that the director of this funeral parade, the future bishop Étienne Marilley, was the presumed successor of Vuarin. Although he had not signed Vuarin's famous 1835 *Mémoire*, Marilley was more or less cut from the same cloth. To avoid perpetuating an atmosphere of conflict, the *Conseil d'État* decided not to accept him as bishop. But faced with resistance, the *Conseil* was obliged to bring him *manu militari* to the border on June 15, 1844.[16]

The schools, as one may have already suspected, constituted one of the Catholic clergy's preferred battlegrounds. Such was the case in the city of Geneva or in Hermance (now a suburb of Geneva) during Vuarin's time, when tragicomic incidents revolved around the allocation of classrooms as keys were spirited away to stop the teacher from entering. During the same period similar incidents happened at cemeteries when the Catholic Church refused access to several funeral processions—the deceased was judged unworthy of being buried in "holy land."

In that regard, the consequences of the 1846 radical revolution were probably more significant. The very progressive democratic Constitution of May 24, 1847, still in effect today (1996), laid the foundation for a new system: "Religious instruction is distinct from other educational fields to guarantee to all Genevans entry into the Canton's various institutions of public education [article 137]." This measure required the creation of a secular public school system. In the name of toleration, the instruction given there had to bear no denominational stripe. One realizes that such a view did not satisfy the profoundly religious, for whom all instruction must be enlivened by the spirit of the Gospel. Protestants, such as historian Ernest Naville, were convinced of this. They established a few private institutions where religion inspired the entire curriculum, but even if these schools wanted to be Christian and biblical—the students read the New Testament in Greek because it bespoke a non-dogmatic, non-denominational, and ecumenical Christianity.

Nothing of the sort was found among the Catholics. In his *Mémoire adressé à S. G. Mgr. Marilley, évêque de Lausanne et de Genève, sur le nouveau réglement des Écoles primaires du canton de Genève* of July 10, 1849, Joseph-Victor Dunoyer, general vicar and curate of Geneva, decried, on the one hand, the secularization of teaching and the purely civil direction in public education; on the other hand, he revealed his resolutely anti-Protestant colors. The mutual support among denominations, as postulated by the government, found no favor in Dunoyer's eyes. He exclaimed: "By the word toleration is the master required to preach that all religions, whatever they may be, are equally good; to preach religious indifference as a doctrine and the destruction of fundamental and non-fundamental doctrines? As such, he would be a Protestant!"[17] In his mouth, the term "Protestant" is by no means a compliment. Farther in the text it is placed beside such words as "deist" and "Jew." It is a term associated with the short prayer the master said at the beginning and the end of the school day. Much to the alarm of the Catholic Church, the prayer's content had to approved by the Department of Education. In short, the term depicted everything in the government's plan that contravened the unchangeable principles of the Roman Catholic Church.

The *Revue de Genève*, voice of the radicals, made no mistake in assessing this pamphlet. The editor would not read the bittersweet prose of Geneva's curate. September 1, 1849, he wrote: "If one had published a pamphlet on the application of the education bill, signed by Mr. Dunoyer, citizen of Geneva, a citizen whom we respect, we would have rushed to have given him all our attention; but a text written by a curate for a bishop falls outside the scope of our activities."[18]

This irony did not stop many Catholics from following the instructions of their clergy. In several districts, children were detained by catechism instruction, which had been deliberately placed first thing in the morning. They arrived at school between 9:45 and 10 o'clock instead of 8 o'clock or 8:30, and as a consequence classes were dropped. Because both radicals and conservatives vied for votes among the Catholic ranks to get elected, the political and religious conflict lost its acuity only with the law of 1872, which put obligatory religious instruction solely in the hands of the priests and pastors, and in the law of 1907, which permanently separated instruction from church and state.

COUNTER-REFORMATION AND THE CATHOLIC PRESS

At the time of the Revolution of 1846, Catholicism asserted itself through the successive, but unsuccessful, publication of three weekly or biweekly newspapers: *La Sentinelle catholique de Genève, La Voix catholique de Genève*, and *L'Obserateur de Genève*. Following the marked failure of these papers, the future cardinal Gaspard Mermillod, an editor of exceptional scope, a preacher with access to high society, and a convertor of Protestants, launched a monthly, *Les Annales catholique de Genève*. It was published from 1852 to 1862.[19]

The aim of the journal was clear. Faced with an unbelieving or Protestant people—synonymous descriptions in the journal's view—individuals who proclaimed their liberty through a radical poet like Albert Richard,[20] the *Annales* was to assert the superiority of Catholics, Switzerland's eldest sons, and to attract Protestants. More specifically, the goal was to set up Geneva as an autonomous bishopric and to break the Protestant triangle of London-Berlin-Geneva. The journal provided a "periodical apology" of Catholicism as the "divine reality," as the total and perfect expression of Christianity; other denominations represented only a "mutilated fragment of truth." Would not lucid, serious Protestants, Mermillod insinuated, turn to Rome "like a plant towards the sun?"[21]

In fact, in his systematic denigrations of Protestantism, the vicar of Geneva had an easy time denouncing a decadence that was all too apparent. Had not Protestantism prepared its own decline by abandoning the founding principles of the Reformation, as expressed in its confessions of faith? In Geneva, this had happened at an early date—in 1725. If, in the name of reason or history, one eliminates from Scripture all miracles and the fragments, even complete chapters and books, judged to have questionable authenticity, how can one claim their unique and absolute authority? The Reformer's mottoes—grace alone, faith alone, and Christ alone—had been abandoned.

In his approval of the *Annales* publication, which appeared to have more and more influence abroad, Mgr. Rendu, bishop of Annecy, noted this "leprosy of doubt" that plagued Geneva. He wrote to the abbé Mermillod on November 4, 1852: "When, in 1835 the Jubilee of the Reformation brought together deputies from all of the Protestant sects, they tried to find a truth that could serve as a tie between them, and it was impossible to find one. . . . Distillation of all the aberrations created by European Protestantism, the city of Calvin is the seat of a dogmatic anarchy impossible to describe." Addressing Reformed Protestants, the bishop added: "*Eh quoi!* for three centuries you have been using extensively your freedom to examine everything, for three centuries you have examined every part of the Word of God, every teaching of the Church, every legacy of tradition; for three centuries you have ceased to drag Christ and his Church before the court of individual reason, and you are consequently left with trying to fin Truth!"[22] The critique is severe. Admittedly what was mentioned concerning the abandonment of the sixteenth- and seventeenth-century confessions gives some credence to this critique. But the bishop's purple prose, repeating "three centuries" in an oratorical style common among the clergy shows little concern for truth. He writes as if the Reformers and their followers had all been terrible rationalists.[23]

Indeed, it is easy to recognize the degree to which, for the good of their cause, the editors of the *Annales* idealize the Geneva of the Middle Ages. Conveniently forgetting the heavy hand the bishop and the dukes of Savoy used on the city, as well as the considerable costs a clergy of several hundred priests weighed upon the people, the *Annales* describe the Geneva of that time as being democratic, egalitarian, and Christian. By contrast the sixteenth-century Reformation is depicted as dictatorial, violent alone, and strict, having established the strictest, craftiest form of inquisition during 200 years. Admittedly these views of Geneva's evolution (and that of many other Protestant countries) are the fruit of completely fanciful a priori judgments, which no evidence confirms. The same can be said of the authors' attempt to provide, general observations. The bishop of Annecy wrote, for example, to the count of Montalembert: "If there is any freedom in the world, its due to Catholics."[24]

The *Annales* continued nonetheless, unchangeable in its approach: "Thus the Catholic clergy, which fights with so much energy for freedom of religion"—one should say, when it is a minority fighting for the freedom of Catholics—"fights in the same fight for every freedom." The journal added "To persist . . . error needs force: true religion only needs freedom."[25] And how does this hymnal passage conclude? The *Annales* ends with an exultant approval of the Statut of February 8, 1848, decreed by the king of Sardinia Charles-Albert de Savoie. The Statut's first article states that the *religion catholique, apostolique et romaine* is the only religion in the state. The *Annales*'s editor saw in this decision "a return to the ancient freedoms that the Church and the people had enjoyed before the sixteenth century."[26] In fact, everything in this publication, blending cleverness and spite, was written in more or less the same style. As noted, the *Annales* contained critiques of contemporary Protestantism that corresponded, no doubt, to reality, but as soon as its articles involved an historical a case or an interpretation of current affairs, misrepresentations were blatant. Further, when dealing with what appeared as a positive element in Protestant thinking, the journal compared Protestantism to the most highly criticized political movement of the time. During a mission that led to a polemic with the pastor Louis Gaussen, founder of the *Société évangélique*, Abbé Combalot wrote in the *Annales*: "The Protestant freedom to examine everything creates an irreparable anarchy, consecrates every error, sanctions every form of fanaticism, resolves itself into pure rationalism, to become lost in the bottomless pit of socialism."[27]

In 1831 as much as during the middle of the century, at a time when the adoption of universal suffrage coincided with the destruction of city walls and the inhabitants of different countries were vigorously mixed together, the Counter-Reformation's goals undergirded the politics of Rome. Although no doubt suffering from the temptations of false modernity and adrift with regard to the Reformation, Protestantism was still a positive force; as its missions and the *Alliance évangélique* gained a ally: Meeting in Geneva in 1861, the first of all the ecumenical movements, the *Unions chrétiennes de Jeunes gens*, founded by Jean-Henri Dunant in Geneva, ventured off to conquer the world's youth.[28]

NOTES

1. See Danielle Coudray, *L'Abbé Vuarin, cure de Genève, 1769–1843*, 4 vols. (Fribourg: D. Coudray, 1984–1987).

2. See Otto Karmin, *Documents sur l'histoire religieuse de Genève à l'époque de la Restoration* (Geneva: SHAG, 1918), 33ff.

3. Marc-Antoine Fazy-Pasteur, *Mémorial des séances du Conseil représentatif (1er mai au décembre 1837)* (Geneva: Abraham Cherbuliez, 1837), 58–88.

4. Alphonse de Candolle, *Lettre à un des MM. les conseillers d'Etat sur la question des étrangeurs qui sejourment ou qui s'établissement dans le canton de Genève* (Geneva: Charles Gruaz, 1837), 5.

5. See *Mémorial*, vol. 19, 51ff. and, vol. 20, 128ff.; Gabriel Mützenberg, *Genève 1830. Restauration de l'école* (Lausanne: Édition du Grand-Pont, 1974), 31.

6. See *Chronique de Genève*, 2 tomes in 4 vol. (Geneva: J.-G. Fick, 1831 [1531]); *BPU*, MS fr. 3175, folio 20ff., 3176, folios 1–8; Gabriel Mützenberg, "David Dunant, oncle et précurseur du fondateur de la Croix-Rouge," *RSH* 30 (1980): 369–376, and *Henry Dunant le prédestiné: Du nouveau sur la famille, la jeunesse, la destinée spirituelle du fondateur de la Croix-Rouge* (Geneva: Robert Éstienne, 1984), 46ff.

7. Gabriel Mützenberg, *L'obsession calviniste* (Geneva: Labor et Fides, 1979), 99–110.

8. Paul Waeber, *La Formation du canton de Genève, 1814-1816* (Geneva: V. Chevalier, 1974), 12. See also *L'abbé Vuarin et la formation de Genève, canton mixte (1801–1809)*, *AEG*, Manuscipt histoire, 252, iii.

9. Otto Karmin, *Sir Francis d'Ivernois, sa vie, son temps (1757–1842)* (Geneva: Revue historique de la Révolution française et de l'Europe, 1920), 611.

10. Charles Pictet de Rochement, *Documents sur l'histoire religieuse de Genève à l'époque de la Restauration* (Geneva: SHAG, 1918), 74–75. See Charles Pictet de Rochemont, *Fragmens de M. Pictet de Rochemont, ministre plenipotentaire de la Conféderation Suisse, à Paris et à Turin en 1815 et 1816* (Geneva: SHAG, 1840).

11. Talleyrand, as cited in Amédée Roget, *La Question catholique à Genève de 1815 à 1870* (Geneva: Carey, 1874), 6.

12. See François Vuarin, Gaspard Greffier, and François Baillard, eds., *Mémoire présenté à Mgr l'évêque de Lausanne et de Genève par le clergé catholique de Genève sur les pièges tendus par l'hérésie à la foi de la population catholique* (Geneva: A. L. Vignier, 1835).

13. See Vuarin, *Mémoire*, 25ff., 32ff..

14. Roger de Candolle, ed., *L'Europe de 1830. Vue à travers la correspondance d'Augustin Pyamus de Candolle et de Madame de Circourt* (Geneva: A. Jullien, 1966), 143.

15. Jean-Jacques Rigaud, *Mémoires*, II, 453 (*BPU*, Mss. Suppl. 1290–1292). See Jean Adrien Naville-Rigaud, ed., *Jean-Jacques Rigaud, ancien premier syndic de Genève: notice biographique* (Geneva: H. Georg; A. Cherbuliez, 1879).

16. Ibid.

17. Joseph-Victor Dunoyer, *Mémoire adressé à S. G. Mgr. Marilley, évêque de Lausanne et de Genève, sur le nouveau réglement des Écoles primaires du canton de Genève* (Geneva: n. p., n. d.).

18. Editor, *Revue de Genève* (September 1, 1849).

19. See Mützenberg, *Genève 1830*, 498ff.; and "Révolution genevois de 1846 et pédagogie chrétienne, ou Un grand pas vers l'école laïque," *RSH* 22, 3 (1972): 433—457.

20. In the *Revue de Genève* (June 16, 1847), Richard wrote: "The sovereign people is not a populace/ That any discipline causes to become impatient and tired; A blind plebeian, without will . . . / But a nation . . ."

21. Gaspard Mermillod, *Les Annales catholique de Genève* (n. p., n. d.).

22. Mgr. Rendu, *Annales* (November 4, 1852), 13—14.

23. See Anne Sylvie Noyer, *Le protestantisme genevois vu à travers les Annales catholiques de Genève, 1852—1862, AEG*, Man. hist. 252/290. 13ff.; and Gabriel Mützenberg, *A l'écoute du Réveil* (St-Léger: Éditions Emmaüs, 1989), 24ff..

24. *Annales* (1852).

25. *Annales* (1852): 345.

26. *Annales* (1852): 89.

27. Abbé Combalot, *Annales* (1852): 200.

28. Established in Great Britain, it had its first meeting in London in 1846, with subsequent meetings in Paris (1855), Berlin (1857), and Geneva (1861). See Jean Henri Merle d'Aubigné, *Septembre 1861 ou l'Alliance évangélique à Genève. Discours prononcé lors l'ouveture de la séance annuelle de la société évangélique de Genève, le juin 1861.* (Geneva and Paris: Société évangélique, 1861); David Tissot, ed., *Les Conférences de Genève, 1861: Rapports et discours publiés au nom du comité de l'Alliance évangélique*, 2 vols. (Geneva: H. Georg, 1861).

12

Education and Modernity in Restoration Geneva

William Edgar

> *Chaque pays a ses usages. A Paris, on va de bal en bal, à Genève, de cours en*
> *cours. Ce n'est pas aussi fatigant, et du moins il en reste quelque chose dans*
> *l'esprit.*
>
> Every country has its customs. In Paris one goes from ball to ball, in Geneva,
> from course to course. This is not as tiring, and at least something remains in the
> mind.[1]

Among European cities, Paris and London are usually considered the great
examples of modernity in an urban setting. The rational philosophy as well as the
spirit of revolution engendered in the Enlightenment became an urban reality in
the architecture and plan of those two cities during the nineteenth century.
Dramatically rising populations and increasing mechanization of life were
accommodated, more deliberately in Paris, and more gradually in London.[2] But
by the second half of the century both had become quintessentially modern cities.

Yet Geneva holds a significant place as well, one that has often been
neglected by historians. That city also represents the coming of modernity in
certain areas, ones that became models for other cities around the world. Insofar
as Geneva was a center of various trades, of industry, of banking, the transition
to a modern urban setting was parallel to other European cities. But there were
unique attributes to this transition because of Geneva's particular history. Geneva
had a self-consciousness about its role, as we can judge from many documents
during the eighteenth and nineteenth centuries. And though we could study
Genevan identity through a number of lenses, one that allows us to focus on that
self-consciousness in a forceful way is education.

Here we will concentrate on the first half of the century, and specifically the
period between 1815 and 1848, known as the Restoration. It is then that the
foundations of modern Europe were laid. To discover the principal themes of

modernity for which education in Geneva is a showcase, we must begin with a few remarks about the enigmatic nature of modernity itself.

THE MODE OF MODERNITY

Modernity is not so much a series of events or themes as it is a value. It is the assertion of a condition. Simply put, modernity favors the new over the ancient. It is the result of what Paul Hazard calls the "crisis of European consciousness," combining psychological shifts and critical judgment with an attempt to build a new world, one that no longer directly relies on revealed religion and church authority.[3] Modernity is thus a mode of civilization, and not simply a series of historical events that may mark a turning point. In fact, because of its insistence on the new (*modo*), one could legitimately ask whether the truly modern is not enslaved to the new altogether. There is always a counterpoint to the new, however, that prevents such captivity.

The term *modernity* as we now use it emerged with Charles Beaudelaire around 1850. He was fascinated by the way in which the arts, especially painting, revealed a critical distance from the present that kept it safe from idolizing the new. Modernity, which for him found its counterpart in the beautiful, is always twofold, or dialectical. First, it must exist in this world. Its "theater" is the historical dimension, the world of fashions and the market economy. But second, it has an eternal, or timeless quality. Accordingly, the posture of modernity is eschatological.[4] Thus, Baudelaire encapsulates the essence of modernity, and explains why it has a life of its own. Slavery to the new is avoided because there are two sides to the dialectic. Although various definitions may stress either the transitory or the absolute, the dialogue itself ensures vitality, albeit an unstable one.

If modernity is not a particular historical episode, when did the shift from the ancient to the new mode occur? Historian Jacques Le Goff argues, correctly, that pitting the new against the ancient is a permanent theme in European history, beginning with the Greeks and with avatars throughout the Middle Ages and down to the present.[5]   There are, nevertheless, major stages that make Baudelaire's semantic awareness singular. Three stages can be identified in the recent emergence of the modern consciousness. The first is during the Renaissance and the Reformation, when the center of cultural gravity moved from heaven down to earth. In theology and science, as well as in the arts, greater stress was laid on the individual, on this world, and on the diversity of the Created order than previously. The second is in the Enlightenment, when significant shift occurred from a theocentric universe to a more geocentric or anthropocentric one. Generally at that time critical reason became the great presupposition underlying human thought. The third, however, is during the first half of the nineteenth century, when modernity really took root. It is then that the social fabric itself was modified in order to accommodate the various contours of our modernity.

Modernity is a mode, then, because it is more than a series of ideas or events that have emerged. Of course, ideas and events put flesh on the bones of mode. Paul Johnson lists myriad personalities and movements that contributed to the rise of the modern world in the short period between 1815 and 1830, including the prophets of romanticism, the statesmen and soldiers who brought an enduring international order, and the entrepreneurs who established industry and transportation as we know them today.[6] But the whole is greater than the sum of the parts. What surfaces from the various parts of the fabric amount to an eschatology? A detailed examination of the several traits of this nineteenth-century development is beyond the scope of a brief chapter, but we should at least mention the key themes, since they are the very subjects at stake in our study.

THE TRAITS OF MODERNITY

First, and at its heart, what characterizes modernity is the complex phenomenon of secularization. The term is broad and needs to be further defined by two others. The first is *laicization*. During the evolution of many European countries toward the modern state, the church as an institution was uncoupled from the central sectors of society. This uncoupling meant the end of an *ancien régime* where ecclesiastical power was so mingled with every other institution that one could not navigate in life without taking the church into account. When this kind of secularization occurs, differentiation of various sectors follows. Thus religions or communities of faith may have their own legitimacy. So do educational, commercial, and medical institutions, however, the state assumes its own identity, and the law is no longer determined by the rules of Christendom. The French Civil Code of 1804 sets the tone in Europe by omitting mention of the church altogether, unless it is as preterit.[7] The logic of laicization does not necessarily entail a lack of concern for the church by the state, nor does it imply silencing the church from its prophetic role in society. The scenario was played out in different ways in different countries.

The second term in further defining secularization is *secularism*. This refers to a secularist philosophy rather than to social differentiation. Strictly applied, the skepticism of many Enlightenment thinkers should have led to a decline of religion, substituting unaided reason for faith. Some of that did occur, making modernity partly the portend of Max Weber's "iron mask" of rationalization. But countertrends arose, proving that human nature requires religion, whether Christian or not: Various folk religions that had always been there survived laicization, and new religious movements emerged either despite secularism or perhaps precisely because of the threat from a loss of religion.[8]

A second key theme of modernity is individual freedom. Perhaps it would be better to call it the freedom of the individual, since a principal emphasis in the world of modernity is personal value and fulfillment. Tied to some extent to Protestantism but coming into its own in the Enlightenment, individualism has implications in many areas, including law, economics, career, and, of course, education. Jean-Jacques Rousseau (1712—1778), who so affected the concept of education, wrestled with a proper definition of the individual's integrity. In his discussions of the tension between the individual and the social group, he leaned against defining individualism as merely the consequence of property or citizenship. Rather, it was the conscience that defined the integrity of the person.[9] Only those beings with a well-developed individual conscience are able to participate either in society or in history. Advocates of modern individual freedom stress the role of persuasion and argument in defining the future direction of a society. In the early nineteenth century, Protestants in France and Switzerland, no doubt naively, believed that if only reading the Bible were promoted, people would be persuaded by the right use of reason that its message is true, and each country would soon become Evangelical!

The opposite side of the coin of individual freedom is the coming of the centralized, bureaucratic state. This third theme of modernity ties in with secularization in that the joint authorities of the church and baroque monarchies are replaced by a more democratic self-rule. This could lead in a number of different directions. The nineteenth century witnessed the transition between the older, confessionally oriented governments and a modern "procedural" state, where government exist only to ensure order in society and is neutral on moral and religious questions. Subjects became citizens, kingdoms became nations, and governors were replaced by popular sovereignty. According to Hegel, the state must be "reason in action."[10] History becomes the playground for the human spirit's creative energies. In the bargain, the decisions of the state may take on an authority not unlike the despotic rules modernity wanted to challenge. At best, pure democracy is balanced by a system of checks and balances. Debate and parliamentary compromise within the rules of civility issue in policies the greatest number can live by. At worst, socialism overwhelms the individual in the name of a higher principle, such as the judgment of history. Revolution rather than debate determines legitimacy.

A fourth trend is the free market economy. This trait of modernity cannot be separated from the others, in that it represents not only a rationalization of the market but a kind of belief in ultimate freedom as well. In the classic vision of Adam Smith (1723—1790) to seek individual and corporate prosperity is necessarily to seek the advantage of society as a whole. According to Smith's Deistic philosophy, a "hidden hand" guides the market through the ambitions of its investors toward the greatest good for the most people. Of course, the industrial revolution and urbanization posed enormous challenges for Europe, challenges that are still very much with us. Issues were raised in the nineteenth century about the propriety of pure capitalism, and there was a mounting concern over the plight of the emerging working class, their working conditions, and humanitarian justice in the context of enterprise. Geneva will play an important role in exemplifying this concern. Socialism of various kinds emerged as a counterpoint to the free market. It differed with capitalism about the societal basis for the greatest good. It must be the collective will, through a central plan, and at least a temporary denial of the individual's autonomy. Interestingly, though, even Marxist socialism did not abandon the presupposition of belief in progress through industry.[11]

The fifth trend is especially significant for the city of Geneva. It is the development of the natural sciences. Flowing out of the more mathematical models of Galileo, Bacon, and Newton, in the early nineteenth century universal laws were sought to explain a greater and greater set of facts. Although Newton posited a supreme power behind the mechanism of the cosmos, later Buffon would assert that the laws of matter are the same as those governing the heavenly bodies. Laplace would reduce all chemical reactions to the actions of various forces. Technology, the first cousin of modern science, develops in many directions, promoting a more rational and efficient life for the greatest number of people.

The sixth and final theme, the direct result of the fifth, is the dual trend toward rapid communication and rapid transportation. It is during the nineteenth century that such commonplaces today as the popular newspaper, the telegraph, the steamboat, and the railroad, aa well as so many other means of connecting peoples and goods, evolved. The possibility of speedy links of all kinds would change not only the rate with which everything is accomplished but also the mentality regarding many of life's operations as well. This trend will also become crucial in the spread of modernity in Europe and around the world.

GENEVA DURING THE RESTORATION

The coming of modernity in Geneva may be conveniently traced to the three decades between 1815 and 1848. Known as the Restoration because certain parts of the *ancien régime* were restored after Napoleon's aggressive attempts to impose the French Revolution on the rest of Europe were arrested, it was nevertheless not a particularly stable period in history. The Restoration represents a transition, sometimes smooth, sometimes violent, between the older monarchies and the newer secular republics. One may conveniently identify two phases, the first from 1815 to 1830, and the second from 1830 to 1848.

The Treaty of Paris, ending the Congress of Vienna, was signed May 30, 1814. Napoleon's empire was replaced by an uneasy coalition of Europeans facing a future that was much more than a restored past. As Robert Palmer put it so well, "An incongruous alliance of British capitalism and east-European agrarian feudalism, of the British navy and the Russian army, of Spanish clericalism and German nationalism, of divine-right monarchies and newly aroused democrats and liberals, combined at last to bring the Man of Destiny to the ground."[12] In France the inept Bourbon king Louis XVIII was installed, followed in 1824 by his fiercely antirevolutionary brother, Charles X. Although during his reign some of the advances of the modern democratic spirit were muzzled, his attempts at eradicating the nascent liberalism were not ultimately successful.

Geneva had moved progressively toward a representative democracy, establishing a constitutional regime in 1794.[13] Four years later, however, after several French military forays in Switzerland, the city was annexed to Napoleon's France. In spite of the humiliation, it was not an oppressive occupation. Geneva became the capital of a new French *département*, the Léman. The commonweal was entrusted to an independent organization. The Protestant church was left to govern its own affairs, but an official Roman Catholic Church was also established, for the first time since the Reformation. The principal educational institutions, the *Collège* and the *Académie*, were allowed to determine their own programs and policies.

Some hard years followed. Conservatives like Louis Simond describes Genevans as "*redevenus des gens simples et solides*" ("having become simple and solid folks once again") after a half century of moral upheaval.[14] But he overlooks the struggles involved to recover stability. Economic conditions degenerated, leaving massive unemployment and the loss of population in part because of death on the battlefields in Napoleon's army. Life expectancy was fewer than 40 years. Through the leadership of aristocrats such as Ami Lullin, however, Geneva regained its independence in 1814 with a provisional government.

A new constitution, the "*Pacte fédéral*," was composed in 1814, and ratified in 1815. Geneva officially became a member of the Swiss Confederation on May 19, 1815. The transition to being a Swiss canton was not altogether smooth. Among other things Switzerland was concerned about the new Roman Catholic presence in Geneva, and it was afraid of the potential disruptions from its militia. Nevertheless, the city paid an attractive dowry. First, it acquired an enlarged territory giving the country a buffer zone against the Savoie. And second, it adopted a constitution that was in tune with the spirit of the times.

The 1814 Constitution was indeed a conservative document. It represented a reaction against the so-called immortal principles of the French Revolution.[15] Yet it contained certain modern features, and it would be modified over the years to accommodate various more liberal demands. Although it remained paternalistic, placing the power in the hands of the enlightened few, its intention was to protect institutions such as the church and the schools. One effect it had was to keep the population out of involvement with government and thus to stunt the growth of self-consciousness about civic responsibility. Commenting on these ambiguities, François Ruchon states: "The most serious reproach one could make against the Constitution and the political régime of the Restoration is to have brought to Geneva a sort of slumber, a sort of anemia and political indifference, and to have dug a chasm, which would grow wider between a people that would end by realizing it had lost its rights, and a government, kindly to be sure, full of good intentions, but which never knew how to trust a people who asked only to demonstrate its patriotism by freely serving its country."[16] This gap, combined with difficult economic conditions, made the first part of the

Restoration all the more difficult for many in the city of Geneva.

Tensions between the Swiss government and the churches had implications for Geneva. The *Conseil d'Etat* was modern to the extent that it imposed order on society. Thus it insisted on controlling the Roman Catholic Church. The country was divided into five dioceses, with a bishop in each. The bishop of Geneva sat in Fribourg. The city had its own vicar. Even though Catholics were not as submitted to Rome as in other countries, there were nonetheless conflicts with Protestants who were increasingly anxious over the strength of any outside power. At times they asked the government to be even stronger. The tensions were abetted because the theology of Catholicism, in contrast to Protestantism, was not particularly accommodating of modernity.

It is crucial in order to understand the Protestant mentality in Geneva to appreciate the significant renewal that occurred after the French Empire's end.[17] An awakening (*Réveil*) took place, beginning in 1817, largely through Bible studies among students at the Theological Faculty led by the Scotsman Robert Haldane. The Consistory and the Venerable Company of Pastors, nervous about this movement, forbade students to preach on Christology, original sin, grace and predestination. In reaction, the awakened faithful founded a number of churches and many evangelistic and diaconal organizations. Although different emphases could be found within the Evangelical renewal, it was on the whole Calvinistic. In 1832 a theological school was founded in order to counter the teaching of "pre-liberals" like J.-J. Caton Chenevière.

As the movement spread, tensions arose between the "awakened" and the historic church bodies, which began to call themselves the National Church. Perceived as antimodern, the awakened were subject to criticism and even legal sanction. In the Canton neighboring Geneva, the Vaud, the government declared evangelical meetings illegal. The great theologian and literary scholar Alexandre Vinet (1797–1847), though personally not especially drawn to the awakening, strongly protested in the name of liberty of conscience and the separation of church and state. Tensions grew until 1845, when the Free Church was founded. Over half the pastors in the National Church resigned because of pressure to submit the church to political authority rather than to the elders.

THE SECOND HALF OF THE RESTORATION

Slowly, certain physical improvements in the city of Geneva occurred toward the end of the 1820s. Guillaume-Henri Dufour, the chief engineer of the canton of Geneva, built the *Grand-Quai* (today's *Quai Général-Guisan*), and the *Pont des Bergues*. Nevertheless merchants and entrepreneurs were frustrated by the fiscal and juridical obstacles to progress. Many of them wanted the city to spread, however, but it could not because of the ancient ramparts. Though obsolete, the government wanted them kept for reasons that appeared prejudiced against the business community. With growing opposition to this regime at many levels, a change was due.

A dramatic change did occur, first in France and then in other countries. The period from 1830 to 1848, known as the July Monarchy, is the second phase of the Restoration, one that would yield a far more fruitful evolution toward modernization. It followed the "*Trois Glorieuses*" of July 27, 28, and 29, in which Charles X abdicated, and the duc d'Orleans, Louis-Philippe, was called to the throne. He was a "*roi-citoyen*" who desired working through the Chamber of Deputies. It is the era of François Guizot, the enlightened Protestant statesman and historian. His legislation in education was a model for many other countries.

A change occurred in Switzerland as well. As they moved into the 1830s, many cities saw a gradual reversal of misfortunes. Not all the cantons welcomed modernity with open arms. Paradoxically, the country became a refuge for both reactionaries and revolutionaries. The events of 1830 were greeted as an encouragement to reform. A movement known as the *Régénération* surfaced in many parts of the country. As the named implies, it represented a new vision for growth and opposition to conservatism. In many cities, including Geneva, cottage industries, watchmaking, and other trade developed steadily. Larger companies, such as Bautte, begin to employ many more workers. The syndic (mayor) of Geneva, Jean-Jacques Rigaud, inaugurated a program of "progrès graduel" in which various liberal voices could be heard.

Geneva was more aware than most of the plight of laborers. Although trade unions were forbidden, mutual aid societies for various professions were founded that had many of the same functions as unions. In 1833 and 1834 tailors and locksmiths went on strike (among the first in the century). The writings of J.-C.-L. Simonde de Sismondi (1773—1842) eloquently proclaimed the need to protect the working class well before Marx and Engels. Troubled by the contradiction between modern progress and poverty, he asks rhetorically whether individuals are better off since the Industrial Revolution: "Does [the Genevan population] have more confidence in the present, more security about the future? Does it enjoy its freedom more? Is it not only better housed, better clothed, better fed, has it won more leisure and more capacity for its intellectual development?"[18] Sismondi is harshly critical of England, which he reckons, leaves workers in a "frightful distress."[19]

Under the leadership of the radical James Fazy (1794—1878), Geneva became thoroughly modern. The Constitution of 1842 was a vast improvement over that of 1814, with it universal suffrage (exclusively male!) and freedom of the press. Geneva became an independent commune with an elected municipal council. In 1847, the city voted its own constitution, written largely by Fazy.

In July 1846 an event occurred that would thrust Geneva, and the rest of Switzerland, fully into a modern disposition. Seven Roman Catholic cantons, known as the Sonderbund, tried to secede from the Confederacy. Despite pressure from Fazy and the radicals, the Genevan delegation to the Federal Diet refused to vote against the Sonderbund. Thus a Protestant city was defending the rights of Catholics! The movement was squelched four months later. Meanwhile, at the occasion of the resistance of Saint-Gervais (a citadel of Geneva) against government troops, the Genevan Council was dissolved and Fazy came to power, where he would remain until 1861. The Genevan delegation to the Federal Diet could then vote the end of the Sonderbund, following the radicals' philosophy. Ironically, Genevan Catholics were often behind Fazy, though more because they were workers than because of loyalty to Roman doctrine.

Fazy was radical only in name. In fact, he was a left-leaning liberal whose dream was for Geneva to be the beacon of modernity in every sphere. In 1849 the ancient ramparts were destroyed, and Geneva grew into the modern agglomeration hoped for. In the bargain, it was able to employ thousands of victims of the European economic crisis of 1847–1850. The city was on its way to becoming what it is today.

SCHOOLS IN RESTORATION GENEVA

By 1848, with the arrival of the radicals, educational philosophy and politics took the form we know in large part today. To arrive at that point, a number of steps were taken during the Restoration that represented a distinctly modern consciousness. In the earlier part of the century the organizational structures were somewhat loose. Conservative government was not inclined to place the various schools under the aegis of the state, as would their radical successors. In point of fact, public schools kept a marked confessional identity, at least until the first serious laws on public instruction, 1834–1836, which moved toward secularization. The majority were Protestant, from the Ancient Territory. But after the annexation of the New Territory in 1815, the buffer zone mentioned above, a good number of schools with a Roman Catholic character emerged.

Three levels of schools can be noted. There were primary schools, either in town or in the surrounding countryside. In 1827, there were 29 schools with over 700 students. Protestant schools before 1834 were run by the Venerable Company of Pastors. They were strongly confessional, though neither free nor obligatory. After the law of 1834 they were run by a 15-member school commission, of which two had to be from the State Council, the rest were ministers or notables. Fazy would later eliminate such intermediary structures. Officially each commune was to have a school. The law also recognized the need for girls' schools, though they were often relegated to second best. Roman Catholic schools were mainly private, at least until Genevan administration began. The principal purpose of these schools was religious instruction.

The next level is secondary education. The most notable public school, at least until 1830, is the Collège, founded by Calvin in 1559. It had two levels, the primary and the secondary. Although limited to families of means, it formed magistrates, pastors, and professional. In addition, there were schools founded by the Société pour l'instruction de la jeunesse (begun in 1736), which specialized in tutoring young people in Christian knowledge and various skills.

Finally, the Académie, which became the modern *Université de Genève*, also founded by Calvin, represented the main opportunity for higher education. There, in addition to the Theological Faculty, departments in the liberal arts, the sciences, and business were added. It is in this setting that the themes of modernity can be traced.

MODERNITY IN EDUCATION

To anticipate our conclusion, schools in Restoration Geneva made numerous reforms, all with a goal to accommodate, or even promulgate, various aspects of modernity. Yet it was a time of transition, when the ghost of the *ancien régime* was still present and the coming of a new era was seen by many not as a boon but a threat. We can judge this by looking at our six traits of modernity. Although logically separate, these themes are interlinked. In the interest of brevity, we shall explore them in relation to education somewhat interchangeably. And although the three levels of schooling do not necessarily confront modernity in the same ways, we will tend to go back and forth between them, for the sake of unity.

At the *Fête des Promotions* (graduation) of the Collège in 1814, the first since independence, Genevans sensed the historic import of the moment. The students marched into the cathedral, followed by the magistrates, the members of the Académie, and the Venerable Company; and they sat before the dignitaries and the popular syndic Ami Lullin. After a number of speeches, Simonde de Sismondi, mentioned above, rose to give the keynote address. His title was "*De la Philosophie de l'Histoire*," which amounted to a panegyric for the city of Geneva.[20] It was the greatest of the cities of light ("post tenebras lux"), first in religious and civil liberties. With a bow to Divine Providence and a reminder of the breach with "superstitious religion," Sismondi recounts for the young scholars the recent past, when their city had provided the world with its greatest example of tolerance and of the freedom of the individual: "Genevans, this Academy has told you, and it repeats it to you with a noble pride, that you have often been put into the front line of the human race's glorious march."[21]

These are Reformation principles corrected by Enlightenment themes. The schools could not translate them into its curriculum consistently, but they certainly moved in that direction. Walo Hutmacher speaks of a "révolution culturelle" characterizing the secondary schools in Geneva, which moves from a Medieval worldview to one that affirms, in addition to Christian principles, the need to form a "civilized adult," who can determine his environment through reason and organizational skills.[22] This ideal of a citizenry characterized by an enlightened religion was in keeping with the times. Philippe-Albert Stapfer, minister of the Arts and Sciences, and in charge of religion, just before the Restoration, wanted the church to be subject to the state, but yet with a special calling to moralize its people. Education was one of the principal means to accomplish this.[23]

The law of January 27, 1834, on the administration and the direction of public instruction severed the Venerable Company from any official role in overseeing the schools. It placed that authority instead in a special commission, the Conseil d'Instruction Publique (CIP), which represented the State Council. This law had the effect of laicizing the schools, a step that provoked a good deal of debate. Whereas most in the Venerable Company saw the change as inevitable, some saw it as secularism, a breach with Protestant history.[24] In practicality, the step allowed for a number of significant reforms both in curriculum and in organization of the secondary schools.

One of these is offering, for the first time, elective courses at the Collège. This was in part in order to accommodate the special needs of students headed for industry or trade, not the professions. German was such a course, which had a good signup, at least for the first year. Debates on the curriculum raged between those who thought the change was none too early and those who believed that the classical languages were sufficient for any and all students, whatever their careers. Their point is that the classics impart a great and noble character more than anything else. Religious instruction went on, but there was debate as to who would be best for the task. Some assumed it should be the pastor or the curate. Others argued that laypersons would actually present a more attractive Christianity, since theirs was a less professional faith. In point of fact religious instruction dwindled gradually during the 1840s, often with a bare memorization of the catechism the only requirement. As one history wistfully puts it, "These religious practices later fell into disuse; but it is difficult today to identify exactly the point at which they ceased."[25]

Protestants in Geneva were not concerned for the decline in religious instruction in the schools as long as there were ways to give students a proper sense of independence and the ability to exercise their conscience. The way to do that was often to promote classical education, despite trends toward praxis. Joël Cherbuliez affirms that the best education is not this or that skill but the ability to become an independent agent. When young people learn to be self-directed, then progress can occur in society.[26] To be sure, freedom without education in skills is counterproductive. One of education's primary goals is to form citizens for democracy. But he is critical of democracy's tendency to downplay knowledge. The danger of popular sovereignty is to forget higher authority altogether. A classical education can mitigate that disrespect.[27]

Naturally, the philosophy of Rousseau was ever present in discussions of curriculum. Although Rousseau's *Emile* was nothing if not controversial, his general emphasis on the importance of early education represented a trend many welcomed. Cherbuliez draws from Rousseau such principles as learning by example, the role of mothers in early childhood, and even the need for laws promoting virtue, and not merely peace. He is critical of Rousseau's more exotic views, but he urges educators to adopt his wisdom on the need for character development.[28] One can even see in the educational philosophy of certain thinkers in Geneva a precursor to the modern teaching of virtue through the story. Rudolph Töpfer, for example, wrote *Le Presbytère*, a novel that loosely followed Rousseau's *Nouvelle Héloïse*, a Calvinist tragedy in which there is strong moral instruction for the reader through identification with the hero. Many other examples could be cited.[29]

Attempts were made at the Académie to nurture the spirit of freedom of the individual in a direct manner. Always seen as a consequence of enlightened Protestantism, educational philosophy justified "free examination" as the only proper posture in modern times. J.-E. Cellérier, for example, tells students they are in a "century of progress." He goes on to say that theology can be justified not in itself but alongside other disciplines. Its role is to add a "moral power from on high" to the general trend of liberty.[30] The professor E. Diodati gave a regular course on "l'Individualisme religieux," in which he traced the principle of free examination from the Reformation to the present. In addition to its intellectual value, individualism, with its freedom of conscience, has social virtue. It is in countries that respect this individual freedom that one finds the greatest tolerance, and also the greatest freedom of religion.[31]

Finally, it should be mentioned that one of the most marked discussions in educational circles in Restoration Geneva was whether and how to accommodate the new demands of a market economy and the industrial environment. We briefly alluded above to debates about training nonprofessionals. More needs to be said. In 1821 the Société pour l'avancement des Arts asked the State Council to study its report, "Mémoire sur les moyens d'améliorer l'éducation des jeunes gens destinés aux professions étrangères aux lettres" ("Statement on the Means of Improving the Education of Young People Called to Professions outside the Humanities"). It and other papers alerted the city that present education for laborers was inadequate. Neither the primary schools nor the Collège seemed to acknowledge the rising group of students called to be "industriels" rather than professionals. Proposals were made to start mathematics earlier, to continue the study of French grammar in secondary schools, to do more geometry and science.

An interesting episode occurred around the same time. Scores of brochures were written taking both sides of the issue. One of them used the form of dialogue, with two characters arguing, "Mentor" (representing the bourgeois conservative) and "Technophile" (representing newer demands). Technophile constantly praises the classical method, but says it is not enough. In addition, he argues, we need more courses on special subjects in order to train students for the more specialized world they would inhabit.[32] A series of reactions followed, some approving this new emphasis on specialization, others strongly opposing it. Some advocated a special school for the "industriels." The final result was not massive change, but the gradual integration of courses and tracks for the nonprofessionals.

Geneva may not have been at the avant-garde in every respect. Women's education was slower in being fostered than one might have thought. The special care of orphans or delinquent children developed very slowly. Adjusting to the coming of modernity was by fits and starts. Yet there is no question that the city demonstrated a strong consciousness of the need to accommodate modernity's rise, and a recognition that education was a key place on which to focus to that end. The Restoration period, which was one of tension and ambiguity to begin with, was a crucial era in Geneva's growth. Decisions made and innovations adopted then contributed immeasurably to what Geneva is today, in its own eyes, and in the eyes of the world.

NOTES

1. A French lady, quoted in Joël Cherbuliez, *Genève, ses institutions, ses moeurs* (Geneva: Cherbuliez, 1868), 192.

2. See Leonardo Benevolo, *The European City*, trans. Carl Ibsen (Oxford: Basil Blackwell, 1993), 160–176.

3. Paul Hazard, *La Crise de la conscience européenne 1680–1715* (Paris: Fayard, 1961).

4. Charles Baudelaire, *Oeuvres complètes* (Paris: La Pléiade, 1961), 949–1154.

5. Jacques Le Goff, *La vieille Europe et la nôtre* (Paris: Le Seuil, 1994), 50.

6. Paul Johnson, *The Birth of the Modern: World Society 1915–1830* (New York: HarperCollins, 1991).

7. Jean Carbonnier, "La Sécularisation du droit civil par le Code Civil des français," in *Cristianesimo secolarizzazione e dirito moderno*, ed. L. L. Vaalauri and G. Oilcher (Milan: n. p., 1981), 1008.

8. See Danièle Hervieu-Léger, *Vers un nouveau christianisme?* (Paris: Cerf, 1986); and Roland J. Campiche, "Dilution ou recomposition confessionnelles en Suisse," in *Identités religieuses en Europe*, ed. Grace Davie and Danièle Hervieu-Léger (Paris: La Découverte, 1996), 89–109.

9. See *Les Libéraux*, vol. 1, ed. Pierre Manent (Paris: Hachette/ Pluriel, 1986), 173.

10. G.W.F. Hegel, *Encyklopädie der philosophischen Wissenschaften im Grundisse* (Berlin: n. p., 1817).

11. Bob Goudzwaard, *Capitalism and Progress: A Diagnosis of Western Society* (Toronto: Wedge; Grand Rapids, MI: Eerdmans, 1979), 78.

12. R. R. Palmer, *A History of the Modern World*, 2d ed., rev. (New York: Alfred A. Knopf, 1961), 410.

13. The process was interrupted by the July insurrection, in which a number aristocrats were condemned for conspiring to repress various civil and economic gains. The constitutional government was reestablished in September. It should be noted that citizenship was restricted to Protestants.

14. Louis Simond, "Voyage à Genève en 1818," in *Gaudeamus: Quelques aspects de la vie des étudiants étrangers à Genève* (Geneva: Kundig, 1959), 66.

15. Joseph Des Arts, one of the framers of the Constitution, had written a treatise on political philosophy of which the third section is entitled "Les Principes de la Révolution française sont incompatibles avec l'ordre social" (Paris: J.-J. Paschoud, 1816). He attacks egalitarianism, and defends the propriety of social rank.

16. François Ruchon, *Histoire politique de la République de Genève de la restauration à la suppression de budget des cultes (31 décembre 1813–30 juin 1907)*, vol. 1 (Geneva: A. Jullien, 1953), 79. "Le plus grave reproche qu'on peut faire à la Constitution et au régime politique de la Restauration, c'est d'avoir amené à Genève une sorte d'assoupissement, une sorte d'atonie et d'indifférence politiques, et creusé un fossé, qui ira jusqu'à s'élargissant entre un peuple qui finira par se rendre compte qu'il a été frustré

de ses droits et un gouvernement, paternel certes, animé d'excellentes intentions, mais qui n'avait pas su faire confiance à une population qui ne demandait qu'à montrer son patriotisme en servant librement son pays."

17. For a discussion of the history of French-speaking Protestantism in the ninetenth century, see Edgar, William. *La Carte protestante: Les réformés francophones et l'essor de la modernité (1815—1848)* (Geneva: Labor et Fides, 1997).

18. J.-C.-L. Simonde de Sismondi, *Etudes dur les constitutions des peuples libres*, vol. 1 (Brussels: n. p. 1836), 15. "A-t-il plus de repos dans le présent, plus de sécurité pour l'avenir? Jouit-il plus de son indépendence? Est-il non seulement mieux logé, mieux vêtu, mieux nourri, a-t-il gagné plus de loisir et plus d'aptitude pour son développement intellectuel?"

19. J.-C.-L. Simonde de Sismondi, *Avertissement, Nouveaux principes d'Economio politique*, 2d ed. (Paris: n. p., 1827).

20. An account of this event and the speech may be found in Ruchon, *Histoire politique de la République de Genève*, 40.

21. Simonde de Sismondi, "*De la Philosophie de l'Histoire.*" Although the Magistrates enjoyed his address, Sismondi was urged not to publish the speech because of its incendiary remarks about Catholicism. He eventually had it published in London. "Genevois, cette Académie vous a dit, elle vous répète encore avec un noble orgueil, que vous vous êtes souvent placés au premier rang dans la marche glorieuse de l'espèce humaine."

22. Walo Hutmacher, "Préface," in Eric Moradpour, *École et jeunesse, Esquisse d'une histoire des débats au Parlement genevois, 1846—1961* (Geneva: Cahiers du Service de la Recherche Sociologique, no. 14, July 1981), v.

23. Philippe-Albert Stapfer, *Histoire du christianisme en Suisse, une perspective oecuménique* (Geneva: Labor et Fides; Fribourg: Editions Saint-Paul, 1995), 196.

24. Gabriel Mützenberg, *Genève 1830, Restoration de l'école* (Lausanne: Grand-Pont, 1974), 268, 339—341.

25. *Histoire du Collège de Genève* (Geneva: Département de l'Instruction publique, 1896), 320. "Ces pratiques religieuses [students reciting the catechism on Sundays] sont plus tard tombées en désuétude; mais il est difficile aujourd'hui de préciser à quelle moment elles ont cessé."

26. Joël Cherbuliez, *Genève, ses institutions, ses moeurs* (Geneva: A. Cherbuliez, 1868), 245, 260.

27. Ibid., 258.

28. Ibid., 236—42.

29. J.-B. Bouvier, *Essai sur l'histoire intellectuelle de la Restauration, du Romantisme à Genève* (Paris, Neuchâtel: Victor Attinger, 1930).

30. Jacob-Elyse Cellérier, *Qu'est-ce qu'un serviteur de Jésus-Christ?* (Geneva; Paris, 1832), 63.

31. E. Diodati, *Cours de l'Individualisme religieux*, vol. 155, Drawer 40, Mss, (Geneva: *BPU*, c. 1840—1846), 1—53.

32. Attributed to M. Girard, regent of the Primary School, *Dialogue sur les deux projets relatifs à l'instruction publique* (Geneva: Sestié, 1821).

Selected Bibliography

Ainsworth, Arthur David. *The Relations between Church and State in the City and Canton of Geneva.* Atlanta: Stein Print Co., 1965.

Anspach, Isaac-Salomon. "Discours du citoyen Isaac-Salomon Anspach, prononcé le 28 juin 1793 à la fête de l'anniversaire de la naissance de J.-J. Rousseau." *BPU,* 1793.

Babel, Henri. *Les Quatre Hommes qui ont fait Genève: De Calvin à Beze et de Rousseau à Dunant.* Geneva: Tribune, 1981.

Beardslee, John W., III. "Theological Development at Geneva under Francis and Jean-Alphonse Turretin, 1648–1737." Ph.D. dissertation, Yale University, 1957.

Beeke, Joel R. *Assurance of Faith: Calvin, English Puritanism, and the Dutch Second Reformation.* New York: Peter Lang, 1991.

Beeke, Joel R. *Jehovah Shepherding His Sheep.* Grand Rapids, MI: Eerdmans, 1982.

Betts, Maria. *Life of Giovanni Diodati: Genevese Theologian.* London: Charles J. Thynne, 1905.

Beza, Theodore. *Cours sur les Épitres aux Romains et aux Hébreux 1564–1566 d'après notes de Marcus Widler; Thèses disputées à l'Académie de Genève, 1564–1567.* Ed. Pierre Fraenkel and Luc Perrotet. Geneva: Droz, 1988.

Biéler, André. *La Pensée économique et Sociale de Calvin.* Geneva: H. Georg, 1961.

Binz, Louis. *Brève Histoire de Genève.* 2d ed. Geneva: Chancellerie d'Etat, 1985.

Bonnet, Charles. *Mémoires autobiographiques de Charles Bonnet de Genève.* Ed. Raymond Savioz. Paris: J. Vrin, 1948.

Borgeaud, Charles. *Monument international de la Réformation à Genève: Le groupe centrale.* Geneva: Albert Kündig, 1911.

Bost, Ami. *Mémoirs peuvent servir l'histoire du réveil religieux.* 2 vols. Paris: Meyreuis et C., 1854.

Bourgeaud, Charles. *Histoire de l'université de Genève: L'Académie de Calvin, 1559–1798.* Geneva: H. Georg, 1900.

Bouvier, J.-B. *Essai sur l'histoire intellectuelle de la Restauration, du Romantisme à Genève*. Paris, Neuchâtel: Victor Attinger, 1930.

Bouvier, Nicholas, Gordon A. Craig, and Lionel Gossman. *Geneva, Zürich, Basel: History, Culture, and National Identity*. Intro. Carl E. Schorske. Princeton, NJ: Princeton UP, 1994.

Brütsch, Yves. "Population Genevoise du XVIIIe siècle." *AEG*. Mémoire de licence, 1973.

Budé, Eugène de. *Vie de Bénédict Pictet, théologien genevois (1655–1724)*. Lausanne: Georges Bridel, 1874.

Budé, Eugène de. *Vie de J. A. Turrettini, théologien genevois (1671–1737)*. Lausanne: Georges Bridel, 1880.

Budé, Eugène de. *Vie de Jacob Vernet, théologien genevois (1698–1789)*. Lausanne: Georges Bridel, 1893.

Bulletin de la Société d'histoire et d'archéologie de Genève. Geneva: SHAG.

Burgelin, Pierre. *Jean-Jacques Rousseau et la religion de Genève*. Geneva: Labor et Fides, 1962.

Burn, John. *Livre des anglois à Genève*. London: n. p., 1831.

Campi, Emidio, and Carla Sodini. *Gli oriundi lucchesi di Ginevra e il cardinale Spinola: Una controversia religiosa alla vigilia della revoca dell'Editto di Nantes*. Chicago: Newberry Library, 1988.

Candaux, Jean-Daniel. *Histoire de la famille Pictet*. Geneva: Etienne Braillard, 1974. Vol. 1.

Candolle, Alphonse de. *Lettre à un des MM. les conseillers d'Etat sur la question des étrangeurs qui sejourment ou qui s'établissement dans le canton de Genève*. Geneva: Charles Gruaz, 1837.

Cellérier, Jacob-Elyse. *Qu'est-ce qu'un serviteur de Jésus-Christ?* Geneva: Paris, 1932.

Chastel, Étienne. *Conférences sur l'histoire du christianisme prêchées à Genève*. 2 vols. Valence: Marc Aurel frères, 1839–1847.

Chenevière, J.J.C. *Principaux faits de l'Histoire Sainte et de l'Histoire de L'Église chrétienne*. Geneva: J. J. Paschoud, 1819.

Cherbuliez, Joël. *Genève, ses institutions, ses moeurs*. Geneva: Cherbuliez, 1868.

Choisy, Eugène. *L'état chrétien calviniste à Genève au temps de Théodore de Bèze*. Geneva: Ch. Eggimann, 1902.

Choisy, Eugène. *La théocratie à Genève au temps de Calvin*. Geneva: Ch. Eggimann, 1897.

Chronique de Genève. 2 tomes in 4 vols. Geneva: J.-G. Fick, 1831 [1531].

Claude, Jean. "Claude to Turretin, 20 June 1675." In *Lettre de Monsr. Jean Claude ecrite à Msr. Francois Turretin sur le sujet de "Fomulaire de consentement". . . Repose de Msr. Francois Turretin*. Geneva: n. p., 1676.

Claude, Jean. *Lettre de Monsr. Jean Claude ecrite a Msr. Francois Turretin sur le sujet de "Fomulaire de consentement". . . Repose de Msr. Francois Turretin . . .* Geneva: n. p., 1676.

Committee report, *Récit des principale circonstances qui ont signalé du célébration du 3e Jubilé de la Réformation de Genève en l'an 1835*. Geneva: Abraham Cherbuliez, 1835.

Coudray, Danielle. *L'Abbé Vuarin, cure de Genève, 1769–1843*. 4 vols. Fribourg: D. Coudray, 1984–1987.

Court, Antoine. *L'assemblée de la Baume des Fées, près Nîmes. Relation d'Antoine Court, avec lettres et pièces justificatives.* Ed. C. Saignier. Intro. J. Bonnet. Paris and Nîmes: Grassart et Lavagne-Peyrot, 1891.

Court, Anotine. *Mémoires pour servir à l'histoire et à la vie d'Antoine Court (de 1695 à 1729).* Ed. Pauline Duley-Haour. Intro. Patrick Cabanel. Paris: Les Éditions de Paris, 1995.

De Montbrillant, Madame. *Texte intégral publié pour la première fois . . . par Georges Roth.* Paris: Gallimard, 1951. Excerpted in Jean-Daniel Candaux, Ed. *Voyageurs européens à la découvert de Genève 1685—1792.* Geneva: Impr. Populaire, 1966.

Deonna, W. "Le nom de Genève." *Geneva* 19 (1941): 80—81.

Dictionnaire biographique des Genevois et Vaudois. Geneva: George Bridel, 1877—1878. Vol. 2: 293.

Diodati, E. *Cours de l'Individualisme religieux.* Vol. 155, Drawer 40, Mss. Geneva: *BPU,* c. 1840—1842.

Diodati, John. *Pious and Learned Annotations upon the Holy Bible: Plainly Expounding the Most Difficult Places Thereof.* 3d ed. London: James Flesher for Nichlas Fussell, 1651 (exposition of Rom. 9:20, no pagination).

Dufour, Alain. "Le Mythe de Genève au temps de Calvin." *Histoire politique et psychologie historique.* Geneva: Droz, 1966.

Dumont, Eugène-Louis. *Genève d'autrefois: Cours et escaliers des XVIIe et XVIIIe siècles.* Geneva: Le Pavé, 1969.

Dunoyer, Joseph-Victor. *Mémoire adressé à S. G. Mgr. Marilley, évêque de Lausanne et de Genève, sur le nouveau réglement des Écoles primaires du canton de Genève.* Geneva: n. p., [18?].

Edgar, William. *La Carte protestante: Les réformés francophones et l'essor de la modernité (1815—1848)* Geneva: Labor et Fides, 1997.

Fatio, Olivier. *Méthode et théologie: Lambert Daneau et les débuts de la scholastique réformée.* Geneva: Droz, 1976.

Fatio, Olivier, ed. *Genève protestante en 1831.* Publication de la Faculté de Théologie de l'Université de Genève. No. 6. Geneva: Labor et Fides, 1983.

Fazy, Henri. *James Fazy, Sa Vie et Son Oeuvre.* Geneva: H. Georg, 1887.

Fazy, James. *De la tentative de Napoléon Louis.* Geneva: Imprimerie P.-V. Oursel, 1836.

Fazy, James. *Rapport de la Commission sur le Projet de Constitution du Canton de Genève.* Geneva: Imprimerie de P.-A. Bonnant, 1847.

Fazy-Pasteur, Marc-Antoine. *Mémorial des séances du Conseil représentatif (1er mai au décembre 1837).* Geneva: Abraham Cherbuliez, 1837.

Fleury, L'Abbé. *Calvin à Genève: Quelques pages de sa vie à l'occasion du 300me anniversaire de sa mort par un Genevois.* Geneva: Pfeffer et Puky, 1864.

Frachebourg, Jean-Claude. "James Fazy (1794—1878): L'homme, le démocrate, le magistrat." *Actes de l'Institut National Genevois.* New series of the Bulletin of the Institut National Genevois, no. 23. Geneva: Institut National Genevois, 1979.

Fraenkel, Pierre. *De l'écriture à la dispute: le cas de l'Académie de Genève sous Théodore de Bèze.* Cahiers de la *RTP* 1. Lausanne: *RTP,* 1977.

Gaberel, Jean. "Jacob Vernet et ses relations contemporaines." *Etrennes religieuses* 24 (1883): 120—41.

Gaberel, Jean. *Voltaire et les Genevois.* Paris, Geneva: J. Cherbuliez, 1857.

Gagnebin, Bernard. "Henry Dunant." *IRRC* 3, 27 (June 1963).

Gargett, Graham. *Jacob Vernet, Geneva and the Philosophes: Studies on Voltaire and the Eighteenth Century.* Oxford: Voltaire Foundation, 1995.

Gaussen, Louis, Jean Henri Merle d'Aubigné, et al. *La Direction de l'École de Théologie établie dans L'Église Reformée de Genève.* Geneva: Susanne Guers, 1833.

Giesendorf, Paul-F. *Bibliographie raisonée de l'histoire de Genève des orgines à Genève.* Geneva: Jullien, 1966.

Goltz, Hermann de. *Genève religieuse au dix-neuvième siècle.* Trans. C. Millan-Sillem. Geneva: H. Georg, 1862.

Good, James I. *History of the Swiss Reformed Church Since the Reformation.* Philadelphia: Publication of the Sunday School Board, 1913.

Grandjean, Henri. "La Bourse Française de Genève (1550—1849)." In *Etrennes Genevoises,* 46—60. Geneva: Edition Atar, 1927.

Grohman, Donald D. "The Genevan Reaction to the Saumur Doctrine of Hypothetical Universalism: 1635—1685." Ph.D. dissertation, Knox College, Toronto, 1971.

Guerdan, René. *Histoire de Genève.* Paris: Mazarine, 1981.

Guers, Emile. *Le Premier Réveil et la Première Église Indépendante à Genève.* Geneva: Béroud et Kaufmann, 1871.

Guichonnet, Paul, ed. *Histoire de Genève.* Toulouse: Privat; Lausanne: Payot, 1974.

Haeberli, Laurent. "Le Suicide à Genève au 18e siècle." *Pour une histoire qualititative: études offertes à Sven Stelling-Michaud.* 115—129. Geneva: Presses Universitaires Romandes, 1975.

Heyd, Michael. *Between Orthodoxy and the Enlightenment: Jean-Robert Chouet and the Introduction of Cartesian Science in the Academy of Geneva.* The Hague: Martinus Nijhoff, 1982.

Heyd, Michael. "Un role nouveau pour la science: Jean-Alphonse Turrettini et les débuts de la théologie naturelle Genève." *RTP* 112 (1982): 25—42.

Heyer, Henri. *L'Église de Genève, 1535—1909.* Geneva: A. Jullien, 1909. Reprint, Nieuwkoop: B. De Graaf, 1974.

Higman, Francis. *Diffusion de la Réforme en France, 1520—1565.* Geneva: Labor et Fides, 1992.

Hiler, David. "Recherches sur les finances publiques d'une cité état au XVIIIe siècle. Les Comptes de la Seigneurie de Genève (1714—1781)." Mémoire de licence, Faculté SES, University of Geneva, 1983.

Hiler, David. "Les Sept Jours gras du patriciat genevois. Le livre de ménage de Marie Gallatin." *RVG* 16 (1986).

Hiler, David, and Bernard Lescaze. *Révolution inachevée révolution oubliée; 1842; les promesses de la Genève moderne.* Geneva: Suzanne Hurter, 1992.

Histoire du Collège de Genève. Geneva: Département de l'Instruction publique, 1896.

Hutmacher, Walo. "Préface." In *Ecole et jeunesse, Esquisse d'une histoire des débats au Parlement genevois, 1846—1961.* Ed. Eric Moradpour. Geneva: Cahiers du Service de la Recherche Sociologique, no. 14, July, 1981.

Jullien, Alexandre. *Histoire de Genève, des origines à 1798.* Geneva: SHAG, 1951.

Karmin, Otto. *Documents sur l'histoire religieuse de Genève à l'époque de la Restoration.* Geneva: SHAG, 1918.

Keate, George. *A Short Account of the Ancient History, Present Government and Laws of the Republic of Geneva.* London: n. p., 1761.

Keizer, Gerrit. *François Turrettini: Sa vie, ses oeuvres et le consensus*. Lausanne: Georges Bridel, 1900.

Kingdon, Robert M. "The First Expression of Theodore Beza's Political Ideas." *ARG* 46 (1955): 88—99.

Kingdon, Robert M. *Geneva and the Consolidation of the French Protestant Movement, 1564—1572*. Madison: U Wisconsin P, 1967.

Kingdon, Robert M. "The Geneva Consistory as Established by John Calvin." *On the Way: Occasional Papers of the Wisconsin Conference of the United Church of Christ* 7 (1990): 41.

Kingdon, Robert M. "The Geneva Consistory in the Time of Calvin." In *Calvinism in Europe, 1540—1620*. Ed. Andrew Pettegree, Alastair Duke, and Gillian Lewis. Cambridge: Cambridge UP, 1994.

Kirk, Linda. "Eighteenth-Century Geneva and a Changing Calvinism." In *Religion and National Identity*. Ed. Stewart Mews. Oxford: Basil Blackwell, 1982.

Kirk, Linda. "Genevan Republicanism." In *Republicanism, Liberty, and Commercial Society, 1649—1776*. Ed. David Wootton. Stanford, CA: Stanford UP, 1994.

Klauber, Martin I. *Between Reformed Scholasticism and Pan-Protestantism: Jean-Alphonse Turretin (1671—1737) and Enlightened Orthodoxy at the Academy of Geneva*. Selinsgrove, PA: Susquehanna UP, 1994.

Klauber, Martin I. "Continuity and Discontinuity in Post-Reformation Reformed Theology: An Evaluation of the Muller Thesis." *Journal of the Evangelical Theological Society* 33—34 (December, 1990): 467—475.

Klauber, Martin I. "The Helvetic Formula Consensus: An Introduction and Translation." *Trinity Journal* (Spring, 1990): 103—23.

Klauber, Martin I. "Jean-Alphonse Turrettini and the Abrogation of the Formula Consensus in Geneva." *WTJ* 53 (1991): 325—338.

Klauber, Martin I. "Reason, Revelation and Cartesianism: Louis Tronchin and Enlightened Orthodox in Late Seventeenth-Century Geneva." *Church History* 59 (September 1990): 326—339.

Klauber, Martin I., and Glenn S. Sunshine, "Jean-Alphonse Turrettini on Biblical Accommodation: Calvinist or Socinian?" *CTJ* (April, 1990): 7—27.

Le Mercier, Andrew. *The Church in Geneva in Five Books. . . .* Boston: n. p., 1732.

Lescaze, Bernard, ed. *Sauver l'âme, nourrir le corps, de l'Hôpital général à l'Hospice général de Genève, 1535—1985*. Pref. Jean Imbert. Geneva: Hospice général, Atar, 1985.

Leuba, Jean-Louis. "Rousseau et le milieu calviniste de sa jeunesse." In J.-L. Leuba, et al. *Jean-Jacques Rousseau et la crise contemporaine de la conscience*. Paris: Beauchesne, 1980.

Lewis, Gillian. "Calvinism in Geneva in the time of Calvin and of Beza (1541—1605)." In *International Calvinism, 1541—1715*. Ed. Menna Prestwich. Oxford: Clarendon Press, 1985.

Lewis, Gillian. "The Genevan Academy." In *Calvinism in Europe*. Ed. Pettegree, et al. Cambridge: Cambridge UP, 1994.

"Loi sur l'établissement d'un Hôpital cantonal du 23 juin 1849." In *Notice publiée à l'occasion du cinquantième anniversaire de la fondation de l'Hôpital cantonal de Genève, 1856—1906*. Geneva: n. p., 1906.

Maag, Karin. *Seminary or University? The Genevan Academy and Reformed*

Higher Education, 1560—1620. St. Andrews Studies in Reformation History. Aldershot, UK: Scolar Press, 1995.

Mallet, George. *Genève et les genevois*. Geneva: J. J. Paschoud, 1814.

Martin, L'Abbé François, and l'Abbé Fleury. *Histoire de M. Vuarin et du rétablissement du Catholicisme à Genève*. 2 vols. Geneva: A. Jaquemont, 1861.

Maury, Léon. *Le réveil religieux dans l'Église Reformée à Genève et en France (1810—1850): Étude historique et dogmatique*. 2 vols. Paris: Fischbacher, 1892.

Mayor, Hélène. "La Bourse française de Genève au moment de la révocation de l'Édit de Nantes." Mémoire de licence, University of Geneva, May 1983.

McComish, William A. *The Epigones: A Study of the Theology of the Genevan Academy at the time of the Synod of Dort, with special reference to Giovanni Diodati*. Allison Park, PA: Pickwith, 1989.

Merle d'Aubigné, Jean Henri. *Discourses and Essays*. Ed. Robert Baird. Glasgow and London: William Collins, 1846.

Merle d'Aubigné, Jean Henri. *Histoire de la Réformation en Europe au temps de Calvin*. 8 vols. Paris: Michel Lévy frères, 1863—1878.

Merle d'Aubigné, Jean Henri. *History of the Reformation in Europe in the Time of Calvin*. 8 vols. London: Longman, Green, Roberts, 1863—1878.

Merle d'Aubigné, Jean Henri. *History of the Reformation of the Sixteenth Century*. 5 vols. Grand Rapids, MI: Baker Books, 1976 [1853].

Merle d'Aubigné, Jean Henri. *La pierre sur laquelle l'académie de Genève fut posée en juin 1559*. Geneva: Émile Béroud, 1859.

Merle d'Aubigné, Jean Henri. *Septembre 1861 ou l'Alliance évangélique à Genève*. Geneva and Paris: Société évangélique, 1861.

Merle d'Aubigné, Jean Henri. *A Voice from the Alps: or, a Brief Account of the Evangelical Societies of Paris and Geneva*. Ed. and Intro. Rev. Edward Bickerseth. London: R. B. Seeley and W. Burnside, 1838.

Monnier, Philippe. "Les archives du Comité genevois pour le protestantisme français." *BSHPF* 119 (1973): 575—596.

Montandon, Albert. *L'Évolution théologique a Genève au XVIIe siècle*. Le Cateau: J. Roland, 1894.

Monter, E. William. *Calvin's Geneva*. New York: John Wiley and Sons, 1967.

Montet, Albert de. *Dictionnaire biographique des Genevois et Vaudois*. 2 vols. Geneva: George Bridel, 1877—1878.

Mottu-Weber, Liliane. "Les Activités manufacturières." In *L'Économie genevoise, de la Réforme à la fin de l'Ancien Régime, XVIe—XVIIIe siècles*. 423—499. Ed. Anne-Marie Piuz and Liliane Mottu-Weber. Geneva: SHAG, 1990.

Mottu-Weber, Liliane. "La Conjoncture de l'économie genevoise, XVIe-XVIIIe siècles." In *L'Économie genevoise, de la Réforme à la fin de l'Ancien Régime, XVIe—XVIIIe siècles*. 615—648. Ed. Anne-Marie Piuz and Liliane Mottu-Weber. Geneva: SHAG, 1990.

Moultou, Paul-Claude. "Extrait d'un sermon de M. Moultou, ministre de Genève, sur le luxe." *Annales de la Société Jean-Jacques Rousseau* 17 (1926): 171—178.

Muller, Richard A. *Christ and the Decree: Christology and Predestination in Reformed Theology from Calvin to Perkins*. Grand Rapids: Baker Books, 1988.

Muller, Richard A. *Dictionary of Latin and Greek Theological Terms*. Grand Rapids, MI: Baker Books, 1985.

Muller, Richard A. "The Hermeneutic of Promise and Fulfillment in Calvin's

Exegesis of the Old Testament Prophecies of the Kingdom." In *The Bible in the Sixteenth Century*. 68—82. Ed. and Intro. David C. Steinmetz. Durham, NC: Duke UP, 1990.

Muller, Richard A. "Predestination and Christology in Sixteenth Century Reformed Theology." Ph.D. dissertation, Duke University, 1976.

Mützenberg, Gabriel. "David Dunant, oncle et précurseur du fondateur de la Croix-Rouge." *RSH* 30 (1980): 369—376.

Mützenberg, Gabriel. *A l'écoute du Réveil*. St-Léger: Éditions Emmaüs, 1989.

Mützenberg, Gabriel. *Henry Dunant le prédestiné: Du nouveau sur la famille, la jeunesse, la destinée spirituelle du fondateur de la Croix-Rouge*. Geneva: Robert Éstienne, 1984.

Mützenberg, Gabriel. *L'Obsession calviniste*. Geneva: Labor et Fides, 1979.

Mützenberg, Gabriel. "Révolution genevois de 1846 et pédagogie chrétienne, ou Un grand pas vers l'école laïque." *RSH* 22, 3 (1972): 433—457.

Naphy, William G. "'No History Can Satisfy Everyone': Geneva's Chroniclers and Emerging Religious Identities." In *Protestant History and Identity*. Vol. 1: 23—38. Ed. Bruce Gordon. Aldershot, UK: Scolar Press, 1996.

Naville-Rigaud, Jean Adrien, ed. *Jean-Jacques Rigaud, ancien premier syndic de Genève: notice biographique*. Geneva: H. Georg; A. Cherbuliez, 1879.

Notice publiée à l'occasion du cinquantième anniversaire de la fondation de l'Hôpital cantonal de Genève, 1856—1906. Ed. Commission administrative de l'Hôpital cantonal de Genève. Geneva: Atar, 1906.

Noyer, Anne Sylvie. *Le Protestantisme genevois vu à travers les Annales catholiques de Genève*. 1852—1862. *AEG*, Manuscrit historique 252/290.

Olson, Jeannine. *Calvin and Social Welfare: Deacons and the Bourse Française*. Selinsgrove, PA: Susquehanna UP; London: Associated UP, 1989.

O'Mara, Patrick. "Geneva in the Eighteenth Century. A Socio-Economic Study of the Bourgeois City-State during Its Golden Age. Ph.D. dissertation, University of California, 1954.

Perrenoud, Alfred. *La Population de Genève du seizième au début du dix-neuvième siècle: Étude démographique*. *MDG*. Geneva: A. Jullien, 1979.

Perret, Geneviève. "La Paillardise à Genève, 1760—1764." *AEG*, Mémoire de licence, 1982.

Phillips, Timothy R. "Francis Turretin's Idea of Theology and Its Impact upon His Doctrine of Scripture." Ph.D. dissertation, Vanderbilt University, 1986.

Pictet, Bénédict. *Christian Theology*. Trans. Frederick Reyroux. Philadelphia: Presbyterian Board of Publications, n. d. Originally published in Latin as *Benedicti Picteti in Ecclesia et acad. Genev. pastoris et S.S. Th. professoris Theologia Christiana*.

Pictet, Bénédict. *Lettre contre les mariages bigarrés*. Geneva: n. p., 1701.

Pictet, Bénédict. *Lettre sur ceux qui se croyent inspirez par Benedict Pictet, pasteur et professeur en theologie*. Geneva: Fabri et Barrillot, 1721.

Pictet, Bénédict. *Morale chrétienne ou l'art de bien vivre*. 2 vols. Geneva: La Compagnie des Libraires, 1710.

Pictet, Bénédict. *Traité contre l'indifférence des religions*. Geneva: Cramer et Perrachon, 1716.

Pictet, Bénédict. *Les Vérités de la religion chrétienne*. Geneva: Pierre Jaquier, 1711.

Pictet de Rochement, Charles. *Documents sur l'histoire religieuse de Genève à l'époque de la Restauration.* Geneva: SHAG, 1918.

Pitassi, Maria-Cristina. "L'Apologétique Raisonnable de Jean-Alphonse Turrettini." In *Apologétique 1680—1740: Sauvetage or naufrage de la théologie.* Ed. Olivier Fatio and Maria C. Pitassi. 180—212. Geneva: Publications de la Faculté de Théologie de l'Université de Genève, 1990.

Pitassi, Maria-Cristina. *De l'orthodoxie aux Lumières. Genève 1670—1737.* Geneva: Labor et Fides, 1992.

Pitassi, Maria-Cristina. "Un Manuscrit Genevois du XVIIIe Siècle: La Refutation du Systeme de Spinosa par Mr. Turrettini." *NAKG* 68 (1988): 180—212.

Porret, Michel. *Le crime et ses circonstances. De l'esprit de l'arbitraire au siècle des Lumières selon les réquisitoires des procureurs généraux de Genève.* Geneva: Droz, 1995.

Porret, Michel. "'Mon Père c'est le dernier chagrin que je vous donne': Jeunes suicides à Genève au 18e siècle." *Ethnologie française* 22 (1992).

Puiz, Anne-Marie. "L'Alimentation hospitalière à Genève au XVIIIe siècle." In *A Genève et autour de Genève au XVIIe et XVIIIe siècles.* Lausanne: Payot, 1985.

Puiz, Anne-Marie. "Chertés et disettes." In *L'Économie genevoise, de la Réforme à la fin de l'Ancien Régime, XVIe—XVIIIe siècles.* Ed. Anne-Marie Piuz and Liliane Mottu-Weber. 372—378. Geneva: SHAG, 1990.

Puiz, Anne-Marie. "Le Marché du bétail et la consommation de la viande à Genève au XVIIIe siècle." *RSH* 25 (1975).

Puiz, Anne-Marie. "Jean Vian (vers 1690-1772), ouvrier italien réfugié à Genève. Contribution à la typologie de la pauvreté ancienne." *Studi in memoria di Federigo Melis.* Vol. 4: 395—407. Naples: Giannini, 1978.

Py, Albert, Jean Paul Barbier, and Alain Dufour, *Ronsard et la Rome protestante.* Geneva: BPU, 1985.

Reconnoissance d'Action sur La Salle des Spectacles établie à Genève. AEG. Registre Vénérable Compagnie, April 9, October 1, 1784.

Réflexions sur les moeurs, la religion, et le culte: Par J. Vernet, pasteur & professeur en théologie. Geneva: n. p., 1769.

"Règlement sur l'institution de Diaconies dans la ville de Genève du 4 avril 1850." In Église Nationale Protestante de Genève, *Les Diaconies de la ville de Genève: Leur origine et leur activité de 1850 à 1900.* Geneva: Librairie Henry Kündig, 1901.

Reverdin, Olivier et al. *Genève au temps de la révocation de l'édit de Nantes 1680-1705, MDG,* vol. 50. Geneva: Droz, 1985.

Rieder, Philip. "Les Enfants de la Chaire . . . ou ces chers Enfants. Être Enfant à Genève au XVIIIe siècle." *RVG* (1994).

Rivoire, Emile and Victor van Berchem, eds. *Les Sources du droit du Canton de Genève.* Vol. 4, *1621—1700.* Arau: H. R. Sauerländer, 1935.

Roget, Amédée. *La question catholique à Genève de 1815 à 1870.* Geneva: Carey, 1874.

Roney, John B. *The Inside of History: Jean Henri Merle d'Aubigné and Romantic Historiography.* Westport, CT: Greenwood Press, 1996.

Rousseau, Jean-Jacques. *Lettre à M. D'Alembert sur son article Genève.* Ed. Michel Launay. Paris: Garnier-Flammarion, 1967.

Ruchon, François. *Histoire politique de la République de Genève de la restauration à la suppression du budget des cultes (31 décembre 1813—30 juin 1907).* Vol. 1. Geneva: A. Jullien, 1953.

Saladin, Michel-Jean-Louis. *Mémoire historique sur la vie des ouvrages de Jacob Vernet, ministre de l'Eglise, accompagné de l'Invocation aux Muses, de Montesquieu, et de plusieurs lettres J.-J. Rousseau et Voltaire, qui n'ont pas encore été publiées.* Paris: Bossange; Geneva: F. Dufart, 1790.

Schotel, G.D.J. *Jean Diodati.* The Hague: Noordendoorp, 1844.

Senarclens, Jean de. "Les écrivains politiques." In *Encyclopédie de Genève.* Vol. 4, *Les institutions politiques, judiciaires et militaires.* Ed. Bernard Lescaze and Françoise Hirsch. Geneva: Association de l'Encyclopédie de Genève, 1985.

Simond, Louis. "Voyage à Genève en 1818." In *Gaudeamus: Quelques aspects de la vie des étudiants étrangers à Genève.* Geneva: Kundig, 1959.

Sonaillon, Bernard. "Etude des divorces à Genève dans la seconde moitié du XVIIIe." *AEG,* mémoire de licence, 1975.

Spink, John Stephenson. *Rousseau et Genève.* Paris: Boivin, 1934.

Stauffenegger, Roger. *Église et Société Genève au XVIIe Siècle.* 2 vols. Geneva: Librairie Droz, 1983.

Steinberg, Jonathan. *Why Switzerland?* 2d ed. Cambridge: Cambridge UP, 1996.

Stelling-Michaud, Sven, and Suzanne Stelling-Michaud. *Le Livre du Recteur de l'Académie de Genève (1559—1878).* Vol. 6. Geneva: Droz, 1958—1980.

Tissot, David, ed. *Les Conférences de Genève, 1861: Rapports et discours publiés au nom du comité de l'Alliance évengélique.* 2 vols. Geneva: H. Georg, 1861.

Turretin, Francis. *Francisci Turrettini Opera.* 4 vols. Edinburgh: John Lowe, 1847—1848.

Turretin, Francis. *Institutes of Elenctic Theology.* 3 vols. Ed. James Dennison Trans. George Musgrave Giger. Phillipsburg, NJ: P & R Publishing, 1992—1997.

Turretin, Francis. *Institutio Theologiae Elencticae.* Edinburgh: John Lowe, 1847.

Turretin, Francis. *Sermons sur divers passages de L'Ecriture sainte.* Geneva: Daniel du Chemin, 1676.

Turretin, Francis. "Turretin to Claude, 16 February 1676." In *Lettre de Monsr. Jean Claude écrite à Msr. François Turretin sur le sujet de "Formulaire de consentement"* . . . *Repose de Msr. François Turretin.* . . . Geneva: n. p., 1676.

Turretin, J.-A. *Dilucidationes philosophico-theologico-morales, quibus praecipua capita tam theologiae naturalis, quam revelatae demonstrantur ad praxin christianam commendantur accedunt.* 3 vols. Basel: J. R. Imhoff, 1748.

Turretin, J.-A. *Lettres inédites addressés de 1686-1737 J. A. Turretin, théologien genevois.* 3 vols. Ed. E. Budé. Geneva: Jules Carey, 1887.

Turretin, J.-A. *Opera omnia theologica, philosophica et philologica.* 3 vols. Franeker: H. A. de Chalmot et D. Romar, 1774—1776.

Turretin, Samuel. *Preservatif contre le fanatisme ou refutation des pretendus inspirez des derniers siécles.* Trans. Jacques-Théodore Le Clerc. Geneva: Du Villard et Jacquier, 1723.

Turretine [*sic*]. *Dissertations on Natural Theology.* Belfast: n. p., 1777. *BPU.* Mss. Suppl., 1540, f.59.

Valeri, Mark. "Religion, Discipline, and the Economy in Calvin's Geneva." *Sixteenth Century Journal* 34, 1 (1997): 123—142.

Vernes, Jacob, ed. *Choix Littéraire.* Vol. 1. Geneva: n. p., 1755.

Vernet, Jacob. *An Argument Concerning the Christian Religion Drawn for the Character of the Founders.* London: Hull, 1800.

Vernet, Jacob. *Instruction chrétienne.* 5 vols. Geneva: Henri-Albert Gosse, 1756.

Vernet, Jacob. *Réflexions sur les moeurs, sur la religion et sur le culte.* Geneva: Claude Philibert, 1769.

Vernet, Jacob. *Traité de la verité de la religion chrétienne. Tiré du latin de M. J. Alphonse Turretin.* Geneva: M. M. Bousquet, 1730—1747.

Waeber, Paul. *L'abbé Vuarin et la formation de Genève, canton mixte (1801—1809). AEG.* Manuscipt histoire, n. d.

Waeber, Paul. *La Formation du canton de Genève, 1814—1816.* Geneva: V. Chevalier, 1974.

Watt, Jeffrey R. "The Family, Love and Suicide in Early Modern Geneva." *Journal of Family History* 21, 1 (1996).

Watt, Jeffrey. *The Making of Modern Marriage: Matrimonial Control and the Rise of Sentiment in Neuchâtel, 1550—1800.* Ithaca, NY: Cornell UP, 1992.

Wiedmer, Lawrence. *Pain quotidien et pain de disette, meuniers, boulangers et état nourricier à Genève (XVIIe et XVIIIe siècles).* Geneva: Editions Passé Présent, 1993.

Index

About the Editors and Contributors

JOEL R. BEEKE is Professor of Systematic Theology, Puritan Reformed Theological Seminary, Grand Rapids, Michigan.

WILLIAM EDGAR is Professor of Apologetics, Westminster Theological Seminary, Philadelphia, Pennsylvania.

FRANCIS HIGMAN is Director of the Institut d'Histoire de la Réformation, Geneva.

ROBERT M. KINGDON is Hilldale Professor in the Institute for Research in the Humanities, University of Wisconsin-Madison.

LINDA KIRK is Senior Lecturer in History, the University of Sheffield.

MARTIN I. KLAUBER is Instructor of History and Religious Studies, Barat College, and Visiting Professor of Church History, Trinity Evangelical Divinity School, Deerfield, Illinois.

RICHARD A. MULLER is P. J. Zondervan Professor of Historical Theology, Calvin Theological Seminary, Grand Rapids, Michigan.

GABRIEL MÜTZENBERG is a historian in Geneva.

JEANNINE E. OLSON is Associate Professor of History, Rhode Island College.

TIMOTHY R. PHILLIPS is Associate Professor of Systematic and Historical Theology, Wheaton College Graduate School, Wheaton, Illinois.

JOHN B. RONEY is Associate Professor of History, Sacred Heart University, Fairfield, Connecticut.

OTTO H. SELLES is Associate Professor of French Language and Literature, Calvin College, Grand Rapids, Michigan.

JEFFREY R. WATT is Associate Professor of History, University of Mississippi.